Quark XPress® 6 For Dummies®

Cheat Sheet

Best QuarkXPress 6 Keyboa...

Opening/closing/saving	Macintos...	
New project	⌘+N	
Open file	⌘+O	
Save file	⌘+S	Ctrl+S
Save as	Option+⌘+S	Ctrl+Shift+S
Get text or picture	⌘+E	Ctrl+E
Close current project	⌘+W	Ctrl+F4
Print	⌘+P	Ctrl+P
Quit	⌘+Q	Ctrl+Q or Alt+F4

Undo/Redo	Macintosh	Windows
Undo	⌘+Z	Ctrl+Z
Redo	Shift⌘+Z	Ctrl+Shift+Z

Preferences/setup	Macintosh	Windows
Application preferences	Option+Shift+⌘+Y	Ctrl+Alt+Shift+Y

Views	Macintosh	Windows
100%	⌘+1	Ctrl+1
Fit in window	⌘+0	Ctrl+0
200%	Option+⌘+click	Ctrl+Alt+click
Thumbnails	Shift+F6	Shift+F6
Go to page	⌘+J	Ctrl+J
Show/hide guides	F7	F7
Show/hide baseline grid	Option+F7	Ctrl+F7
Snap to guides	Shift+F7	Shift+F7

Palettes	Macintosh	Windows
Show/hide Tools palette	F8	F8
Show/hide Measurements palette	F9	F9
Show/hide Page Layout palette	F10	F4
Show/hide Style Sheets palette	F11	F11
Show/hide Colors palette	F12	F12

Item commands	Macintosh	Windows
Modify	⌘+M	Ctrl+M
Send to back	Shift+F5	Shift+F5
Bring to front	F5	F5
Send backward	Option+Shift+F5	Ctrl+Shift+F5
Bring forward	Option+F5	Ctrl+F5
Lock/unlock	F6	F6
Group	⌘+G	Ctrl+G
Ungroup	⌘+U	Ctrl+U

Quark XPress® 6 For Dummies®

Cheat Sheet

Best QuarkXPress 6 Keyboard Shortcuts (continued)

Find/change	Macintosh	Windows
Open Find/Change	⌘+F	Ctrl+F
Close Find/Change	Option+⌘+F	Ctrl+Alt+F

Text/paragraph formats	Macintosh	Windows
Edit style sheets	Shift+F11	Shift+F11
Character attributes	Shift+⌘+D	Ctrl+Shift+D
Paragraph attributes	Shift+⌘+F	Ctrl+Shift+F
Normal	Shift+⌘+P	Ctrl+Shift+P
Bold	Shift+⌘+B	Ctrl+Shift+B
Italic	Shift+⌘+I	Ctrl+Shift+I
Underline	Shift+⌘+U	Ctrl+Shift+U
All caps	Shift+⌘+K	Ctrl+Shift+K
Subscript	Shift+⌘+hyphen	Ctrl+Shift+9
Superscript	Shift+⌘+=	Ctrl+Shift+0 (zero)

Special characters/spacing	Macintosh	Windows
Em dash	Option+Shift+hyphen	Ctrl+Shift+=
Nonbreaking em dash	Option+⌘+equal	Ctrl+Alt+Shift+=
En dash	Option+hyphen	Ctrl+Alt+Shift+hyphen
Nonbreaking hyphen	⌘+=	Ctrl+=
Discretionary hyphen	⌘+hyphen	Ctrl+hyphen

Graphics handling	Macintosh	Windows
Center image within box	Shift+⌘+M	Ctrl+Shift+M
Fit image to box	Shift+⌘+F	Ctrl+Shift+F
Fit image proportionally to box	Option+Shift+⌘+F	Ctrl+Alt+Shift+F

For Dummies: Bestselling Book Series for Beginners

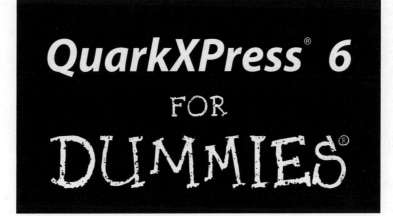

QuarkXPress® 6

FOR

DUMMIES®

by Barbara Assadi and Galen Gruman

WILEY

Wiley Publishing, Inc.

QuarkXPress® 6 For Dummies®

Published by
Wiley Publishing, Inc.
111 River St.
Hoboken, NJ 07030
www.wiley.com

 WILEY is a trademark of Wiley Publishing, Inc.

About the Authors

Barbara Assadi is co-founder and principal of BayCreative, a San Francisco-based advertising and marketing services agency. In that capacity, she manages content creation for client companies' ads, Web sites, direct mail, white papers, and data sheets. In previous positions she was editor-in-chief of Oracle Corporation's Web site, and Editorial Director at Quark, Inc. Barbara has written about software for *Macworld, Publish, InfoWorld,* and *Oracle Magazine,* and has co-authored several other books on desktop publishing, including the *QuarkXPress Bible* (Wiley, Inc.) with Galen Gruman, and has edited several computer books, including *The Macintosh iLife* (Peachpit Press).

Galen Gruman is the editor at *M-Business* magazine, and previously was executive editor at both *Upside* and *Macworld,* as well as West Coast bureau chief of *Computerworld.* A pioneer user of desktop publishing in professional magazine production, Galen adopted the technology in 1986 for a national engineering magazine, *IEEE Software.* He covered desktop publishing technology for the trade weekly *InfoWorld* for 12 years, as well as for other publications. Galen is coauthor with Deke McClelland of several *PageMaker For Dummies* books, with Barbara Assadi the series of *QuarkXPress For Dummies* and *QuarkXPress Bible* books, and with Kelly Anton and John Cruise the *Adobe InDesign 1.0 Bible,* all from Wiley Publishing, Inc.

Dedication

To my "mother" Monavar, with love and appreciation, Barbara

To my brothers Stephen and Darius, Galen

Authors' Acknowledgments

We want to thank Jonathan Woolson for his assistance in updating Chapters 18 and 19 of this book. Special thanks to Pat O'Brien for editing this book and also to Bob Woerner and everyone on the Wiley Editorial and Production staffs for their contributions.

We also thank Arne Hurty for support and encouragement. Special thanks to Fred Ebrahimi and Glen Turpin of Quark, Inc.

Publisher's Acknowledgments

We're proud of this book; please send us your comments through our online registration form located at www.dummies.com/register/.

Some of the people who helped bring this book to market include the following:

Acquisitions, Editorial, and Media Development

Project Editor: Pat O'Brien

(Previous Edition: Christine Berman)

Acquisitions Editor: Bob Woerner

Copy Editors: Teresa Artman, Diana Conover, Barry Childs-Helton

Technical Editor: Jonathan Woolson

Editorial Manager: Kevin Kirschner

Media Development Manager: Laura VanWinkle

Media Development Supervisor: Richard Graves

Editorial Assistant: Amanda Foxworth

Cartoons: Rich Tennant (www.the5thwave.com)

Production

Project Coordinators: Maridee Ennis, Courtney MacIntyre

Layout and Graphics: Amanda Carter, Joyce Haughey, LeAndra Hosier, Lynsey Osborn, Jacque Schneider

Proofreaders: Laura Albert, TECHBOOKS Production Services, Brain H. Walls

Indexer: TECHBOOKS Production Services

Publishing and Editorial for Technology Dummies

Richard Swadley, Vice President and Executive Group Publisher

Andy Cummings, Vice President and Publisher

Mary C. Corder, Editorial Director

Publishing for Consumer Dummies

Diane Graves Steele, Vice President and Publisher

Joyce Pepple, Acquisitions Director

Composition Services

Gerry Fahey, Vice President of Production Services

Debbie Stailey, Director of Composition Services

Contents at a Glance

Table of Contents

Introduction

• •

A man walks down the street when he comes upon a construction site where a group of three brick masons are busily at work. He stops to talk to the first brick mason and asks, "What are you doing?" The brick mason answers, "I'm putting bricks on top of other bricks."

The man continues down the sidewalk until he comes to the second brick mason. Again he asks the same question, "What are you doing?" The second brick mason answers, "I'm putting some bricks together to make a wall."

The man then walks on until he comes face-to-face with the third brick mason. The man poses the same question to the third brick mason: "What are you doing?" The third brick mason answers, "I'm building a beautiful cathedral."

Is QuarkXPress Too High-End for Me?

Right now, you may be wondering why on earth we are telling this story as part of the introduction to a book on QuarkXPress. Good question. But, when you think about it, the people who use QuarkXPress are a lot like those brick masons, and QuarkXPress is a lot like the mortar and bricks used by those brick masons to do their work.

What we are saying is this: There are all kinds of users of QuarkXPress. Some do very simple, one-color layouts. Some do moderately challenging layouts, which include photos, illustrations, and complex charts. Some even create Web pages. Still others — like the third brick mason who was building a cathedral — use QuarkXPress to create polished, highly designed and illustrated works of art.

QuarkXPress — like the mortar and bricks used by the brick masons in our story — is a *tool*. Nothing more, nothing less. It works for the world's most-celebrated graphic designers. It also works for people who create simpler projects, such as school newsletters.

The point is, QuarkXPress can never be too high-end for you, or for anyone else, because you pick and choose which parts of this tool you need to use. Also, keep in mind that if you create *any* type of print or Web layout, you can benefit from the program's features. Sure, it's true that if your layouts are simple, you won't need to use all the sophisticated features in QuarkXPress. But, when you think about it, isn't it nice to know that these features are available when and if you ever need them? And that you won't outgrow the program as you become more proficient with page design? We think so.

How to Use This Book

Although this book has information that any level of publisher needs to know to use QuarkXPress, this book is also for those of you who are fairly new to the field, or who are just becoming familiar with the program. What we try to do is to take the mystery out of QuarkXPress and give you some guidance on how to create a bunch of different types of layouts. Here are some conventions used in this book:

- ✔ **Menu commands** are listed like this: Style➪Type Style➪Bold.

  If we describe a situation in which you need to select one menu and then choose a command from a secondary menu or list box, we do it like this: Choose File➪Get Picture (or press ⌘+E on Mac or Ctrl+E in Windows). After the first mention, we drop the platform reference. This shorthand method of indicating a sequence of commands is often followed by the keyboard shortcut, as shown in this example.

- ✔ **⌘:** This is the Macintosh's Command key — the most-used shortcut key. Its Windows equivalent is **Ctrl.**

- ✔ **Key combinations:** If you're supposed to press several keys together, we indicate that by placing plus signs (+) between them. Thus Shift+⌘+A means press and hold the Shift and ⌘ keys, and then press A. After you've pressed the A key, let go of the other keys. (The last letter in the sequence does not need to be held down.) We also use the plus sign to join keys to mouse movements. For example, Option+drag means to hold the Option key when dragging the mouse.

- ✔ **Panes:** QuarkXPress has an interface feature, tabbed panes, that you may have seen in other applications. This is a method of stuffing several dialog boxes into one dialog box. You see tabs, like those in file folders, and by clicking a tab, the options for that tab come to the front of the dialog box in what is called a *pane*.

- ✔ **Pointer:** The small graphic icon that moves on the screen as you move your mouse is a pointer (also called a cursor). The pointer takes on different shapes depending on the tool you select, the current location of the mouse, and the function you are performing.

- ✔ **Click:** This means to quickly press and release the mouse button once. On most Mac mice, there is only one button, but on some there are two or more. All PC mice have at least two buttons. If you have a multi-button mouse, click the leftmost button when we say to click the mouse.

✔ **Double-click:** This means to quickly press and release the mouse button twice. On some multi-button mice, one of the buttons can function as a double-click. (You click it once; the mouse clicks twice.) If your mouse has this feature, use it; it saves strain on your hand.

✔ **Right-click:** A Windows feature, this means to click the right-hand mouse button. On a Mac's one-button mouse, hold the Control key when clicking the mouse button to do the equivalent of right-clicking in programs that support it. On multi-button Mac mice, assign one of the buttons to the Control+click combination.

✔ **Dragging:** Dragging is used for moving and sizing items in a QuarkXPress layout. To drag an item, position the mouse pointer on the item, press *and hold* down the mouse button, and then slide the mouse across a flat surface.

How This Book Is Organized

We've divided *QuarkXPress 6 For Dummies* into seven parts, not counting this introduction. Each part has anywhere from two to six chapters, so you don't have to wade through too much explanation to get to the information you need. Note that the book covers QuarkXPress on both Macintosh and Windows platforms. Because the application is almost identical on both, we only point out platform-specific information when we need to, or when we remember to, or both.

Part I: Getting Started

Designing a layout is a combination of science and art. The science is in setting up the structure of the page: How many places will hold text and how many will hold graphics? How wide will the margins be? Where will the page numbers appear? And so on. The art is in coming up with creative ways of filling the structure to please your eyes and the eyes of the people who will be looking at your layout.

In this part, we tell you how to navigate your way around QuarkXPress using the program's menus, dialog boxes, and tabbed panes. We also show you how to set up the basic structure of a layout and then how to begin filling the structure with words and pictures. We also tell you how to bring in text and graphics created in separate word processing and graphics applications.

Part II: Adding Style and Substance

Good publishing technique is about more than just getting the words down on paper or Web page. It's also about tweaking the letters and lines — and the space between them — to make your pages shine. This part shows you how to do all that and a lot more, including tips on using Required Components and XTensions to get more out of QuarkXPress and how to get your project out of your computer and onto some other medium, such as film or paper or the Web. We give you some solid suggestions on how to work with all those other people in the world who know how to help you get the job done.

Part III: The Picasso Factor

Let's be honest. Pablo Picasso didn't become famous for realistically portraying people. His claim to fame is based on how he took facial features and then skewed, slanted, stretched, and shrunk them into new forms. Some folks loved his work; others found it hard to figure out. But you had to admire the fact that it was unique.

We named this part of the book after the famous artist because it tells not only how to use QuarkXPress as an illustration tool, but also how to take normal-looking text and graphics and distort them. Why would you want to do this? Good question. The answer could be that, like Picasso, you want to present ideas in a visually interesting way. Either that, or you want to see how your relatives might look with their faces rearranged. QuarkXPress lets you manipulate text and art in interesting ways, and we show you how.

Part IV: Going Long and Linking

QuarkXPress includes features that help you keep track of figure numbers, table numbers, index entries — well, you get the idea. In fact, crafting long projects with QuarkXPress is a piece of cake. In this section, we show you how to handle long projects of all flavors, including those that link together several smaller layouts into a whole.

Part V: Taking QuarkXPress to the Web

QuarkXPress now has features for building both print and Web pages — and when it comes to building Web pages, a lot of the regular QuarkXPress rules don't apply. We show you how to use the new Web features to make some snazzy pages for online use.

Part VI: Guru in Training

After you master the basics, why not pick up some of the tricks the pros use? In this part, we show you how to customize QuarkXPress so that it fits you like a comfortable easy chair. We also explain how QuarkXPress works on PCs that use Windows and on Macs.

Part VII: The Part of Tens

This part of the book is like the chips in the chocolate chip cookies; you could eat the cookies without them, but you'd be missing a really good part. It's a part of extremes, of bests and worsts. It's like a mystery novel that's hard to put down until you read the very last word. In fact, you might even be tempted to start reading here and then go back to Chapter 1, but don't. The concepts in this book will make more sense to you if you read the other six parts of the book first.

Icons Used in This Book

So that you can pick out parts that you really need to pay attention to (or, depending on your taste, to avoid), we've used some symbols, or *icons* in this book.

When you see this icon, it means we are pointing out a feature that's new to Version 6 of QuarkXPress.

This icon points out features that behave a bit differently on Windows machines and Macs.

If you see this icon, it means that we're mentioning some really nifty point or idea that you may want to keep in mind as you use the program.

If you skip all the other icons, pay attention to this one. Why? Because ignoring it could cause something really, really bad or embarrassing to happen, like when you were sitting in your second-grade classroom waiting for the teacher to call on you to answer a question, and you noticed that you still had your pajama shirt on — backwards. We don't want that to happen to you!

This icon tells you that we are about to pontificate on some remote technical bit of information that might help explain a feature in QuarkXPress. The technical info will definitely make you sound impressive if you memorize it and recite it to your friends.

This icon alerts you to a valuable nugget of information you should store in your memory.

Where to Go from Here

QuarkXPress is an extremely versatile publishing tool. The time you take to become familiar with the program's many capabilities will be amply repaid in your ability to create the types of layouts you want and need, from the most basic to the most bizarre. QuarkXPress can take you anywhere you want to go in print or online publishing. So get going!

Part I
Getting Started

The 5th Wave   By Rich Tennant

"Someone want to look at this manuscript I recieved on email called, 'The Embedded Virus That Destroyed the Publisher's Servers When the Manuscript Was Rejected.'?"

In this part . . .

Getting off to a great start with QuarkXPress is what this part is about. We take you from a blank screen to a text-filled layout, helping you navigate your way around QuarkXPress using the program's menus, dialog boxes, views, and tabbed panes. And we explain the basics about how to get QuarkXPress to do what you want it to: First you build a box and then you start to fill it with text or graphics. All this just to get you on your way.

Chapter 1

Introducing QuarkXPress

In This Chapter

▶ Discovering menus, dialog boxes, and keyboard shortcuts

▶ Using the Tool palette and Measurements palette

*W*hen desktop publishing arrived in the 1980s, anyone could be a publisher. Anyone with a message could put it on paper and send it to the world, which revolutionized society in general (and business in particular). If you're about to use or are already using QuarkXPress, you, too, are taking up the cause.

QuarkXPress has become the most used desktop publishing software in the world. Professionals have made QuarkXPress the corporate standard for magazine, newspaper, and catalog publishing. It is also an effective book-publishing tool, thanks to its capability to index documents, and to create tables of contents and multichapter books.

The folks at Quark have upped the ante again with the release of QuarkXPress 6. This latest version, for Mac OS X and Windows 2000/XP, lets you

- ✔ Combine print and Web layouts in the same project

- ✔ Change your mind with the new multiple undo/redo capability

- ✔ Synchronize text so that a change in one text box automatically happens in corresponding text boxes elsewhere

- ✔ Convert print files to HTML format

- ✔ Create PDF files without using additional software

- ✔ See full-resolution previews of pictures in your projects

- ✔ Make production easier with layer locking, paste in place, and more contextual menus

- ✔ Make two-position rollovers and cascading menus for Web pages

- ✔ Gain more control over Web text display through CSS font families

You may feel a little daunted by QuarkXPress. Relax. In this book, we walk you through the program to familiarize you with all it has to offer. You may be intimidated by projects and layouts or by the vast layers of panes, palettes, tools, and menus you see. Don't be. Working with QuarkXPress is like working with a new person at the office. Things may be awkward at first, but after you get to know each other, you find you can do great things together.

The Big Picture

QuarkXPress is a page layout program. You can use it to compose, or *lay out,* print and Web pages. You don't have to be a professional publisher to use QuarkXPress; it works for simple documents, such as letters and flyers that you print out by using your desktop printer. But it's powerful enough to handle high-end projects, like annual reports, magazines, and ads, and is used for such projects by professional publishers and designers around the world.

The paste-up method

QuarkXPress uses a paste-up metaphor for page design. It's ideal for creating text and graphic element blocks, placing them on a page, then resizing and positioning them until you're happy. First, you set up the basic project framework, including the page size and orientation, margins, and columns. You fill that framework with boxes that have text, boxes that contain pictures, and with lines. Figure 1-1 shows a simple page layout in QuarkXPress.

Items and content

QuarkXPress makes a distinction between *items* and *content.*

Items are things you draw on a page — squares, circles, lines, and wavy shapes — and then modify by filling them with color, changing their size or position, and the like. The primary items in QuarkXPress are picture boxes and text boxes, but lines, text paths, and tables are also used. You can import text and graphical content into some of these items.

Figure 1-1:
A layout
created in
Quark-
XPress.

Content is *text* and *pictures.* (QuarkXPress calls any imported graphic a picture, whether the graphic is a logo, chart, line drawing, or photograph.) Content is always placed within an item. You can have items without content but you cannot have content without items.

Projects and layouts

Before QuarkXPress 6, the program's basic layout element was the document. Now *document* has been replaced by *project,* and the difference is significant. True, a QuarkXPress project can include a print document — such as a report or a book chapter — but it can also contain multiple print and Web documents. These documents are all stored in the same file, which is the *project.*

Inside each project are its *layouts*. A layout is a set of pages that have the same basic page setup (such as two-sided, 8½ in-by-10⅞ pages) and content type (print or Web).

Designers like the project/layout concept because it lets them group related components into one file rather than having separate files for a single project. Consider some applications: A print magazine that has a foldout table in an article no longer needs a separate document for the foldout, with its different page settings. A company that creates print and Web versions of its annual report now has both versions in the same file for consistency. A business report can combine two-sided pages with single-page chapter dividers.

Pages and layers

Each project in QuarkXPress is made of pages. Depending on how you've set up the project, the pages may be side-by-side in spreads and may indicate margins and columns visually by blue lines. Usually, each page in a document is a page in a printed piece. You can also have multiple *pages* on a page, such as a page of business cards. Some pages in a project can be Web pages.

You can create layers for pages. These layers function like clear overlays that you can show, hide, and print as necessary. A layer applies to all the pages in a layout. Layers are handy for storing two different versions of text or graphics in the same document. They're also good for isolating so you can work on them without being distracted by other items on a page.

A Familiar Interface

When you first sit down at your computer to start using QuarkXPress, you'll no doubt notice that its interface bears a strong resemblance to that used by other Windows and Macintosh programs. If you use other programs, you already know how to use QuarkXPress components, such as file folders, document icons, and the menus at the top of the project window.

To create a project, choose File⇨New⇨Project. To open an existing project, choose File⇨Open. The program displays a window similar to the ones shown in Figure 1-2.

Close button

Minimize button   Zoom button

Title bar

Pasteboard

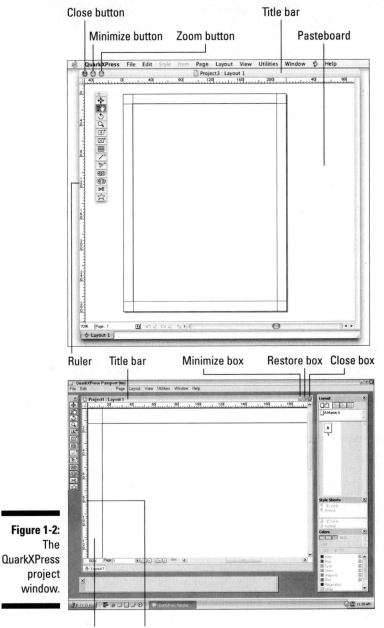

Ruler   Title bar   Minimize box   Restore box   Close box

Figure 1-2:
The
QuarkXPress
project
window.

Pasteboard   Ruler

This book is for both Windows and Macintosh users. We use Mac screen shots, except where the QuarkXPress versions have significant differences. In those cases we show screens from both, as in Figure 1-2.

A project displayed in either Windows or Macintosh has these elements:

✔ The *Ruler Origin box* lets you reset and reposition the ruler origin, which is the point at which the side and top rulers are 0 (zero).

✔ The name of the open project and layout appears on the *title bar,* located below the menu bar on the Mac and above the menu bar in Windows. You can move the project window around in the screen display area by clicking and dragging the title bar.

✔ If you have reduced or enlarged a project, clicking the green *Zoom box* on the Mac, at the top-left corner of the project window, returns to its previous size. In Windows, click the *Restore box,* at the top-right corner of the project window.

✔ You can make a project all but disappear by minimizing it. To minimize a project, click the Minimize box in the document's title bar. On the Mac, it's the yellow button at top left: in Windows, it's the box with a horizontal line in it at top right.

✔ The vertical and horizontal rulers on the left and top of the window reflect the measurement system currently in use.

✔ The *pasteboard* is an area around the page. You can store text boxes, picture boxes, or lines on the pasteboard. Pasteboard items do not print.

✔ QuarkXPress displays a shadow around the page on the Mac, and a line around the page in Windows. These borders indicate the page edges.

✔ If you select Automatic Text Box in the New dialog box (accessed by choosing File⇨New⇨Project and choosing Print from the Default Layout pop-up menu), the first page of the new project has a text box.

✔ The *View Percent* field shows the magnification level of the page that's currently displayed. Press Control+V on the Mac or Ctrl+Alt+V in Windows to highlight the View Percent field. To change the magnification level, enter a value between 10 and 800 percent in the field; then press the Return key on a Mac or the Enter key on Windows (or just click elsewhere on the screen).

✔ Switch pages by using the *page pop-up* at the lower-left corner of the QuarkXPress project window. To use this pop-up, click the triangle.

✔ Use the *scroll bars, boxes,* and *arrows* to shift the page around within the project window.

    If you hold down the Option or Alt key while you drag the scroll box, the view of the page is refreshed as you scroll the page.

✔ Close a project by clicking its Close box (the red close button at the upper-left corner of your open project window on the Mac; in Windows, the box that contains an X in the upper-right corner of the open window).

Macs also have the shortcut ⌘+W; in Windows, use Alt+F4.

Menus

The menu bar appears across the top of the project window. To display a menu, click the menu's title. From the menu, you can choose any of the active menu commands. QuarkXPress displays inactive menu commands with dimmed (grayed-out) letters. When commands are dimmed, it means that these commands are not currently available to you — they're inactive.

To choose one of the active menu commands, hold down the mouse button as you slide through the menu selections. (You can skip using menus by using the keyboard equivalents for menu selections instead. Keyboard equivalents are displayed to the right of the command names in the menu.)

If an arrow appears to the right of a menu command, QuarkXPress displays a second, associated menu when you choose that command. Sometimes this secondary menu appears automatically when you highlight the first menu command. Just click the arrow to make the submenu appear. Figure 1-3 shows the Style menu and the secondary menu that appears when you choose the Size menu command.

Style	Item	Page	Layout	View	Utilities	Wind

Font ▶	t 1
Size ▶	Other... ⇧⌘\
Type Style ▶	7 pt
Color ▶	9 pt
Shade ▶	10 pt
Horizontal/Vertical Scale...	✓ 12 pt
Kern...	14 pt
Baseline Shift...	18 pt
Character... ⇧⌘D	24 pt
Character Style Sheet ▶	36 pt
Text to Box	48 pt
	60 pt
Alignment ▶	72 pt
Leading... ⇧⌘E	
Formats... ⇧⌘F	
Tabs... ⇧⌘T	
Rules... ⇧⌘N	
Paragraph Style Sheet ▶	
Flip Horizontal	
Flip Vertical	
Synchronize Text...	
Unsynchronize Text...	
Hyperlink ▶	
Anchor ▶	
Underline Styles ▶	

Figure 1-3: Choosing menu and submenu options in QuarkX-Press.

Dialog boxes

Some menu commands are followed by a series of dots called an ellipsis (...). If you choose a menu command whose name is followed by an ellipsis, a dialog box appears. Dialog boxes give you a great deal of control over how QuarkXPress applies specific features or functions to your project.

Some dialog boxes also contain submenus. If a menu has a submenu associated with it, an arrowhead appears to the right of the menu entry. In addition to submenus, pop-up menus appear when you make certain selections in a dialog box. Figure 1-4 shows a pop-up menu for text alignment.

QuarkXPress uses *panes,* a type of dialog box that merges several dialog boxes into one. In fact, you often see six or seven of these panes (similar to a file folder in an office cabinet) in a single dialog box. Like the file folders in an office cabinet, these panes organize a large amount of stuff in one tidy spot. Click a pane's tab (it looks just like a paper folder's tab), and the pane comes to the forefront, showing you the options for that pane. You see three tabs (Formats, Tabs, and Rules) on top of the dialog box shown in Figure 1-4.

Figure 1-4:
The
Paragraph
Attributes
dialog box,
showing the
Alignment
pop-up
menu on the
Formats
pane.

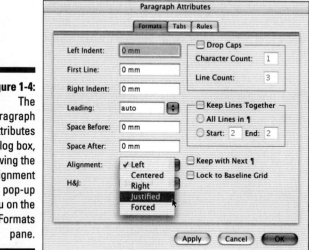

Working with contextual menus

Windows and Macs use a technique called *contextual menus* to save you time. By right-clicking an object in Windows, or Control+clicking on the Mac, you get a menu of options just for that item. This saves you time going through menus, dialog boxes, and palettes. QuarkXPress 6 has added a number of new contextual menus, which you can use in relation to virtually everything in and around a QuarkXPress project. To use a contextual menu, simply press and hold the appropriate keyboard command and then click on the object you want to modify.

✔ On the Mac, the default keyboard command to launch a contextual menu is Control+click. You can, however, change this keyboard command to Control+Shift+click by clicking Zoom in the Control Key area of the Preferences pane (QuarkXPress⇨Preferences⇨Interactive). If you have a third-party multi-button mouse, Mac OS X automatically sets the right-hand mouse button to be the Control+click or Control+Shift+click command.

✔ To display a contextual menu in Windows, just right-click on the object you want to modify.

Because contextual menus require less mouse movement and menu searching and require less brain power (something we all want to conserve), contextual menus may soon replace keyboard shortcuts as the beeline of choice among QuarkXPress users.

Keyboard shortcuts

You can select some QuarkXPress functions through pull-down menus, some through palettes, some through keyboard shortcuts, and some through all three options. Most new users use menus. As you become comfortable, you can save time by using the other options (particularly keyboard shortcuts).

You can download our free, printable list, in PDF format, of keyboard shortcuts from this book's companion Web site, www.QXcentral.com.

Want to move from page one of a layout to page three? You can change pages by choosing Go To from the Page menu, or you can use the keyboard shortcut: Press and hold the Command key (⌘) or Ctrl key while you press the J key. In this book, we write this combination like this: ⌘+J or Ctrl+J. The Macintosh shortcut appears first, followed by the Windows shortcut. If the platforms use the same shortcut, we list the shortcut just once.

In most cases, the Mac's ⌘ key and the Windows Ctrl key are the same, as are the Mac's Option key and the Windows Alt key. Shift is the same on both, whereas the Control key exists only on the Mac and has no Windows equivalent. The Mac's Return key is the same as the Windows Enter key. (Some Mac keyboards call this key Enter and some Windows keyboards call this key Return — no matter what it's called on your keyboard, don't confuse it with the keypad Enter key on the numeric keypad. To avoid confusion, we say *Return or Enter* for the key that inserts a new paragraph or activates a command, and we say *keypad Enter* for the key on the numeric keypad.)

The Tool and Measurements Palettes

One of the coolest features of the QuarkXPress interface is its set of palettes, which let you perform a wide range of functions on a layout without having to access pull-down menus. Like contextual menus and keyboard shortcuts, palettes are huge timesavers, and you'll undoubtedly find yourself using them all the time. Without a doubt, the Tools palette (see Figure 1-5) and the Measurements palette are the most commonly used. In fact, you'll probably keep these two palettes open all the time. You can find both palettes by choosing Window⇨Show Tools and Window⇨Show Measurements. The following text describes the contents of the two palettes.

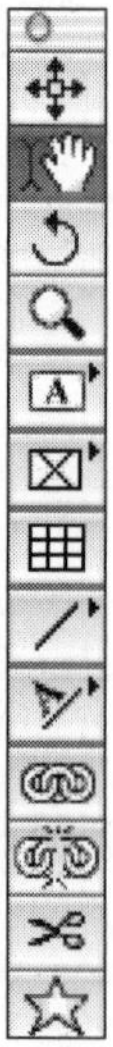

Figure 1-5:
The QuarkX-
Press Tools
palette.

The Tools palette

To use a tool on the palette, you first need to activate the tool. To activate a tool, simply click it. Depending on which tool you select, the cursor takes on a different look to reflect the function the tool performs. When you click the Linking tool, for example, the cursor looks like links in a chain.

Throughout the book, we explain in detail many of the functions you can perform with the Tools palette. The following sections are brief descriptions.

Item tool

The Item tool controls the size and positioning of items. In other words, when you want to change the shape, location, or presence of a text box, picture box, or line, you use the Item tool. (We discuss text boxes, picture boxes, and the like in detail later in this book.) For now, just keep in mind that the Item tool lets you create, select, move, group, ungroup, cut, copy, and paste text boxes, picture boxes, lines, and groups. When you select the Item tool and click on a box, the box becomes *active,* which means that you can change or move the box. Sizing handles appear on the sides of the active box; you can click and drag these handles to make the box a different size.

Content tool

The Content tool controls the *internal* aspects of items on a page. Functions that you can perform with the Content tool include *importing* (putting text into a text box or putting a picture into a picture box), cutting, copying, pasting, and editing text.

To edit text in a text box, select the Content tool. Then select the areas of text you want to edit by clicking and dragging the mouse to highlight the text or by using different numbers of mouse button clicks, as follows:

- ✔ **To position the cursor:** Use the mouse to move the I-beam pointer (it looks like a large capital *I*) to the desired location and click the mouse button once.

- ✔ **To select a single word:** Use the mouse to position the pointer within the word and click the mouse button twice.

- ✔ **To select a line of text:** Use the mouse to move the pointer within the line and click the mouse button three times.

- ✔ **To select an entire paragraph:** Use the mouse to move the pointer within the paragraph and click the mouse button four times.

- ✔ **To select the entire document:** Use the mouse to move the cursor anywhere within the document and click the mouse button five times.

When the Content tool cursor changes to a hand shape, you can use the tool to move the contents of the picture box around the inside the picture box. You can also use it to manipulate the picture's contents, such as applying shades, colors, or printing effects. Again, we discuss the ins and outs of text boxes and picture boxes in more detail in Chapter 5.

Rotation tool

 Use the Rotation tool to rotate items on a page. Just click a text box, picture box, or line, and rotate it by dragging it to the angle you want. You also can rotate items on a page in other ways, such as entering rotation information in the Measurements palette and using the Modify command in the Item menu.

Zoom tool

You may want to change the magnification of a page on-screen. For example, you may need to make edits on text that is set in 8-point type; increasing the displayed size of the text makes seeing what you are doing as you work easier. The Zoom tool lets you reduce or enlarge the view you see in the project window. When you select the Zoom tool, the cursor looks like a magnifying glass; when you hold the cursor over the project window and click the mouse button, magnification of that section of the screen increases or decreases in increments of 25 percent. (To increase magnification, select the Zoom tool and click on the page. To decrease magnification, select the Zoom tool, hold the Option or Alt key, and click on the page.)

Another way to change the magnification of the page is to enter a percentage value in the bottom-left corner of the project window; when a page is displayed at actual size, the percentage is 100 (refer to the Mac screenshot in Figure 1-2, which shows 70 percent). QuarkXPress lets you select any viewing percentage, including those in fractions of a percent (such as 49.5 percent), as long as you stay within the range of 10 to 800 percent.

Text Box tools

QuarkXPress needs to have a text box on the page before it lets you type text onto a layout or import text from a word processing file. You can instruct QuarkXPress to create text boxes automatically on each page of the document, or you can create text boxes manually by using the Text Box tools. We discuss Text Box tools more in Chapter 3.

To create a text box, select the desired Text Box tool and place the cursor where you want the box to appear. Click the mouse button and hold it down as you drag the box to the desired size.

The arrow to the right of the Text Box tool's icon indicates that if you click and hold down on the Text Box tool, a pop-up menu shows other Text Box tools. Select any of these other tools, and it becomes the default tool of the Tool palette. The Text Box tools (as shown in Figure 1-6) function as follows:

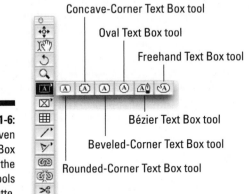

Concave-Corner Text Box tool

Oval Text Box tool

Freehand Text Box tool

Bézier Text Box tool

Beveled-Corner Text Box tool

Rounded-Corner Text Box tool

Figure 1-6: The seven Text Box tools in the Tools palette.

- **Rectangle Text Box tool:** Produces the standard rectangles in which most text is placed. The Rectangle Text Box tool should be the default tool for most users. To get a perfectly square text box, hold down the Shift key while drawing.

- **Rounded-Corner Text Box tool:** Produces text boxes with rounded corners. You can adjust the degree of rounding (the *corner radius)* in the Modify section of the Tools section of the Preferences dialog box. (Choose QuarkXPress⇨Preferences⇨Tools on the Mac or Edit⇨ Preferences⇨Tools in Windows, and then click Modify.) To get a perfectly square text box, hold down the Shift key while you draw it.

- **Oval Text Box tool:** Produces a text box shaped as an ellipse. To create a perfect circle, hold down the Shift key while drawing your oval.

- **Concave-Corner Text Box tool:** Produces text boxes that are *notched out* in the corners. You can adjust the degree of notching, technically referred to as *modifying the corner radius,* in the Modify section of the Tools pane in the Preferences dialog box. (Choose QuarkXPress⇨ Preferences⇨Tools on the Mac or Edit⇨Preferences⇨Tools, and then click Modify.) To get a perfect square with concave corners, hold down the Shift key while drawing.

- **Beveled-Corner Text Box tool:** Produces boxes with beveled corners, which appear as if they've been sheared off by diagonal lines. You can adjust the degree of *shearing,* also referred to as the *corner radius,* in the

Modify section of the Tool pane in the Preferences dialog box. (Choose QuarkXPress⇨Preferences⇨Tools on the Mac or Edit⇨Preferences⇨ Tools, and then click Modify.) For a perfectly square beveled text box, hold down the Shift key while drawing the box.

✔ **Bézier Text Box tool:** Named after the renowned French engineer Pierre Bézier, this tool lets you produce *polygons* (shapes composed of a series of flat sides) and *polycurves* (shapes composed of a series of curves) as well as shapes that combine both sides and curves. This tool works differently than the other Text Box tools: Rather than holding down the mouse, you click and release at each corner (or *node,* in graphics-speak). To complete the box, return to your first node and click on it (the mouse pointer changes from the default cross to an oval).

If you click and drag a little at each desired node, the Bézier control handles appear. These handles let you create a curve. You can have both straight and curved sides based on how you use the mouse at each node. The best way to learn to use Bézier curves (unless you are Bézier himself) is to experiment with them and get a feel for how they work.

✔ **Freehand Text Box tool:** Produces curved shapes composed of a series of curves. The box takes shape as you move the mouse, as if your mouse were a pen on paper. To complete the box, you usually bring the mouse back to the origin point and then release the mouse button. (Notice how the pointer changes to a circle from the normal cross.) If you release the mouse button before you return to the origin point, QuarkXPress automatically draws a straight line from where you released the mouse to the origin point. Using this tool, too, requires practice and a steady hand.

Picture Box tools

Picture boxes hold graphics that you import from graphics programs. As with text, QuarkXPress needs a box (in this case a picture box) on the page before you can import and manipulate a graphic on a page. You can create a picture box manually, using one of the QuarkXPress Picture Box tools. You select the Picture Box tool to use from the Picture Box pop-up menu in the Tools palette, place the cursor where you want the box, click and hold the mouse button, and drag the box to size. (We talk more about this in Chapter 3.) The following Picture Box tools work like their Text Box tool equivalents:

✔ **Rectangle Picture Box tool**

✔ **Rounded-Rectangle Picture Box tool**

✔ **Oval Picture Box tool**

✔ **Concave-Corner Picture Box tool**.

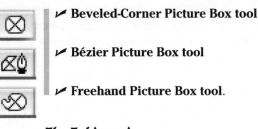

✓ **Beveled-Corner Picture Box tool**

✓ **Bézier Picture Box tool**

✓ **Freehand Picture Box tool**.

The Table tool

The Table tool lets you organize data into rows and columns (a *table,* if you will). Creating a table is much like creating a text or picture box. You select the Table tool in the Tools palette, place the cursor where you want the table, click and hold the mouse button, and drag it until the table is the approximate size you want. The Table Properties dialog box appears, asking you the number of rows and columns you want to include in your table and whether you want to fill the individual spaces of the table, called *cells,* with text or picture boxes. After you create your table, you can adjust it by choosing Item⇨ Modify and selecting options in the Modify dialog box and/or choosing Item⇨ Table and selecting options in the Table pop-up menu that appears. Chapter 8 covers creating and modifying tables in more detail.

The Line tools

The four Line tools in the Line Tools pop-up palette let you draw — you guessed it — lines. After you draw a line, you can change its thickness (*weight*) and/or style (line style is, for example, a dotted line).

✓ **Orthogonal Line tool:** Produces straight lines that are completely horizontal or vertical.

✓ **Diagonal Line tool:** Produces straight lines at any desired angle. If you hold down the Shift key while drawing with it, the line is constrained to be perfectly horizontal, perfectly vertical, or at a perfect 45-degree angle. (The QuarkXPress manual just calls this the Line tool; we use the name Diagonal Line so that you don't mix it up with the other Line tools.)

✓ **Bézier Line tool:** Produces straight and curved lines, like edges created with the Bézier Text Box and Bézier Picture Box tools. A line section is straight or curved, depending on how you use the mouse at each node.

✓ **Freehand Line tool:** Produces curved lines that follow the motion of your mouse, similar to drawing with a pen on paper.

As with the Text Box and Picture Box pop-up palettes, you can change the arrangement of the Tools palette's Line tools to suit your style.

To use any of the Line tools, click the tool to select it and position the cursor at the point where you want the line to begin.

✔ For the Diagonal Line, Orthogonal Line, and Freehand Line tools, click and hold down the mouse button as you draw the line. When the line is approximately the length you want, release the mouse button.

✔ For the Bézier Line tool, click at each point, as described for the Bézier Picture Box and Bézier Text Box tools. If you click and drag for a little bit at each desired node, you see the Bézier control handles appear that let you create a curve. You can have both straight and curved sides based on how you use the mouse at each node. Again, we suggest that you play around with this tool to get the hang of it. After you draw a line, use the Measurements palette to select the line weight and line style.

Text Path tools

You can draw four kinds of *text paths* — lines that text will follow — to create text that flows in any direction instead of being confined within a text box. The Text Path tools work much like the Line tools; like the line tools, they are in their own pop-up palette in the Tools palette. (Because they work like their Line tool equivalents, we won't repeat the details.) They are:

✔ **Freehand Text Path tool**

✔ **Orthogonal Text Path tool**

✔ **Bézier Text Path tool**

✔ **Line (or Diagonal) Text Path tool**

Linking and Unlinking tools

Directly beneath the Tools palette are the Linking tool (above) and the Unlinking tool (below). The Linking tool lets you link text boxes together so that extra text flows from one text box into another. The Unlinking tool breaks the link between text boxes. Linking is very useful when you want to "jump" text; for example, when a story starts on page one and jumps to (continues on) page four. Chapter 3 covers linking and unlinking text boxes.

Scissors tool

The Scissors tool lets you *cut* shapes you have created with the Text Box, Picture Box, or Line tools. For example, you can use the Scissors tool to split a single line into two separate lines or to remove the corner of a box. This tool also comes in handy when you want to edit a shape you've created with the Freehand Text Box, Freehand Picture Box, or Freehand Line tool. You can cut lines made with the Text Path tools, too, although any text on the text path will remain linked, even if it is split into two entirely separate parts.

Starburst tool

The Starburst tool lets you create a picture box in a star shape. This is used as a graphical element to draw attention to something on the page. A starburst shouts "Look at me!" For example, if you are designing a flyer about a new product, you can put a starburst with the word *New!* at the top of the page.

The Measurements palette

The Measurements palette is one of the most significant desktop publishing innovations; you'll use it all the time. It shows the precise position and attributes of any selected page element; you can enter values to change those specifications. To see the Measurements palette, you need a document open as you choose Window⇨Show Measurements or press F9.

The information in the Measurements palette depends on the element currently selected. When you select a text box, the Measurements palette displays the text box position coordinates (X and Y), size (W and H), amount of rotation, and number of columns (Cols), as shown in Figure 1-7. By clicking the up and down arrows on the palette, you can modify the *leading* (space between the lines of text) of the text box (or you can simply type a value in the space next to the arrows); click the right and left arrows to adjust *kerning* or *tracking* (space between letters) for selected text.

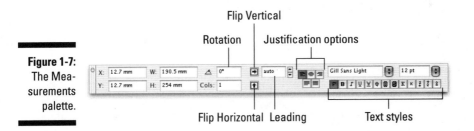

Figure 1-7: The Measurements palette.

Specify text alignment (left, center, right, justified, or force-justified) by using the alignment icons. In the type section of the palette, you can control the font, size, and type style of selected text.

For a picture box, the Measurements palette displays different information. In Figure 1-8, the Measurements palette shows the box position of the (X and Y), its size (W and H), the amount it is rotated, its corner radius, its repositioning coordinates (X+ and Y+), the amount of picture rotation within the box, and the amount of slant.

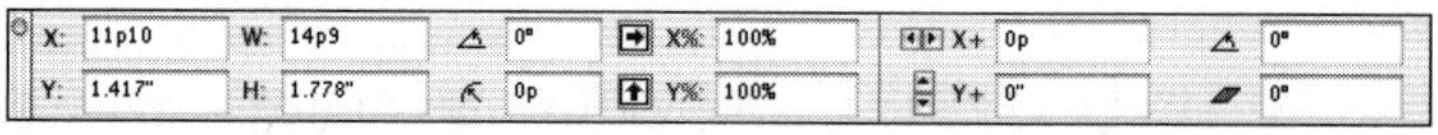

Figure 1-8:
The Measurements palette when a text box is selected.

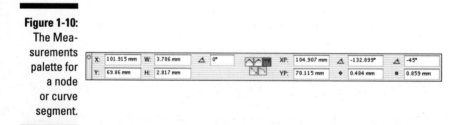

For a line or text path, the Measurements palette (as shown in Figure 1-9) displays the location coordinates (X and Y), line width, line style, and end-point (line ending) style. The line style pop-up menu lets you select the style for the line. (If you use a freehand or Bézier line, an icon to control the line's rotation replaces the Endpoints section of the Measurements palette.)

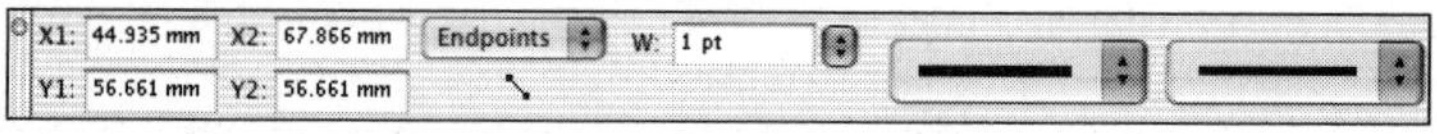

Figure 1-9:
The Measurements palette for a straight line or text path.

If you select a Bézier or freehand element's node or curve, you get controls for the nodes, as in Figure 1-10. Chapter 12 explains what the controls do.

Figure 1-10:
The Measurements palette for a node or curve segment.

Chapter 2

Have It Your Way

*I*s sitting in front of a computer all those hours is affecting your eyesight? Do you find yourself nose to screen, trying to read the really small print? Well, you're not alone. And those nice people who brought you QuarkXPress are doing their part to save your eyes by providing some nifty ways for you to change the way that layouts appear onscreen. For example, you can zoom in to make things larger or create thumbnail pages so you can see how well (or in some case, not so well) your layouts work together. Another set of timesaving features in the program's interface, *palettes,* lets you perform a wide range of functions without having to access pull-down menus.

This chapter helps you get started with QuarkXPress. We begin by showing you how to create your first project and by giving you tips on taking control by using the settings in the View menu and the palettes in the Window menu.

Creating Your First Project

Think of a *project* as a big, fat file folder that holds all the layouts and individual items for one, well, project. A project can hold up to 25 layouts. Enough talk about projects. To really get a feel for how they work, you need to create a new project and get started. These steps create a new project:

1. **Choose File⇨New⇨Project, or press ⌘+N or Ctrl+N.**

   When you first choose File⇨New, a list appears, showing things like Web, Library, and XML. Don't panic! Just select Project. We talk about that stuff later in this book.

The New Project dialog box appears (as shown in Figure 2-1), offering you a whole bunch of other options. You can choose the Layout Type, which will be either Web or Print. If this truly is your first project, we suggest you start with Print. You can also choose other attributes for your project, such as an automatic text box to hold the text, how many columns of text your pages must have, and how big your margins are.

2. **After you have all those settings to your liking, click OK.**

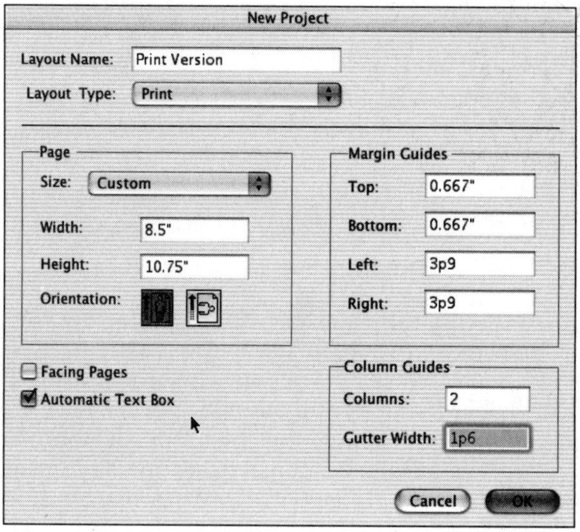

Figure 2-1:
The New
Project
dialog box.

Congratulations! You've just given birth to your first QuarkXPress project. Here, have a cigar.

The View Menu

After you create a project, the View menu (as shown in Figure 2-2) lets you control the display of items onscreen.

The View menu also provides commands that control the display of positioning aids: guides, baseline grid, rulers, and invisibles (such as tabs and returns). It also lets you turn full-resolution previews off and on. You can toggle features on and off; if a command is active, its option changes from Show to Hide or a check mark appears next to its name.

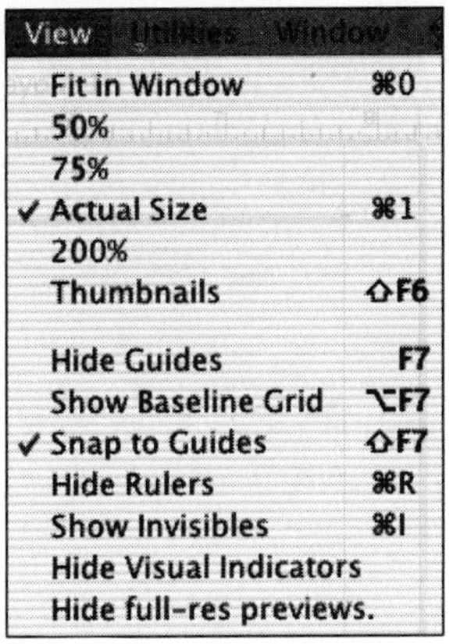

View	Utilities	Window
Fit in Window		⌘0
50%		
75%		
✓ Actual Size		⌘1
200%		
Thumbnails		⇧F6
Hide Guides		F7
Show Baseline Grid		⌥F7
✓ Snap to Guides		⇧F7
Hide Rulers		⌘R
Show Invisibles		⌘I
Hide Visual Indicators		
Hide full-res previews.		

Figure 2-2:
The View
menu.

Using the preset options

Menu commands in the View menu scale the project view to a set of sizes preset by QuarkXPress. The preset view options in the View menu are

- **Fit in Window (⌘+0 [zero] or Ctrl+0 [zero]):** Fits the page into the area of the project window.

- **50%:** Displays the page at half its actual size.

- **75%:** Displays the page at three-fourths its actual size.

- **Actual Size (⌘+1 or Ctrl+1):** Displays the page at actual size (100%). With this setting, depending on the physical size of your monitor, you may see only part of the page on-screen.

- **200%:** Displays the page at twice its actual size.

- **Thumbnails (Shift+F6):** Displays miniature versions of the pages. Figure 2-3 shows a thumbnail view of a layout.

View-changing tips and tricks

In addition to the view commands in the preceding section, QuarkXPress offers other ways of changing views. The following methods are very useful:

- To increase the page view in 25-percent increments, select the Zoom tool. (It looks like a magnifying glass.) When you place the mouse pointer in the layout with the Zoom tool selected, the pointer changes to a magnifying glass. Each time you click the mouse button, the view increases in 25-percent increments up to a maximum of 800 percent. To decrease the page view in 25-percent increments, hold down the Option or Alt key as you click the mouse button.

✔ To zoom in on a specific area, click the Zoom tool, select a corner of the area you want to zoom in on, hold down the mouse button, drag to the opposite corner of the specified area, and release the mouse button.

✔ Another way to change your view is by using the View Percentage field in the bottom leftmost corner of the layout window. You can highlight the current value with the mouse and enter a new value in that field. A quicker way is to use the keyboard shortcut (Control+V or Ctrl+Alt+V) to highlight the current value, then enter a new view percentage (you don't need to enter the % symbol) and press Enter or Return. For the thumbnail view, enter **T** instead of a percentage.

You can change the increment for all these Zoom tool options from its default of 25 percent by making changes in the Preferences dialog box's Tool pane.

1. **To access the Preferences dialog box, choose QuarkXPress⇨ Preferences on the Mac or Edit⇨Preferences in Windows.**

The Preferences dialog box opens.

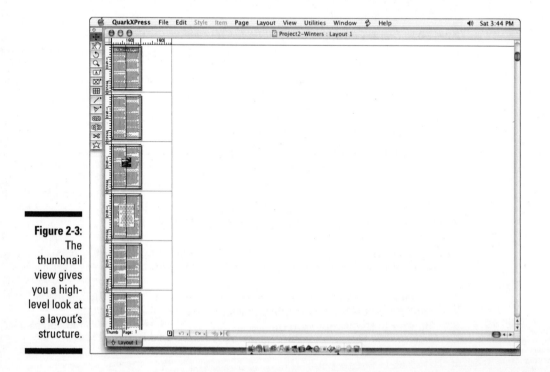

Figure 2-3:
The thumbnail view gives you a high-level look at a layout's structure.

2. **In the Preferences dialog box, select Tools.**

   The Tool Defaults pane appears.

3. **In the Tool Defaults pane, click the Zoom tool icon.**

4. **In the Preferences dialog box, click the Modify button to open a dialog box that lets you change the zoom increment. Click OK to save the change.**

Chapter 20 covers changing default layout and application preferences to gain still more control over the way QuarkXPress handles your projects.

Palettes: Here, There, and Everywhere!

In Chapter 1, we introduce you to the Tools and Measurements palettes, which are the palettes you use most often in QuarkXPress. But the program comes with a slew of other palettes, including palettes for color management, page layout, style sheets, hyperlinks, and (with the introduction of synchronized text in QuarkXPress 6) a palette for synchronizing text.

In earlier versions of QuarkXPress, the following palettes were in the View menu; now they are in the Window menu.

The following sections give you the lowdown on these palettes and explain how they can help you with creating projects as you become more adept with the program. The palettes are listed in the Window menu.

Opening and closing palettes and panes

To open a palette or pane, choose its menu command (such as Window⇨ Show Colors). Some palettes or panes have keyboard shortcuts: If so, the shortcut is shown in the menu. To close a palette, click its Close box in the upper-left corner (Macintosh) or upper-right corner (Windows). You can also choose its menu command (such as Window⇨Hide Colors).

The Page Layout palette

Earlier versions of QuarkXPress featured a Document Layout palette. This has been renamed the Page Layout palette, as shown in Figure 2-4. Use it to create, name, delete, move, and apply master pages, or to move layout pages. *Master pages* hold page elements (such as graphics and margins) that

QuarkXPress can apply automatically to new pages, much as a style sheet works to apply standardized formatting to text. You also can add, delete, and move pages. To display the Page Layout palette, choose Window⇨Show Page Layout or press F10. We explain master pages in Chapter 16.

The Style Sheets palette

The Style Sheets palette, shown in Figure 2-5, lists the names of the style tags (names of styles) attached to currently selected paragraphs and characters, and it also lets you apply style sheets to paragraphs and characters. To display the Style Sheets palette, choose Window⇨Show Style Sheets or press F11. We cover Style sheets in depth in Chapter 6.

The Colors palette

The Colors palette lets you designate the color and *shade* (percentage of color) you want to apply to text, pictures, and backgrounds of text and picture boxes. You also can produce color blends, using one or two colors, to apply to box backgrounds. To display the Colors palette, as shown in Figure 2-6, choose Window⇨Show Colors or press F12.

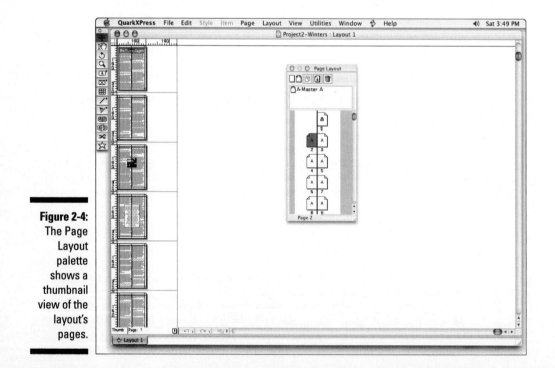

Figure 2-4:
The Page Layout palette shows a thumbnail view of the layout's pages.

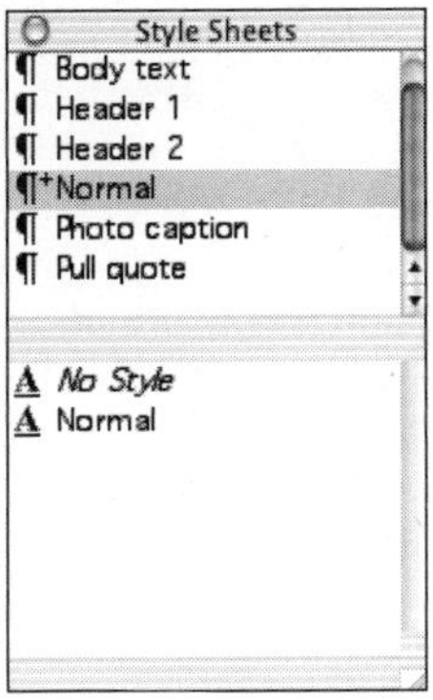

Figure 2-5:
The Style
Sheets
palette
displays
the names
of style
tags
attached
to any
currently
selected
paragraphs
and
characters.

A *spot color* is a single color (or process color) applied at one or more places on a page. You can use more than one spot color per page.

Process color refers to any of the four primary colors used in publishing: cyan, magenta, yellow, and black (known as a group as CMYK).

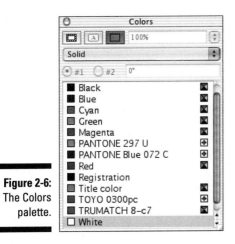

Figure 2-6:
The Colors
palette.

In QuarkXPress, you can create both process and spot colors; both display in your Colors palette. Spot and process colors are distinguished by the Spot Color and Process Color buttons, which appear on the right side of the palette next to the color name. (A spot color will have a small printer's registration mark — a crosshair. A process separation color will have a square with four triangles of color next to it.) This feature makes keeping your project's color palette organized easy because you can view the colors in a list.

The Synchronized Text palette

Synchronized text is used in multiple places. If text is synchronized, changes in one place (a text box or a text path) are reflected everywhere that text is used. The Synchronized Text palette (shown in Figure 2-7) lets you identify text to be synchronized and place copies of the text elsewhere in your project. This handles *boilerplate* text (like the blurb that describes your company and legal disclaimers) and text that may *change* (such as names of products under development) while you're developing the project. To display the Synchronized Text palette, choose Window⇨Show Synchronized Text.

Figure 2-7:
The Synch-
ronized Text
palette.

The Trap Information palette

A feature that makes QuarkXPress the program of choice among professional publishers is one that you never worry about: trapping. *Trapping* is the technique of extending a color so that it slightly overlaps an adjoining color, preventing gaps between two abutting colors that result from misalignment on a printing press. The Trap Information palette, you can set or change trapping specifications for selected items. To display the palette, choose Window⇨ Show Trap Information or press Option+F12 or Ctrl+F12.

Don't use the Trap Information palette unless you know what you're doing. This is an expert feature. As such, it is beyond the scope of this book. Using it inexpertly can produce uneven results when you print your document.

The Lists palette

You can create lists based on paragraph styles — styles that you can use to build tables of contents, tables of figures, and so on. In the Lists palette, you can set or change list settings. To see the palette, choose Window⬄Show Lists or press Option+F11 or Ctrl+F11. Chapter 17 covers list creation.

The Layers palette

The Layers palette, shown in Figure 2-8, lets you create layers (tiers) of objects in layouts. You can use this feature to isolate items that otherwise might cause unnecessary clutter. Or you can use it to hold different variations (for example, one layer for Spanish text and one for English text in a brochure that has the same images for both versions.) If items need to be in a document but should not print, such as crop marks or output instructions, you can place them on a *hidden* layer, completely separate from the document to be printed. To display the Layers palette, choose Window⬄Show Layers.

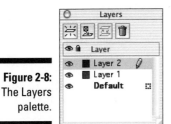

Figure 2-8:
The Layers
palette.

The Profile Information palette

Another expert feature is the Profile Information palette, used to set or change color profiles for selected items. Color profiles make slight adjustments to an object's colors to compensate for differences among color input and output devices. Most users don't have to worry about this feature, and if they do, their service bureau will let them know when to worry about it. To display this palette, choose Window⬄Show Profile Information.

Don't use the Profile Information palette unless you know what you're doing. The Profile Information palette is an expert feature of QuarkXPress that we don't go into detail about in this book. Using it without knowing precisely why you use it can produce uneven results when you print your document.

The Hyperlinks palette

You can think of hyperlinks as *the things people click on* in Web layouts. The Hyperlinks palette (as shown in Figure 2-9) contains a list of hyperlinks to Web pages and to layout pages used in the current QuarkXPress Web layout. To display the Hyperlinks palette, choose Window⇨Show Hyperlinks. We explain more about the Hyperlinks palette in Chapter 18.

Figure 2-9:
The
Hyperlinks
palette.

The Index palette

QuarkXPress lets you mark words in a layout as you are creating it or reading it. The Index palette, shown in Figure 2-10, copies the marked text and makes an alphabetized, hierarchical index. When the Index palette has all the entries, build the index by choosing Utilities⇨Build Index. To display the Index palette, choose Window⇨Show Index or press Option+⌘+I or Ctrl+Alt+I. You can find out more about indexes in Chapter 16.

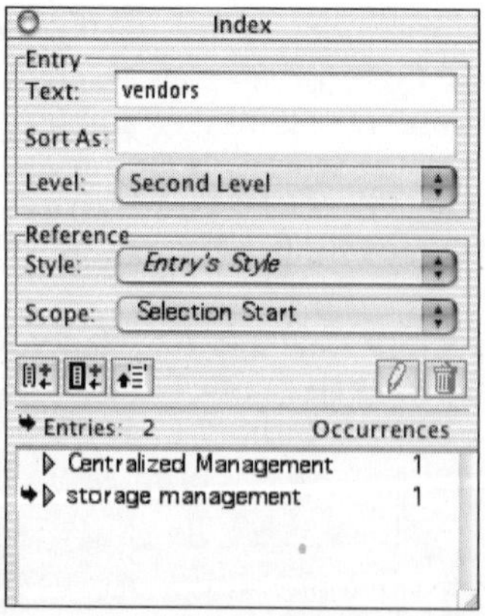

Figure 2-10:
The Index
palette.

The Web Tools palette

The Web Tools palette, shown in Figure 2-11, appears only when you are working in a Web layout. It has tools for creating and editing Web layouts, including form control and image map tools. You open the Web Tools palette by using Show Web Tools in the Tools pop-up menu (Window⇨Tools⇨Show Web Tools). Chapter 18 covers the Web Tools palette.

Figure 2-11:
The Web
Tools
palette.

Sequences palette

The Sequences palette (as shown in Figure 2-12) builds a list of objects to be displayed or linked to in a Web page. The sequence created in this palette is essentially a miniprogram that displays certain items in a certain order. To display the Sequences palette, choose Window⇨Show Sequences.

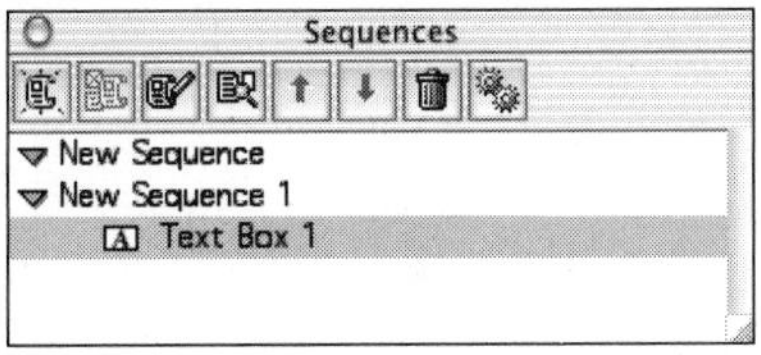

Figure 2-12:
The
Sequences
palette.

Sequences
▽ New Sequence
▽ New Sequence 1
[A] Text Box 1

Library palettes

You can store layout elements (text or picture boxes, lines, or groups) in *library palettes.* To use this feature, select the element that you want to store from the layout or the pasteboard and drag it into an open library palette. You can have several library palettes (each library is in its own palette), so you can group items into libraries (such as one for each project or one for logos and one for employee photos). You can use items from the library in other layouts. To create a library palette, choose File⇨New⇨Library.

The Placeholders palette

The Placeholders palette is used in creating XML files. (XML is a database language that is used to produce structured Web content.) The Placeholders palette shows the records defined in a particular XML file. To display the palette, choose Window⇨Show Placeholders.

A Myriad of Mouse Pointers

In addition to the many palettes in QuarkXPress, you'll find a bunch of mouse pointer icons as you begin working with the program's features. These pointers are visual hints about what tool you're using. For example, when you choose the Rotation tool, you find that the pointer, or *cursor,* becomes the *Rotation pointer.* Expect to see these mouse pointers in QuarkXPress:

- ✔ **Standard pointer:** Appears as you move through dialog boxes, menus, and windows, and as you move over nonselected elements. The standard pointer is the most common pointer.

- ✔ **Creation pointer:** Appears if you have selected a box or line tool. Use this pointer to draw boxes and lines.

- ✔ **Sizing pointer:** Appears if you select a handle on a text or picture box (with the Item or Content tool selected) or on a line. You can resize the item by holding down the mouse button and dragging the handle.

- ✔ **Item pointer:** Appears if the Item tool is selected and you have selected a box or line. You can move the selected item by holding down the mouse button and dragging the item.

- ✔ **Lock pointer:** Appears if the Item tool is selected and a locked text box, picture box, or line is selected. The Lock pointer indicates that you can't move the box by to dragging it. (You can move it by altering coordinates in the Measurements palette or by choosing Item⇨Modify or pressing ⌘+M or Ctrl+M.)

- ✔ **I-beam (text) pointer:** Appears if the Content tool is selected and you select a text box. If the cursor is blinking, any text you type inserts where the cursor appears. If the cursor is not blinking, you must click at the location in the text box where you want to edit text.

✔ **Grabber pointer (also known as the page-grabber hand):** Appears if the Content tool is selected and you have selected a picture box containing a graphic. You can move the graphic within the box by holding down the mouse button and dragging the item.

✔ **Rotation pointer:** Appears if you select the Rotation tool in the Tools palette. After you select the tool, hold down the mouse button and drag the pointer until the object is rotated to the angle you want. You can actually see the object rotating as you drag the pointer across the page.

✔ **Zoom-in pointer:** Appears if you select the Zoom tool and click the mouse button. (Clicking the mouse button zooms in on the image by the predefined amount, which by default is 25 percent.) You can also select an area to zoom into by clicking one corner of the area of interest, holding down the mouse button, dragging the mouse to the opposite corner, and then releasing the button.

✔ **Zoom-out pointer:** Appears if you select the Zoom tool and hold down the Option or Alt key while clicking the mouse button. (Clicking the mouse button zooms out by a defined amount; by default it's 25 percent.)

✔ **Link pointer:** Appears if you select the Link tool. Click the pointer on the first text box and then on the second text box in the chain of boxes through which you want text to flow. If there are more boxes, repeat the process (for example, link box two to box three and then link box three to box four and so on). You can switch pages while this tool is active to flow text from one box to another across pages.

✔ **Unlink pointer:** Appears if you select the Unlink tool. Click the pointer on the first text box and then on the second text box in the chain of boxes that have the link that you want to break. If there are more boxes to unlink, repeat this process for each pair of boxes to be unlinked. You can switch pages while this tool is active to unlink text flow across pages.

Chapter 3

Boxes and Text Unite!

• •

• •

*L*et's face it: When you think of a flat piece of paper or a Web page with
words and pictures on it, you don't intuitively know that those words
and pictures are held in boxes, right? Not if you're like most people we know.
And the boxes that we're talking about now are not your typical supermarket
boxes. In fact, they are unlike any three-dimensional boxes that you may be
familiar with. About the only way in which QuarkXPress boxes are similar to
those you're familiar with is that they also hold stuff. But the stuff in
QuarkXPress boxes is two-dimensional text and pictures.

Surprised? You're not alone. Brand-new QuarkXPress users are amazed that
just about everything on a page produced in this program must be placed into
a box. QuarkXPress boxes may not hold a great deal of memorabilia, but they
are pretty powerful just the same; they serve as the placeholders for the text
and pictures that you use to build a page. These boxes not only define the
layout of a page by controlling the size and placement of pictures, but they
also delineate the white space between an illustration and its caption, and
they identify the portion of a page's real estate that is covered with words.

Yes, these boxes do a lot. And if you spend any time at all working with
QuarkXPress, you'll get comfortable with its text boxes and picture boxes
in no time flat. This chapter focuses on creating text boxes. In Chapter 4,
we concentrate on building and modifying picture boxes.

Revisiting Text Box Tools

Composing a page in QuarkXPress involves arranging and rearranging the program's basic building blocks, among them *text boxes*. In Chapter 1, we show you the QuarkXPress Tools palette. That the Tools palette contains seven box-related tools (the Rectangle Text Box tool, the Rounded-Corner Text Box tool, the Oval Text Box tool, the Concave-Corner Text Box tool, the Beveled-Corner Text Box Tool, the Bézier Text Box tool, and the Freehand Text Box tool) reflects how important they are to page design in QuarkXPress.

You use these seven tools (as shown in Figure 3-1) to make text boxes. (You also can tell QuarkXPress to automatically create a single text box on each page, which we describe in the section "Using automatic text boxes" later in this chapter.) After you create a text box, you can enter text directly into it by either typing on your keyboard or importing text from a word processor file.

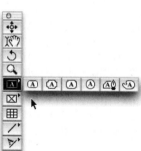

Figure 3-1:
QuarkXPress offers seven tools for creating text boxes.

Building Text Boxes

To create a text box, you just choose a tool in the Text Box Tools palette and use the mouse to draw the box. Later, you can change things about the box, such as its size, its placement on the page, and the width of its margins. Creating a text box is easy. Just follow these steps:

1. **Select the Rectangle Text Box tool from the Tools palette.**

   The Rectangle Text Box tool is a rectangle with a capital A in its center. When you move the mouse pointer into the layout page, the mouse pointer changes to look like a crosshair.

2. **Hold down the mouse button and drag the mouse across your page until you've drawn a text box the size you want.**

3. **Release the mouse button.**

Now step back and admire your work. It doesn't get any easier than that.

Active and inactive boxes

If you draw a text box and decide that it's too small and too high on the page, what can you do? Do you scrap the box and start over, hoping for better luck the next time you create it? No, because deleting the box and redrawing it takes too long, plus (to be honest about it) it means that you're chickening out. Be brave! You can fix that box. We show you how in the "Taming the wild text box" section, later in this chapter. Before you can do anything to the box, you must *activate* it.

Selecting an item by using the Content tool or the Item tool is the same as *activating* it. Before you can make changes in a text box, or any item for that matter, you must select or activate it so that QuarkXPress knows what part of your layout to work on next.

Figure 3-2 shows two boxes. The box on the left is inactive, or unselected. The box on the right is active, or selected. Activating the box lets you modify it in many ways. As shown, determining that a box is active is easy because little black boxes, called *sizing handles,* appear on its sides and corners.

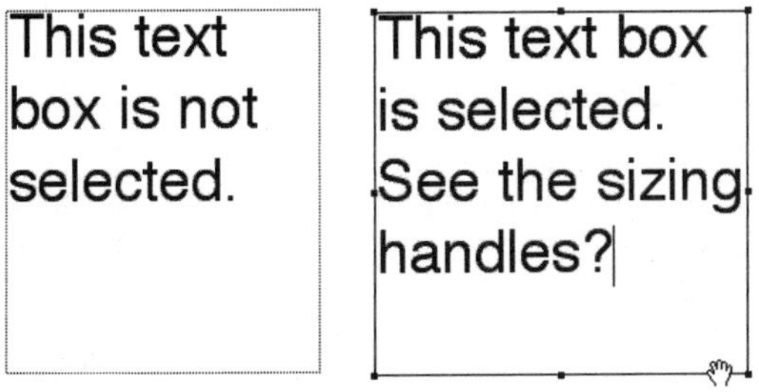

Figure 3-2:
The sizing handles on the box on the right show that it's selected, or active.

This text box is not selected.

This text box is selected. See the sizing handles?

Taming the wild text box

You probably know a control freak: A friend who goes berserk when a piece of paper on his desk is at an angle instead of being perfectly aligned with the stapler, or a boss who insists on reading every word you write and knowing where you are each minute of the day. (It's also called micromanaging.)

Generally, being a control freak isn't a thing to be proud of. You won't find it on many résumés (although you may run across *micromanager* from time to time). In desktop publishing, taking control is a necessary and valued trait. Striving for perfection takes over even if you aren't a control freak. Soon you find yourself spending hours tweaking each little element on a layout.

So when you're building a page, being a control freak is perfectly okay. Honestly, half the fun of using QuarkXPress is the unbelievable amount of control it gives you over everything in a page layout.

You have complete control over text boxes when you use QuarkXPress. After you create a text box, you can control it by using the Modify dialog box.

Here's how you make the Modify dialog box appear:

1. **Make sure that the text box is active.**

   Look for the sizing handles around it. Activate it by either the Content tool or the Item tool and then clicking on the text box with your mouse.

2. **Choose Item⇨Modify to display the Modify dialog box for text boxes, as shown in Figure 3-3, or press ⌘+M or Ctrl+M.**

The four panes of the Modify dialog box let you tweak a text box. By entering values, choosing items from pop-up menus, and checking or unchecking boxes, you can modify the box's appearance and set other box properties.

The Box pane lets you adjust the position and appearance of a text box, including the following:

- The box's size and position on the page
- The angle of the box's rotation
- The *skew angle* (or slant) of the box and the text within
- The amount of roundness applied to the box's corners
- The color (or colors, in the case of a two-color blend) and shade applied to the box's background

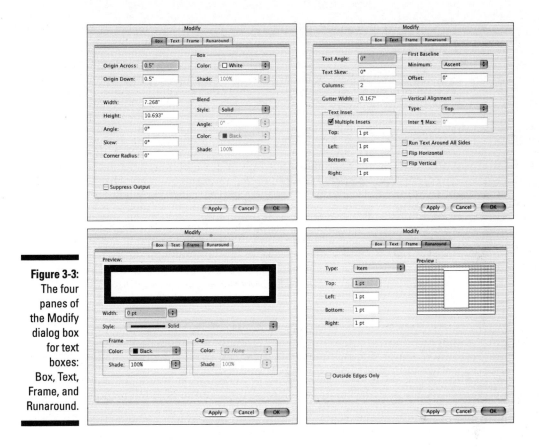

Figure 3-3:
The four
panes of
the Modify
dialog box
for text
boxes:
Box, Text,
Frame, and
Runaround.

The Text pane lets you adjust the placement and appearance of the text in
the box, including the following:

- The number of columns and the space between columns
- The distance between the edge of the box and the text within
- The angle of the lines of text within the box
- The skew angle of the text
- The placement of the first line of text relative to the top of the box
- The vertical alignment of the text
- How text flows within the box when an item is placed in front of the box
- The option to flip the text in a box along a vertical and/or horizontal axis

The Frame pane lets you apply a frame around a text box and to specify the style, width, color, and shade of the frame, as well as the color and shade applied to the gap between dotted, dashed, and multiple-line frames.

The Runaround pane (covered in Chapter 5) controls the flow of text in a box in relation to another box. If you want text in a text box to flow around the edge of a picture, you go to the Runaround pane to do it. We explain many of these modifications in Chapter 5. For now, just be aware that they exist.

Creating irregular text boxes

QuarkXPress offers two tools — the Bézier Text Box tool and the Freehand Text Box tool — for creating irregular boxes that have straight or curved edges. You also can convert any box shape into any other shape. (We explain this in Chapter 12.) Be careful, though. A layout full of irregularly shaped text boxes can at best be described as *hodgepodge*. Don't make your layout ugly just because you can. Figure 3-4 shows two irregular text boxes.

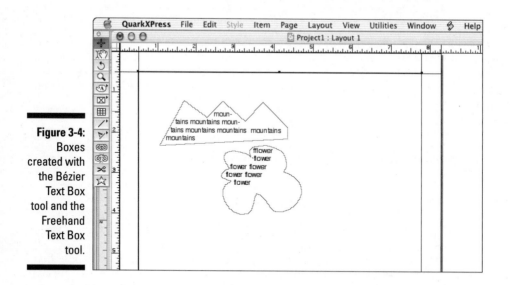

Figure 3-4:
Boxes created with the Bézier Text Box tool and the Freehand Text Box tool.

Follow these steps to create a straight-edged (polygon) Bézier text box by using the Bézier Text Box tool:

1. **Select the Bézier Text Box tool.**

2. **Click and release the mouse button to create the box's first point.**

3. **Move the mouse to where you want to establish the next point; then click and release the mouse button.**

4. **Continue to establish the points of your box by moving the mouse and then clicking and releasing the mouse button.**

5. **Close the box by clicking on the first point that you created. You can also close a box by double-clicking anywhere to create a final point.**

   When you double-click, QuarkXPress creates a final point and automatically draws a final segment back to the first point.

Here's how to create a curved-edged Bézier text box with the Freehand Text Box tool:

1. **Select the Freehand Text Box tool.**

2. **Hold down the mouse button and then drag the mouse, using it like a pencil to create any shape you want.**

3. **Close the box by dragging the crosshair mouse pointer back to the first point and releasing the mouse button.**

   You can also release the mouse button at any time to have QuarkXPress create the final segment by drawing a line from the current position of the crosshair mouse pointer to the point of origin.

Bézier boxes can contain three kinds of points (corner points, smooth points, and symmetrical points) and two kinds of segments (curved and straight). You can change any kind of point or segment into any other kind. In addition, you can split a segment into one or more segments by using the Scissors tool. Chapter 12 has more information about modifying lines.

Using automatic text boxes

QuarkXPress text boxes accommodate different work styles. For example, Howie likes to tinker with page layout to see exactly how everything works. He can spend hours in front of the computer, getting all his layout ducks in a row, luxuriating in the depth and breadth of controls offered by QuarkXPress.

Pamela, on the other hand, is always rushed. In her job, she's responsible for producing two newsletters — one print and one online — every week. She collects QuarkXPress shortcuts the way that some kids collect baseball cards.

Although Howie is perfectly comfortable with manually creating every text box that appears in his layout, Pamela would go crazy at the very thought of such a time-consuming approach. She has found a way to make QuarkXPress automatically and precisely create a text box for her on every page. She uses the program's Automatic Text Box feature each time she creates a new layout.

Suppose that Pamela is going to create a two-page, printed newsletter and she wants the text to appear on each page in two columns. She starts a new project (by choosing File➪New➪Project or by pressing ⌘+N or Ctrl+N) and makes sure that the Layout Type pop-up menu is set to Print, which opens the New Project dialog box (shown in Figure 3-5). In the Column Guides area, she specifies two columns. She also makes sure that the Automatic Text Box check box is checked.

New Project	
Layout Name:	Pamela's newsletter
Layout Type:	Print

Page
Size:	A4 Letter
Width:	8.268"
Height:	11.693"
Orientation:	

Margin Guides
Top:	0.5"
Bottom:	0.5"
Inside:	0.5"
Outside:	0.5"

☑ Facing Pages
☑ Automatic Text Box

Column Guides
Columns:	2
Gutter Width:	0.167"

Cancel   OK

Figure 3-5:
You create automatic text boxes in the New Project dialog box.

That's all Pamela has to do. QuarkXPress takes care of the rest, automatically creating a two-column text box on each page of her newsletter.

What's more, when Automatic Text Box is checked, QuarkXPress automatically inserts new pages when text overflows the boundaries of an automatic text box. Each of these new pages has its own automatic text box.

If you want QuarkXPress to insert new pages automatically, you must first make sure that the Auto Page Insertion option is set to End of Story (as shown in Figure 3-6). To select that option, follow these steps:

1. **Choose QuarkXPress➪Preferences on the Mac or Edit➪Preferences in Windows (or press Option+Shift+⌘+Y or Ctrl+Alt+Shift+Y).**

   The Preferences dialog box appears.

2. **In the Preferences dialog box, choose General in the list on the left side of the dialog box.**

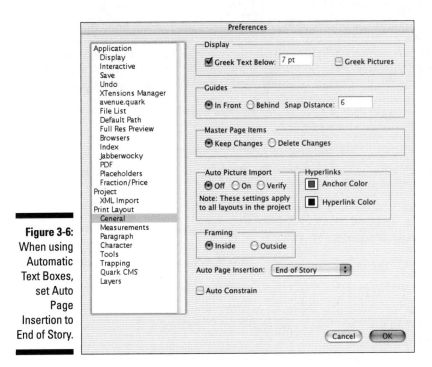

Figure 3-6:
When using
Automatic
Text Boxes,
set Auto
Page
Insertion to
End of Story.

3. **Use the Auto Page Insertion arrows to make sure that the Auto Page Insertion option is set to End of Story.**

   If you don't use automatic text boxes, you have to draw all the text boxes manually and link them before you can bring text into them.

This, of course, leads to the obvious question: "What the #%@# is *linking*?" Hold your horses. (And watch your language!) We cover that next.

Linking and unlinking text boxes

Automatic text boxes are great for creating multipage layouts in which text automatically flows from page to page. In other situations, however, text must flow not from one page to the next page, but from one page to a different, nonconsecutive page or from one box to another within a single page. A newsletter layout may require a story that begins on page 1 to finish on page 4. How do you make this *jump* (or "continued on" instance)? *Link* the boxes.

To remember linking in QuarkXPress, think of text boxes as links in a chain, just like a metal chain with connected links. The only difference is that QuarkXPress links boxes that hold text. Because you can't link a text box to another box that already contains text, however, you need to do your linking before you fill the boxes with text. Here's how you link empty text boxes:

1. **Go to the page that contains the first text box that you want to use in the linked chain of text boxes.**

   To get to that page, choose Page➪Go To (or press ⌘+J or Ctrl+J).

2. **Click the Linking tool (the third tool from the bottom of the Tools palette; it looks like a piece of chain) to select it.**

3. **Position the mouse pointer anywhere inside the text box that will be the first box in the chain.**

   Notice that the mouse pointer changes to look like a chain link.

4. **Click the mouse button.**

   Notice that the text box has a moving dashed line around it, a *marquee* to be exact, which tells you that this box is the start of the chain.

5. **Go to the page that contains the text box that will be the next box in the chain.**

6. **Position the mouse pointer in the next text box that you want to use in the chain; then click the mouse button.**

   The second text box is now linked to the first. If you enter or import more text into the first box than it can hold, the overflow text continues in the second box, even if several pages separate the two text boxes. As text is entered or imported, it flows to the next box in the text chain until there is no text left over.

7. **Repeat Steps 2 through 6 until all the text boxes that you want to use in the chain are linked.**

How do you know whether two text boxes are linked? Activate either of the boxes; then select the Linking tool and look for the large gray arrow pointing to or from the next box in the chain. Figure 3-7 shows this linking arrow.

As nice as it is to link text boxes, it's nice to be able to change your mind about how the text flows or doesn't flow, meaning that you want to be able to unlink two or more linked text boxes, too. Here's how:

1. **Go to the page that contains the text box that you want to unlink from a chain.**

2. **Click the Unlinking tool (the tool that is third from the bottom in the Tool palette) to select it.**

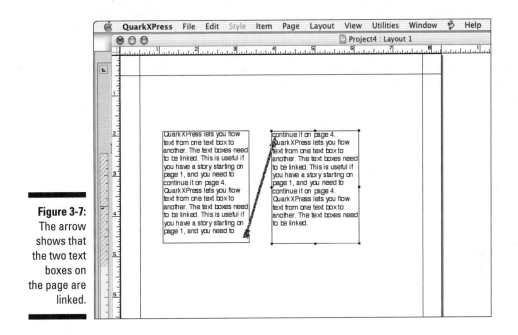

Figure 3-7:
The arrow
shows that
the two text
boxes on
the page are
linked.

3. **Position the mouse pointer in the text box, hold down the Shift key, and then click the mouse button.**

   This step unlinks the selected text box from the chain while retaining links between the preceding box, and the following box, in the chain. To break the chain entirely, click the arrowhead on the top-left side of the box. To take it another step, click the arrow's tail feathers on the bottom-right corner of the first box; this also breaks the link to the following box. (In this instance, holding down the Shift key isn't necessary.)

4. **To unlink additional text boxes, repeat Steps 2 and 3.**

Filling the Text Box with Text

After you create a QuarkXPress layout, add text boxes, and link the text boxes the way you want them, you're ready to fill those boxes with some text!

As we mentioned earlier, you can fill text boxes in one of two ways: One way is to enter text directly in QuarkXPress. (You simply activate a text box by clicking on it, select the Content tool, click inside the activated box, and start typing). The other way is to import text from a word processor into the text box. Follow these steps to import the text:

1. **With the QuarkXPress layout open, select the Content tool.**

2. **Click (or activate) the text box where you want to import the text.**

   If the text box is empty, the flashing I-beam pointer appears in the top-left corner.

   If the text box already contains text, click where you want the imported text to begin; text is always imported wherever the I-beam pointer is flashing. Importing text does not remove the text already in the text box; importing text simply bumps the text that follows the I-beam pointer.

3. **Choose File⇨Get Text (or press ⌘+E or Ctrl+E) to display the Get Text dialog box.**

4. **Select the text file that you want to place in the text box.**

5. **Check the Convert Quotes check box if you want QuarkXPress to automatically change typewriter-type double dashes, straight quotation marks, and apostrophes to their typographic equivalents.**

6. **To include the style sheets used in the word processor, check the Include Style Sheets box.**

   We talk much more about style sheets in Chapter 6.

7. **Click OK.**

   The text flows into the text box or the linked chain of text boxes.

It doesn't get any easier than that. Unfortunately, as is the case with most things in life, importing text files into QuarkXPress isn't always as cut and dried as the preceding steps may suggest. There can be snags. The good news is, if you make a few adjustments to your text files before you import them, you should be able to import text with minimum brain damage.

More about Word-Processor Files

You can import a whole bunch of different kinds of word-processor files into QuarkXPress. However, QuarkXPress doesn't necessarily read the latest versions of Word or WordPerfect. The latest versions supported are Word 97/2000 (Windows) or 98/2001 (Mac) and WordPerfect 6 (Windows) or 3.5 (Mac). (Note that Word 2002 for Windows uses the same format as Word 97/2000 and that Word X for the Mac uses the same format as Word 98/2001.) QuarkXPress can also import Rich Text Format (RTF), Hypertext Markup Language (HTML), and text-only (ASCII) files.

If you have a later version of Word or WordPerfect, either save your files in a supported version or see whether Quark has an updated import filter on its Web site. If you use those newer programs, you need to save your files in a previous format supported by QuarkXPress: Windows Word 97/2000 (8.0), 95 (7.0), or 6.0; Mac Word 98/2001, 6.0, 5.*x*, 4.0, or 3.0; Windows WordPerfect 6.*x* and 5.*x*; and Mac WordPerfect 3.*x*.

Getting text ready to import

Suppose that you're familiar with formatting text in your computer's word processing program. That is, you know how to create text, flow it into two columns, add a header and footer, and italicize and bold selected sections of text. Doing as much as possible within the word processing file and then importing the text into QuarkXPress may seem to be a good thing to do.

But is this a good thing to do? No way. Unless you plan ahead, you risk losing some of the work — such as formatting — that you did in the word processor, such as that boldface text, after you import the text into QuarkXPress. Why waste your time?

Keeping it simple: All you need is text

Here's a good guideline: When using a word processor to create a file that you intend to import into QuarkXPress, remember that you'll be importing only *text*. If you keep that thought in mind, you'll resist the temptation to do more formatting than necessary in the word processor. To make the most of your investment, use the power of QuarkXPress for your *layout* formatting. With that said, what word-processing features should you go ahead and use?

If you tell QuarkXPress to keep style sheets from Microsoft Word and WordPerfect when you import text, the style sheets come across, along with their associated text. Figure 3-8 shows the Get Text dialog box that appears when you import text from a word processor. Be sure to check Include Style Sheets when you import your text; otherwise, your style sheets won't import along with the text. We explain more about style sheets in Chapter 6.

To successfully import text into QuarkXPress, avoid using the graphics and layout features of the word processor. Limit your word-processor text formatting to the kind that will enhance the reader's understanding or that places emphasis, such as boldfacing, italicizing, and varying type styles.

If you use Microsoft Word, by far the most popular word processor in use today, rest assured that these formats import into QuarkXPress:

- ✔ Boldfaced, outlined, italicized, and shadow characters
- ✔ Underlining (in Word, all underlining changes to a single underline)

- ✔ Color
- ✔ Font changes
- ✔ Varied point sizes
- ✔ Small caps
- ✔ Strikethrough characters
- ✔ Subscript
- ✔ Superscript
- ✔ Special characters

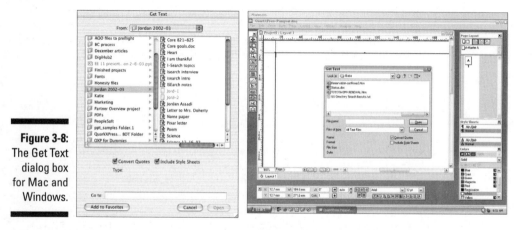

Figure 3-8:
The Get Text
dialog box
for Mac and
Windows.

If you use a different word processor supported by QuarkXPress, these same features should import, but there's no guarantee, so do a test before using a format other than Word. After QuarkXPress takes care of the characters in your text, you can deal with issues on a bigger scale: tables, headers and footers, and more that you may have included in your word-processor files. Can any be saved? The sections that follow let you know what to expect.

Tables: Don't bother

If you decide to create a table in a word-processor file and then import the file into QuarkXPress, be forewarned that the table will disappear. Ergo, take heed: If you like tables in your layouts, wait until you're using QuarkXPress to format them. QuarkXPress has its own table-making tool, which has been improved in Version 6. We discuss tables in Chapter 8.

On the other hand, if you format a table with tabs (whether or not you make the tabs line up properly by using style sheets), you can import the table into QuarkXPress along with the rest of the text in the file and can then modify the table in QuarkXPress as needed. Basically, to create a table that can be imported by QuarkXPress, you need to separate each column with a tab and each row with a paragraph return. If your word processor uses style sheets, make sure that the table text uses a unique style so you can set up the tabs in QuarkXPress just once (in that table text's style) and have all the table text use those tabs automatically. (Chapter 6 covers style sheets in depth.)

If you create a table in a spreadsheet or database program (such as Microsoft Excel or FileMaker Pro), you can import the table into QuarkXPress, but not smoothly. You choose between saving the files as tab-delimited ASCII text or as graphics. If you save the files as tab-delimited ASCII text, you need to do some work inside the QuarkXPress layout, setting tab stops to line up everything (as you would with tabbed text imported from a word processor). If you save the files as graphics, you can't change the data in QuarkXPress.

Headers and footers: Forget it

Headers are pieces of information, such as the name of the current chapter, at the tops of pages. *Footers* are at the bottoms of pages and usually include information such as the current page number and the name of the document.

As a QuarkXPress user, get into the habit of thinking about headers and footers as layout issues, not text issues. Because these elements are layout issues, wait until you're working on your project in QuarkXPress before you worry about them. For one thing, your project will invariably paginate differently in QuarkXPress; when it does, the page elements in your headers and/or footers will be useless, even if they did import into QuarkXPress (which they don't). However, keep in mind that Quark's master pages make it easy to establish headers and footers. We explain master pages in Chapter 16.

Footnotes: Nope!

Some word processors include a footnote feature that lets you do two things:

- ✔ Mark spots in text with a number
- ✔ Display the number and some corresponding text at the bottom of the page containing the footnote

If you import a word-processor file with footnotes into QuarkXPress, the footnotes no longer appear on the same page as the text that they reference. Instead, footnotes are at the end of the imported text. Also, the superscript or subscript footnote indicators in the project may not import correctly.

In-line graphics: Difficult, not impossible

Most Macintosh and Windows word processors support *in-line graphics*, which are pictures that you import into your word processor and associate with certain sections of text. QuarkXPress usually can import in-line graphics with your text, particularly if these graphics were formatted in Microsoft Word or WordPerfect. You may need to experiment if you use another word processor that allows in-line graphics. Embedded graphics that use Object Linking and Embedding (OLE, a dynamic-linking feature from Microsoft) in a word-processor document cannot be imported into QuarkXPress.

In-line graphics import into QuarkXPress in the form of their previews, not as their original formats — when they import at all. Because of this, the versions of the in-line graphics that end up in your QuarkXPress layout probably will have a lower resolution in your QuarkXPress layout than in their original word-processor file. To get them back to their proper resolution, *relink* them in the Pictures pane of the Usage dialog box (choose Utilities➪Usage).

Style sheets: Absolutely, positively!

Okay, now for the good news. QuarkXPress lets you import styles created in Microsoft Word and WordPerfect *if* you check the Include Style Sheets check box in the Get Text dialog box, but only if you remember to check the Include Style Sheets Box *before* you import the text. (To display this dialog box, choose File➪Get Text or press ⌘+E or Ctrl+E.) In fact, even if you don't always use style sheets in your word processor, checking the Include Style Sheets box when you import text is a good idea; you may end up saving important text formatting you forgot that you'd even applied.

We tell you more about style sheets in Chapter 6.

XPress Tags: Your secret code

Keen on secret codes? QuarkXPress has them in a nifty, although tough-to-learn, feature that lets you insert tags into text that you're preparing to import into QuarkXPress. These codes are *XPress Tags;* you can use them to give QuarkXPress instructions on formatting text that's being imported into a QuarkXPress layout. XPress Tags are ASCII (text-only) text containing embedded codes that tell QuarkXPress which formatting to apply. XPress Tags are like the codes used in the Web's HTML language, or in the ancient versions of WordPerfect. You embed tags in your word-processor text.

Word-processing mistakes to avoid

After you figure out that QuarkXPress does a good job of importing text from your word processor, be careful not to fall victim to the temptation of using all the features of the word processor simply because they exist. Here are some pointers to keep in mind:

✔ **Don't do extensive formatting in your word processor.** A word processor's style sheets are much less sophisticated, with fewer options than the effects you can achieve in QuarkXPress. Avoid using layout-related features (such as page numbers, headers and footers, and multiple columns) in the word processor. QuarkXPress simply ignores them.

✔ **Don't use the word processor as though it were a manual typewriter.** In other words, don't press the Return or Enter key at the end of each line of text, only do so at the end of a paragraph. If you forget to skip this old-standby task, you'll spend considerable time in QuarkXPress removing all the unnecessary returns, which can clutter an otherwise tidy layout. Also, don't use two spaces between sentences; professional typesetters never do this. Of course, you can fix many of these sorts of mistakes within QuarkXPress by using the find-and-replace feature, but it's better not to make the mistake in the first place.

✔ **Don't try to use multiple word spaces or multiple paragraph returns to align words or lines of text on-screen.** Use QuarkXPress to tweak the spacing of words and characters; it's easier and much more precise.

✔ **Notice the version number of your word processor.** If your word-processing program is a couple of versions older or newer than those that QuarkXPress supports, you may have trouble importing text files. If in doubt, create a test text file using all the features that you're likely to use and import it into a text box in a test QuarkXPress project. You may you need to change the list of word processing features that you can use with QuarkXPress.

✔ **Don't use the fast-save option on files that you plan to import into QuarkXPress.** This note of caution applies if your word processor has a *fast-save option* (an option that writes information about what's been changed in a text file at the end of the file instead of rewriting the entire file each time you do a save). Microsoft Word has this feature, and it's active by default. The fast-save option can cause problems with the text file when you import it. We suggest that you turn off the fast-save feature for files that you plan to import into QuarkXPress (refer to your word processor's user manual or online help file for instructions on how to do this). With today's super-speedy hard drives, the time that you gain by using fast-save is barely noticeable anyway.

The point of all these points is this: If you want to use a separate word processor, use it. But you should limit what you do in that program to plain old text entry, saving the fancy stuff for adding after you import the text into QuarkXPress.

Synchronizing Text

A major publishing headache is keeping *boilerplate* text identical in layouts and projects. Whether it's a copyright line, a legal notice, business cards with several copies on the same page, or chapter headings in folios, such text is repeated in a project and must be changed at every location consistently. QuarkXPress 6 offers *synchronization*. You can have one source for repeated text, so changes to any of the text's instances are updated to all copies.

How to synchronize text

The process of text synchronization is simple:

1. **Create a text box or text path that contains the text you want synchronized with other text boxes and/or text paths.**

   Only the entire text in text boxes and text paths can be synchronized, not text snippets.

2. **Point and click anywhere inside the text box or text path using the Content tool to activate the text box or text path.**

3. **Either choose Window⇨Synchronized Text and click the Synchronize Text icon on the palette that opens, or choose Style⇨Synchronize Text.**

   Figure 3-9 shows the Synch Content dialog box that appears.

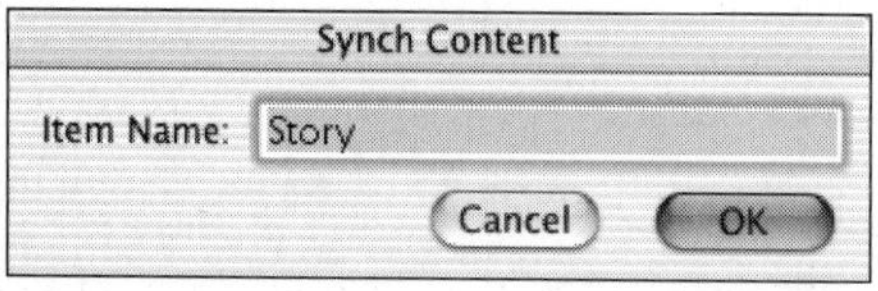

Figure 3-9:
The Synch
Content
dialog box.

Synch Content
Item Name: Story
Cancel   OK

4. **You'll be asked to name the synchronized content; give it a name that is meaningful, not the default Story1, Story2, and the like.**

5. **Click OK.**

   The text box's or path's handles change to diagonal blue stripes. This indicates that the box or path contains synchronized text.

6. **Go to another location in your project — it does not have to be in the same layout (we used the same layout for our example in Figure 3-9) — and click a text box or path to contain the same text.**

7. **Again, use the Content tool and click on the box or path to select it.**

8. **Click the Insert Text button (the second button from the left) on the Synchronized Text palette. Or you can simply drag the story icon from the Synchronized Text palette onto the target text box or path.**

   The target text box or path now contains the synchronized text.

Now when you change the first (source) synchronized text box or path, those changes automatically happen in the second (target) text box or path. You can synchronize a source text box or path to multiple target boxes and/or paths.

You cannot synchronize text across multiple projects, such as in a book. But you can synchronize text across multiple layouts in the same project.

Working with synchronized text

The Synchronized Text palette contains all synchronized-text sources for the current project. You can manage all your synchronized text from one location.

After you've synchronized text to multiple boxes and paths, any edits you make to the text will be automatically reflected in all synchronized boxes and paths — you don't have to edit the original box or path to make the changes synchronize throughout the project.

If you make major edits to synchronized text, such as adding or removing many words, the text boxes holding that text may no longer be the right size for the revised text. That may not be a big deal if you delete text. If you add a lot of text, the multiple target text boxes and paths may not hold all the new text. In this case, you'll have to adjust the text box and paths containing synchronized text throughout your project so all the text is displayed.

When you synchronize text to a new text box or path, the text copy picks up the attributes of the original text box or path *at the time you first synchronized it*. But you can also *reformat* the text in synchronized boxes and paths— formatting color, style sheets, character attributes, and so on. This formatting does *not* synchronize across the other text boxes and paths. This lets you style any instance without affecting style of the other instances.

Replacing, unsynchronizing, and deleting synchronized text

You can replace synchronized text in a path or box with another synchronized story (replacing one boilerplate paragraph with another). That's easy:

1. **Just drag the new synchronized story from the Synchronized Text palette, or select the target box or path with the Content tool.**

2. **Click the Insert Text button on the Synchronized text palette.**

   You get a warning dialog box, asking if you're sure that you want to replace the synchronized text.

3. **Click OK in the warning dialog box to replace the synchronized text, or click Cancel if you've changed your mind.**

You also may want to unsynchronize a specific text box or path so that it's no longer automatically updated. That, too, is easy: Just select the box or path with the Content tool and choose Style⇨Unsynchronize Text. The text won't be deleted, but it will no longer be automatically updated.

To unsynchronize *all* instances of synchronized text, click the story name in the Synchronized Text palette, then click the Unsynchronize All button. You get a confirmation dialog box; you can also undo the action if you click OK by accident. (We cover the Undo feature in Chapter 8.) You can delete the story from the palette with the Remove Item button, which unsynchronizes all instances and also removes the story from the palette. Either way, text boxes and paths retain the existing text, but they aren't automatically updated.

Finally, you can delete specific synchronized text boxes and paths at any time by selecting the box or path with the Item tool and choosing Edit⇨Cut or ⌘+X or Ctrl+X. Other synchronized boxes and paths are unaffected.

Chapter 4

A Picture Is Worth . . .

. . . .

In This Chapter

▶ Building picture boxes

▶ Importing pictures into boxes

▶ Managing and viewing pictures in a QuarkXPress project

. . . .

A picture may not always be worth a thousand words, but we encourage you to consider adding one or more to each QuarkXPress project. Any project that you would go to the trouble of laying out is likely to benefit from a graphic or two. The graphic may be as simple as a logo or as complex as a series of annotated photos. When all is said and done, graphics are integral parts of professional-looking print and Web publications. But how do you get those graphics ready for use in QuarkXPress, and how do you get them into the layout after they're prepped? That's what this chapter's all about.

Building Boxes for Pictures

If you know how to create text boxes, you've probably already made a thousand or two of them (or maybe just five or six). But when you look at a layout with nothing but text boxes on it, you start to realize that it looks . . . well, kind of *boring*. What you need is a picture or two. Pictures, or graphics, do more than just add visual interest to a page. A well-designed graphic actually can convey more information than a block of text. A photo, drawing, or chart can convey some very meaningful ideas.

Okay, you're convinced. It's time to start adding some pictures to your layout. You do this by creating picture boxes and filling them with pictures.

First, you need to select one of the seven picture-box tools in the Tools palette. As we mention in Chapter 1, the picture-box tools found in the Tools palette (as shown in Figure 4-1) are similar to those found in the Tools palette for text boxes: Rectangle, Rounded-Corner, Beveled-Corner, Concave-Corner, Oval, Bézier, and Freehand.

Figure 4-1:
The Tools
palette
includes
seven tools
for drawing
picture
boxes in a
variety of
shapes.

Chapter 1 explains how to create these picture boxes — it's the same process as for the Text Box tools explained there.

The only real way to tell the difference between a picture box and a text box is that a picture box has a big X inside of it, and a text box doesn't. If you turn off the guides in the View Menu (choose View⇨Hide Guides, or press F7), the X disappears, and there is really *no* way of telling one from the other. But don't fret about getting the two types of boxes mixed up; QuarkXPress won't let you put text inside a picture box or a picture inside a text box. You can *change* a picture box into a text box (and vice versa) by choosing Item⇨Content and then choosing Text (or Picture) from the Content submenu.

Setting picture box specifications

As it does with text boxes, QuarkXPress lets you be pretty darned picky about every part of a picture box. To establish a bunch of parameters for your picture box, use the five panes of the Modify dialog box for picture boxes. Figure 4-2 shows the Picture, Runaround, and Clipping panes. (The Box and Frame panes are alike for text boxes and picture boxes. See Chapter 3.)

The Picture pane of the Modify dialog box lets you size and position a picture box precisely, rotate it, scale it, flip it, color its background, and *skew* (slant) it. In these ways, the picture box options in the Modify dialog box are similar to those of the text box options. One thing you can do to a picture box that you can't do to a text box is position or crop the image *inside* the picture box.

If you specify custom values in the Picture pane of the Modify dialog box before you import a graphic into it, the settings are applied to the imported graphic. But if, for some reason, you *reimport* the graphic (or any other) into the picture box, QuarkXPress ignores the custom settings and uses the default settings. In other words, you must reenter your settings all over again.

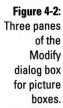

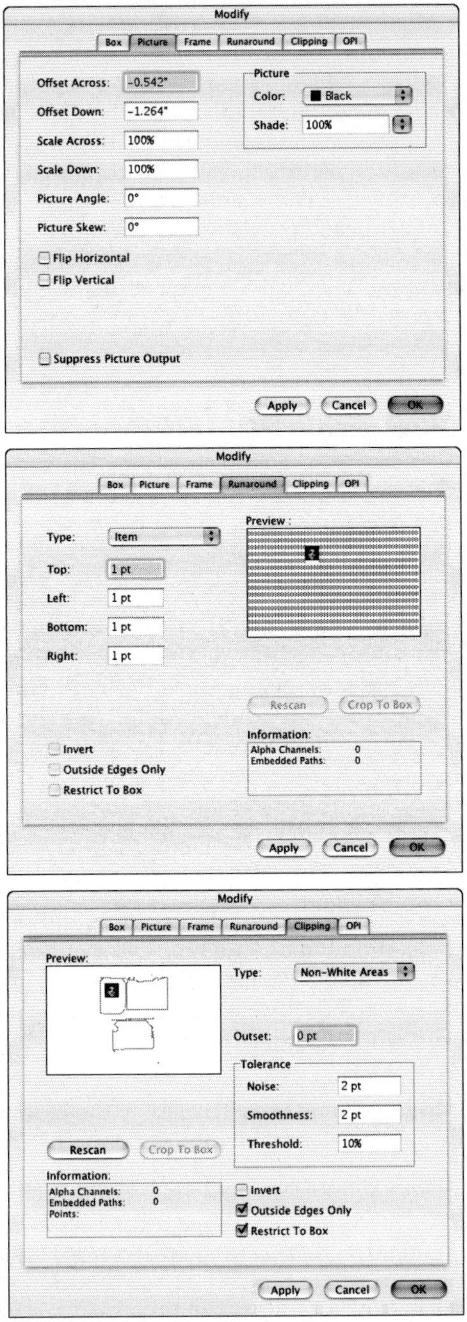

Figure 4-2:
Three panes
of the
Modify
dialog box
for picture
boxes.

The Runaround pane of the Modify dialog box controls how text wraps around the picture. You control the amount of space between the picture box and the text wrapping around it by entering distance values in the Top, Left, Bottom, and Right fields. The Clipping pane of the Modify dialog box lets you control the parts of the picture that appear in the layout; this is the *clipping path*. Clipping doesn't change the source picture file, just its copy that is used in the specific layout you're working on. There's also the OPI pane, an advanced feature used only in some server-based publishing environments.

The Clipping and OPI panes of the Modify dialog box appear only when you already have a picture placed inside the picture box.

Changing the size and position of a picture box

After you draw a picture box, you can tweak it in many ways. The most common way is by using the options in the Measurements palette (choose Window⇨Show Measurements, or press F9), where you can change the size of the box by entering different W (width) and H (height) values. You also can change the position of the box by entering different X (horizontal) and Y (vertical) coordinates. You can make the same changes in a Bézier picture box; and when you activate an individual *point* (the *corners* connecting the sides of the Bézier bar) by clicking it, the Measurements palette lets you adjust the point and its control handles.

QuarkXPress gives you a rich selection of ways to change the size and position of a picture box:

- **The Measurements palette.** This palette lets you enter different values in the X and Y fields to position the picture box; enter different values in the W and H fields to resize the box; enter a different value in the Angle field to rotate the box; and press Return or Enter to exit the palette and apply the new values (this method is our favorite because it lets you see the result of your work as it happens).

- **The Box pane of the Modify dialog box.** To display the Modify dialog box (refer to Figure 4-2), choose Item⇨Modify, or press ⌘+M or Ctrl+M:

  - Enter values in the Origin Across and Origin Down fields to control the position of the box.

  - Enter values in the Width and Height fields to control the size of the picture box.

  - Enter values in the Angle and Skew fields to rotate and slant the picture box. (More about this in Chapter 5.)

  To see the results of changed values, click the Apply button.

This method works fine, but we aren't enthusiastic. The Modify dialog box takes a great deal of space on the screen, which can make it difficult to see how the new values you're entering change the picture box.

✔ **The Item tool.** Use this tool to drag the box into position, and then grab the handles of the box to resize it.

Creating odd shapes

On occasion, to add visual interest to a page, you may want to import a graphic into a nonrectangular picture box, such as an oval, a circle, a straight-edged polygon, a starburst, or a curved shape. But as with irregular text boxes, we recommend that you use this trick sparingly. More than that, we recommend that you *not* use irregular boxes unless you are using them for a well-reasoned and well-planned effect. Okay, okay, you've heard the lecture. Now exactly how *do* you create irregular picture boxes? Exactly the same way that you create irregular text boxes, as we explained in Chapter 1.

You can also use the Starburst tool (the bottommost tool on the Tools palette) to draw picture boxes in the shape of a five-pointed star; actually, any sort of star or starburst — just double-click the tool to select the number of points and types of spikes.

Once created, you can resize any picture box.

Keep these things in mind as you change the shape of a Bézier box:

✔ Before you adjust a Bézier box, make sure that a check mark appears before the Shape command in the Item⇨Edit submenu.

✔ If Shape is checked when you click anywhere on or within a Bézier box, the entire box becomes active, and all points are displayed. You can then drag the point or segment that you want to move.

✔ To move multiple points at the same time, hold down the Shift key and click the points; then drag any of the selected points.

✔ If you want to drag the points in a straight, perfectly even line — in other words, if you want to *constrain* the direction you are dragging the points — continue to hold down the Shift key as you drag them.

✔ If you pause a moment before dragging a point or segment, QuarkXPress redraws the contents of the box as you drag.

✔ To add new points, hold down the Option or Alt key and click a segment at the place where you want the point to appear.

✔ To delete a point, hold down the Option or Alt key and click on the point.

Like Bézier text boxes, Bézier picture boxes can contain three kinds of points (corner points, smooth points, and symmetrical points) and two kinds of segments (curved and straight). And (as in Bézier text boxes) you can change any kind of point or segment in a Bézier picture box into any other kind of point or segment. You can also split the segments into more segments by using the Scissors tool.

Pick a Format, Any Format

Okay, you may have used the Starburst tool to create a picture box. You've resized it and moved its various points about a million times, and now you're ready to import a picture. Right? Well, not exactly. QuarkXPress is designed to handle a slew of graphics types, including some that you may not have heard of. We suggest that you take some time to get acquainted with these file formats before you begin importing anything.

QuarkXPress imports the following file formats. If your program's format is not on this list, chances are high that it can save as (or export to) one of these formats. In the following list, the code in *monofont* (equally spaced letters) is the filename extension common for these files on PCs:

- BMP, the Windows bitmap format. `.BMP`, `.DIB`

- EPS, the Encapsulated PostScript vector format favored by professional publishers — also Adobe Illustrator's native format. `.EPS`, `.AI`

  QuarkXPress also supports the DCS color-separated variant of `EPS`. Its full name is Document Color Separation. `.DCS`

- GIF, the Graphics Interchange Format common in Web projects. `.GIF`

- JPEG, the Joint Photographers Expert Group compressed bitmap format often used on the Web. `.JPG`

- Photo CD, the Kodak format used for photo finishing on CDs and popular for image catalogs. `.PCD`

- PICT, the Mac's former native graphics format (it can be bitmap or vector); common for inexpensive clip art. `.PCT`

- Portable Document Format (PDF), also known as Acrobat format, used for distributing formatted documents. `.PDF`

- Portable Network Graphics (PNG), a recent bitmap format from Adobe Systems that's designed for use on the Web. `.PNG`

- RLE, Run Length Encoded bitmap, the OS/2 variant of BMP. `.RLE`

- Scitex CT, the continuous-tone bitmap format used on Scitex prepress systems. `.CT`

✔ TIFF, the Tagged Image File Format, the bitmap standard for professional image editors and publishers. `.TIF` or `.TIFF`

✔ WMF, the Windows Metafile Format native to Windows but little used in professional documents. `.WMF`

QuarkXPress 6 no longer supports some graphic formats: the little-used MacPaint, PCX (PC Paintbrush), and Targa file formats. The program also does not support the Enhanced Windows Metafile Format (files have the extension `.EMF`) now standard in Microsoft Office for Windows applications. Be sure to use the older WMF format instead in such applications.

If QuarkXPress refuses to import the supported formats listed above, QuarkXPress probably thumbed its nose at you for one of two reasons:

✔ Embarrassingly obvious: The file isn't in the format that you think it's in (or it's corrupt).

✔ Not so obvious: The QuarkXPress import filter for the file type isn't installed in your XTension folder. If you are using PDF, Photo CD, PNG, or compressed TIFF files in QuarkXPress, you must manually install the filters. See Chapter 10 for information on how to install XTensions.

Although QuarkXPress supports all these file formats, we recommend that you stick to just two formats for your graphics — TIFF and EPS (including DCS) — because they offer the most flexibility and the best output. Runners-up are Photo CD, PICT, and Windows Metafile. If you're creating a Web page, we recommend JPEG and GIF files exclusively. For the rest, use them if you have them, but ask your artists (or the person who buys your clip art and stock photos) to convert the images into a recommended format.

EPS files provide the best-quality output, allow you to embed fonts, and better support color separations than any other drawing format. The only downside to EPS files is that they need a PostScript printer to print at high resolution; many Windows users may not have such a printer. (The PCL printer format is popular in Windows.) PICTs, Photo CDs, and Windows Metafiles are good second choices because they're common, but their formats don't offer the same capabilities for high-end output as TIFF and EPS.

If you're building a Web layout in QuarkXPress, there really isn't much to debate. GIFs and JPEGs are the only reliable graphics file formats available. The Web doesn't recognize any of the other file formats mentioned; although more Web applications are supporting the PNG format, still not enough do.

Pouring In the Picture

After you check out the picture you want to use in your QuarkXPress layout, you're ready to import it. Follow these steps:

1. **Open the project to the page that holds the picture box that you want to fill with a picture; then click the picture box to activate it.**

2. **Click the Content tool if it's not already selected.**

3. **Choose File➪Get Picture (or press ⌘+E or Ctrl+E).**

   The Get Picture dialog box appears, as shown in Figure 4-3.

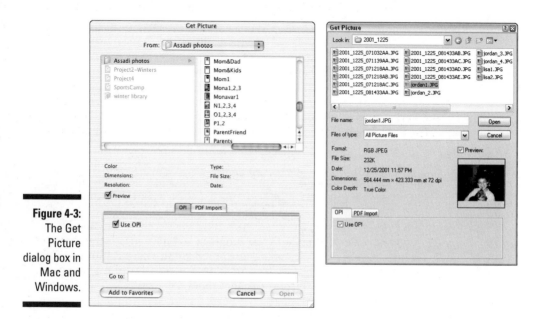

Figure 4-3: The Get Picture dialog box in Mac and Windows.

4. **Navigate the folders and drives until you find the image that you want to import.**

   If the Preview box is checked, QuarkXPress displays a thumbnail version of the image when you click the filename; this preview is meant to help you see whether it's the one you want. The preview may take a few moments to display after you select an image.

5. **Click Open.**

   The active picture box shows the picture. Sometimes, QuarkXPress takes a few moments to load the file, particularly if it is more than 200K, has millions of colors, or is a compressed file (such as JPEG or Photo CD).

QuarkXPress treats objects differently, depending on the selected tool. To change the contents of a box — text or graphics — select the Content tool.

If you click the Item tool, you can work with the box itself. Thus, to move an image within its box, click the Content tool; to move the box and the image inside it, select the Item tool.

You should always import graphics from external files as described above. In addition to importing pictures into picture boxes, you can copy a picture from a box and paste it into another. Although you can also copy pictures from other programs to the Clipboard, switch to QuarkXPress, and paste the picture into a picture box, you should avoid using this method; the original image file is not used for the image on the printed layout. Copying and pasting images this way will cause problems and cost you time and extra charges when you send the QuarkXPress project to a service bureau for output.

Making the Graphics Fit

What if you import an image and the image doesn't fit the box? How do you fit the image correctly? QuarkXPress imports a graphic at the graphic's original size. If the original is 6 inches square, QuarkXPress makes the image 6 inches square, no matter the size of the box that it's being placed in.

Following are a couple of ways to get your graphic to fit:

- ✔ Drag the handles (the little boxes that appear around the picture box when it's selected) to resize the picture box to fit the image.

- ✔ If you want the graphic to fit the box's current size, make sure that the Content tool or the Item tool is selected; then press Shift+Option+⌘+F or Ctrl+Alt+Shift+F. That finger-wrenching keyboard shortcut makes QuarkXPress resize the image so that it fits the box. Make sure that you press all four keys.

   If you miss the Option or Alt key and press just Shift+⌘+F or Ctrl+Shift+F, you get a distorted version of the image. It will be resized differently along the length than along the width. (No, we don't know why the more common option has the harder-to-use key combination.)

   The difference? The first shortcut keeps the image's original proportions, whereas the second makes the image fit the size of the box, distorting it if necessary. Figure 4-4 shows what happens when you use each option.

Sounds ugly? Fear not! You can avoid this conundrum entirely, thanks to some menu options in the Style menu in QuarkXPress. The Fit Picture to Box (Proportionally) command (Style➪Fit Picture to Box [Proportionally]) lets you resize an image so that it fits in a box without distortion.

You can also resize the picture box to the size of the picture with the Fit Box To Picture command (Style➪Fit Box to Picture). This option adjusts the picture box to fit around the picture instead of vice versa.

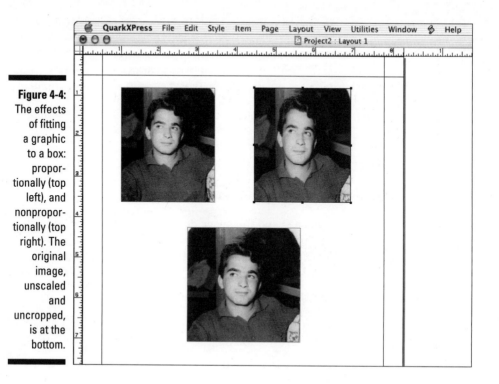

Figure 4-4:
The effects
of fitting
a graphic
to a box:
propor-
tionally (top
left), and
nonpropor-
tionally (top
right). The
original
image,
unscaled
and
uncropped,
is at the
bottom.

Another keyboard shortcut — Shift+⌘+M or Ctrl+Shift+M — centers a
graphic in the box. This shortcut won't resize your image; you'll probably
use Option+Shift+⌘+F or Ctrl+Alt+Shift+F to fit your image in the box. You
can also choose Style⇨Center Picture.

In addition to taking advantage of the automatic controls in QuarkXPress,
you can manually reposition, or *crop*, a graphic so it fits as you'd like it to
within a box. The easiest way to reposition a graphic manually is to start
with the Content tool active. Then just click the graphic and move it. The
pointer becomes a hand (called the grabber hand) when you position it over
the graphic. Hold down the mouse button and move the mouse — you'll see
the graphic move within the box. Release the mouse button when you're done.

You also can specify how much you want the image to move within the box.
You use the Measurements palette to control text attributes, graphics attributes, and box attributes. Figure 4-5 shows the Measurements palette with the
settings for the picture box that's in the top-left corner of the page.

The X% and Y% values show the amount of scaling (90 percent in Figure 4-5).
You can change those values by typing new ones in the boxes and then pressing Enter or Return.

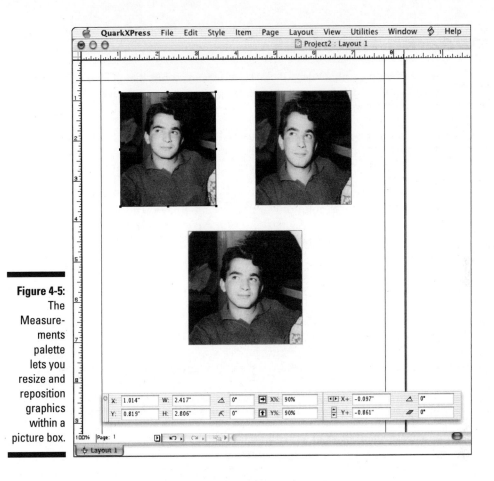

Figure 4-5:
The
Measure-
ments
palette
lets you
resize and
reposition
graphics
within a
picture box.

You also can change the position of a graphic by changing the X+ and Y+ values. A positive number moves the image to the right for X+ and down for Y+. Another method is to click the arrows to the right of the X+ and Y+ boxes. These arrows nudge the image up, down, left, or right, depending on which arrow you click. (Hold down the Option or Alt key to nudge an image in tiny steps: 0.001 unit of the current measurement, such as inches or picas.) You can, of course, use a combination of these techniques. Use the grabber hand to roughly position the graphic and then fine-tune the placement by clicking nudge arrows and/or changing the X+ and Y+ values manually. Another option is to choose Item⇨Modify (or press ⌘+M or Ctrl+M) and then click the Picture tab to get to the Picture pane of the Modify dialog box. There, you can change the Scale Across, Scale Down, Offset Down, and Offset Across values. That method is a bit of work, though.

When your graphics are placed in the box, sized, and positioned the way you like them, you can move on to using graphics as embellishments.

Managing Graphics

Getting pictures into QuarkXPress layouts is easy, but that is only part of the job. You also must keep track of your imported pictures during the production process so everything goes smoothly when it's time to output final pages.

When you import a picture into QuarkXPress, you don't actually import the entire picture file. If QuarkXPress added imported picture files to projects every time that you imported a picture, the project sizes would get out of hand. A few high-resolution scans could produce a single QuarkXPress layout that exceeds 50MB. So instead of importing entire graphic files, QuarkXPress imports only a low-resolution version of each image. This image is what you see when you rotate, crop, resize, or otherwise alter a picture. When you print the picture, the original image file is sent to the printer.

Dealing with modified pictures

After you import a picture, you should be aware of several pitfalls. First, if somebody modifies a picture that you imported into a QuarkXPress layout, you want to reimport the picture before you print it. If you don't update a picture that's been modified, QuarkXPress warns you when you print it and gives you a chance to update the graphic. If you update the graphic, however, you won't get to see the modified graphic before it's printed, and you may be in for a surprise. You have two options for updating modified pictures:

✔ You can update individual pictures manually in the Pictures pane of the Usage dialog box. (To display this dialog box, choose Utilities⇨Usage and then click the Pictures tab. See Figure 4-6.) The scroll list displays information on an imported TIFF file that was modified after it was imported. If you click the More Information button, QuarkXPress displays additional information about the picture whose name is highlighted in the scroll list. To update a modified picture, click its name and then click Update. To update multiple pictures, hold down the ⌘ or Ctrl key when you click.

✔ QuarkXPress can automatically update modified pictures for you. The Auto Picture Import list in the Preferences dialog box provides two choices — On and On (Verify) — that automatically update modified pictures when you open a layout. (To see the Preferences pane, choose QuarkXPress⇨Preferences on the Mac or Edit⇨Preferences in Windows, and choose General from the list at the left, or press Option+Shift+⌘+Y or Ctrl+Alt+Shift+Y.) If you choose On or Verify, a dialog box displays when QuarkXPress updates a modified picture.

Figure 4-6:
Pictures
imported
into Quark-
XPress are
managed in
the Picture
pane of
the Usage
dialog box.

		Usage for Layout 1		
	Fonts	Pictures	Profiles	OPI	Placeholders

Print	Name	Page	Type	Status
☑	Macintosh HD:...:GARDEN2.jpg	1	JPEG	OK
☑	Macintosh HD:...:Tday3.tif	1	TIFF	OK
☑	Macintosh HD:...:AA7,AA8	1	JPEG	OK

☐ More Information   (Done)   (Show)   (Update...)

Dealing with moved pictures

Sometimes, pictures get modified after you import them; other times, they get moved from their original locations. When you import a picture, QuarkXPress records its storage location so that it knows where the picture file is located when it's time to print your layout or post it to the Web. But if you move a picture file after you import it, QuarkXPress won't be able to find it. If this happens, QuarkXPress warns you when you try to print the picture and provides you the option of reestablishing the link to the missing file.

You can also reestablish links to missing pictures by choosing Utilities⇨ Usage, and then clicking on the Pictures tab to display the Pictures pane. To update a missing picture, click it and then click Update in the Pictures pane. QuarkXPress displays a standard Open dialog box that lets you locate and select the missing file. Sorry, but you must do this part yourself; QuarkXPress isn't smart enough to figure out the location of missing picture files.

Keeping track of picture files is particularly important if you use a printer pre-press house to produce final output. In addition to providing your QuarkXPress layouts to your printer, you must provide all imported pictures for those documents. If you don't include picture files, your service provider can still output your documents, but the low-resolution previews will be used instead of the original high-resolution picture files. Not a pretty picture.

Full-resolution preview

A new feature in QuarkXPress displays images at their full resolution, rather than at screen resolution. Full-resolution preview produces higher fidelity for clipping paths and when you zoom in, but it takes more computer horsepower and can slow down display.

QuarkXPress 6 lets you import a full-resolution version of images during import by checking Create Full Resolution Preview in the Get Picture dialog box's Full Resolution pane. If an imported image is no longer available and you used this option when importing it, it will still output at full resolution because the full file has been copied into the QuarkXPress project file. Also, you can turn on or off full-resolution preview for a selected image by choosing Item⇨Preview Resolution.

If you didn't register your copy of QuarkXPress 6, you won't have the Full-Resolution Preview feature available.

Collecting pictures for output

In layouts that contain many pictures, keeping track of all the pictures can be tricky, but collecting them all manually in preparation for output could challenge your sanity. Fortunately, QuarkXPress does this job for you. Just choose File⇨Collect for Output. In addition to collecting picture files, QuarkXPress generates a report that contains printing-related information about the document, including a list of fonts used, XTensions required for output, and the document's page size.

The Collect for Output feature also lets you pick and choose which pictures you want QuarkXPress to collect (as well as fonts and ICC color profiles). For more about the QuarkXPress Collect for Output feature, see Chapter 11.

Chapter 5

Getting Tricky with Boxes

*I*f you've read the preceding chapters, you've conquered the text box. You've uncovered the hidden secrets of the picture box. You've even dabbled with XPress Tags. (Okay. If you skipped XPress Tags, we won't hold it against you.) Now it's time to get creative! Let your hair down!

In this chapter, we show you some cool things to do with text and picture boxes that can add some flair to your projects. After all, you bought QuarkXPress to become a print and/or Web publisher, right? No self-respecting publisher would be caught without a bag of layout tricks. Discovering how to create tricky effects with text and picture boxes is worth your while and lets you create layouts that look very professional.

For example, QuarkXPress lets you wrap text around the contours of a picture: just one example of a layout trick that helps you establish — or solidify — the relationship between form and content in your layout designs.

Keep in mind that this chapter covers just a small part of what you can do with text and pictures in QuarkXPress — indeed, entire books have been written about manipulating (and remanipulating) layouts in QuarkXPress. You must go a long way to truly unleash the powers of this program. But that doesn't mean you can't have some fun now. Start filling that bag of tricks!

Running Around

In Chapter 3, we introduced the Runaround pane of the Modify dialog box. This section covers the Runaround pane in more detail.

In QuarkXPress, when text wraps around the edges of something — for example, a picture box, another text box, or something within a picture — it's called a *runaround.* You may know this effect as a *text wrap,* so try to adjust your vocabulary to *runaround* when using QuarkXPress. Keep these factors in mind when you create a runaround:

- ✔ You need two things: some text in a box (or on a text path) and an *obstructing item.* The obstructing item is the item the text runs around.
- ✔ The obstructing item must be in front of the text box in the page's stacking order. To bring an item in front of a text box, choose Item⇨Bring to Front or press F5.

Text runaround actually occurs by default any time you place an item in front of a text box. This default text runaround can easily be turned on or off to meet your needs, so you need to know how to create and adjust a runaround.

Follow these steps to create a runaround:

1. **Create a text box on the page and fill it with text.**

2. **Create an additional item for the text to wrap around — this is the obstructing item. Alternately, select an item on the page and choose Item⇨Bring to Front to be sure that it's in front of the text box.**

3. **Choose Item⇨Modify and then click the Runaround tab (or press ⌘+T or Ctrl+T) to open the Runaround pane, as shown in Figure 5-1.**

4. **In the Runaround pane, make sure that Item is selected from the Type menu.**

   (If you're trying to turn Runaround off, choose None.)

5. **Enter point values in the Outset, Top, Bottom, Left, and Right fields to specify how much white space to leave between the item and text runaround.**

   If the item is not rectangular, you can specify only a single runaround value in the Outset field. If the obstructing item has any holes (for example, a box shaped like the letter *O*), the Outside Edges Only option is available. If you check it, text cannot flow into and out of the holes.

6. **Look in the Preview area of the Runaround pane and click the Apply button to see whether you like the runaround. When you're satisfied, click OK.**

The Runaround pane of the Modify dialog box varies, based on the type of item around which you are wrapping text. Figure 5-1 shows the Runaround pane for a text box, a graphic, and a line.

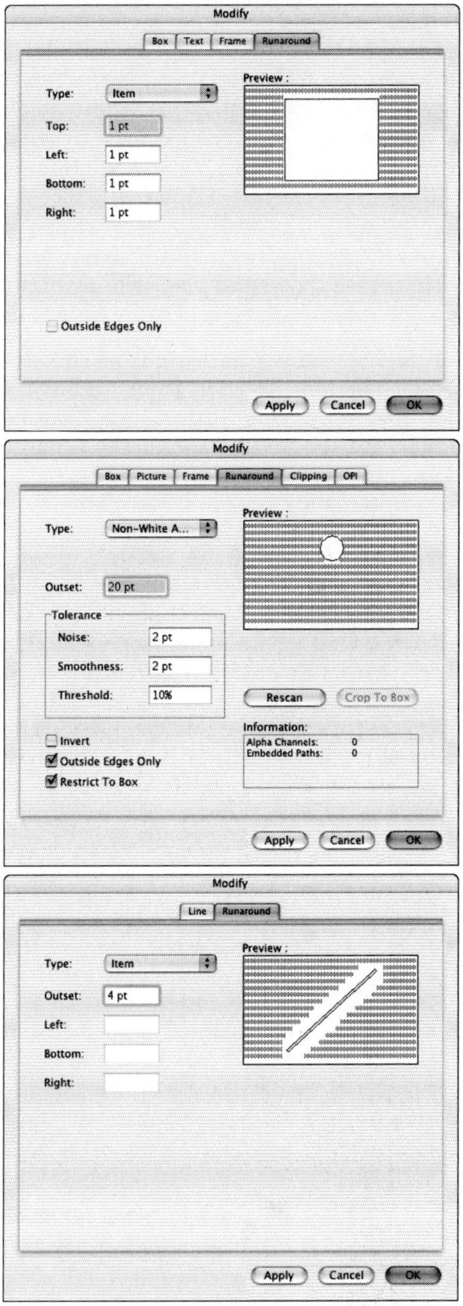

Figure 5-1:
The Runaround pane of the Modify dialog box.

QuarkXPress has two runaround options (None or Item) for text boxes, three options (None, Item, or Manual) for lines and text paths, and several options for picture boxes. You choose an option by selecting it in the Type pop-up menu in the Runaround pane of the Modify dialog box. After you choose an option, look at the Preview window of the Runaround pane to get an idea about how the text will flow. Here are the choices for flowing text around text boxes and boxes:

✔ **None.** QuarkXPress flows the text behind the active box as though no item appeared there. Figure 5-2 shows the overprinting of text that occurs when you choose a runaround type of None for a text box.

✔ **Item.** Flows the text around the edges of the item, as shown in Figure 5-3. Notice that you can determine how far away from the box the text will flow by entering values in the Top, Left, Bottom, and Right fields of the Runaround pane. In the figure, we set this amount as 1 point.

You can choose among three options for lines and text paths:

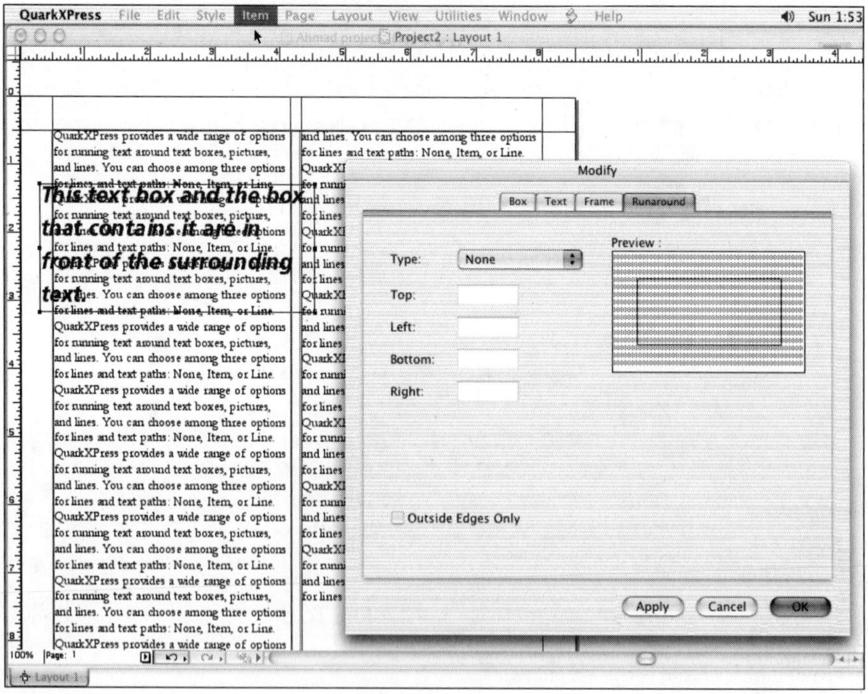

Figure 5-2:
Selecting
None as the
text box
runaround
type creates
this effect.

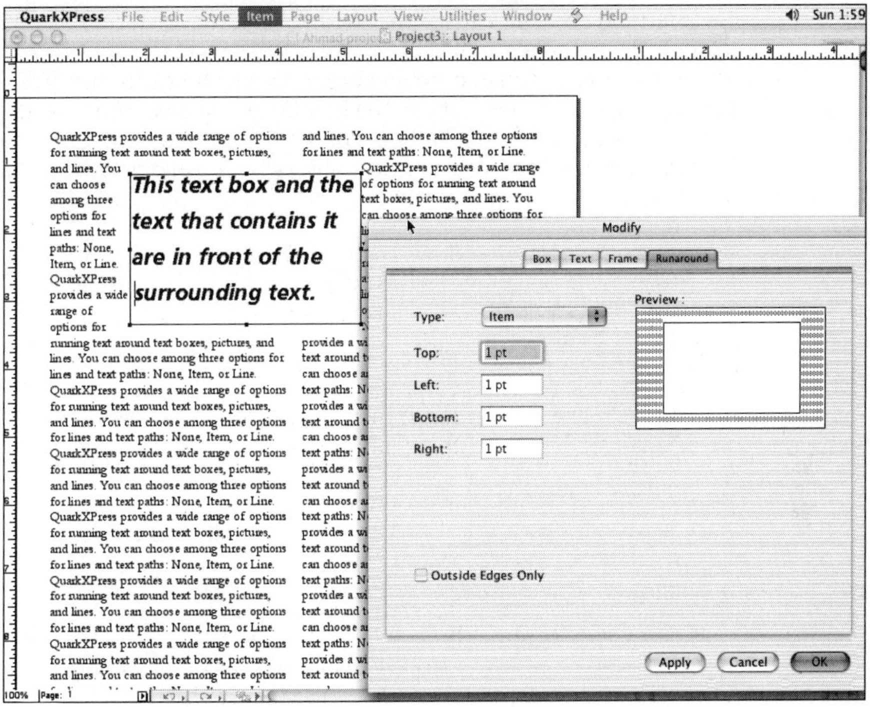

Figure 5-3:
An example
of the Item
runaround
for a text
box.

The figure shows a QuarkXPress screen with a Modify dialog box open on the Runaround tab, containing:
- Type: Item
- Top: 1 pt
- Left: 1 pt
- Bottom: 1 pt
- Right: 1 pt
- Outside Edges Only checkbox
- Preview area
- Apply, Cancel, OK buttons

The text box in the layout reads: "This text box and the text that contains it are in front of the surrounding text."

- ✓ **None.** Flows the text behind the active line or text path.

- ✓ **Item.** Flows text around the active line or text path. Note that if the active item is a text path, the runaround text behind is not affected by the text on the path — only by the path itself. As a result, the text on the path can overlap and obscure the text that's behind.

- ✓ **Manual.** Flows text around the image as it does when you choose Item.

If you choose Manual, QuarkXPress creates an editable shape, called a *runaround path,* around the active line or text path. If you activate the line or text path, you can edit the runaround by choosing Item➪Edit➪Runaround (or pressing Option+F4 or Ctrl+F10) and then dragging points, control handles, and segments.

You can also run text around tables. To do so, follow these steps:

1. **Select the table.**

2. **Choose Item➪Modify, or press ⌘+M or Ctrl+M, to open the Modify pane.**

3. **Choose the Text tab to display the Text pane, and make sure that the Run Text Around All Sides box is checked.**

Here are the choices for picture boxes:

- ✔ **None.** Flows the text behind the active picture box and picture.
- ✔ **Item.** Flows text around the active box.
- ✔ **Auto Image.** Creates a runaround path around the image within the box and flows text around the runaround path. Figure 5-4 shows an Auto Image runaround.
- ✔ **Embedded Path.** Creates a runaround path based on a picture-embedded clipping path (drawn in Adobe Photoshop) and runs text around the path.
- ✔ **Alpha Channel.** Creates a runaround path based on an alpha channel built into a TIFF image by a photo-editing application and runs text around this path. (An *alpha channel* is an invisible outline picture used to edit the image to which it is attached.) If you have more than one alpha channel embedded in your image, QuarkXPress lets you choose the alpha channel you want to run the text around.
- ✔ **Non-White Areas.** Creates a runaround path based on the picture's contrast. If you choose Non-White Areas, the Outset and Tolerance controls allow you to customize the runaround path.
- ✔ **Same as Clipping.** Runs text around the clipping path specified in the Clipping pane of the Modify dialog box. (A *clipping path* is a shape, created in an image-editing program, that isolates a portion of a picture.)
- ✔ **Picture Bounds.** Creates a runaround path based on the rectangular shape of the imported graphic. The runaround area includes the white background of the original picture file.

When you choose a picture box, you get additional runaround controls in the Runaround pane, including Outset, Tolerance, and Invert options. To use the extra controls, you need to be familiar with sophisticated image-editing techniques, so we don't cover them here. (If you want to try using these options, watch how the preview window shows the effects of your settings.)

The Outside Edges Only check box in the lower-left corner of the Runaround pane (refer to Figure 5-1) should normally be checked because it prevents text from getting inside a shape's interior gaps (for example, in the hollow part of a doughnut shape). The Outside Edges Only box does not apply to lines.

The Restrict To Box check box, also in the lower-left corner of the Runaround pane (refer to Figure 5-1), should usually be checked, too. If that box is unchecked, your text would wrap around any part of the image cropped by the box. (In other words, if your picture is larger than the picture box containing it, the part visible in the box is the cropped portion. The rest of the picture still exists but won't display or print. If the Restrict To Box is not checked, QuarkXPress assumes that you want the text to wrap around the entire picture, not just the part visible in the picture box. Although at times you may want such a *ghost wrap,* those times are rare.)

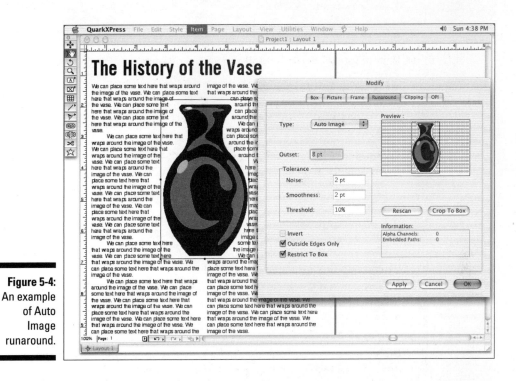

Figure 5-4:
An example
of Auto
Image
runaround.

If you run text around an item that's placed in front of a single column of text, by default QuarkXPress runs text on only one side of the item — the side that holds more text. For the text to run around both sides of an obstructing item, you must select the box that contains the runaround text, display the Text pane of the Modify dialog box (choose Item⇨Modify, or press ⌘+M or Ctrl+M), and check the Run Text Around All Sides check box.

Rotating Boxes

You can rotate both text boxes and picture boxes in QuarkXPress. Used well, rotated boxes add spark to the appearance of a page. For example, you can rotate a *sale* banner and splash it diagonally across an advertisement. As with the other layout tricks, use rotation sparingly for best results.

Figure 5-5 shows text boxes unrotated, rotated at 45 degrees, and rotated at 90 degrees.

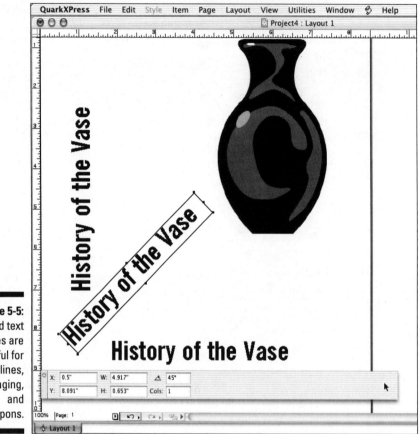

Figure 5-5:
Rotated text
boxes are
useful for
credit lines,
packaging,
and
coupons.

You can control the rotation of selected text boxes, picture boxes, or no-content boxes in three ways:

✔ Choose Item➪Modify, or press ⌘+M or Ctrl+M to display the Modify dialog box. If necessary, go to the Box pane. Then enter a rotation amount between 360 (degrees) and –360 in the Angle field. To rotate the box clockwise, use a negative value in the Angle field; to rotate the box counterclockwise, use a positive value in the Angle field.

✔ Click the Rotation tool in the Tool palette to select it. Position the mouse pointer at the point around which you want to rotate the box. (Click the center of the box to rotate it around its center, for example.) Then hold down the mouse button and move the mouse pointer away from the point where you clicked. Continue to hold down the mouse button as you drag in a circular direction, clockwise or counterclockwise.

✔ Enter a rotation value in the Angle box of the Measurements palette.

No single, correct way exists to rotate boxes. Experiment with all three options to see which method is most comfortable for you.

Skew, too!

The Box pane of the Modify dialog box also lets you enter an amount in another field called the Skew field. Not to be confused with the Angle box, which deals strictly with the rotation of a box, the Skew box applies an actual *slant* to the shape and contents of the box, as shown in Figure 5-6. The slanted text box in this example was achieved by entering a value of 20 in the Skew field in the Box pane of the Modify dialog box.

To skew a box, do the following:

1. **Open the project to the layout that holds the text box or picture box that you want to slant.**

2. **Click the box to make it active.**

3. **Choose Item⇨Modify, or press ⌘+M or Ctrl+M.**

   The Modify dialog box appears.

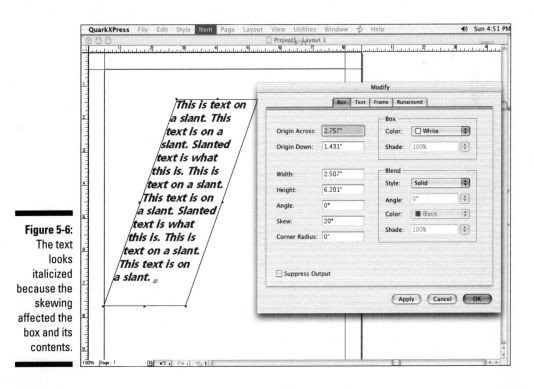

Figure 5-6:
The text looks italicized because the skewing affected the box and its contents.

4. **Go to the Box pane if it's not already open.**

5. **In the Skew field, enter a value between 75 and –75.**

   A positive number slants the box to the right; a negative number slants the box to the left.

If you apply a skew value to a box, any text or picture within the box is also slanted. You can also specify a skew value for only the contents of the box — text or picture — by displaying the Text or Picture pane of the Modify dialog box and entering a value in the Skew field.

Anchoring boxes within text

In the old days of publishing, graphic designers used wax or glue and a rubber roller to adhere galleys of text and halftones to paste-up boards. QuarkXPress not only frees you from such manual drudgery, but it also enables you to do something that wasn't possible before the advent of electronic publishing.

You have the option to anchor picture boxes and text boxes, as well as lines and text paths, within text so that the boxes move with the text if editing causes the text to reflow (change position as a result of edits that lengthen or shorten the text). This feature is great if, for example, you create catalogs that contain product pictures. You can paste a picture box within each product description. If the text is edited later, you don't have to worry about having to reposition all the pictures, because the pictures have been anchored and flow right along with the text. You can also anchor any and all grouped items, including grouped pictures, grouped text boxes, and any combination thereof.

Anchoring an item within text isn't difficult: Using the Content tool, click within a text box at the point in the text where you want to paste the copied or cut box, then choose Edit⇨Paste, or press ⌘+V or Ctrl+V.

You can anchor any box, including Bézier boxes and boxes that have been rotated or skewed. After you anchor a box within text, you can modify the contents of the box the same way that you modify the contents of an unanchored box. One thing that you can't do, however, is move an anchored box with the Item tool, because QuarkXPress treats an anchored box in much the same way as a character within text.

To delete an anchored box, click to its right with the Content tool to place the cursor next to it; then press Backspace or Delete. You can also delete an anchored box by highlighting it as you would a text character and then pressing Backspace or Delete.

If you click an anchored box, a pair of small icons appears on the left edge of the Measurements palette. If you click the top button (Align with Text Ascent), the top of an anchored box aligns with the top of the characters on the line that contains it; if you click the bottom button (Align with Text Baseline), the bottom of an anchored box aligns with the baseline of the line that contains it. The Box pane of the Measurements palette also lets you specify the alignment of an anchored box, and it offers an Offset box where you can adjust the position of baseline-aligned anchored boxes.

Here are some pitfalls to watch for when you anchor boxes within text:

- ✔ If the item that you're anchoring is wider than the column you're pasting it into, the item won't fit. When you paste, you create a text overflow. To avoid this problem, make sure that the item you're anchoring is narrower than the column that will contain it.

- ✔ If the item that you're anchoring is taller than the *leading* (space between lines) of the paragraph that you paste it into, the anchored item can cause uneven leading or obscure some of the surrounding text.

- ✔ If you want to anchor a box that's taller than the leading of the paragraph that will contain it, the safest practice is to anchor the box at the beginning of the paragraph (that is, make the anchored box the first character of the paragraph).

In Figure 5-7, the picture boxes in the left and right margins have been anchored in a two-column text box. The anchored box in the left column is a simple rectangle. The box was pasted at the beginning of the paragraph; the top of the box is aligned with the baseline of the first line. The anchored box on the right is aligned with the baseline of the first line of a paragraph. Note that you can apply rotation and skew to a box after you anchor it, too.

QuarkXPress also lets you anchor lines into text; anchoring lines works just like anchoring boxes.

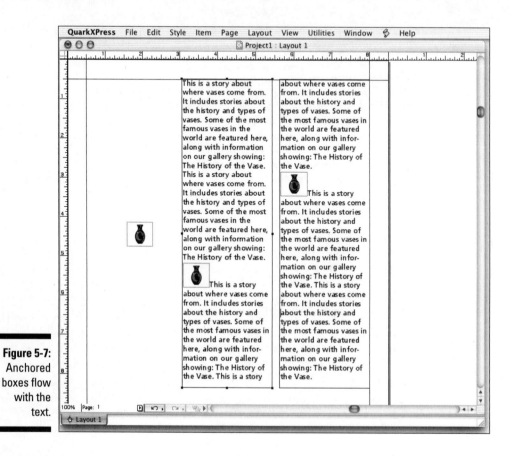

Figure 5-7:
Anchored
boxes flow
with the
text.

Part II
Adding Style and Substance

The 5th Wave   By Rich Tennant

@RICHTENNANT.COM

Gee, Richard, you'll have to show me where on the toolbar you found an icon labeled "Overkill".

In this part . . .

Good publishing technique is about more than just getting the words on paper or onscreen. It's also about tweaking the letters and lines — and the space between them — to make your pages shine. This part shows you how to do a lot, including how to get your QuarkXPress project out of your computer and onto some other medium, such as paper (later on in the book, we show you how to put pages on the Web). We tell you how to use XTensions — plug-ins to the program that beef up its capabilities. We also give you some solid suggestions on printing and working with all those other people in the world who know how to help you get the job done.

Chapter 6

You've Got Real Style

In This Chapter

▶ Using style sheets to format paragraphs in your layouts

▶ Creating, changing, and applying styles

▶ Importing styles from other projects

*H*alf the fun of desktop publishing is being able to automate some of the tasks that used to take so long. QuarkXPress makes setting up styles easy. Best of all, using style sheets saves you tons of time and helps you keep your formatting consistent throughout a layout.

Style sheets define basic specifications for your text: typefaces, type sizes, justification settings, and tab settings. If you select a paragraph and apply a style sheet, the paragraph automatically formats itself to the style sheet font and size. Even better, you can apply styles to any text selection, not just whole paragraphs. Even individual characters can have style.

Just think of all the time style sheets save you. Instead of applying each attribute to text individually, you can just tell QuarkXPress that you want particular swaths of text to take on all the formatting attributes established in a style tag. Then, with one click of the mouse, you send QuarkXPress on its merry way to format your layout quicker than you can take a sip of coffee.

Like many features of publishing, style sheets come with their own jargon:

✔ **Style sheet:** The group of formatting attributes (styles) in a layout. It's called a *sheet* because, before electronic publishing, typesetters had sheets that listed the formatting attributes they had to apply to specific kinds of text, such as body copy, captions, and headlines. QuarkXPress lets you define style sheets that apply to every layout in a project and to copy (also called *append*) those style sheets from one project to another.

✔ **Style or style tag:** A group of formatting attributes that you apply to one or more paragraphs or to selected text. You name the group, or style, so that you can apply all the attributes to the layout at once. For example, in text styled Body Text, you may indicate the typeface, type size, leading, and so on, as part of that Body Text style. The word *tag* means that you *tag* selected paragraphs or selected text with the style you want to apply. Because the word *style* also sometimes refers to a character attribute, such as italics or underline, many people use *style tag* to refer to the group of attributes. This distinction helps you avoid confusing the two meanings. (QuarkXPress uses the phrase *style sheet* for what we call a style or style tag; we use the industry-standard term, not Quark's term.)

Styles work in two places: Either *selected paragraphs or text* in your layout or in the word processing text you plan to import. We explain both.

Paragraph versus Character Styles

In addition to specifying styles for paragraphs, you can also specify styles that let you save the attributes for selected characters. Paragraph and character styles are not an either/or proposition. You can use both:

- The timesaving part about paragraph styles is that you apply them to whole paragraphs. For example, first-level heads might have a Header 1 style; captions, a Caption style; bylines, a Byline style; body text, a Body Text style, and so on. Specifying a style for all paragraph types that you often use is a great idea. With a paragraph style, all the text in the paragraph receives the same settings, such as font, size, and leading.

- The character styles feature can ensure consistent typography throughout your project. A paragraph style does that for entire paragraphs, but layouts often have pieces of text that always get the same formatting. For example, the first few words after a bullet might always appear bold. A character style with the settings for those specific characters can ensure that you always apply the correct settings. Before character styles, you had to apply each setting yourself and hoped that you remembered and used the correct settings each time. With character styles, QuarkXPress remembers for you. And as with paragraph styles, if you change the style sheet's settings, all the text using the style automatically updates throughout your project. Cool!

To distinguish between paragraph and character styles, QuarkXPress precedes the names of styles with either a ¶ to indicate a paragraph style or an **A** to indicate a character style. You see these symbols in the Style Sheets dialog box (see the following section, "Styling Your Style Sheets"), in the Append dialog box (see the section "Copying styles between layouts"), and in the Style Sheets palette (covered in "Making styles happen" in this chapter).

Styling Your Style Sheets

You find the keys to creating, changing, and applying styles in one spot — the Style Sheets dialog box, which you access by choosing Edit⇨Style Sheets or by pressing Shift+F11 (see Figure 6-1).

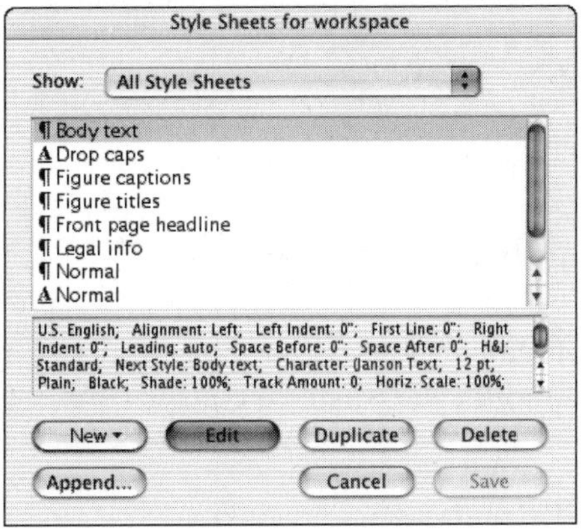

Figure 6-1:
The Style
Sheets
dialog box.

You set two style-related functions outside the Style Sheets dialog box:

✔ Set hyphenation controls in the H&Js dialog box by choosing Edit⇨H&Js.

✔ Control character and space scaling by accessing the Character pane in the Preferences dialog box. (Choose QuarkXPress⇨Preferences on the Mac or Edit⇨Preferences in Windows, or press Option+Shift+⌘+Y or Ctrl+Alt+Shift+Y.)

We cover style-related functions in detail in Chapter 8. If you're new to style sheets, experiment. You can delete any style sheet by highlighting the style in the Style Sheets dialog box and clicking the Delete button.

You can also use the new multiple Undo/Redo feature in QuarkXPress to cancel and reinstate changes to style sheets, so feel free to experiment. We cover the Undo/Redo feature in Chapter 8.

We *told* you it was easy!

Delving into the Style Sheets dialog box

The Style Sheets dialog box (refer to Figure 6-1) gives you several choices for editing style sheets:

✔ **New.** Lets you create a new style from scratch or create a new style based on an existing style. Note that the New button is a drop-down button — if you click it, it becomes a pop-up menu with two choices: ¶ Paragraph and **A** Character. You need to tell QuarkXPress whether you want to create a paragraph or character style.

Did you just define text settings through the Measurements palette or Style menu? You can turn these settings into a style. Just position your text cursor anywhere on the text that has the settings. Then open the Style Sheets dialog box and choose New. All settings automatically appear in the new style you create. Alternatively, you can Control+click or right-click any style name in the Style Sheets palette (open it by choosing Window⇨Show Style Sheets or by pressing F11) to get a pop-up menu that shows the New command; when you click New, the Style Sheets dialog box opens to let you create the new style.

✔ **Append.** Lets you copy a style from another project. Styles are at the project level in QuarkXPress.

✔ **Edit.** Lets you make changes to an existing style. Alternatively, you can Control+click or right-click any style name in the Style Sheets palette (open it by choosing Window⇨Show Style Sheets or by pressing F11) to get a pop-up menu that shows the Edit command.

✔ **Duplicate.** Makes copies of all the attributes of an existing style and gives the duplicate style the name *Copy of* name.

✔ **Delete.** Lets you delete existing styles. Any text using a deleted style retains the style's attributes, but the Style Sheets palette and Style menu show these paragraphs as having No Style. Alternatively, you can Control+click or right-click any style name in the Style Sheets palette to get a pop-up menu that has the Delete command in it. Note that if you delete a style sheet that you applied to text, QuarkXPress asks you which style sheet to apply instead. You can choose No Style, which leaves the text formatting untouched while removing the style sheet, or you can pick another style sheet and apply it to the text.

✔ **Save.** Saves all the style changes you make in the Style Sheets dialog box. If you forget to save styles when leaving the dialog box, the changes won't take effect, so try to remember to save, okay?

✔ **Cancel.** Makes the program ignore all style changes you made in the Style Sheets dialog box since you last saved changes.

Notice how QuarkXPress shows you the settings for the selected paragraph or character style in the Description area near the bottom of the Style Sheets dialog box? Reading this area is a great way to double-check your settings.

Using the Character Attributes dialog box

The best place to start creating styles for a layout is with character attributes. Paragraph styles use character attributes to format their paragraphs' text. Even if a paragraph uses a particular character style, you can use that same character style for selected text. Doing this saves you effort when you're creating paragraph styles because you can create several similar paragraph styles that all use the same character attributes; you define the text formatting once in the Character Attributes dialog box and just change the paragraph formatting (such as indentation or space above) in the various paragraph styles based on it. We talk about editing paragraph styles in the next section.

The default setting for Normal is left-aligned, 12-point Helvetica (Arial in Windows) with automatic leading. To change any attributes of the Normal style, close all open layouts, choose Edit⇔Style Sheets (or press Shift+F11) and edit the Normal style as we describe in the following two sections. These settings become the new defaults for all future new layouts. Any style tag created without a project open becomes part of the default style sheet for all new projects.

Figure 6-2 shows the Character Attributes dialog box, where much of the action of setting up styles happens.

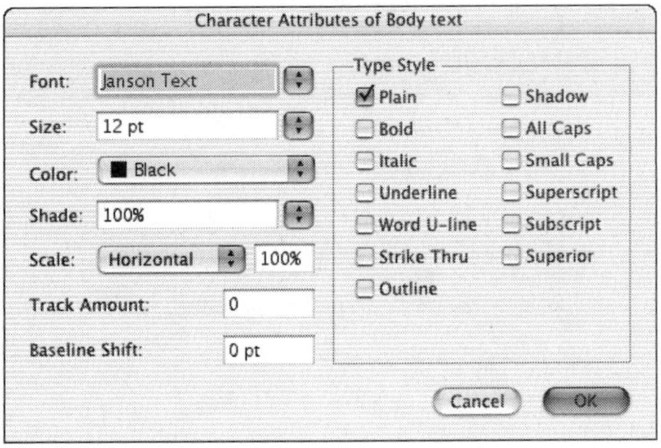

Figure 6-2:
The
Character
Attributes
dialog box.

> Character Attributes of Body text
>
> Font: Janson Text
> Size: 12 pt
> Color: ■ Black
> Shade: 100%
> Scale: Horizontal 100%
> Track Amount: 0
> Baseline Shift: 0 pt
>
> Type Style
> ☑ Plain   ☐ Shadow
> ☐ Bold   ☐ All Caps
> ☐ Italic   ☐ Small Caps
> ☐ Underline ☐ Superscript
> ☐ Word U-line ☐ Subscript
> ☐ Strike Thru ☐ Superior
> ☐ Outline
>
> Cancel   OK

Following are explanations of the fields in the Character Attributes dialog box:

✔ **Font** is where you choose the typeface. The pop-up menu shows all the fonts installed in your system, as shown in Figure 6-3. If you type the first few letters of a font's name, the menu automatically scrolls to the first font whose name begins with those letters.

In Windows, QuarkXPress adds a code before each font name:

- **T1:** *Type 1 PostScript* fonts (best when outputting to film)

- **O:** The new *OpenType* format (fine for laser and inkjet printers; okay for film if your service bureau supports OpenType)

- **TT:** *TrueType* fonts (fine for laser and inkjet printers)

✔ **Size** lets you pick the type size in *points* (the standard measurement for text size, of which there are 72 to an inch). You can pick from the pop-up menu's sizes or simply type any size you want in the Size field. (You can specify type size to three decimal places, such as 12.123 points. If you enter more decimal places than that, QuarkXPress ignores them.)

✔ **Color** lets you choose the color for text. Any color defined in the project appears in this list.

✔ **Shade** lets you determine how dark the selected color (including black) appears. You can pick from the pop-up menu's percentages or enter your own figure (up to three decimal places).

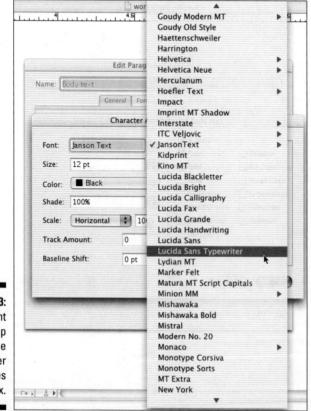

Figure 6-3:
The Font pop-up menu in the Character Attributes dialog box.

✔ **Scale** lets you scrunch type either horizontally (width) or vertically (height). Pick what you want from the pop-up menu. Then enter a percentage value for how much you want to expand (widen) or condense (compress) the size. Values less than 100% condense the type; values greater than 100% expand the type.

✔ **Track Amount** adjusts the spacing between all characters, moving them closer together (a negative number) or farther apart (a positive number). See Chapter 8 for more on tracking and its cousin, kerning.

✔ **Baseline Shift** lets you move text up or down relative to other text on the line. (The *baseline* is the imaginary line that type rests on.) A positive number moves the text up; a negative number moves it down.

✔ **Type Style** is where you set the typeface settings. Check all the appropriate boxes. Note that some settings disallow others: Underline and Word Underline override each other, as do All Caps and Small Caps, and Subscript and Superscript. Selecting Plain deselects everything else.

QuarkXPress dialog boxes often include pop-up menus to help you make selections faster. For example, in the Character Attributes dialog box, Font, Size, Color, and Shade all offer pop-up menus. You also can enter the value you want directly into the box.

When you finish selecting the character formatting for your new or edited character style sheet, click OK. You return to the Style Sheets dialog box (refer to Figure 6-1).

Checking out the Edit Paragraph Style Sheet dialog box

After you work with character styles, you can create or edit the paragraph style sheet. In the Style Sheet dialog box, use the New button to create a new paragraph style sheet. To change an existing paragraph style, click the style and then click the Edit button. The Edit Paragraph Style Sheet dialog box, shown in Figure 6-4, appears. In the sections that follow, we cover the four panes of Edit Paragraph Style Sheet dialog box in order. You can use these Edit Paragraph Style Sheet features in any order and ignore the ones that don't apply to the current style.

The General pane

The first pane is the General pane (refer to Figure 6-4).

The first two options are

- ✔ **Keyboard Equivalent** lets you assign a shortcut key (what QuarkXPress calls a *hot key*) to a paragraph style.

- ✔ **Based On** lets you make the paragraph style use a previously created style sheet's settings (and update the current style sheet if the style sheet it's based on is changed in the future).

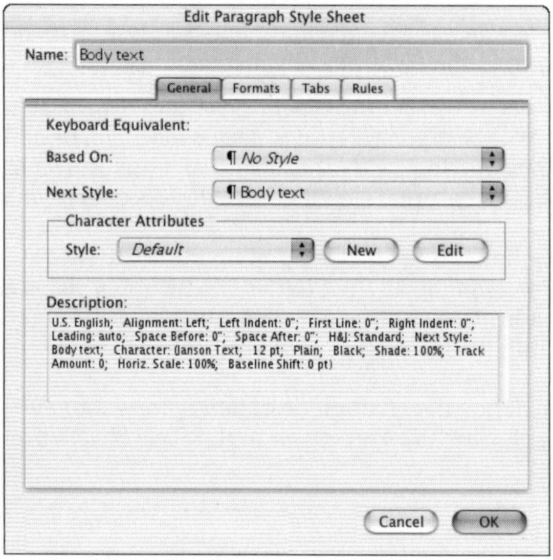

Figure 6-4:
The General pane of the Edit Paragraph Style Sheet dialog box.

> **Edit Paragraph Style Sheet**
>
> Name: Body text
>
> [General | Formats | Tabs | Rules]
>
> Keyboard Equivalent:
>
> Based On: ¶ No Style
>
> Next Style: ¶ Body text
>
> Character Attributes
>
> Style: Default   (New) (Edit)
>
> Description:
> U.S. English; Alignment: Left; Left Indent: 0"; First Line: 0"; Right Indent: 0"; Leading: auto; Space Before: 0"; Space After: 0"; H&J: Standard; Next Style: Body text; Character: (Janson Text; 12 pt; Plain; Black; Shade: 100%; Track Amount: 0; Horiz. Scale: 100%; Baseline Shift: 0 pt)
>
> (Cancel) (OK)

The other settings are unique to the Edit Paragraph Style Sheet dialog box:

- ✔ **Next Style** lets you establish linked styles. For example, suppose that you specify that a headline style should always be followed by a byline style, which will always be followed by a body text style. If you choose Next Style, here's what happens after you enter a headline: As you type text into the QuarkXPress page, every time you enter a paragraph return after typing a byline, the style automatically changes to the Body Text style. If your style is used on paragraphs typically followed by other paragraphs using the same style, such as body text, leave Next Style set to Self.

- ✔ **Style** tells QuarkXPress which character style to use in this paragraph style. (That's why we suggest that you create the character styles first.) If you want to create a new character style, you can do so by clicking the New button. You can also edit an existing character style by picking it from the Style pop-up menu and then clicking the Edit button.

The Formats pane

Most of the work that goes into creating a paragraph style occurs in the Formats pane. Figure 6-5 shows this pane.

Edit Paragraph Style Sheet

Name: Body text

General | Formats | Tabs | Rules

Left Indent: 0"	☐ Drop Caps
	Character Count: 1
First Line: 0"	Line Count: 3
Right Indent: 0"	
Leading: auto	☐ Keep Lines Together
	☐ All Lines in ¶
Space Before: 0"	☐ Start: 2 End: 2
Space After: 0"	
Alignment: Left	☐ Keep with Next ¶
H&J: Standard	☐ Lock to Baseline Grid

Cancel   OK

Figure 6-5: The Formats pane of the Edit Paragraph Style Sheet dialog box.

Here are the options:

- ✔ **Left Indent** indents the entire paragraph's left margin by the amount you specify.

- ✔ **First Line** indents the first line of a paragraph — a common thing to do with body text. A typical setting makes the indent the same as the text's point size (equal to an em space).

- ✔ **Right Indent** indents the entire paragraph's right margin by the amount you specify.

You don't have to use the same measurement system in this — or any — dialog box. The Left Indent and Right Indent could appear in inches, whereas the First Line could appear in picas and points. For example, if you want the first line to be an em space, which is the same as the point size, you can enter **0p9**, which means 0 picas and 9 points, instead of figuring out its equivalent in inches. You could easily enter **9 pt** to indicate 9 points.

- **Leading** sets the space between lines. Enter the leading value in the Preferences dialog box's Paragraph pane (or select a pre-set leading amount in the Paragraph pane's Leading pop-up) by choosing QuarkXPress⇨Preferences on the Mac or Edit⇨Preferences in Windows or by pressing Option+Shift+⌘+Y or Ctrl+Alt+Shift+Y.

- **Space Before** lets you insert a fixed amount of space before the paragraph. This space is not inserted if the paragraph happens to start at the top of a page, column, or text box. An example of when to use this setting is for headlines within a story, where you typically want some space between the text and the headline.

- **Space After** is like Space Before, except it adds space after a paragraph. It's pretty rare that you use both settings on the same paragraph.

- **Alignment** tells QuarkXPress whether to align the text to the left or right margin, to center the text, or to align the text against both right and left margins (justified). Note that Force Justify makes the last line of a paragraph align against both margins (rarely used), while the regular Justify option leaves the last line aligned only to the left.

- **H&J** is where you pick the hyphenation and tracking settings for the paragraph. You create H&J sets (hyphenation and justification controls) by choosing Edit⇨H&Js or by pressing Option+Shift+F11 or Ctrl+Shift+F11. Chapter 8 covers hyphenation in detail.

We recommend that you always create an H&J set called None that has hyphenation disabled. For several types of text, such as headlines, bylines, company names, and product names, you won't want the text to be hyphenated. An H&J set with hyphenation disabled does the trick.

- **Drop Caps** lets you make the first character or characters in a paragraph large and dropped down into the text, as shown in Figure 6-6. This is popular for introductions and conclusions. Check the Character Count box for how many characters are to be oversized and dropped down (1 is typical); use Line Count to set how deep the drop is (2, 3, and 4 are typical). Drop caps are more effective if you boldface the dropped character(s) or change the font, as in the last two examples in Figure 6-6. If you have a huge drop cap, as in the bottom of the figure, you may not need a bold drop cap — it's a question of judgment and taste.

Including a drop cap in a different font than the rest of the paragraph is a common technique in publishing, so it's puzzling to see that QuarkXPress still can't set the paragraph style to make this font change for you. That means that you need to create a drop cap character style and then, after you've applied the drop cap paragraph style, apply the character style to the dropped cap letter itself manually each time. (You could change the drop cap's font each time by using the Measurements palette, by choosing Style⇨Character, or by pressing Shift+⌘+D or Ctrl+Shift+D; but using the character style ensures that every drop cap will have exactly the same settings.)

✓ **Keep Lines Together** ensures that a paragraph's lines are kept together rather than split at a column break or page break. You can set this field so all lines are kept together by selecting the All Lines in ¶ button. Another way to keep lines together is to specify how many lines in the beginning and end of a paragraph must be kept together; enter the values in the Start and End boxes and click the button next to the Start box.

Many typographers hate orphans and widows — not people who are orphaned or widowed, but text isolated from the rest of its paragraph. An *orphan* is the first line of text in a paragraph that is at the bottom of a column or page, isolated from the rest of its paragraph (on the next column or page); a *widow* is the last line of a paragraph that is by itself at the top of a page or column (see Figure 6-7). To prevent these typographic horrors, the typographically correct set likes to set the Start and End fields to 2 to force QuarkXPress to avoid such lonely lines. However, incorporating those settings means that the bottoms of your columns may not align, because QuarkXPress may have to move text from the bottom of a column to prevent a widow or an orphan.

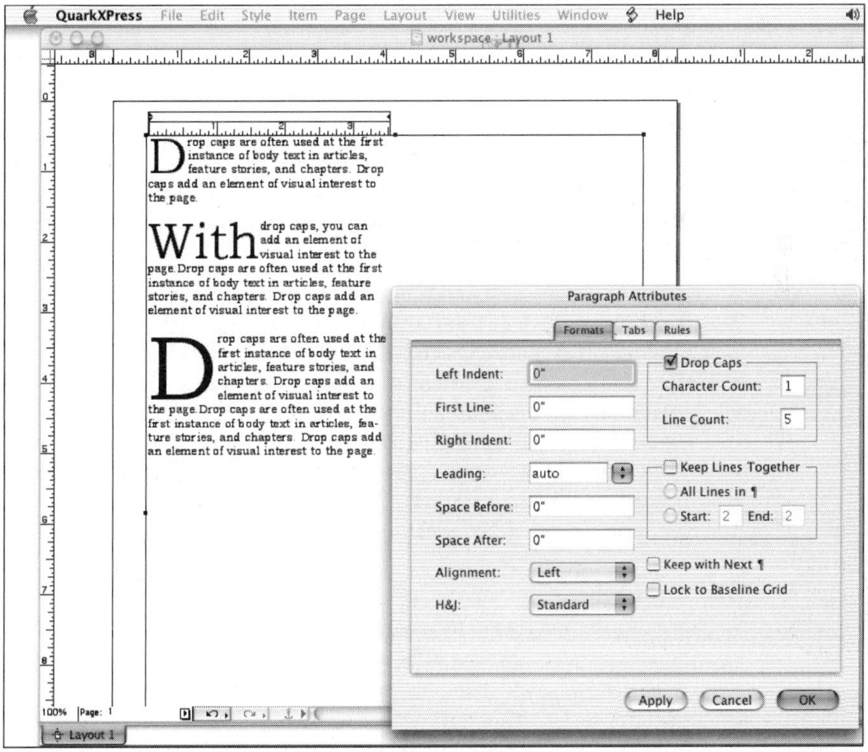

Figure 6-6:
Examples of
drop cap
settings.

We agree that widows are bad things when it comes to printing, but we think orphans are usually fine, so we recommend that you leave Start at 1 and set End at 2. To avoid the uneven column bottoms that result when QuarkXPress moves widowed text, add a few words to each of your layouts' shorter columns — QuarkXPress puts back a line of text at the bottom of each column so all of your text aligns properly.

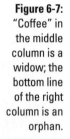

Figure 6-7: "Coffee" in the middle column is a widow; the bottom line of the right column is an orphan.

widow

Typographers avoid widows and orphans because they are isolated lines that seem to be cut off from the rest of the paragraph. This can interfere with the reader's comprehension because widows and orphans are isolated from their context. You can usually fix widows quicker than you can take a sip of

coffee.

Typographers avoid widows and orphans because they are isolated lines that seem to be cut off from the rest of the paragraph. This can interfere with the reader's comprehension because widows and orphans are isolated from their context. Once you learn how, you can

fix widows and orphans quicker than you can take a sip of coffee.

Widows and orphans are isolated lines that seem to be cut off from the rest of the paragraph. Avoid them by paying attention to the beginnings and endings of columns.

You can fix widows and

orphan

✔ **Keep with Next ¶** ensures that a paragraph does not separate from the paragraph that follows. For example, you wouldn't want a headline at the bottom of a column or page; to make sure that the headline doesn't separate from the body text that follows, check Keep with Next ¶ in your headline paragraph style.

✔ **Lock to Baseline Grid** ensures that all text aligns to the baseline grid that you set up in the Paragraph pane of the Preferences dialog box. (Access the dialog by QuarkXPress⇨Preferences on the Mac or Edit⇨ Preferences in Windows or by pressing Option+Shift+⌘+Y or Ctrl+ Alt+Shift+Y). Locking a paragraph to the baseline grid means that QuarkXPress ignores the leading specifications, if necessary, to ensure that text aligns from column to column. If you use this feature, make sure you set the Increment amount the same as your body text's leading so you don't get awkward gaps between paragraphs.

The Tabs pane

The Tabs pane lets you set up tabs in your paragraphs — handy for creating simple tables and aligning bullets and the text that follows them. Figure 6-8 shows the Tabs pane.

In the Tabs pane, you see a ruler that you use to set your tabs. Under the ruler, you see buttons for each kind of tab: left-aligned, center-aligned, right-aligned, decimal-aligned, comma-aligned, and character-aligned (Align On).

(If you choose Align On, enter the character you want the tab to align to in the Align On field.) The text aligns to the tab's location based on the type of alignment you choose. Figure 6-9 shows some tab alignment examples.

Click the button for the alignment you want; then click the ruler at the spot where you want that tab. If you miss the spot you want, click the tab location and (holding down the mouse button) move the mouse to the left or right until you get to the desired location. The Position box shows the current location.

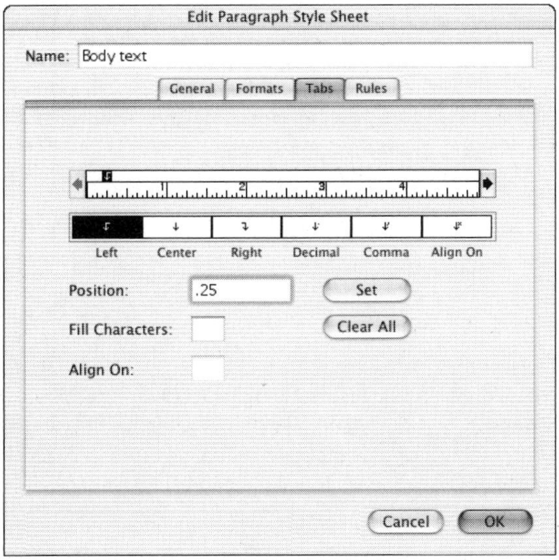

Figure 6-8:
The Tabs
pane of
the Edit
Paragraph
Style Sheet
dialog box.

If you prefer to be exact, you can just click the appropriate alignment button and then enter the position you want in the Position box. Enter a new number to change its position if you got it wrong the first time. When the new tab is where you want it, click the Set button to tell QuarkXPress that you're finished specifying that tab and are ready to enter a new position for a new tab. You can alter a tab's position by clicking it in the ruler and entering a new value in the Position box.

Regardless of how you set the position, you can change the alignment by selecting the tab and clicking a new alignment button.

If you create several tabs and want to get rid of them all, just click the Clear All button. To delete an individual tab, select it with the mouse, hold down the mouse button, and drag the tab outside of the ruler. Release the mouse button, and the tab disappears. Or select the tab and press the Backspace key or the Delete or Del key.

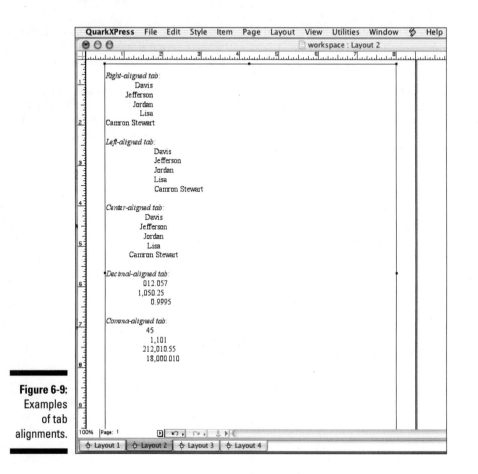

Figure 6-9:
Examples
of tab
alignments.

When creating a tab, you may want a *leader* or *fill* character. For example, to get a series of dots between text in a table of contents and its page number, you'd have a tab between the text and the number. By giving that tab a fill character of a period (.), you get your row of dots. You can enter two fill characters in QuarkXPress; the tab alternates the two characters. For example, entering += as the fill characters results in a leader like +=+=+=+=+=+=. More commonly, you would have a period and a space as your two leader characters, so the periods are not packed too tightly together.

The Rules pane

By using the Rules pane, you can insert ruling lines above and/or below your paragraphs (see Figure 6-10). This feature is handy especially for separating kickers (small-print text that appears below headlines), headlines, and other such elements. You can use the underline settings in the Edit Character Style

Sheet dialog box, but those settings give you no control over the type of under-line, its position, color, or pattern. In the Rules pane, you set the rules for these rules. And the Rules pane also lets you put a rule above a paragraph.

First, decide whether you want the rules above and/or below your paragraph. Check the Rule Above and Rule Below boxes as appropriate. You can set the two rules independently, which is why you see the exact same specifications twice — once for each rule. You're not seeing double — QuarkXPress is simply giving you identical controls for each rule.

The Rules pane gives you control over the following:

✔ **Length** lets you choose between Text, which makes the rule the same width as the text (if the paragraph has multiple lines, the length of the rule will match the top line if you use Rule Above; the length of the rule will match the length of the last line of text if you use Rule Below) or Indents, which makes the rule a specific length.

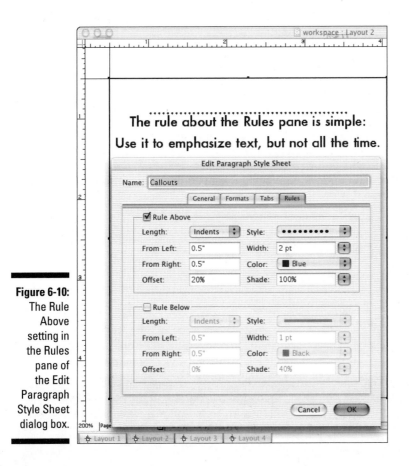

Figure 6-10:
The Rule
Above
setting in
the Rules
pane of
the Edit
Paragraph
Style Sheet
dialog box.

- ✔ **From Left** tells QuarkXPress how far from the column's left margin to start the rule, if you selected Indents in the Length pop-up menu.

- ✔ **From Right** tells QuarkXPress how far from the column's right margin to end the rule, if you selected Indents in the Length pop-up menu.

- ✔ **Offset** is tricky. You can enter a percentage from 0% to 100% to move the rule away from the text, but the difference between 0% and 100% is just a point or two. Or you can enter a value like 1.0 pt or –9 pt to position the rule relative to the text. Larger positive numbers move the rule above the text's baseline; a value of 0 puts the rule at the baseline, while a negative number moves the rule below the baseline. (The maximum and minimum values depend on the point size and leading; QuarkXPress tells you when you exceed the specific text's limits.) Experiment with these settings until you get what you want.

- ✔ **Style** lets you select the rule style. The pop-up menu displays any rule styles defined in the Dashes & Stripes dialog box (Edit⇨Dashes & Stripes); Chapter 12 covers this in detail.

- ✔ **Width** is the rule's thickness. Choose from the pop-up menu's sizes or enter your own in the field.

- ✔ **Color** lets you select a color for the rule. Any color defined in the project appears in this list.

- ✔ **Shade** lets you set the percentage of the color selected (including black). Choose from the pop-up menu's sizes or enter your own in the field.

The QuarkXPress Style Sheets dialog box has a nifty feature that makes style management incredibly simple. In the Show pop-up menu, you can choose which style sheets you want to display: All Style Sheets, Paragraph Style Sheets, Character Style Sheets, Style Sheets in Use, and Style Sheets Not Used. Those last two come in really handy.

Making styles happen

You can apply a style in one of three ways:

- ✔ Use the Paragraph Style Sheet and Character Style Sheet menu options in the Style menu.

- ✔ Use the Style Sheets palette (at the right side of Figure 6-11) by choosing Window⇨Show Style Sheets or by pressing F11. This option is our favorite way to apply styles in most cases.

- ✔ Use the keyboard shortcut, if you defined one in the Style Sheets dialog box. (In Figure 6-11, we did not invoke a shortcut key.) Although this option is the fastest method, use it only for very commonly used styles because you need to remember the keyboard shortcuts that you assign.

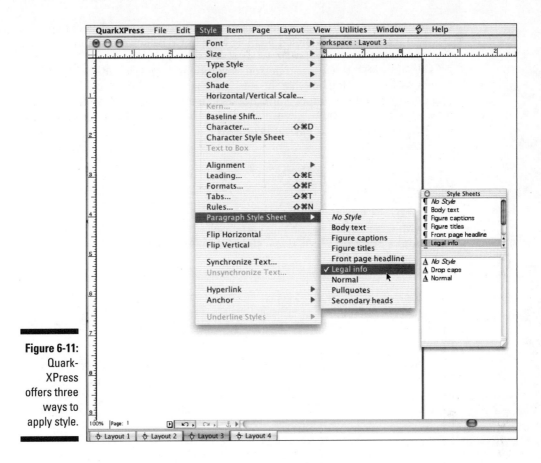

Figure 6-11:
Quark-
XPress
offers three
ways to
apply style.

If you aren't convinced that style sheets can save you a great deal of time, take a few minutes and give them a try and then compare formatting a layout with them to formatting a layout without them. Most publishers find style sheets to be terrific timesavers, and we think that you will, too.

Altering Styles

Just when you think you've created a great style, you decide to make some little changes to make it even better — you know, add a point to the size of your headline, make your byline italic, or change the body copy leading.

Again, you can make changes to a style easily: Simply open the Style Sheets dialog box (press Shift+F11), select the style sheet you want to change, and click Edit. You then can change attributes as you want. You also can use this approach to create new styles based on current ones or to create duplicate styles and modify them to make new ones.

To compare two styles, a great feature makes comparing easy. Select two styles in the Style Sheets dialog box (⌘+click or Ctrl+click the second style so that the first style remains selected as well). Then hold down the Option or Alt key and watch the Append button become the Compare button. Click Compare, and a dialog box like the one shown in Figure 6-12 appears. With this Compare feature, you can now determine quickly how styles differ, making it easier for you to identify the styles that you need to alter to ensure typographic consistency in your layout.

Based-on styles

When you create styles for a layout, you may want several similar styles, perhaps with some styles even being variations of others. For example, you may want both a Body Text style *and* a style for bulleted lists that's based on the Body Text style.

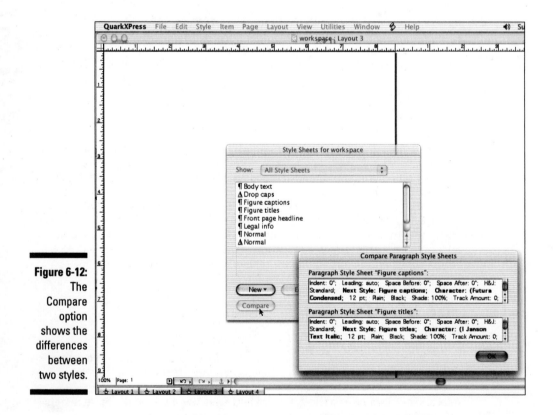

Figure 6-12:
The Compare option shows the differences between two styles.

No problem. QuarkXPress uses a technique called *based-on formatting* in its styles. By selecting the Based On option in the Edit Character Style Sheet dialog box, you can tell QuarkXPress to base the Bulleted Text character style on the Body Text character style (in which you defined typeface, point size, leading, justification, hyphenation, indentation, tabs, and other attributes). You then modify the Bulleted Text character style to accommodate bullets — by changing the indentation, for example. The great thing about based-on formatting is that if you later decide to change the typeface in Body Text, the typeface automatically changes in Bulleted Text and in all other character styles that you created or edited based on Body Text. Think of it as a shortcut that saves you a great deal of work in maintaining consistent styles.

Duplicating styles

Another nifty way to change an existing style or create a new one is to duplicate an existing style and then edit the attributes in that duplicate.

Duplicating a style is like creating a based-on style, except that the new style does not automatically update if you modify the style it is duplicated from — unless you base the style that you duplicated or edited on another style.

Replacing styles

You can replace style sheets in your layout as easily as you can change text. In fact, you use the same method — choose Edit⇨Find/Change, or press ⌘+F or Ctrl+F. When you use this feature, you may wonder how you can replace style sheets because you see no obvious option to do so. The trick is to uncheck the Ignore Attributes check box; doing so enlarges the dialog box to make room for new options (see Figure 6-13).

Note that Find/Change does not search all layouts in the project, only the active layout. (The *active layout* is the one you have open to work on.)

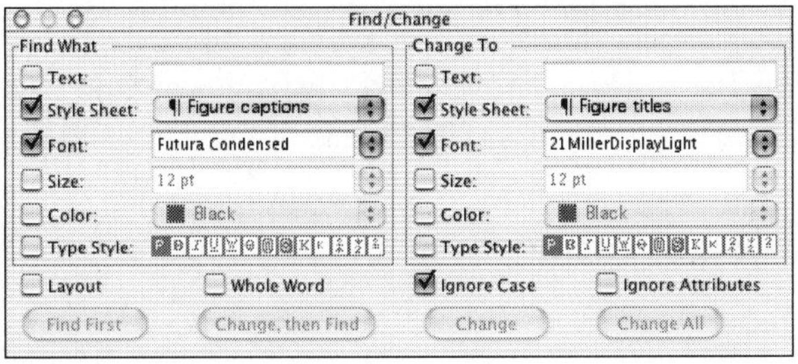

Figure 6-13:
The Find/
Change
dialog box.

To replace one style sheet with another, check the Style Sheet check boxes in the Find What and Change To sections of the Find/Change dialog box and then use the pop-up menus to specify which style sheet should replace another. When you do this, make sure that you're at the beginning of your layout or story — QuarkXPress only searches from the text cursor's location, ignoring text before it. (*Story* is the QuarkXPress term for text in the current text box and any text boxes linked to it.) To replace the style throughout the layout, make sure that the Layout check box is selected; to replace the style only in the current story, make sure the Layout check box is unchecked.

Click the Find First button to find the first occurrence of the style you want to replace. Then click Change All to have QuarkXPress replace all occurrences of that style from that point on; or click Change Then Find to replace the found text's style and look for the next occurrence; or click Change to change the found text's style but not look for the next occurrence.

Replacing a style sheet does not get rid of that style sheet — it simply retags all the text that uses the original style sheet with the new style sheet.

Importing Styles

Sometimes you find yourself in a situation where you already have style sheets in one QuarkXPress layout that are *just right* for what you need in another one. Have no fear — you don't need to start the process all over again. Just copy styles from one layout to another.

Copying styles between layouts

You copy styles between layouts by clicking the Append button in the Style Sheets dialog box to open the Append Style Sheets dialog box (see Figure 6-14). You can change drives and directories as needed to select the QuarkXPress layout that has the style sheet you want. You can also append style sheets through the Append dialog box (choose File➪Append), which also lets you append other settings, such as color definitions.

To append a style (or styles), simply select the names of individual styles you want to copy. If a style you select to append has the same name as one already in the current layout, you get to choose whether to override the current style with the one you want to copy, cancel the appending of that style, or append the style anyhow but give it a new name.

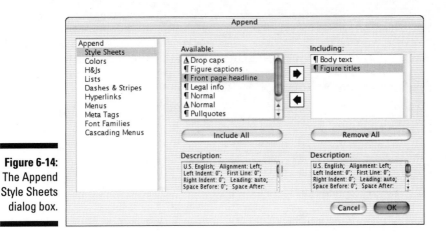

Figure 6-14:
The Append
Style Sheets
dialog box.

Importing styles from a word processor

Some people create text by entering it directly into the text boxes of a
QuarkXPress layout. Others prefer to use a separate word-processing program for drafting the text, and then they import the text into QuarkXPress
later. Either works fine, and both methods let you take advantage of style
sheets.

QuarkXPress lets you import paragraph styles created in Microsoft Word and
Corel WordPerfect. To make the process of importing text files that include
style sheets work smoothly, we suggest that you first put a check mark in the
Include Style Sheets box at the bottom of the Get Text box (see Figure 6-15).

You also use the Include Style Sheets option if you want to import text saved
in the XPress Tags format. Although the purpose of the XPress Tags format
is to embed style tags and other formatting information in your text, you
still must remind QuarkXPress to read those tags during import. Otherwise,
QuarkXPress imports your text as an ASCII file and treats all the embedded
tags as regular text without acting on them. (If you want to find out more
about XPress Tags, refer to the QuarkXPress documentation or our
QuarkXPress 6 Bible, also published by Wiley Publishing, Inc.)

If you check the Include Style Sheets check box for word-processor formats
that have no style sheets, QuarkXPress ignores the setting. Thus, if you usually import style sheets with your text, always check this box; checking the
box causes no problems when importing other text formats.

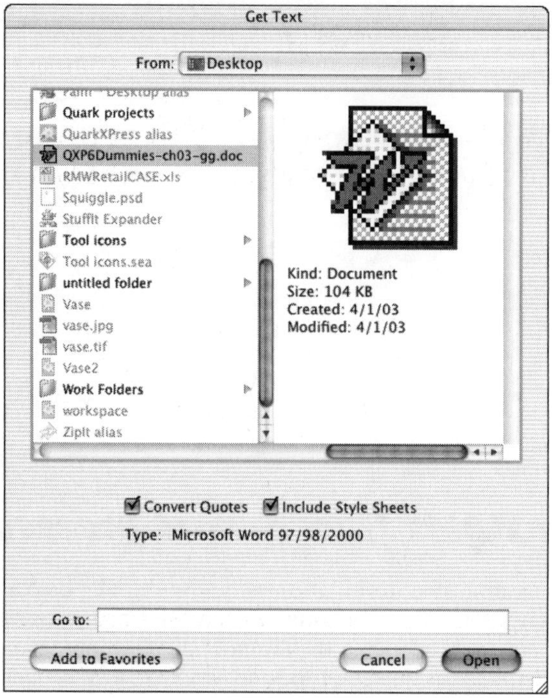

Figure 6-15:
The Include
Style Sheets
option
imports
word-
processor
documents
with style
sheets.

If the imported style sheet has a style tag that uses a name already in use by the QuarkXPress layout, you can either rename the imported style tag or ignore it and use the existing QuarkXPress style tag in its place. This capability is just one more reason to use style sheets.

We recommend checking the Convert Quotes box so that quotation marks in imported text convert to the curly quotes favored by professional typesetters.

As you can tell, we are style-sheet fans to the core. Style sheets save you time. Saving time saves you money. And saving money is a good thing.

Chapter 7

Working with Special Characters

*B*efore desktop publishing, you could distinguish homegrown layouts from the professionally produced kind by the difference in typography. Homegrown publications were often typewritten; professional publications were typeset. Anyone could spot the difference: Homegrown publications, for example, contained two hyphens (--) as a dash, whereas professional publications used the — dash character. Professionally produced publications also featured accents — when appropriate — on letters, different styles of characters, a wide variety of symbols, and even characters of different sizes.

Special Characters

With desktop publishing, anyone with a desktop computer had access to the same typeset characters. The only problem was that most people didn't know how to use these characters. You could use all sorts of keyboard commands to get these characters, but who could remember them all? So you kept seeing --, ', and " in documents that looked professional; you could tell that the documents had come off of someone's laser printer because of those telltale typewriter characters.

Working with special characters soon became simpler with the advent of QuarkXPress. For example, the program can generate those quotation characters as you type text. Automating the quotes goes a long way toward helping your publications look professionally produced.

Unfortunately, you still have to type in em dashes the hard way — by using special keyboard commands (Option+Shift+– (hyphen) or Ctrl+Shift+=).

Most versions of Microsoft Word have a default setting that converts two hyphens to an en dash (–) rather than an em dash (—), which is simply wrong typographically. (Word 98 for Mac and Word 2002/XP for Windows don't have this problem.) Worse, in some cases, QuarkXPress for Mac reads the Word-for-Windows-created en dash as the æ character, which can really mess up your file. To solve these two problems, we recommend that you turn off Word's automatic conversion of two hyphens to a dash (Tools⇨AutoCorrect⇨AutoFormat as You Type). Instead, enter two hyphens in the Replace box in the AutoCorrect dialog box's AutoCorrect pane, place an em dash (Option+Shift+–(hyphen) on the Mac or Alt+0151 in Windows) in the With box, and then click the Add button. Doing this makes Word substitute the correct dash when you type two consecutive hyphens.

If you did a double-take at the preceding Windows shortcut *(Alt+0151? I don't have that many fingers!)*, you read it right. The upcoming sidebar "Windows and Mac special-character shortcuts" explains how it's done.

Typographic Characters

Your otherwise-humble authors are typographic snobs, so we think everyone should use the curly quotes and the correct kinds of dashes. Why? Because professional typographers always use them, and they've become synonymous with professionalism. And they're so easy to use that you have no excuse not to use them. Table 7-1 shows the typographic and typewriter characters that you'll care about most often. It also shows shortcuts for quotes and dashes in Windows and on a Mac.

Table 7-1	Typographic and Typewriter Characters	
Character	*Typographic Character*	*Typewriter Character*
Em dash	—	- - (two hyphens)
En dash	–	- (single hyphen)

Character	Typographic Character	Typewriter Character
Apostrophe	'	'
Single quotes	"	''
Double quotes	""	"

Quotes and dashes

One of the first things you should do in QuarkXPress is configure it to type in the professional characters for you automatically. In addition, make sure QuarkXPress is set to convert quotes and double hyphens immediately on import.

Entering curly quotes

To set up automatic curly quotes, choose QuarkXPress⇨Preferences on the Mac or Edit⇨Preferences in Windows, or press Option+Shift+⌘+Y or Ctrl+Alt+Shift+Y, and activate the Interactive pane from the list on the left side of the Preferences dialog box (see Figure 7-1). Smart Quotes should be checked by default; if it isn't, be sure to check the Smart Quotes option so QuarkXPress will convert quotes as you type. If you're not publishing in English, you can select a different set of quote characters through the Format pop-up menu, also shown in Figure 7-1.

For many preferences, to make them affect all QuarkXPress layouts, you have to make sure that no project is open before you change the preferences. Otherwise, the changed preferences will apply only to that project. But any preferences set in the Interactive pane of the Preferences dialog box affect all layouts, whether or not a project was open when you set those preferences.

Converting quotes and dashes

In text files that you import, you can ensure that QuarkXPress converts the quotes and, yes, even the double hyphens to dashes, by checking the Convert Quotes box in the Get Text dialog box. You can access the Get Text dialog box by choosing File⇨Get Text, or by pressing ⌘+E or Ctrl+E. Once checked, you don't have to keep checking the Convert Quotes check box; QuarkXPress leaves the box checked for all future imports until, of course, you uncheck it. Figure 7-2 shows how the Get Text dialog box looks with the Convert Quotes box checked.

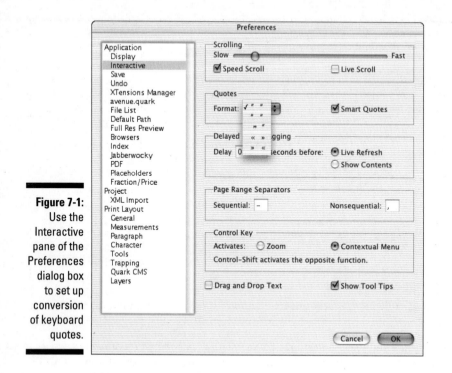

Figure 7-1:
Use the
Interactive
pane of the
Preferences
dialog box
to set up
conversion
of keyboard
quotes.

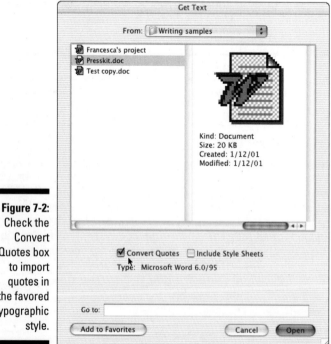

Figure 7-2:
Check the
Convert
Quotes box
to import
quotes in
the favored
typographic
style.

Windows and Mac special-character shortcuts

The Mac has many built-in shortcuts for special characters and symbols; QuarkXPress adds its own. Windows also supports many symbols (though it uses special codes for most, rather than keyboard shortcuts). When you use keyboard shortcuts, keep the following conditions in mind:

✔ **Not all keyboard shortcuts are available in all programs.** This is truer in Windows than on the Mac, because Windows programs are generally less consistent than Mac programs.

✔ **Not all symbols are supported in all fonts.** For symbols listed as not supported, you

may be able to find a symbol font (also called pi font) that includes the symbol (as used here, not supported means that the symbol is not available in standard fonts).

✔ **The Windows codes require special, four-digit key combinations using Alt.** To use the Windows codes, press and hold the Alt key and enter the four-digit numeral code from the numeric keypad, not from the numbers on the keyboard (above the letters). The Mac doesn't use an equivalent numeric system; instead, all characters are accessible through some shortcut combination.

When a double hyphen converts to an em dash, you get a *breaking em dash* — it can separate from its preceding text and appear as the first character in a line. Most editors prefer not to start a line with a dash, so they manually enter nonbreaking em dashes. Table 7-2 lists the keyboard shortcuts for quotes and nonbreaking (and breaking) em dashes in Windows and on a Mac.

Table 7-2	Shortcuts for Quotes and Dashes	
Character	*Mac Shortcut*	*Windows Shortcut*
Open double quote (")	Option+[	Shift+Alt+[or Alt+0147
Close double quote (")	Option+Shift+[	Shift+Alt+] or Alt+0148
Open French double quote («)	Option+\	Ctrl+Alt+[or Alt+0171
Close French double quote (»)	Option+Shift+\	Ctrl+Alt+] or Alt+0187
Open single quote (')	Option+]	Alt+[
Close single quote (')	Option+Shift+]	Alt+]

(continued)

Table 7-2 *(continued)*		
Character	*Mac Shortcut*	*Windows Shortcut*
Breaking em dash (—)	Option+Shift+– (hyphen)	Ctrl+Shift+= or Alt+0151
Nonbreaking en dash (–)	Option+– (hyphen)	Ctrl+= or Alt+0150
Nonbreaking em dash (—)	Option+⌘+=	Ctrl+Shift+Alt+=

Ligatures

Ligatures are linked-together characters in many higher-end publications (magazines, books, and the like) where you find the combination of *f* and *i* typeset not as *fi* but as *fi*. Such a combination avoids having the dot on the *i* get in the way of the top curve or the bar of the *f*. In QuarkXPress for Mac, you also have automatic access to an *fl* ligature, an *ffi* ligature, and an *ffl* ligature.

QuarkXPress for Windows doesn't support ligatures. When you open a Mac file that has ligatures into QuarkXPress for Windows, QuarkXPress translates the ligatures back to regular characters. If you move the file back to the Mac, the ligatures reappear. There's a slight chance that such translations could affect the line length of text in your layout, so double-check to make sure you don't gain or lose a line or two if you try this.

If you're working in a cross-platform publishing environment, save yourself (and your colleagues) some headaches: Don't use ligatures.

Figure 7-3 shows some ligatures. Other ligatures than these occur in some fonts, but the Mac version of QuarkXPress automatically handles only these four. For others (assuming that the font supports other ligatures), you have to enter the ligature code manually (see Table 7-3).

To use ligatures consistently with a Mac in all your publications, first make sure no projects are open. Then follow these steps:

1. **Open the Preferences dialog box.**

   To get there, choose QuarkXPress⇨Preferences or press Option+Shift+⌘+Y.

   The Preferences dialog box opens.

2. **Use the Character pane to set up your treatment of ligatures.**

   Figure 7-4 shows the pane with the ligature section highlighted.

TECHNICAL STUFF

Now you see them, now you don't

If you use ligatures, you may find that sometimes the combined characters appear as a ligature — and sometimes they don't. The variation comes about because of the spacing computations used by QuarkXPress.

Ligatures make sense when characters are close together, because that's when pieces of the characters may overlap (ironically, that's the problem ligatures were designed to solve in the first place). But when text is spaced more widely, the characters won't overprint. In such a case, you have no practical reason to combine characters — in fact, if you do combine them, your layout would look weird: most letters would have space between them except for the ligatures.

QuarkXPress automatically figures out when the characters should be combined into ligatures and when they shouldn't, so don't worry about it. In fact, QuarkXPress is so smart that if you did a search for the word first and the fi was a ligature in your text, QuarkXPress would find the ligature even though you entered fi as two letters in the Find dialog box.

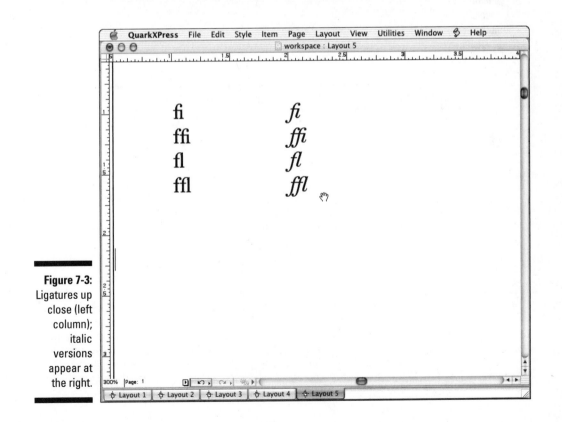

Figure 7-3:
Ligatures up close (left column); italic versions appear at the right.

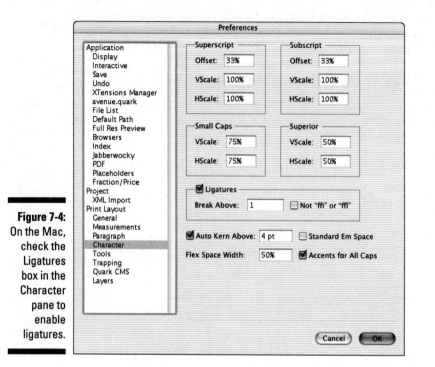

Figure 7-4:
On the Mac,
check the
Ligatures
box in the
Character
pane to
enable
ligatures.

Table 7-3	Shortcuts for Ligatures	
Character	*Mac Shortcut*	*Windows Shortcut*
fi	Option+Shift+5	not supported
fl	Option+Shift+6	not supported
ffi	no shortcut	not supported
ffl	no shortcut	not supported

When you use the codes in Table 7-3, you actually enter the ligature character manually; when QuarkXPress generates the ligatures for you, it remembers the actual letters in your layout but substitutes the ligature characters for them both onscreen and when printing. Note that these coded ligature characters may appear in your Find dialog box as a square. That's okay: QuarkXPress still searches for the actual character. Also note that using codes to generate ligatures, rather than using the QuarkXPress automatic ligature feature, causes the spell checker to flag words with the coded-in ligatures as suspect words. The bottom line: For the vast majority of cases, don't use those codes to create ligatures. It's not worth the hassle.

Accented and Foreign Characters

You don't have to use accents for words like *café* that came to English from another language. *Cafe* is quite acceptable. But adding the accent to the *e* gives the word a bit more sophistication (plus it helps people pronounce it *ka-fay* rather than *kayfe!*). Of course, if your publication is international or multilingual, you want to use the international characters and accents.

First, decide how you want to treat accents on capital letters. If you use accents, you always use them on lowercase letters, but they're optional for uppercase letters — as long as you're consistent (within the same publication) and either *always* use the accents on capitalized letters or *never* use them. QuarkXPress makes consistent decisions on accents easy:

✔ If you select the Accents for All Caps option in the Character pane of the Preferences dialog box, all accented letters keep their accents when capitalized.

✔ If you don't select Accents for All Caps, the accent is removed when the letters are capitalized — and reinstated when the letters are lowercased. With this handy option, you can always add the accents as you type and let QuarkXPress handle the uppercase letters.

So how do you get the accents, as shown in Table 7-4, to appear in the first place? Read on. (Windows supports hundreds more special characters and accented characters, available through Word's Insert Symbol feature. We don't include these because they don't have special codes and aren't supported in QuarkXPress, Windows or Mac, unless you have fonts with those characters.)

Table 7-4	Accent and Foreign Character Shortcuts	
Character	*Mac Shortcut*	*Windows Shortcut*
acute (´)	Option+E letter	' letter
cedilla (¸)	See C and c	' letter
circumflex (ˆ)	Option+I letter	∧ letter
grave (`)	Option+` letter	` letter
tilde (~)	Option+N letter	~ letter
trema (¨)	Option+U letter	" letter
umlaut (¨)	Option+U letter	" letter

(continued)

Table 7-4 *(continued)*

Character	Mac Shortcut	Windows Shortcut
Á	Option+E A	" A or Alt+0193
á	Option+E a	' a or Alt+0225
À	Option+` A	` A or Alt+0192
à	Option+` a	` a or Alt+0224
Ä	Option+U A	" A or Alt+0196
ä	Option+U a	" a or Alt+0228
Ã	Option+N A	~ A or Alt+0195
ã	Option+N a	~ a or Alt+0227
Â	Option+I A	^ A or Alt+0194
â	Option+I a	^ a or Alt+0226
Å	Option+Shift+A	Alt+0197
å	Option+A	Alt+0229
Æ	Option+Shift+`	Alt+0198
æ	Option+`	Alt+0230 or Ctrl+Alt+Z
Ç	Option+Shift+C	" C or Alt+0199
ç	Option+C	' c or Alt+0231 or Ctrl+Alt+,
Ð	not supported	Alt+0208
ð	not supported	Alt+0240
É	Option+E E	' E or Alt+0201
é	Option+E e	' e or Alt+0233
È	Option+` E	` E or Alt+0200
è	Option+` e	` e or Alt+0232
Ë	Option+U E	" E or Alt+0203
ë	Option+U e	" e or Alt+0235
Ê	Option+I E	^ E or Alt+0202
ê	Option+I e	^ e or Alt+0234

Character	Mac Shortcut	Windows Shortcut
Í	Option+E I	' I or Alt+-205
í	Option+E i	' i or Alt+0237
Ì	Option+ ` I	` I or Alt+0204
ì	Option+` i	` i or Alt+0236
Ï	Option+U I	" I or Alt+0207
ï	Option+U i	" I or Alt+0239
Î	Option+I I	^ I or Alt+0206
î	Option+I i	^ I or Alt+0238
Ñ	Option+N N	~ N or Alt+0209
ñ	Option+N n	~ n or Alt+0241
Ó	Option+E O	" O or Alt+0211
ó	Option+E o	' o or Alt+0243 or Ctrl+Alt+O
Ò	Option+` O	` O or Alt+0210
ò	Option+` o	` o or Alt+0242
Ö	Option+U O	" O or Alt+0214
ö	Option+U o	" o or Alt+0246
Õ	Option+N O	~ O or Alt+0213
õ	Option+N o	~ o or Alt+0245
Ô	Option+I O	^ O or Alt+0212
ô	Option+I o	^ o or Alt+0244
Ø	Option+Shift+O	Alt+0216
ø	Option+O	Alt+0248 or Ctrl+Alt+L
Œ	Option+Shift+Q	Alt+0140
œ	Option+Q	Alt+0156
Þ	not supported	Alt+0222
þ	not supported	Alt+0254
ß	Option+S	Ctrl+Alt+S or Alt+0223

(continued)

Table 7-4 *(continued)*

Character	Mac Shortcut	Windows Shortcut
Š	not supported	Alt+0138
š	not supported	Alt+0154
Ú	Option+E U	' U or Alt+0218
ú	Option+E u	' u or Alt+0250 or Ctrl+Alt+U
Ù	Option+` U	` U or Alt+0217
ù	Option+` u	` u or Alt+0249
Ü	Option+U U	" U or Alt+0220
ü	Option+U u	" u or Alt+0252
Û	Option+I U	^ U or Alt+0219
û	Option+I u	^ u or Alt+0251
Ý	not supported	' Y or Alt+0221
ý	not supported	' y or Alt+0253
Ÿ	Option+U Y	" Y or Alt+0159
ÿ	Option+U y	" y or Alt+0255
Ž	not supported	Alt+0142
ž	not supported	Alt+0158
Spanish open exclamation (¡)	Option+1	Ctrl+Alt+1 or Alt+-0161
Spanish open question (¿)	Option+Shift+/	Ctrl+Alt+/ or Alt+0191
French open double quote («)	Option+\	Ctrl+Alt+[or Alt+0171
French close double quote (»)	Option+Shift+\	Ctrl+Alt+] or Alt+0187

Accessing characters

On the Mac, you can find and produce all the characters in each font installed on your computer by using Key Caps, which comes with Mac OS X (it's in the Utilities folder in the Applications folder). Here's how:

1. **Choose Font.**

   The Font menu appears.

2. **Choose a font.**

   The font is highlighted, and Key Caps displays the lowercase characters and numbers; press the Shift key to see the uppercase characters and the symbols above the numbers. Press Option to see a variety of special symbols, and Option+Shift to see more such symbols.

3. **Click a character to make it appear in the display field at the top of the Key Caps window.**

   You can use these steps to copy and paste characters from the Key Caps display field into your QuarkXPress layout.

An even greater tool for accessing special characters on the Macintosh is PopChar X. It adds a spot next to the Apple logo that when clicked opens a palette of all available characters for the current font. (This book's companion Web site, www.QXCentral.com, links to this software.)

A similar Windows utility, Character Map, is available by choosing Start⇨ Programs⇨Accessories⇨System Tools⇨Character Map. Figure 7-5 shows the Windows Character Map. (If Character Map isn't available in your Start menu, search for the filename Character Map; if you still don't find it, run Windows Setup and select it for installation.)

Ç and ç and such: Which can I make automatic?

Fortunately, you can get your computer to help you cope with the blizzard of international punctuation. Here's a quick-and-dirty guide:

✔ **Accents (acute, circumflex, grave), cedillas, and umlauts:** On the Mac, enter the shortcut for the accent and then type the letter to be accented. For example, to get é, type Option+E and then the letter e. In Windows, if the keyboard layout is set to United States-International — via the Keyboard icon in the Windows Control Panel — you can enter the accent signifier and then type the letter (for example, type

` and then the letter e to get è). To avoid an accent (for example, if you want the begin a quote — such as "A man" rather than have Ä man" — type a space after the accent character — for example, " then space then A, rather than "then A.

✔ **French double quotes:** These are automatically generated if the Smart Quotes option is selected in the Interactive pane of the Preferences dialog box (QuarkX-Press⇨Preferences on the Mac and Edit⇨ Preferences in Windows) and the French quotes are selected in the Quote pop-up list.

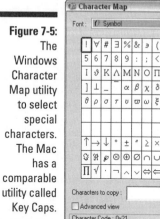

Character Map magnifies the character that your pointer is currently on and displays the code for the selected character. You can select and copy characters to the Windows Clipboard so that you can paste them into your text. You can even change fonts if the character you want is available in a different font than your text uses. A choice of fonts comes in very handy when inserting foreign characters (like Greek or Cyrillic) that aren't available in standard fonts.

When you create text, you can also use the special symbol feature (Insert⇨ Symbol) that comes with Microsoft Word, versions 6.0 and later. Using the symbol feature in Word, you can insert characters from a list or assign your own shortcuts for symbols and foreign characters (for use within Word only). Figure 7-6 shows the Symbol dialog box in Word. For example, you might want to set up Alt+8 to insert the shortcut for a bullet point (•), to be consistent with the Mac's Option+8 shortcut for the bullet character.

Figure 7-6:
The Symbol
dialog box in
Microsoft
Word.

Special Punctuation

You can use some tricks to access special punctuation in addition to the typographic versions of quotes and dashes we cover earlier in this chapter. You can't automate the other punctuation you may need — QuarkXPress won't substitute, for example, an ellipsis (...) when you type three periods (. . .). Besides, you may not even have ready access to these characters — they may not even be on your computer. The sections that follow how to get those characters. Table 7-5 lists the shortcuts that get them into your layout.

Table 7-5	Shortcuts for Other Punctuation	
Character	*Mac Shortcut*	*Windows Shortcut*
Ellipsis (...)	Option+; (semicolon)	Ctrl+Alt+. (period) or Alt+0133
En bullet (·)	Option+8	Alt+0149
Nonbreaking hyphen (-)	⌘+=	Ctrl+=
Discretionary (soft) hyphen (-)	⌘+– (hyphen)	Ctrl+– (hyphen)
Nonbreaking en dash(–)	Option+– (hyphen)	Ctrl+Alt+Shift+– (hyphen) or Alt+0150
Nonbreaking space	⌘+spacebar	Ctrl+5
Breaking en space	Option+spacebar	Ctrl+Shift+6
Nonbreaking en space	Option+⌘+spacebar	Ctrl+Alt+Shift+6
Breaking punctuation space	Shift+spacebar	Shift+spacebar
Nonbreaking punctuation space	Shift+⌘+spacebar	Ctrl+Shift+spacebar
Breaking flexible space	Option+Shift+spacebar	Ctrl+Shift+5
Nonbreaking flexible space	Option+⌘+spacebar	Ctrl+Alt+Shift+5

Bullets (all nonlethal)

A *bullet* is a form of punctuation that starts an element in a list. On a typewriter, you use an asterisk (*) to indicate a bullet. But in desktop publishing (and in modern word processing), you have the real thing: the character that typographers call an *en bullet* (•).

You can find *many* more bullets than the en bullet we all know and love. Bullets don't even have to be round. They can be any shape — squares, stars, arrows, or triangles. They can be hollow or solid. They can be a small version of a corporate logo. They could be some other symbol — anything that clearly demarcates the start of a new item. Take a look at:

✔ Symbol characters in Table 7-5

✔ Characters in the Symbol and Zapf Dingbats fonts on your computer

A *dingbat* is a symbol that ends a story or serves as an embellishment for a certain type of text. It's sort of like a bullet — one that you can use, for example, at the beginning of each byline, at the beginning of a continued line, or at the end of the text so that you know a story is over.

✔ Both the Windows and Mac versions of Microsoft Word and Microsoft Office include the Wingdings font.

Figure 7-7 shows some example bullets.

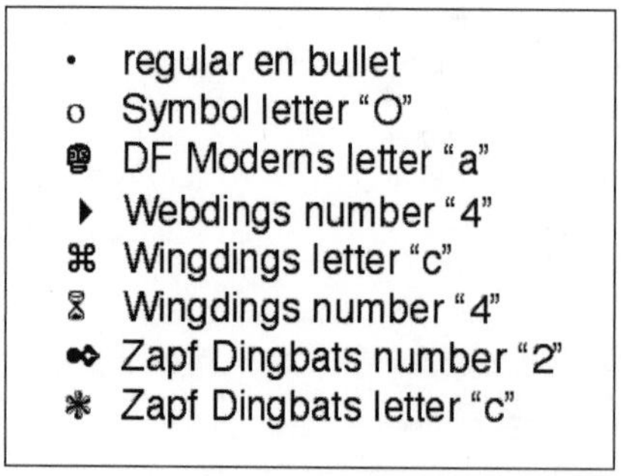

Figure 7-7:
Bullets can come in all shapes, not just the standard en bullet (•).

•	regular en bullet
o	Symbol letter "O"
☻	DF Moderns letter "a"
▶	Webdings number "4"
⌘	Wingdings letter "c"
⌛	Wingdings number "4"
❖	Zapf Dingbats number "2"
✳	Zapf Dingbats letter "c"

You can use tons of symbols as bullets, so feel free to experiment. With all these options, just make sure you don't use an asterisk when you can use a bullet — that would be too tacky for words.

The Mac uses Option+8 as the shortcut to a bullet for all applications. You can set Word for Windows to use a shortcut for the bullet character:

1. **Choose Insert➪Symbol.**

2. **Select your bullet character from the palette of special characters that appears.**

3. **Click the Shortcut Key button.**

4. **In the Press New Shortcut Key field, enter your preferred shortcut (we prefer Alt+8 for the bullet), then click the Assign button.**

5. **Close the dialog boxes to return to Word.**

Ellipses

On a typewriter, you use three periods — some people put spaces around them, others don't — to indicate an *ellipsis,* the character (...) that stands in for missing text, particularly in quoted material. You can also use it to show when a speaker trailed off while talking.

The nice thing about using the actual ellipsis character is that the periods stay together. Otherwise, as text moves within a column, some of the periods won't appear at the end of one line; they end up loitering at the beginning of the next line. Of course, you can get around that design *faux pas* by typing the three periods with no spaces, which would make QuarkXPress see them as a single "word." But if you do that, then the spacing within the ellipsis could be too tight or too loose if you use the QuarkXPress justification feature to stretch or compress the other words to fit on a justified line. If you use the ellipsis character, the space between its constituent dots can't change, so the ellipsis always looks like it belongs there (and isn't made of rubber).

If you just don't like the look of three consecutive periods *or* a font's ellipsis character, you have a third option: Use nonbreaking spaces between the periods. Spaces are covered in this chapter in the "Spaces" section.

Hyphens and en dashes

Normally, a hyphen's a hyphen, right? Not always. If you want to hyphenate two words to a third, such as in *San Francisco–like,* the proper typographic style, according to the World Typography Police, is to use an *en dash* instead of a hyphen (compare *San Francisco–like* to *San Francisco-like*). Chapter 8 describes hyphens in more detail.

The distinction is subtle, but it matters: To a reader, a hyphen looks like a hyphen and an en dash looks like an en dash.

Spaces

A *space* is one of those characters you take for granted. But professional publishers know that there are different kinds of spaces. As with hyphens, the basic reason to use different kinds of spaces is to affect positioning. What you need to know is that you can use several fixed-size spaces that come in really handy when you try to align numbers in a table. An *en space* is the width of most numerals (or yeah, okay, the lowercase letter *n*), and a *punctuation space* (also called a *thin space*) is the width of a comma or period.

The difference is actually pretty handy. Some popular fonts (such as New Century Schoolbook) use an en space for punctuation as well as for numerals. In a few decorative fonts, the numerals and punctuation don't correspond to *any* of the fixed spaces' widths. If you were using one of those fonts and trying to decimal-align *10,000* and *50.12* against the left margin, you'd have to put three en spaces and a punctuation space in front of *50.12*.

You can define another type of fixed space — the *flexible space* (*flex space* for short) — to fit where it's needed:

1. **In the Flex Space Width field of the Character pane, choose QuarkXPress⇨Preferences on the Mac or Edit⇨Preferences in Windows.**

   Alternatively, you can press Option+Shift+⌘+Y or Ctrl+Alt+Shift+Y.

   The Preferences dialog box appears.

2. **In the Character pane, click the Flex Space Width field.**

3. **Enter a value in terms of the percentage of an en space.**

   To get a punctuation (thin) space, you'd enter 50%; to get an em space, you'd enter 200%. Or you can create your own type of space and enter another value from 1% to 400%.

You can't use these fixed spaces when right-aligning text. Want to decimal-align *10,000* and *50.12* against the right margin? You'd expect to put a punctuation space and two en spaces after the *10,000* before right-justifying the two numbers. But that doesn't work. QuarkXPress ignores spaces at the end of a line when it right-aligns (it sees them when centering, however). To get Quark to space correctly (rather than just space out) when you right-align, you have to use the Tab feature instead (explained in Chapter 8).

Working with Symbols

The number of special characters is amazing. You get more than 100 with each regular font — and scores of fonts (*symbol* or *pi* fonts) contain only symbols. Some people use symbols all the time; others rarely. Your own use of symbols depends on the text you work with. Table 7-6 shows the shortcuts for the symbols in most Mac and Windows fonts. For symbol and pi fonts, you must use the font's documentation or a keyboard-character program (like the Mac's Key Caps utility, the $29 PopChar X shareware program for Macs, or the Windows Character Map utility) to see what's available.

Table 7-6	Shortcuts for Symbols	
Character	*Mac Shortcut*	*Windows Shortcut*
Legal		
Copyright (©)	Option+G	Alt+Shift+C or Ctrl+Alt+C or Alt+0169
Registered trademark (®)	Option+R	Alt+Shift+R or Alt+0174
Trademark (™)	Option+2	Alt+Shift+2 or Alt+0153
Paragraph (¶)	Option+7	Alt+Shift+7 or Ctrl+Alt+; or Alt+0182
Section (§)	Option+6	Alt+Shift+6 or Alt+0167
Dagger (†)	Option+T	Alt+Shift+T or Alt+0134
Double dagger (‡)	Option+Shift+T	Alt+0135
Currency		
Cent (¢)	Option+4	Alt+0162
Euro (€)	Option+Shift+2	Ctrl+Alt+5
Pound sterling (£)	Option+3	Alt+0163
Yen (¥)	Option+Y	Ctrl+Alt+– (hyphen) or Alt+0165
Punctuation		
En bullet (•)	Option+8	Alt+8 or Alt+0149
Thin bullet (·)	not supported	Alt+0183
Ellipsis (...)	Option+; (semicolon)	Alt+0133
Measurement		
Foot (')	Control+"	Ctrl+"
Inch (")	Control+Shift+"	Ctrl+Alt+"

(continued)

Table 7-6 *(continued)*

Character	*Mac Shortcut*	*Windows Shortcut*
Mathematics		
One-half fraction (½)	not supported	Ctrl+Alt+6 or Alt+0189
One-quarter fraction (¼)	not supported	Ctrl+Alt+7 or Alt+0188
Three-quarters fraction (¾)	not supported	Ctrl+Alt+8 or Alt+0190
Infinity (∞)	Option+5	not supported
Multiplication (×)	not supported	Ctrl+Alt+= or Alt+0215
Division (÷)	Option+/	Alt+0247
Root (√)	Option+V	not supported
Greater than or equal (≥)	Option+>	not supported
Less than or equal (≤)	Option+<	not supported
Inequality (≠)	Option+=	not supported
Rough equivalence (≈)	Option+X	not supported
Plus or minus (±)	Option+Shift+=	Alt+0177
Logical not (¬)	Option+L	Ctrl+Alt+\ or Alt+0172
Per mil (‰)	Option+Shift+R	Alt+0137
Degree (°)	Option+Shift+8	Alt+0176
Function (f)	Option+F	Alt+0131
Integral (∫)	Option+B	not supported
Variation (∂)	Option+D	not supported
Greek beta (β)	not supported	not supported
Greek mu (μ)	Option+M	Alt+0181
Greek Pi (∏)	Option+Shift+P	not supported
Greek pi (π)	Option+P	not supported
Greek Sigma (∑)	Option+W	not supported
Greek Omega (Ω)	Option+Z	not supported

Character	*Mac Shortcut*	*Windows Shortcut*
Miscellaneous		
Apple logo ( )	Option+Shift+K	not supported
Light (ą)	not supported	Ctrl+Alt+4 or Alt+0164
Open diamond (◊)	Option+Shift+V	not supported

Why dingbats are smart

In publishing, a dingbat is no scatterbrain — it's a visual marker. As with bullets, a host of choices are available. Many people use a square (hollow or solid), but you can be more creative. You can use a version of your company or publication logo. Or you even could use a stylized letter.

When you use dingbats, remember that you can choose how you use them. To end a story, you usually have the dingbat follow the last of the text, with an en space or em space separating them. If your text is justified against both margins, it's common to put the dingbat flush right in the last line of the story. To make it flush right, you set up a tab stop equal to the width of your column. So if your column is 2½ inches wide, you would set up a right-aligned tab at 2½ inches. (Chapters 6 and 8 cover how to set up tabs.) A shortcut is to use Option+Tab or Shift+Tab, which sets up a right-aligned tab at the right edge of the column.

You would use the same techniques to place, say, a square before the text *Continued on page 14* or perhaps place a hollow square before a byline.

Chapter 8

Devil in the Details

• •

• •

Creating cool layouts with QuarkXPress is exhilarating, but keep in mind that a necessary part of publishing is the proofreading and attention to small text details, whether setting tabs so they align on a decimal or remembering to use italics whenever appropriate. Details get missed. In all too many magazines, books, and Web sites, there's at least one typo or inconsistency in formatting. No matter how many people look at a layout, errors amazingly get through.

Although there's no magic cure for these errors, you can substantially reduce them. Old-fashioned proofreading by a fresh pair of eyes — not the author's, not the editor's, and not the layout artist's — is the first and best line of defense so that all concerned have a chance to find and replace incorrect text, fix spelling errors, and fit copy. A close second is to use the program's built-in spell checker. Although technically not mistakes, check for poor spacing and justification that can lead the reader to misread text, which is as bad as a typo because it causes a problem for the reader.

If you follow the advice in this chapter, you'll minimize — and maybe on a good day even eliminate — imprecision and errors. We also show you how to create tables that help to give structure to information, which is another way of helping your audience understand what you're trying to say.

Replacing and Correcting Text

One of the most used text editing features is correcting text by replacing a word or a section of text with another word or chunk of text. Sometimes you want to replace just one instance of a word or phrase; other times, you want to replace a word or phrase every time that it occurs in the layout.

For example, imagine that you're working on a layout that describes tours to the Greek islands. You decide that you need to change each instance of the word *Naxos* to *Santorini*. What's the best way to do this? Use the QuarkXPress built-in replace function. Access it through the Find/Change palette by choosing Edit⇨Find/Change, or pressing ⌘+F or Ctrl+F. This palette is shown in Figure 8-1.

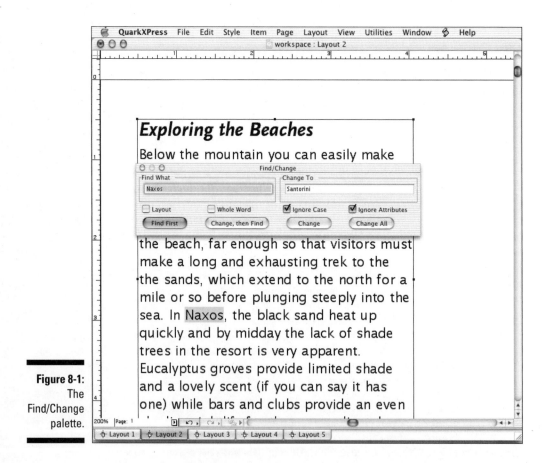

Figure 8-1:
The
Find/Change
palette.

As you can see, the QuarkXPress replace function works like the standard search and replace tool found in most word processing programs. You can search for whole words or for words whose capitalization matches the words or characters that you type in the Find What field.

The Find/Change palette lets you choose whether QuarkXPress should look for a whole word, such as *Quark* as a standalone word but not as part of *QuarkXPress*. (If the Whole Word check box is unchecked, the program finds the string of characters wherever it appears, such as the letters *Sant* inside the name *Santa*.) You can have the program fine and replace a word, regardless of its capitalization, by enabling the Ignore Case check box. If the Layout check box is enabled, the replace affects all stories and text in your layout. Note that Find/Change only works for the active layout — not for all other layouts within the project. The other buttons in the Find/Change dialog box, such as Find First or Find Next, work like they do in word processing programs.

Changing text attributes

The Find/Change palette has another incredibly cool function. You can find and replace text attributes, typefaces, and sizes. You can also find and replace text that's set according to a specific paragraph or character style.

These Find/Change capabilities can be useful if, for example, you want to change all instances of 12-point Helvetica to 11.5-point Bookman Old Style.

To access these options, clear the Ignore Attributes check box in the Find/Change palette. When Ignore Attributes is deselected, the palette expands and offers you attribute-replacement options. Figure 8-2 shows text in 12-point Helvetica will be replaced with 11.5-point Bookman Old Style.

You can select specific *text, typeface,* and *styles* for the search and replace functions by checking the Text, Style Sheet, Font, Size, and Type Style check boxes in the Find What and Change To columns of the dialog box.

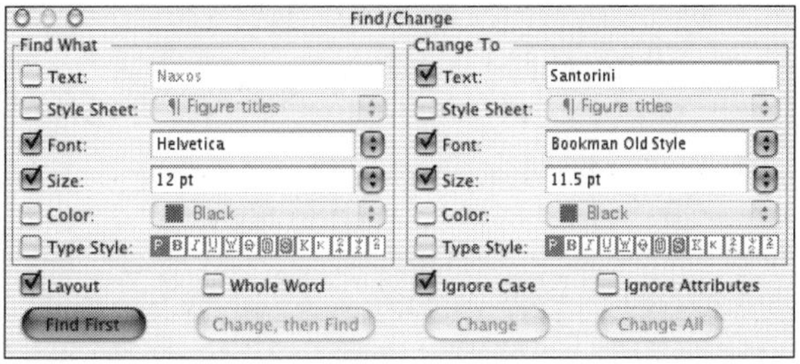

Figure 8-2:
The expanded
Find/Change
palette.

The Type Style area of the palette has several controls:

- Click an attribute box once to make it gray, which means you don't care about the attribute in your search. For example, if QuarkXPress finds italic text, it leaves it italic.

- Click an attribute box again to turn the attribute on, meaning that you want to find text with that attribute (on the Find What side) or apply that attribute (on the Change To side).

- Click an attribute box yet again to turn it off. This means that you don't want to find text with this attribute applied (on the Find What side) or that you want to remove it (on the Change To side).

Removing carriage returns

It's not uncommon for QuarkXPress users to receive text files for typesetting that have several extra carriage returns entered between paragraphs. The Find/Change feature in QuarkXPress gives you an easy way to remove these unwanted carriage returns (also known as hard returns).

Enter two consecutive return symbols, **\p\p**, in the Find What field and then enter one return symbol, **\p**, in the Change To field. Figure 8-3 shows what the Find/Change palette should look like when you are about to begin removing unwanted carriage returns. (If the text that you're working with has multiple carriage returns between paragraphs, you may need to repeat this Find/Change procedure a number of times.)

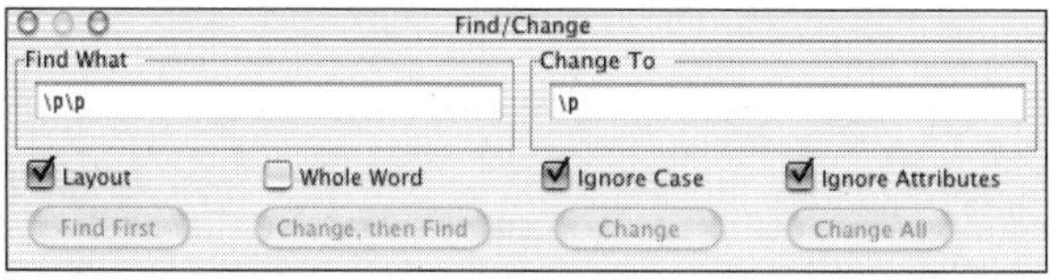

Figure 8-3:
Stripping
hard returns
from a file.

What do you do if a hard return exists at the end of each line of text, in addition to the extra hard returns between paragraphs? If you simply delete all the hard returns by using a Find/Change procedure similar to the one shown in Figure 8-3 (only in this case, search for \p and replace it with nothing), you would lose all paragraph breaks. So you need to follow a two-step procedure:

1. **Search for paragraph breaks that are marked by two hard returns (\p\p) and replace the paragraph breaks with a string of characters that's not used in the layout, such as #!#.**

2. **Search for all hard returns and replace them with nothing. That is, enter \p in the Find What field and leave the Change To field blank.**

After you delete the hard returns, you need to reinsert the paragraph breaks. To do this, enter the character(s) that you used to replace the paragraph breaks (**#!#** in our example) in the Find What field, enter **\p** in the Change To field, and then perform Find/Change again.

Setting Tabs

Tabs are useful for lining up text into columns to create lists and other columnar data. QuarkXPress provides six paragraph tab options: Left, Center, Right, Decimal, Comma, and Align On. Tabs can be tricky, and using them effectively takes some practice.

If you've ever used a typewriter, you're familiar with typewriter tabs, which are left-aligned only: You press the Tab key, and the carriage moves to a new left margin. But QuarkXPress offers a wide variety of tabs through the Paragraph Attributes pane, which you access by choosing Style⇨Tabs (or by pressing Shift+⌘+T or Ctrl+Shift+T). Each type of tab has its own mark on the tab ruler, which appears when you set tabs. Figure 8-4 shows the Paragraph Attributes dialog box.

Copy in an open layout can be set with six different tab settings. The tab settings, which you click on to enable, are as follows:

- ✔ **Left:** Text typed after the tab will align to the tab as if the tab were a left margin. This is, by far, the most popular tab setting.
- ✔ **Center:** Typed text will be centered; the tab stop is the center of the text.
- ✔ **Right:** Text typed after the tab will align to the tab as if the tab were a right margin. The right tab setting is often used with tables of numbers because the numbers align with all their rightmost digits in a row.
- ✔ **Decimal:** Numbers with a decimal (.) that are typed after the tab will align on the decimal. This tab setting is useful if you have columns of numbers that include decimal places.
- ✔ **Comma:** Numbers with a comma (,) that are typed after the tab will align on the comma. This tab setting is handy if you have some numbers with decimal places, such as 31.001, and some without, such as 2,339.
- ✔ **Align On:** With this option, you type in the character you want the text to align on. In the example in Figure 8-4, we aligned a column of numbers with the closing parenthesis.

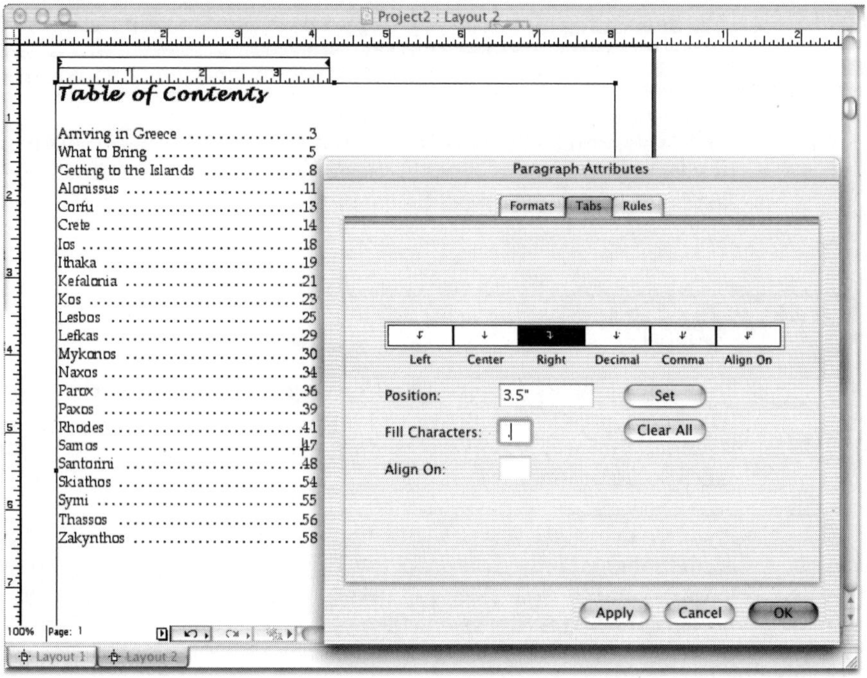

Figure 8-4:
Set tab
leader
characters
by entering
up to two
characters
in the Fill
Characters
field in the
Tabs pane.

The default for tabs is one left tab every half inch. If you want to apply differ-
ent tab settings that you can use throughout the layout, choose Edit⇨Style
Sheets (or press Shift+F11) and then select the Tabs pane. If you're working
on a specific paragraph or want to override a style for one paragraph, choose
Style⇨Tabs (or press Shift+⌘+T or Ctrl+Shift+T) to access the Paragraph
Attributes pane.

You can place thousands of tabs in a paragraph, and you can use any printing
character to fill the space between tabs.

Specifying your own tabs

After you access the Paragraph Attributes pane, here's how you set tabs:

1. **Select the alignment that you want (Left, Center, Right, Decimal,
   Comma, Align On).**

2. **Type the numeric position for the tab in the Position box or move
   your mouse to the Tab ruler and click to set the position of the tab.**

You can also specify tabs for a selected paragraph or range of paragraphs by choosing Style⇨Formats (or press Shift+⌘+F or Ctrl+Shift+F), selecting the Tabs pane, and then clicking the ruler above the box or column.

Setting tabs in QuarkXPress is simple but takes a bit of practice. For example, it takes time to learn how using tabs with the various Alignment options affects your layout. We recommend that you take a few minutes to practice setting some tabs so that you'll be comfortable with the process.

Using leader characters in tabs

A *leader character,* also known as a *tab leader,* is a series of characters that runs from text to text within tabular material. An example is the series of dots (periods) between a table of contents entry and its matching page number. A tab leader guides the reader's eye, especially across the width of a page.

QuarkXPress calls a tab leader a *fill character.* To define a leader, enter up to two characters in the Fill Characters box of the Tabs pane of the Paragraph Attributes pane. If you enter two characters, they alternate to fill the space between the defined tab stop and the place where you pressed the Tab key. Refer to Figure 8-4 to see a space and a period as the two fill characters.

Note that in Figure 8-4, we've left the Paragraph Attributes pane open so that you can see the entries that we made. You can see the resulting tab leaders at the left side of the open layout, above the Paragraph Attributes pane.

Making tables in QuarkXPress

QuarkXPress has a table feature that's easy to use — it's flexible and efficient, as well — and it has been enhanced in QuarkXPress 6. Individual table boxes (cells) can handle text, pictures, colors, and blends.

If you're creating just a simple table, consider using tabs instead of the table feature in QuarkXPress. The simpler your table, the easier it is to use tabs, as we describe earlier in this chapter.

Before you start drawing tables, consider what you're going to fill the table with. If you fill the table with text, figure out what format the text is currently in. If you're going to enter the text into the QuarkXPress table, go ahead and draw the table. But if the table already exists — for example, in a word processing file — you'll be much better off importing the text into a text box and then converting it into a table. See the section, "Converting text to a table and vice versa," later in this chapter for more information.

It also helps to understand how the program handles tables. A QuarkXPress table is a collection of rectangular text boxes, picture boxes, and/or no-content boxes, all grouped together to function as a single unit, as shown in Figure 8-5. Each box is a table cell. Each cell can have content that you format with the Style menu and properties that you specify in the Modify dialog box. These tables can look great but do not have the power of spreadsheets, like those you create in programs such as Microsoft Excel. (For example, you cannot set a QuarkXPress table to calculate data.)

Creating a table

Creating a table in QuarkXPress is much like creating a picture or text box in QuarkXPress. You simply click the Table tool and use the mouse to draw a table. After you draw a table, the Table Properties dialog box appears (see Figure 8-6), asking you how many rows and columns you want in your table as well as whether you want the table to contain text or picture boxes. Because this chapter focuses on tweaking text, we focus for now on text, but keep in mind that QuarkXPress also lets you place pictures in table cells. Select the Text Cells radio button and then click OK. Instant table!

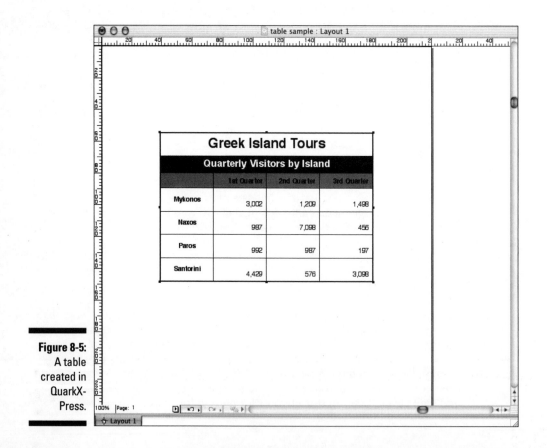

Greek Island Tours		
Quarterly Visitors by Island		
	1st Quarter	2nd Quarter	3rd Quarter
Mykonos	3,002	1,209	1,498
Naxos	987	7,098	456
Paros	992	987	197
Santorini	4,429	576	3,098

Figure 8-5:
A table created in QuarkX-Press.

Of course, at this point, the table looks a bit empty. You need to put some text in it. No problem. A table works pretty much like a text (or picture) box. In fact, it is basically just several text (or picture) boxes joined together. The first thing to do is type some text into the first box, or cell. From there, you apply all the attributes that you can apply to standard text box: leading, ascent, color, and even text skew. Then you click in the next cell and do the same. Some boxes may be more time consuming than others, depending on the number of cells involved. Nevertheless, the results will be stunning.

A table in QuarkXPress is essentially a kind of box. That means it won't flow with the rest of your text. If you want the table to move with your text, treat it like any other box that you want anchored in text. Select the table with the Item tool, cut it, and then switch to the Content tool. Click within text where you want to insert the table box and paste the box.

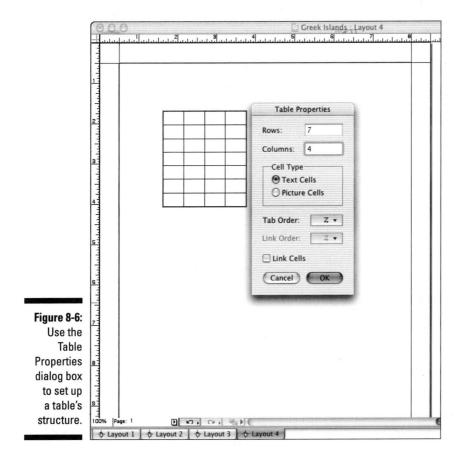

Figure 8-6:
Use the
Table
Properties
dialog box
to set up
a table's
structure.

Converting text to a table and vice versa

Creating a table from scratch is fine if it's a new element. But what if that table already exists, either in your text document or in an older QuarkXPress layout as a series of tabbed text? Quark thought of that, too. Or you may want to simply type your table text into a text box — with tabs between columns and a paragraph return at the end of each row — and convert it to a table.

When you convert highlighted text to a table, the following things happen:

- By default, tabs in the text mark new cells. Paragraph returns mark new rows. Tabs and paragraph returns are then stripped from the text inside the cells. (You can specify the actual characters used to separate your data during the conversion process.)

- Character attributes, including character style sheets, are retained.

- Paragraph attributes are retained except those specified in the Tabs pane of the Paragraph Attributes dialog box (choose Style⇨Formats, or press Shift+⌘+F or Ctrl+Shift+F).

  In QuarkXPress 6, ruling lines are retained during text-to-table conversion. Ruling lines above the text will not display, just like they do not display whenever they are at the top of a text box.

- Lines or text paths anchored in text will end up in the text's cell.

- Picture boxes anchored in text will become picture cells in the table.

- Text that you convert to a table is copied (not cut) from the document.

To convert a section of text to a table, select the text — with the elements that you want in table cells separated by tabs, spaces, paragraphs, or commas — and then choose Item⇨Convert Text to Table, as shown in Figure 8-7.

In the Convert Text to Table dialog box, you have several options, although the default works for tabbed text:

- You can specify in the pop-up menus what separates rows and columns. Your options are Commas, Tabs, Spaces, and Paragraphs. Almost always, you'd choose Paragraphs as the separators for rows. For columns, you'd typically choose either tabs or commas. Most people use tabs in Word and QuarkXPress to set up tables; when you save Excel files to text, tabs are used as well. But a common format exists for separating data — comma-separated value (CSV) — which uses commas instead. Spaces are also used; however, we don't recommend using this option because distinguishing a space separating two cells from a space used with a cell's text can be hard. In the Separate Columns With pop-up menu, simply select whatever separates the data in your source text.

✔ The Rows and Columns options change for what you select in Separate Rows With and Separate Columns With. If you type different values, QuarkXPress creates cells or skips cells, depending on whether the values are more or less than the actual cells in your source text.

✔ Cell Fill Order tells QuarkXPress how to determine how the source text maps to your intended table. The default is to read from left to right for a row's column contents and then to the next line (paragraph return) for the next row. That's the option that looks like a Z. But you could select the other options to change the table's appearance. For example, selecting the reversed Z essentially puts the first piece of data in your source text's first "row" at the end of the table's row. Selecting the option that looks like an N basically swaps the columns and rows, which may be a more efficient way to convert the source text into a table.

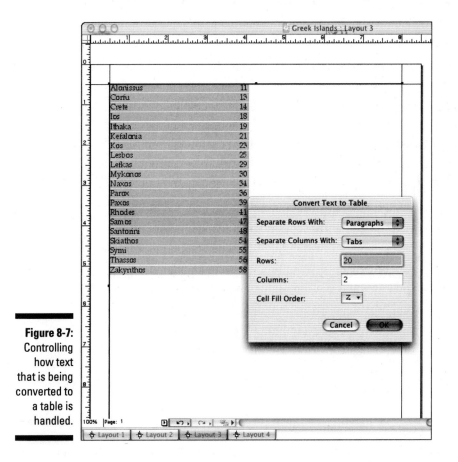

Figure 8-7:
Controlling how text that is being converted to a table is handled.

You can also convert a QuarkXPress table to text. With the text that you want to convert to a table selected, choose Item⇨Convert Table to Text, which reveals a dialog box almost like the Convert Text to Table dialog box. Specify how columns and rows should be exported (separated by tabs, commas, and so on), what order the data should be extracted in, and whether the original table should be deleted. That's it!

Working with rows and columns

Any time that the data in your table changes, or you want to change its design, you can change its rows and columns accordingly. You can resize rows and columns, add them, and delete them.

To resize an individual row or column, just grab its grid line with the Content tool. The pointer lets you drag the grid line up and down. When you drag grid lines, the remaining rows or columns are resized accordingly.

Modifying a table

After a table is finished, you're not stuck with it. You can resize rows and columns, change the number of rows and columns, apply colored back-grounds to cells, format the grid lines and frame, combine cells, and more. The tools that you use to accomplish these tasks include the following:

- **Content tool:** The Content tool lets you work inside a table: selecting cells, rows, and columns; dragging grid lines; and editing cell contents.

- **Item tool:** The Item tool lets you work with the entire table: moving it, resizing it, and scaling it.

- **Modify dialog box:** The Modify dialog box (choose Item⇨Modify, or press ⌘+M or Ctrl+M) provides the Table pane for positioning the table; the Runaround pane for controlling how the table affects surrounding text; the Grid pane for formatting the lines and frame; the Cell pane for formatting cells; and the Text or Picture pane for working with cell contents. As with other items, the controls in the Modify dialog box vary according to what you've selected in the table.

- **Measurements palette:** The Measurements palette lets you size and position a table by using the X, Y, W, and H fields. When text within a table is selected with the Content tool, you can format the text with the Measurements palette, including setting the font, size, alignment, leading, tracking, and style, as well as flipping the text within the cell horizontally and vertically.

- **Table submenu, Item menu:** The Table submenu of the Item menu gives you commands for adding and deleting rows and columns and for combining or splitting cells.

✔ **Contextual menu:** The contextual menu provides all the options applicable to the part of the table that you click. For example, if you click a picture cell when the Content tool is selected, you have options for modifying the graphic in addition to gaining access to commands for formatting the table.

- Windows users just right-click to display the contextual menu.

- Macintosh users either press Control+Shift or Control+click to display the contextual menu (depending on the Control Key preferences in the Interactive pane of the Preferences dialog box).

Just like it does with other boxes in QuarkXPress, the Modify dialog box gives you a lot of power over tables. The Table pane controls the width, height, and placement of the table on the page; the Cell pane controls the width and height of the cells and their background colors; and the Text pane controls how text is placed within the cells.

One key feature about the Table tool is its capability of containing pictures in addition to text. Of course, looking at the Table Properties dialog box, you'd think that you choose either text or pictures. And because this chapter focuses on text, it just doesn't seem right to get into the whole picture thing right now. But the truth is that you don't have to choose between one format or the other. As is the case with picture boxes and text boxes, you can actually change the content of a particular cell at will. It works basically the same way that it does with other boxes. Just put the cursor in the cell that you want to change, choose Item⇨Content, and change the text cell to a picture cell or vice versa. Who knows? You may want to drop a picture into your otherwise tedious text chart to grab some attention. This feature lets you do it!

Linking text cells

A new feature in QuarkXPress 6 lets you link text cells in a table to other text cells or to text boxes. This is handy for when you want text to flow from one spot to another as edits are made. To link text cells, do the following:

1. **With the Table tool, draw a table.**

   When you let go of the mouse button, a Table Properties dialog box appears.

   If you want to link text cells in an existing table, select the table, choose Item⇨Modify, and then select the Table tab.

2. **Click the Text Cells radio button to specify that the cells in the table will hold text (instead of pictures) and then click the Link Cells check box.**

3. **From the Link Order list, choose the direction for text to link.**

   For example, choose Left to Right, Top Down to set up the links from the top, left cell that continue across the top row to the far right.

You can manually link text cells in a table. To do so, select the Linking tool (it looks like a little link of chain), click the first cell in the table, and then click the subsequent cells to which you want the text to flow. To unlink text cells, click the Unlink tool and clear the text boxes that you want to unlink.

Applying color to cells and tables

QuarkXPress 6 lets you add color to individual table cells, to the overall table that contains all the cells, and to the gridlines that divide up the table. To apply color to a table cell, select the cell with the Content tool and choose Item⇨Modify. In the Cell area, choose a color and shade for the cell and then click OK.

A similar technique changes the color of the gridlines. With the Content tool, Shift+click to select a gridline and then choose Item⇨Modify. In the Line area, choose a color and shade for the gridline and then click OK.

Black is the default color of the table box *frame* (the outside frame holding the cells of the table). To change the color, use the Item tool, select the table, and choose Item⇨Modify. In the Frame area, choose a color and shade for the frame and then click OK.

Getting Copy to Fit

Copy fitting is what it sounds like — the process of fitting text into the layout. Sometimes it's like squeezing 20 pounds of lemons into a 5-pound bag. If your original, unmodified text fits the layout the first time, consider it a stroke of luck because that's not what usually happens.

Copy fitting can make your layout look professional. It can also save you money. For example, you may have the budget to produce an eight-page print layout. You flow your text and find there is a little more than eight pages of content to deal with. Good copy fitting can make the text fit into eight pages and save the expense and hassle of adding pages to your booklet.

You can make copy fit onto a page or within a column in a number of ways. Sometimes you can use just one method; sometimes you have to use a combination of methods to make text fit in the available space.

Having more text than space is common. Therefore, the following tips assume that the goal is to shorten text. But you can use the same procedures in reverse to expand text. (Use the last two tips only if you can't make text fit using the first few.)

✔ **Edit text** to remove extra lines. Watch for lines at the end of a paragraph that have only a few characters. Getting rid of a few characters somewhere else in the paragraph may eliminate these short lines, thus reducing the amount of page space needed while keeping the amount of text removed to a minimum.

✔ **Adjust the tracking of the text** so that the text occupies less space and, especially, so that short lines are eliminated.

✔ **Tighten the leading** by a half or quarter point. Because this is such a small change, the average reader won't notice it; it may even save you a few lines per column, which can add up quickly.

✔ **Reduce the point size** by a half point. This action saves more space than is first apparent because it lets you place a few more lines on the page and put a bit more text in each line. You can change point size in the style sheet or select text and use the type size controls in the Measurements palette.

✔ **Reduce the horizontal scale** of text to a slightly smaller percentage (perhaps 85 percent) to squeeze more text in each line by entering a percent value in the Horizontal Scale field. (With the text selected, choose Modify from the Item menu.)

✔ **Vary the size of columns** by setting slightly narrower column gutters or slightly wider margins.

Winning the Spelling Bee

Many people dread spelling; that's why word processors and publishing programs come with spell checkers. But there's a catch: Spell checkers work by being based on lists of words. Sure, spelling dictionaries sometimes contain 500,000-odd words (QuarkXPress has a "mere" 120,000), but industry-specific terms like *G4* or people's names rarely show up in these dictionaries, so you can't completely automate spell-checking. Sorry, but you need to have another dictionary somewhere around for referral.

If you're not content with the 120,000-word dictionary in QuarkXPress, you can add words to an auxiliary dictionary. Technical words for your company or industry are candidates for an auxiliary dictionary, as are proper names.

One nice thing about auxiliary dictionaries is that you can pretty much put the files where you want them. Auxiliary dictionaries don't have to reside in the same file as the documents accessing them. You can create as many auxiliary dictionaries as you need, you can use the dictionaries with multiple projects, and you can create copies of the dictionaries to share with other users. However, you can only use one auxiliary dictionary with a project at a time.

You can't automate spell-checking, but you can make it part of your routine. You should spell-check your text in the word processor before laying it out in QuarkXPress. You also should spell-check it again in QuarkXPress after you finish your layout but before you print it. You'll be surprised how much text gets added or changed in the layout, after the text is officially "done."

You can access the QuarkXPress internal spell checker by choosing Utilities⟹ Check Spelling, as shown in Figure 8-8. Check Spelling has three submenus: Word, Story, and Layout. You can jump directly to these options by pressing ⌘+L or Ctrl+W for Word, Option+⌘+L or Ctrl+Alt+W for Story, and Option+Shift+⌘+L or Ctrl+Alt+Shift+W for Layout. Chances are that you'll use the Story and Layout options the most — naturally, the ones with the hardest-to-remember shortcuts. (A *story* is all text in the current text box and in all text boxes linked to that text box. A story is often the contents of an imported text file.)

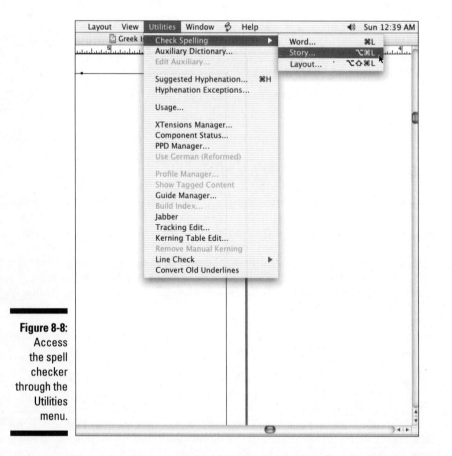

Figure 8-8:
Access
the spell
checker
through the
Utilities
menu.

To access the Story or Word options, you have to have the Content tool active and the text pointer on a piece of text. You don't have to select a word to spell-check it; just have the text pointer somewhere on the word. You can't spell-check a highlighted range of words. If you select multiple words and use the Word spell-checking option, QuarkXPress checks only the first word.

Running the spell checker

If you spell-check an entire layout or the current story, you see the dialog box shown in Figure 8-9.

Word Count
Document
Total: 178
Unique: 119
Suspect: 5
Cancel   OK

Click OK to continue, which displays the dialog box shown in Figure 8-10.

To spell-check a single word, highlight the word and press ⌘+L or Ctrl+W. The dialog box shown in Figure 8-11 appears.

The dialog boxes shown in Figures 8-10 and 8-11 differ in a number of ways:

- ✔ The Check Word dialog box has no capability of moving on (when you click the Skip button) to the next suspect word (an option that doesn't make sense for one-word spell-checking) like the Check Story or Check Document dialog boxes do.

- ✔ The Check Word dialog box automatically looks for possible correct words to replace the suspect word; the other dialog boxes require that you click the Look Up button to get a list of possible replacements. If one of those words is the correct one, just click it and then click Replace, or just double-click the word in the list.

- ✔ The Check Word dialog box has an Add button, which lets you add words to your auxiliary dictionary (which we explain in this section).

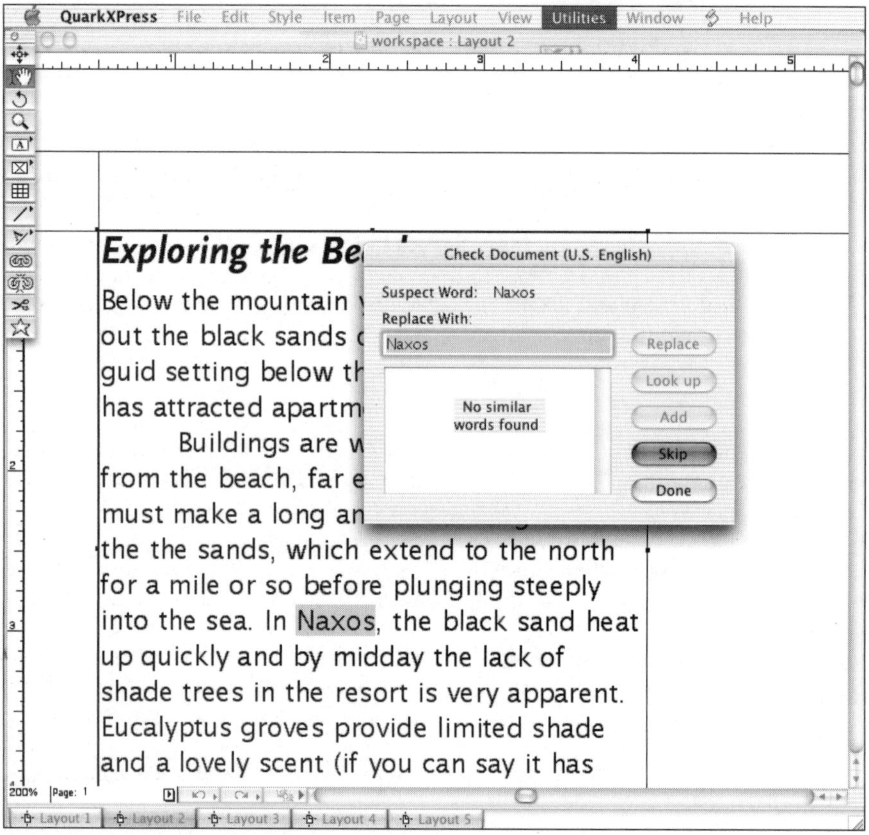

Figure 8-10:
QuarkXPress
shows
you each
suspect
word in turn.

In the spell-checking dialog boxes, you can select a new word and click the Replace button to ask QuarkXPress to make the replacement. If the word appears several times, QuarkXPress tells you how many times the word is used and then replaces all instances when you click Replace.

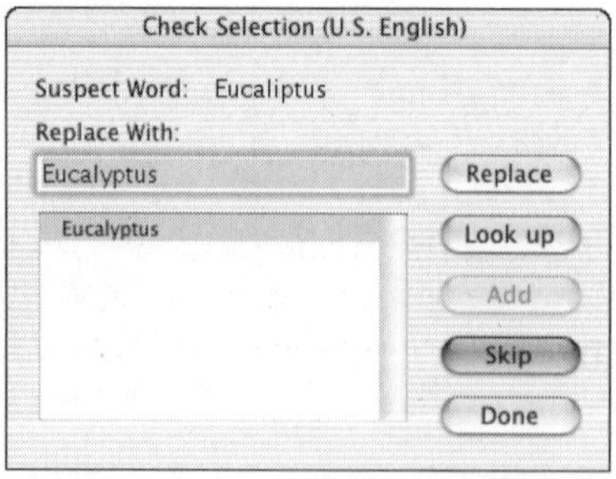

Figure 8-11:
When spell-
checking a
single word,
you see
this version
of the
dialog box.

You can also spell-check a selection of highlighted text from the Selection dialog box, which you access by choosing Utilities⇨Check Spelling⇨ Selection.

Setting up your personal dictionaries

If you've experimented with the QuarkXPress spell checker, you probably noticed that the Add button stays gray. So what's it there for? For the Add button to become active, you need to set up an auxiliary dictionary: a personal dictionary of words that the QuarkXPress dictionary doesn't know about.

If you open an auxiliary dictionary when a layout is open, QuarkXPress associates the two; when you open or switch to the layout in the future, the layout can access the auxiliary dictionary. (Other layouts in the project won't be associated with that dictionary — you'll have to open the dictionary for each layout manually.) If you want an auxiliary dictionary available in all projects' initial layouts that you subsequently create, open the auxiliary dictionary when no projects are open (as we explain in the following items).

In previous versions of QuarkXPress, only one auxiliary dictionary could be associated with a document. In QuarkXPress 6, a project can be associated with multiple auxiliary dictionaries. But only one auxiliary dictionary can be associated with each layout. When you add new layouts, no auxiliary dictionary is automatically associated — you have to do it each time.

To set up an auxiliary dictionary, choose Utilities⇨Auxiliary Dictionary, which displays the dialog box shown in Figure 8-12. Any existing dictionaries in the current folder are displayed. You can select one of them, move to a different directory to select a different dictionary, or click the New button to create a new auxiliary dictionary.

In Figure 8-12, we had previously set up an auxiliary dictionary on Greek island terms for the current layout, so the name of that dictionary is displayed in the Current Auxiliary Dictionary field.

The Windows QuarkXPress Auxiliary Dictionary dialog box looks a little different than its Mac counterpart because it follows the Windows conventions for an Open or a Save dialog box, but it has all the same features and buttons. You need to know one other thing about the auxiliary dictionaries in Windows QuarkXPress: Although the main dictionary (XPress Dictionary. dct) uses the extension .dct, the auxiliary dictionaries use the extension .qdt (such as Computer.qdt).

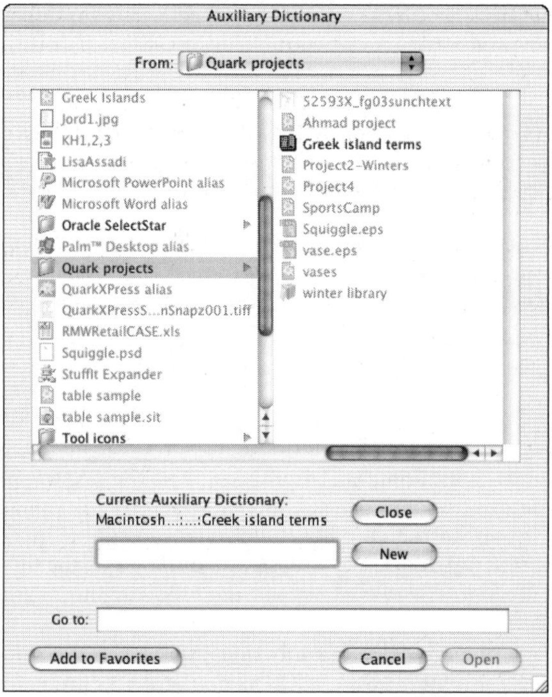

Auxiliary Dictionary

From: [Quark projects]

Greek Islands	52593X_fg03sunchtext
Jord1.jpg	Ahmad project
KH1,2,3	**Greek island terms**
LisaAssadi	Project2-Winters
Microsoft PowerPoint alias	Project4
Microsoft Word alias	SportsCamp
Oracle SelectStar	Squiggle.eps
Palm™ Desktop alias	vase.eps
Quark projects	vases
QuarkXPress alias	winter library
QuarkXPressS...nSnapz001.tiff	
RMWRetailCASE.xls	
Squiggle.psd	
StuffIt Expander	
table sample	
table sample.sit	
Tool icons	

Current Auxiliary Dictionary:
Macintosh...:...:Greek island terms [Close]

[ ] [New]

Go to: [ ]

[Add to Favorites] [Cancel] [Open]

Figure 8-12:
Create or switch spelling dictionaries with the Auxiliary Dictionary dialog box.

After you create the auxiliary dictionary, you have to add words to it. Actually, you don't have to add them right then; you just add words when you find them in the spell checker by clicking the Add button when you come across a word like *Naxos* that is correct but unknown to QuarkXPress. Or, if you already know some of the words that you want to add, you can choose Utilities⇨Edit Auxiliary to invoke the dialog box shown in Figure 8-13. You also can use this dialog box to remove incorrect words. (Maybe someone was too fast on the trigger and clicked Add by accident.)

Click the Save button after making changes to your auxiliary dictionary.

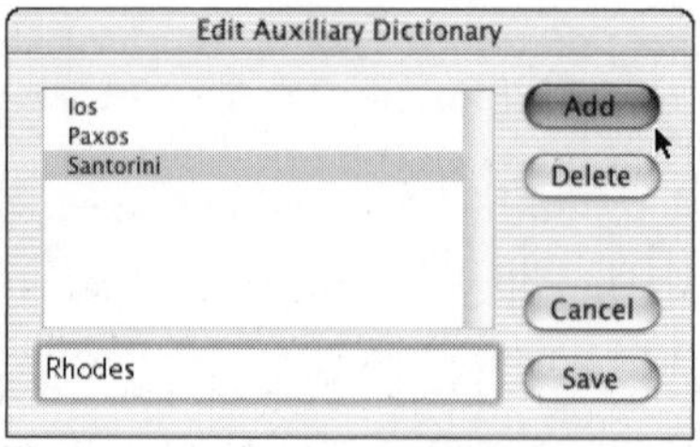

Edit Auxiliary Dictionary

Ios	[Add]
Paxos	
Santorini	[Delete]
	[Cancel]
Rhodes	[Save]

Figure 8-13:
Add spelling variations to the Edit Auxiliary Dictionary.

When you add words, case doesn't matter. So QuarkXPress enters all text as lowercase characters, no matter how you type it, to ensure that the word won't be flagged as incorrect if it were typed in all caps. Your word processor probably has *case-sensitive spell-checking* (which means that it looks at the *capitalization* of words, not just the sequence of letters), but QuarkXPress doesn't. That's another reason to do a spell-check in your word processor before importing the text into QuarkXPress.

Because auxiliary dictionaries are files, you can share them over a network; it's a great way to maintain spelling consistency among several users. You also can have different dictionaries for different projects. But you can't share dictionaries between Windows and Macintosh users. The two dictionary formats aren't compatible, and there's no way to translate to the other format.

Maintaining an up-to-date spelling dictionary and spell-checking at key points in the editing and layout process can reduce typographical mistakes. Some typos (such words that are spelled correctly but used incorrectly) won't be caught this way, so you still need a person to proofread. But the obvious mistakes will have been caught by the time a proofreader sees your text.

Hyphenating the Right Way

Hyphenation settings can make or break the look of every line and paragraph of text in a letter, a two-column newsletter, or a design-intensive ad with text wrapping around items and images. For example, if you have justified text without hyphenation, you can get big gaps in text. Or, if you wrap text around the edges of an item, you may need hyphens to improve the wrap.

But hyphenation is even harder for many people than spelling. Where do you break a word? Between two consonants? After a syllable? You can follow rules, but the English language is so full of exceptions that you may think that it's hardly worth learning the rules unless you're a professional copy editor.

Like it does for spell-checking, QuarkXPress offers automatic hyphenation, as well as controls to customize how it works.

Creating hyphenation sets

Any ink-stained newspaper person can tell you what an H&J set is. In case you don't have an ink-stained newsperson nearby, we'll clue you in: An *H&J set* is newspaper lingo for a hyphenation and justification set — the specifications for how words are divided across lines and how the text in each line is spaced. We cover some of the spacing features later in this chapter.

To set up hyphenation settings, choose Edit➪H&Js, or press or Option+
Shift+F11 or Ctrl+Shift+F11 to display the Edit Hyphenation & Justification
dialog box. When you first open this dialog box, you see just one listing in the
H&J list: Standard. Edit this listing first so that you can establish the hyphen-
ation settings that you want as the default for your text styles. After you edit
Standard to your liking, you can create additional H&J sets for other needs.
For example, you may want an H&J set called No Hyphen for text (like head-
lines and bylines) that should have no hyphenation.

Like other global preferences, QuarkXPress works differently if no project is
open than if one is. If you create or change H&J sets when no layout is open,
QuarkXPress uses that H&J set for all future projects until you change the
dictionary again. If a project is open, the H&J set is created or changed just
for that project. You can tell whether the H&Js are being edited globally for
all new projects or locally for the currently opened one: If the dialog box
reads Default H&Js (the settings as shown in Figure 8-14), you're changing the
global settings; if it reads H&Js for *project name,* you're changing the settings
locally for whatever *project name*'s real name is (the real name will display in
the title, not *project name*).

To edit an existing H&J set, select its name from the list and double-click it.
To create an H&J set, click the New button. Either way, you get the Edit
Hyphenation & Justification dialog box as shown in Figure 8-14. The fields at
the left are the ones that affect hyphenation.

Edit Hyphenation & Justification		
Name: New H&J	**Justification Method**	
		Min. Opt. Max.
☑ Auto Hyphenation	Space: 85% 110% 250%	
Smallest Word: 6	Char: 0% 0% 4%	
Minimum Before: 3	Flush Zone: 0"	
Minimum After: 2		
☐ Break Capitalized Words	☑ Single Word Justify	
Hyphens in a Row: unlimited		
Hyphenation Zone: 0"	Cancel OK	

Figure 8-14:
The Edit
Hyphen-
ation &
Justification
dialog box.

Compare the values in Figure 8-14 with the values in your copy of
QuarkXPress. Our values differ from yours because we edited the Standard
settings in our copy of QuarkXPress to work best in such multicolumn layouts
as newsletters, newspapers, and magazines. Here's how each setting works:

✔ **Name:** If you clicked New, enter the name for the H&J set here. (H&J sets are named, just like style sheets are.) If you clicked Edit to edit the Standard H&J set, you won't be able to edit the name.

✔ **Auto Hyphenation:** If this check box is enabled, hyphenation is turned on for any style sheet that uses this H&J set. If the check box is clear, hyphenation is turned off for any style sheet that uses this H&J set.

✔ **Smallest Word:** This field tells QuarkXPress to ignore words with fewer characters than that field's value. The default is 6, so any word of five or fewer characters won't be hyphenated. The default value of 6 is a good choice because few words of six or fewer letters are unable to fit on a line with other text or will look good if they are split across two lines, so there's little reason to change this default value. (One possible instance to change it would be if you had wide columns — for example, six inches or more — in which case there's plenty of room for words, so a value of 8 would be fine.)

✔ **Minimum Before:** This field tells QuarkXPress how many characters in the word must precede a hyphen. Thus, if you leave the value set to the default of 3, QuarkXPress will not hyphenate the word *Rolodex* as *Ro-lodex,* even though that's a legal hyphenation for the word. The first place that QuarkXPress will hyphenate would be after the *l*, but that's an incorrect hyphenation point, so QuarkXPress inserts a hyphen after *Rolo.*

✔ **Minimum After:** This field is like Minimum Before except that it tells QuarkXPress the minimum number of characters in a word that must follow the hyphen. The default is 2, although many people change that to 3 so that QuarkXPress won't hyphenate verbs before the *-ed*, as in *edit-ed.* Many publishers think that looks tacky. It's a personal choice.

✔ **Hyphens in a Row:** The default is Unlimited, which means that theoretically, every line could end in a hyphen. Having too many end-of-line hyphens in a row makes the text hard to read because it's difficult to keep track of what line to move to next. We suggest 3 as a good setting, although 2 and 4 are fine, too. The smaller the number, the greater the chance that QuarkXPress will have trouble spacing text in a line; a line that could really use a hyphen wouldn't have one just because it happened to come after that maximum number of consecutive hyphenated lines. (For example: If you set Hyphens in a Row to 2 and a particular paragraph turns out to have two hyphens in a row somewhere, even though the third line needs a hyphen to avoid awkward spacing, QuarkXPress won't hyphenate that line.)

When you confront this spacing situation, don't despair — and don't change the settings in your H&J set. Just type a regular hyphen followed by a space. If you try to use the soft hyphen — ⌘+- (hyphen) or Ctrl+- (hyphen) — to create a break on that third line, QuarkXPress won't add the hyphen because soft hyphens respect the Hyphens in a Row setting.

Add a regular hyphen and space only when everything else in the layout is finished. If your text were to reflow, you might find a hyphen and space in the middle of a word in the middle of a line. Oops! This cheat lets you get around the H&J limitations without changing a standard that works most of the time. And, if you're unsure where to hyphenate a word (and no dictionary is handy), just click the word and then choose Utilities➪Suggested Hyphenation (or press ⌘+H or Ctrl+H) to have QuarkXPress show you where hyphens may be added.

✔ **Break Capitalized Words:** This check box does what it says. Some typographers frown on hyphenating proper names, like *Macworld* or *Alexander.* Unless you're in a situation where you need to avoid hyphen-ating proper names — for example, if your company's rules require that its product names are not hyphenated — check this check box. We prefer a broken name, not awkward spacing.

✔ **Hyphenation Zone:** For text that is left aligned, right aligned, or cen-tered, this check box tells QuarkXPress how far from the outside margin to look for opportunities to hyphenate. Hyphenation Zone helps you pre-vent awkward gaps — something that looks like a kid's smile with no front top teeth — because a word happened to hyphenate halfway into the line. Set the zone to at least 10 percent of the column width (15 per-cent is better) but to no less than 0.2 inches. Thus, for a 1.5-inch-wide line, a good setting would be 0.225 inch (although you can round that to 0.2 or 0.25); that's 1.5 (inches) times 0.15 (percent). For justified or force-justified text, this setting has no effect, however, because all the text is aligned to both the left and right margins, which means that the text has no possible gaps for you to worry about.

When you click the New button, the new H&J set takes the attributes of the Standard H&J set, so it's best to edit Standard to your liking before creating new sets. That way, attributes that you've specified in several sets (such as checking. Auto Hyphenation and Break Capitalized Words) are automatically copied into the new sets. If you want to duplicate an H&J set and then make slight modifications to it (perhaps two sets are identical except for the Hyphenation Zone settings), select one of the sets in the H&J dialog box, click the Duplicate button, and then modify (and rename) that duplicate set.

Figure 8-15 shows the effects of different hyphenation settings. The figure shows really skinny columns because thin columns emphasize the differ-ences between hyphenation settings. The wider the columns, the less notice-able the differences; QuarkXPress has more text to play in while adjusting spacing.

Click OK when you're finished creating or modifying an H&J set (or click Cancel if you want to abort those settings). QuarkXPress displays the H&Js

dialog box, from which you can create or edit other H&J sets. ***Reminder:*** When you're done, be sure to click Save to save all the work you've done — if you click Cancel, your work is lost.

When you travel to the Greek islands, remember to bring your camera. You won't want to miss the shots of glorious sunsets, black sand beaches, and whitewashed buildings. Each time you visit the Volcano Vista Apartments will be a highlight.	When you travel to the Greek islands, remember to bring your camera. You won't want to miss the shots of glorious sunsets, black sand beaches, and whitewashed buildings. Each time you visit the Vol-cano Vista Apartments will be a highlight.

If you created H&J sets in another project, you can import those sets into the current QuarkXPress project by using this mini-procedure: Click the Append button (it really should be named Import — Append makes it sound like it will copy the current H&J set to another set, not *from* it); then navigate the dialog box to find the project that you're importing from.

All H&J sets in that project will be imported into your current project with one exception: If both projects have H&J sets with the same name, importing sets into the current project will not affect its H&J set. For example, suppose that the current project has the H&J sets Standard and No Hyphen, while the other project has the H&J sets Standard and Masthead. When you import H&J sets from the other project, Masthead will be copied into the current project, but Standard won't be copied, and the current project's Standard H&J set will remain unaffected.

If you want to copy H&J sets from another project and make them the default for all future projects, make sure that no project is open in your copy of QuarkXPress before you import H&J sets. This is a great way to, for example, copy standards from a client's system to your system.

After you set up your H&J sets — and many projects will have just two: Standard and No Hyphen — edit your style sheets so that each style uses the appropriate H&J set. Headlines, bylines, and other categories of display type usually are not hyphenated, but body text, bios, captions, and sidebars usually *are* hyphenated. You also can apply an H&J set to a selected paragraph (or several selected paragraphs) in the Paragraph Attributes pane. Choose Style➪Formats (or press Shift+⌘+F or Ctrl+Shift+F) and change the H&J value to the H&J set that you want to apply.

Personalizing hyphenation

Like a spelling dictionary, your own personal hyphenation dictionaries can

- ✔ Tell QuarkXPress how to hyphenate words that it doesn't know about.
- ✔ Change the default hyphenation of words that are hyphenated differently based on their usage (such as the verb pro-*ject* versus the noun *proj*-ect) or on the rules in the particular reference book you've chosen.

To add your own hyphenation, choose Utilities⇨Hyphenation Exceptions. The dialog box shown in Figure 8-16 appears. (Looks a lot like the dialog box for spelling exceptions, doesn't it?)

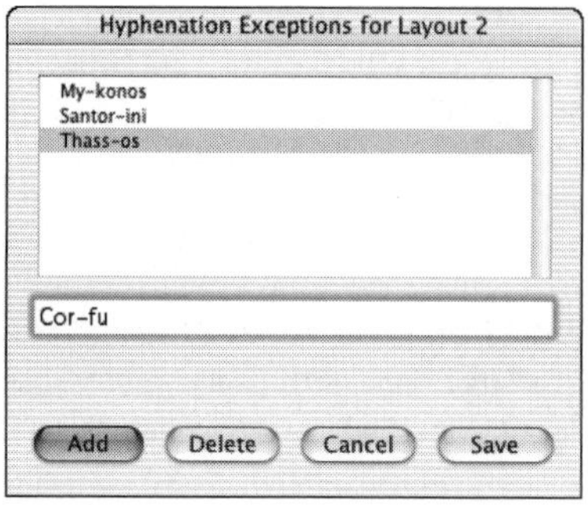

Figure 8-16: The Hyphenation Exceptions dialog box.

Hyphenation Exceptions for Layout 2

My-konos
Santor-ini
Thass-os

Cor-fu

Add   Delete   Cancel   Save

Simply enter into the Hyphenation Exceptions dialog box the word whose hyphenation you want to personalize, include hyphens where it's okay for QuarkXPress to hyphenate the word, and click Add. (To prevent a word from being hyphenated, enter it with no hyphens.) To delete a word, select it from the list and then click Delete.

After you're finished, click Save. Clicking Cancel wipes out your changes.

Preserving Readability

The other half of the H&J set — the *J*, or justification — controls the spacing of text. It's easy to overlook this aspect of typography and just go with the defaults. But you don't want to do that. How you set your spacing has a subtle but important effect on readability. QuarkXPress assumes that you're doing single-column-wide layouts, which is fine for reports and price lists. But for multicolumn layouts, the default settings can result in spacing that leaves awkward gaps between words and can make the space between characters in words open enough that you may not be sure whether the characters make one word or two.

Default spacing

Quark set the default spacing in the Edit Hyphenation & Justification dialog box to work for most basic columns of text. (Basically, the settings for spacing rely on the typeface, size, column width, and other factors in use.) Nonetheless, you can improve on the defaults, as shown in Figure 8-17.

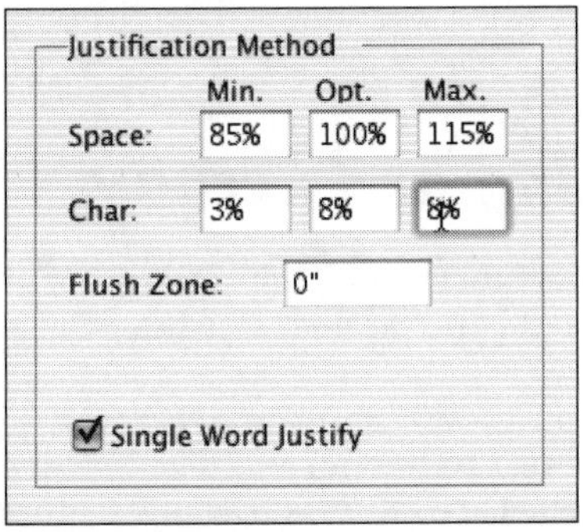

Figure 8-17: The justification half of the dialog box contains the authors' preferred settings.

Justification Method

	Min.	Opt.	Max.
Space:	85%	100%	115%
Char:	3%	8%	8%

Flush Zone: 0"

☑ Single Word Justify

With the settings shown in Figure 8-17, the results are that the characters in a word are closer together and no unsightly gaps remain between words. You can experiment with the values, but before you do that, read on to find out what those values mean.

All settings for justification are in the Justification Method section of the dialog box. At the top are six fields that determine how your text is spaced between characters and words; the spacing of text between characters and words is letter spacing and word spacing, respectively. The first row (Space) determines the space between words; the second row (Char) controls the space between characters within a word. Generally, you want tighter space within a word than between words so that words look unified and the space between them is easily discernible. The three columns determine the rules by which QuarkXPress spaces characters and words.

The spacing columns behave differently depending on how the text is aligned. If text is left aligned, right aligned, or centered, QuarkXPress always uses the Opt. (optimum, or target) values. If the text is justified or force justified, QuarkXPress tries to meet the Opt. values; if it can't meet those values, it uses a value in the range between the Min. (minimum) and Max. (maximum) values. If that doesn't work, it uses a value greater than the Max. value. QuarkXPress *never* uses less than the Min. settings.

Setting the Opt. values to 100% for words and 0% for characters works best. Those particular Opt. values tell QuarkXPress to use the defaults from the font's internal spacing specifications. (Presumably, the font's designers picked those specs for a good reason.)

For the Min. settings, we prefer 85% for words and –3% for characters. That prevents words and letters from getting too close, but it also helps balance any spaced-out text with slightly cramped text, thus keeping the overall average closer to the Opt. values. For Max., we allow a greater difference from Opt. than from Min. because the human eye handles extra space better than too little space.

Local space: Tracking and kerning

But wait, there's more! You can override the spacing settings for selected text or even with a style sheet. Why would you do this? Consider these scenarios:

- ✔ Some text is too spacey, or you know that if some text were just a little closer together, you'd get the text to rewrap and take one line less. Here's where you would use the QuarkXPress tracking feature to tighten (or loosen) the space among characters in a selected block of text.

- ✔ Standard H&J sets justification settings work fine for your body text but not for your headlines. Rather than create a new H&J set for headlines, you just adjust the tracking settings in your Headlines style sheet to compensate for the difference.

- ✔ Here and there, a couple of letters in a word seem to be too close or too far apart. Just use the QuarkXPress kerning feature to adjust the space between those two characters.

Tracking and *kerning* are pretty much the same thing — ways to adjust the spacing between characters. So what's the difference? The scope of the adjustments that they make. *Kerning* adjusts spacing between just two characters, and *tracking* adjusts spacing between all characters selected. QuarkXPress uses the same menus for these two features because they are variations of the same feature. You see the Kern command in the Style menu if your text pointer happens to be between two characters, but it's replaced by the Track command if you select several characters. Similarly, the horizontal arrows on the Measurements palette adjust kerning if the pointer is between two characters, and they adjust tracking when several characters are selected.

The Character Attributes pane appears when you choose Style⇨Kern or Style⇨Track. It's where you control kerning and tracking specifications. Figure 8-18 shows how you can modify kerning or tracking from the Measurements palette.

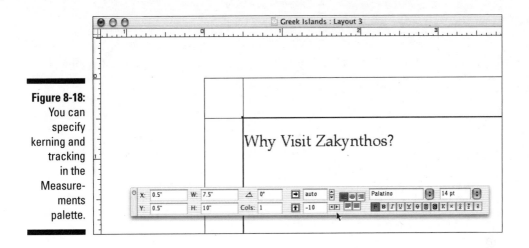

Why Visit Zakynthos?

| X: 0.5" | W: 7.5" | △ 0° | auto | Palatino | 14 pt |
| Y: 0.5" | H: 10" | Cols: 1 | -10 | | |

Figure 8-18:
You can specify kerning and tracking in the Measurements palette.

Use the keyboard shortcuts or the Measurements palette to adjust tracking and kerning; you can see the effects of your changes while you make them. (Otherwise, you must make the effort of opening a dialog box, entering a value, closing the dialog box, seeing the result, reopening the dialog box to further adjust the spacing, and so on.) Press Shift+⌘+] or Ctrl+Shift+] to increase spacing in ¹⁄₂₀ increments and Shift+⌘+Option+] or Ctrl+Alt+Shift+] to increase spacing in ¹⁄₂₀₀ increments. To decrease spacing, press Shift+⌘+[or Option+Shift+⌘+[on the Mac or press Ctrl+Shift+[or Ctrl+Shift+[or Ctrl+Alt+Shift+[in Windows.

The values that QuarkXPress uses for tracking and kerning are not percentages like they are for the H&J sets' spacing options. For tracking and kerning, QuarkXPress uses a unit of measurement called (of all things) a *unit* — a handy little length that measures all of ¹⁄₂₀₀ of an em space. An *em space* is as wide as a font is high; thus, an em space for 9-point type is 9 points wide. That means that a unit is ⁹⁄₂₀₀ of a point for 9-point type, ⁸⁄₂₀₀ (or ¹⁄₅₀) of a point for 8-point type, and so on.

As you can see, a unit really is another way to express a percentage: 0.05% (that's the decimal way to represent ¹⁄₂₀₀). That's a pretty small value. So, in the Measurements palette, QuarkXPress jumps in 10-unit increments when you click the left and right arrows to adjust tracking or kerning. Of course, you can select your own precise values by entering a number. A positive number adds space; a negative number removes it.

Undos and Redos

QuarkXPress 6 introduces a long-requested feature: multiple undos and redos. Repeatedly choosing Edit⇨Undo (or the shortcut ⌘+Z or Ctrl+Z) undoes each previous action in turn. Likewise, repeatedly choosing Edit⇨ Redo (or Shift+⌘+Z or Ctrl+Shift+Z) redoes each previous action in turn.

In addition to the menu items and keyboard shortcuts, there are also icons at the bottom of the project window to undo and redo. Those icons actually are *pop-up menus* that let you select a range of undo and redo actions.

Although you can redo and undo up to 30 consecutive actions (depending on your Preferences), you must start with the most recent action — you cannot undo, say, only the action taken four steps ago.

QuarkXPress lets you set the preferred keyboard command for redo in the Preferences dialog box (choose QuarkPress⇨Preferences on the Mac or Edit⇨Preferences in Windows, or press Option+Shift+⌘+Y or Ctrl+Alt+ Shift+Y) to ⌘+Y or Ctrl+Y, ⌘+Z or Ctrl+Z, or the default of Shift+⌘+Z or Ctrl+Shift+Z. You can also set how many actions can be undone or redone — up to 30.

Chapter 9

A Touch of Color

C olor is everywhere, so we tend to take it for granted. Most of us don't usually spend much time thinking about color theory or color physics. (And we don't spend much time on those topics in this chapter, either.)

In the world of computers, color is the rule, not the exception. You can get high-quality color inkjet printers for as little as $100. They're great for limited-run output (for a few dozen copies or for use in a color copier). You can also buy more expensive color printers (for $5,000 to $20,000) that use technologies with intimidating names such as *dye sublimation* and *thermal wax.* These printers are for professional publishers who perform color proofing of publications, such as magazines and catalogs, to be reproduced at a commercial printing plant. Or you can have your work printed by a commercial printer that does color work, in which case, your lowly grayscale laser printer is just a proofing device for your text and image placement.

This chapter focuses on color in printing (see Chapter 18 for information about using color in Web layouts). The color tools in QuarkXPress are definitely designed for professionals. (Check out *QuarkXPress 6 Bible* — by the authors of this book and also published by Wiley Publishing, Inc. — which delves into professional color in detail.) But you can benefit from color as well. After all, who can resist using color in print layouts, especially if you have one of those inexpensive color inkjet printers? But before you can make the best use of color, you need a quick look into how color happens — and that process is a lot more complicated than you may think.

Heading off to Color Class

Prepare to see all sorts of acronyms when you explore color. Color theory is like the military — capital letters and confusion everywhere.

RGB versus CMYK

For desktop publishing, color comes in two basic types: RGB (red, green, and blue) and CMYK (cyan, magenta, yellow, and black). Computer monitors use RGB, whereas printers use CMYK. Because the color types differ, what you see on-screen usually looks different from what your printed output looks like. (Sometimes you don't even receive a close match.) These types of color schemes are called *color models;* the model is the physics behind the colors.

The different physics of RGB and CMYK mean that the colors they produce don't always match. RGB tends to create brighter colors and does well in the orange and green ranges; CMYK tends to create deeper colors and does poorly with greens and oranges — but very well with subtle, dark shades like eggplant and indigo. Therefore the color you create on-screen may not look much like the one that ends up on your printed page.

The RGB (red, green, and blue) model is composed of the three colors of light that a monitor or television uses to create all colors. As a kid, you probably played with prisms, which split white light into its constituent colors. White light goes in one side of the prism, and a rainbow comes out the other side. In a monitor or television, the opposite occurs: red, green, and blue colors go in one side and combine to form white at the other side. You can think of a monitor as working like a prism in reverse. Green and red combine to produce yellow. Red and green light have different frequencies, and as they merge, they change to the frequency of yellow light. These colors are known technically as *subtractive colors.* Figure 9-1 shows how subtractive colors combine. Figure 9-2 shows how additive colors combine.

Keep in mind that the colors depicted in Figure 9-1 are the basic ones. (You have to use your imagination because these examples are in black and white.) Whereas green and red combine to make yellow, the actual color could be yellow-green (more mustardy) or orange (more flamelike), depending on the proportion of each light being combined. You can get a better understanding of this process from the color wheel to the right of the drawing in Figure 9-1, which shows the intersections of the three colors of light.

As we mention previously, CMYK stands for cyan, magenta, yellow, and black. (The *K* in CMYK represents the *k* in black. Publishers don't use *B* because it usually indicates blue.) *Cyan* is an electric sky-blue, the color of some mints, mouthwashes, and sapphires. *Magenta* is a hot pink, like cycling shorts and highlighter markers. By mixing the colors in the CMYK combination, you can simulate most colors that the human eye can discern.

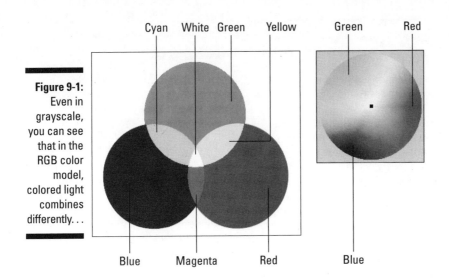

Cyan White Green Yellow   Green Red

Figure 9-1:
Even in
grayscale,
you can see
that in the
RGB color
model,
colored light
combines
differently...

Blue Magenta Red   Blue

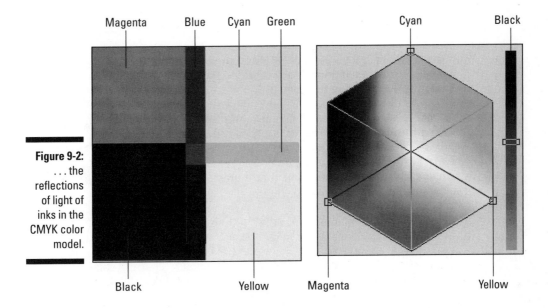

Magenta Blue Cyan Green   Cyan Black

Figure 9-2:
...the
reflections
of light of
inks in the
CMYK color
model.

Black Yellow Magenta Yellow

Unlike RGB, CMYK does not combine colored light to create colors; instead, it reflects light off ink and combines the reflections to form colors. Yellow ink, for example, actually absorbs all other colors, so only yellow is reflected to your eye. As a kid, when you played with fingerpaints or crayons, mixing colors together probably gave you dark grays and browns. As with crayons, adding the CMYK colors together on paper causes the colors to become darker (because more colors of light are absorbed), so adding all four makes a solid black. These colors are known as *additive colors.*

Spot colors versus process colors

Commercial color printing presses and most office color printers (such as inkjet printers) use CMYK. In publishing lingo, CMYK colors are known as *process colors.* But other special inks are available to create colors that are impossible to make by mixing cyan, magenta, yellow, and black in any amount. Pastel, metallic, neon, and frosted colors, for example, can't be accurately produced in CMYK. In printing a photo, you may not mind using CMYK because a photo has so much color that the human eye compensates for the few that are off. But if you're creating a drawing or using a tint, you'll have to settle for the closest color that you can get (such as a yellowish orange for gold or a light gray for silver), or use special inks. These special inks are called *spot colors* because they are usually used on just part of a page (a spot).

If you work with artists or publishers, you've probably heard the word *Pantone* or the acronym *PMS.* Both are shorthand for the Pantone Matching System, the most popular set of spot-color inks. Pantone has color sets for uncoated (rough) paper, for matte (slightly textured) paper, and for coated (glossy) paper. QuarkXPress can work with these colors, along with such colors as Trumatch, Focoltone, DIC (Dainippon Ink & Chemical), Pantone Hexachrome, and Toyo.

At the right of Figure 9-2 is a cube that represents how the cyan, magenta, and yellow colors combine; black is added through a slider, lightening or darkening the colors in the cube.

Because the color you see on the printed page is based on how light is filtered through and reflects off ink, the type and quality of ink determines the color that you see. That's why a flesh tone in a magazine looks better than a flesh tone in a newspaper, and a green printed on an expensive dye-sublimation printer looks better than a green printed on an inexpensive inkjet printer.

Although QuarkXPress lets you create colors in several models — RGB, HSB (hue, saturation, and brightness — a variant of RGB), and LAB (*luminosity, a* axis, *b* axis; an international color standard) — few printers accurately reproduce them. Use these models only when you're creating colors for a computer-generated slide show. If you're printing, think strictly CMYK.

We cover only a speck, nay a scintilla, of color theory and its applications. If you want to find out more about color and how it applies to printing, we suggest you pick up a copy of *Pocket Pal: A Graphic Arts Production Handbook,* edited by Michael H. Bruno.

QuarkXPress 6 adds four Pantone color variants: two pastel color sets, one set of metallic colors, and one set for European inks. The Hexachrome Solid in Process Coated color set also is new; it's used when your commercial printer uses high-fidelity inks from a company other than Pantone.

Use spot colors only if you're printing on a commercial printing press — and supply a separate negative for each color used (one for each of the CMYK process colors and one for each spot color). If you print a spot color on a printer that supports only CMYK, the spot color is translated to the nearest CMYK combination. The process is automatic; you can't do anything about it. Talk with your commercial printer first about any project you plan that contains any spot color.

If you're using only black and one or two spot colors (maybe for just a logo and some tints behind text boxes) and no other color (no color photos or drawings), then you don't need to have the CMYK negatives created. If you're using both process and spot colors, keep in mind that many commercial printers can't handle more than six colors on a page — even six may not be possible on small-run jobs or at small printing plants. Again, consult with your printer before submitting the job for printing.

Just to make things a little weirder, the Trumatch brand of spot colors is based on CMYK, so any Trumatch color can be faithfully converted (*color-separated,* in publishing lingo) into process colors. (That's why the system is called *Trumatch.*) With Trumatch, you can use a premixed CMYK color for spot colors (cheaper than CMYK if you print fewer than four colors total, including black). If you end up using more than three colors, you can have QuarkXPress convert all Trumatch spot colors to CMYK combinations during output — and know you'll get an accurate rendition. The folks at Pantone created a color model called *Pantone Process,* which is a set of the Pantone colors that have faithful CMYK equivalents. QuarkXPress includes the three variations, for different kinds of paper, of the Pantone Process model as well.

Figure 9-3 shows colors that don't match their equivalent CMYK combinations. Again, using your imagination to view the color, you see the standard green that QuarkXPress includes as a default in all layouts. (Don't worry yet about where this dialog box is or what it does; we cover that in the section, "Creating Color," later in this chapter.) In the figure, the color model has been changed from the RGB model that QuarkXPress uses to the CMYK color model. You can see the two color swatches next to the section labels *New* and *Original.* New is the green converted to CMYK; Original is the original green. (QuarkXPress shows you the effects of a conversion so you can cancel, adjust, or pick a different color.) Even in grayscale reproduction, these colors don't match up. (Amazing, isn't it?)

Just above the arrow pointer in Figure 9-3, you see a small square in the color wheel, which is the green color's position in the color model. If you click the small square and drag it through the color wheel, you see the new swatch's color change. Release the mouse button, and the square indicates the new color's location in the color wheel. The slider bar at the far right is like a dimmer switch.

The brighter an RGB color, the less chance that CMYK can print it correctly.

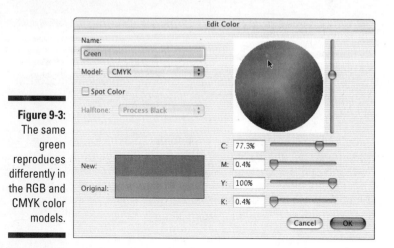

Figure 9-3:
The same
green
reproduces
differently in
the RGB and
CMYK color
models.

Creating Color

Okay, okay, you slackers in the back can start paying attention now! This is
the part of the book where we actually create and use colors in QuarkXPress.
You create colors in three ways:

- ✔ Define the colors within QuarkXPress itself
- ✔ Import the colors defined in another QuarkXPress project
- ✔ Import the colors defined in an EPS file

No matter how you define them, the available colors display in the Colors
palette and in all dialog boxes that let you apply color. If the Colors palette is
not visible, you can display it by choosing Window➪Show Colors or by
pressing F12. Figure 9-4 shows the default Colors palette.

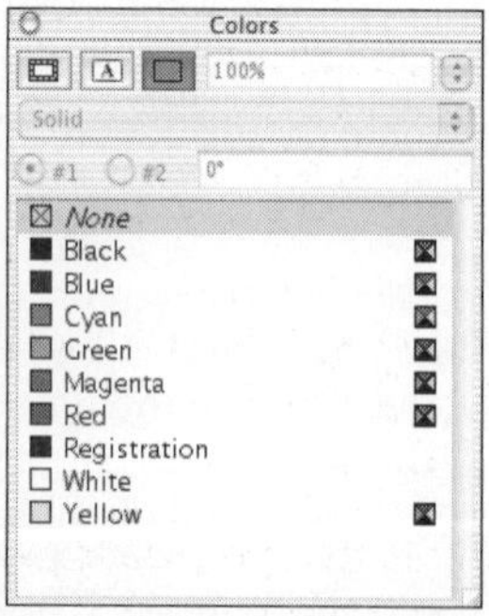

Figure 9-4:
The Colors
palette
shows
available
colors.

Defining colors in QuarkXPress

To define, alter, or remove the colors in a project, choose Edit⇨Colors to display the Colors dialog box (shown in Figure 9-5). Here's a rundown of your choices at the bottom of the screen:

- ✔ **New:** Creates a new color
- ✔ **Edit:** Changes an existing color
- ✔ **Duplicate:** Copies an existing color, for example to use one color as both a process color and a spot color
- ✔ **Delete:** Removes unwanted colors
- ✔ **Append:** Imports colors from other QuarkXPress projects

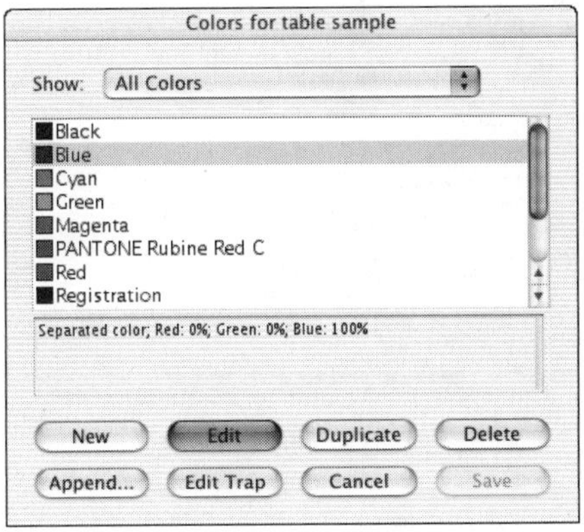

Figure 9-5:
The Colors dialog box lets you add new colors and modify existing colors.

```
                    Colors for table sample

Show:   All Colors                           ▼

  ■ Black
  ■ Blue
  □ Cyan
  □ Green
  ■ Magenta
  ■ PANTONE Rubine Red C
  ■ Red
  ■ Registration

  Separated color; Red: 0%; Green: 0%; Blue: 100%


   ( New )  ( Edit )  ( Duplicate )  ( Delete )
   ( Append... )  ( Edit Trap )  ( Cancel )  ( Save )
```

Don't worry about the Edit Trap button. Using it changes how colors print when they are side by side, and the QuarkXPress defaults are generally fine for the work most people do. When they aren't, skilled and knowledgeable color publishers can fiddle with the trap. You, on the other hand, can file it in your brain under "More Technical Weirdness" and move on.

The Edit and Delete buttons are sometimes grayed out. That's because some basic colors (cyan, magenta, yellow, black, and white) cannot be altered.

Also in the list of color choices in the Colors dialog box is the color swatch *Registration,* which looks like black — but isn't. This color can be altered but not deleted. Registration serves two purposes:

- ✔ **It provides a consistent color for elements that you want to appear on all your negatives (such as crop marks and file names).** If you define Registration to be 100 percent cyan, magenta, yellow, or black, anything in the Registration color prints on all those negatives.

✔ **You can use Registration to create a rich black — something that looks like licorice, not flat like what you get from a marker.** To create a rich black (known as *superblack*), use 100 percent black and either 100 percent magenta or 100 percent yellow. Combining black with either of these colors makes the black richer and more appealing when printed.

Creating a new process color

Whether you click New or Edit, the Edit Color dialog box appears, as shown in Figure 9-6. (If this dialog box looks familiar, that's because it's similar to the one in Figure 9-3.) You can use the Edit Color dialog box to create or modify process and spot colors. We show you how to work with both.

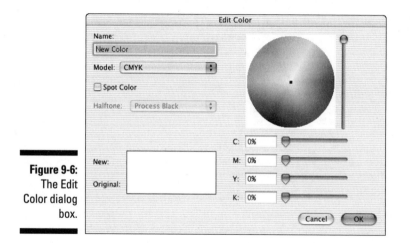

Figure 9-6: The Edit Color dialog box.

Here's how to create a process color:

1. **Click the Edit button in the Colors dialog box to display the Edit Color dialog box; then choose CMYK from the Model pop-up menu.**

2. **Uncheck the Spot Color check box (if it's already checked) if you are using a commercial printer and are producing CMYK negatives.**

3. **Change the color to the one you want (either by using the CMYK color wheel or the Pantone swatches) — in both cases, click the desired color (as in Figure 9-7), or change the value in the Cyan, Magenta, Yellow, and Black boxes. You can also use the sliders beneath each color.**

4. **Give the color a name in the Name field, unless you're using a Pantone swatch and are comfortable with using the swatch name to identify the color.**

5. **Click OK to add the CMYK color to your palette and return to the Colors dialog box.**

While the Colors dialog box is displayed, you can create additional colors by clicking the New button, or you can modify any existing color by clicking the color's name and clicking Edit.

6. **Click Save in the Colors dialog box when you're finished creating or modifying colors.**

   Your Colors palette reflects the new colors.

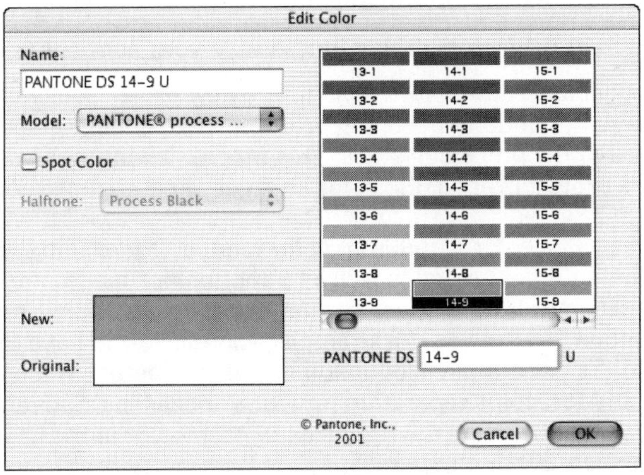

Figure 9-7: Pantone spot colors are shown in swatches, not in a color wheel.

You can convert a color defined in any model to the CMYK, RGB, LAB, or HSB models simply by selecting one of those models after you define the color. But note that colors defined in one model and converted to another may not reproduce exactly the same because each model was designed for use in a different medium (such as paper or a video monitor).

Creating a new spot color

Creating a spot color is a lot like creating a process color, with some important differences. Here's how you add a new spot color:

1. **Click the Edit button in the Colors dialog box to display the Edit Color dialog box; then choose a spot color model.**

   For example, you can choose Pantone pastel coated or Pantone solid uncoated from the Model pop-up menu. After you choose, a picker appears in the right side of the Edit Color dialog box.

2. **If it's not already checked, check the Spot Color box.**

   If you check this box, the color you create prints on a *single* color plate when you print color separations. If you don't check it, the color is converted into CMYK components and printed on *multiple* plates when you print separations.

3. **Click a color swatch in the color picker or enter a number in the field below the swatches.**

Check a color swatchbook before you create a spot color (so you know exactly what color you're choosing on-screen) is a good idea. If you don't have a swatchbook, we recommend you purchase one. Pantone swatchbooks are available at www.pantone.com. Go to www.QXCentral.com for other swatchbook sources.

4. **Click OK in the Edit Color dialog box.**

5. **Click Save in the Colors dialog box to save your spot color.**

To add or change new colors to all future new projects, launch QuarkXPress, but don't open any projects. Then change colors as described in the preceding steps. This process changes the default settings. If a project is open, the color changes affect that project only.

If you have the same color in different color models (for example, using Pantone 145 as a process color as well as a spot color), make sure that the color names reflect this difference. You may have colors named Pantone 145 Spot and Pantone 145 Process, for example. Therefore, you have to choose the right color for accurate reproduction based on whether you plan to print the color as a CMYK color separation or with a special ink. Spot and Process Color icons, which reside on the right side of each color in the Colors palette, also help you identify which is which.

The Quark CMS (Color Management System, covered later in this chapter) helps ensure consistency between the colors displayed on-screen and the final printed colors, but there are noticeable differences between color monitors and colored printing inks. Comparing the colors of a Pantone color swatch book with their on-screen counterparts shows the differences — more with some colors, less with others. If you're using Pantone colors or colors from any other color-matching system, we want to re-emphasize that you should use a swatchbook when choosing colors. Don't rely on the colors displayed in the Edit Color dialog box and the Pantone color picker.

Web color models

QuarkXPress has two Web-oriented color models:

- ✔ **Web Named Colors:** A set of colors for use on the Web by current Windows and Mac Web browsers.

- ✔ **Web Safe Colors:** A set of colors designed to reproduce accurately on any Web browser.

See Chapter 18 for more information about Web colors.

Importing colors

You can import colors defined in other QuarkXPress layouts or in an EPS file. Doing so saves work and could reduce errors in defining a color differently in QuarkXPress than in, say, Adobe Illustrator. Here's how you import a color from a QuarkXPress layout:

1. **Click the Append button in the Colors dialog box.**

   The Append Colors dialog box shown in Figure 9-8 appears.

2. **Click the color in the scroll list that you want to append, ⌘+click or Ctrl+click to select multiple colors, or click Include All to append all colors.**

   When you click a color, the Description section displays color-separation information about the color.

It's clear why you may need to import a color defined in another QuarkXPress layout, but would you need to import a color defined in an EPS file? Yes, for two reasons: You may have a color for a logo or other image that you want to use, or perhaps the color in the EPS file is defined as a spot color but you want to print it as a process color. By importing the color definition into QuarkXPress, you can edit that color in QuarkXPress to be a process color. You can import the color definition automatically when you import the EPS file if you choose File➪Get Picture, or press ⌘+E or Ctrl+E. Your Colors dialog box is then updated to reflect the imported colors as soon as the image has been imported. (Pretty easy, huh?)

Actually, there's a third reason for importing a color defined in an EPS file: If EPS colors didn't import into QuarkXPress, QuarkXPress wouldn't be able to color-separate them.

Figure 9-8:
In the
Append
Colors
dialog box,
choose the
layout
containing
the colors
that you
want to
append.

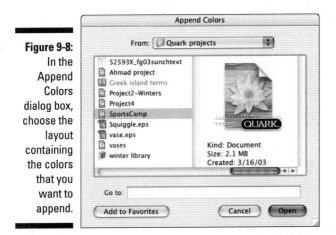

Using the Color Management System to correct color

Color calibration can make or break the way your project looks when it's printed. Your final published piece may depend on it. No matter how carefully you calibrate the hardware required for color publishing, the range of colors produced by scanning devices, computer monitors, color printers, and color printing presses vary from device to device. Luckily, QuarkXPress offers a tool that helps ensure accurate printing of the colors in your layout — colors that you create within QuarkXPress and colors in imported pictures.

Some service bureaus, prepress houses, and commercial printers will insist that you turn off the color management feature because they do their own color adjustments. Be sure to ask your service provider before you use QuarkXPress's built-in color management system.

The Quark CMS (Color Management System) XTension tracks the colors in imported picture files, the colors that your monitor can display, and the colors your printer can produce. To activate the Quark CMS, follow these steps:

1. **Choose Utilities⇨XTensions Manager to make sure the Quark CMS XTension is active.**

2. **Choose QuarkXPress⇨Preferences on the Mac or Edit⇨Preferences in Windows.**

   Alternatively, you can press Option+Shift+⌘+Y or Ctrl+Alt+Shift+Y.

3. **Select Quark CMS from the list on the left, and then check the box next to Color Management Active.**

   If your monitor or printer can't produce a particular color, Quark CMS substitutes the closest simulation of the color.

Quark CMS offers choices for rendering intents, which let you indicate color properties the Color Management Module should preserve when it performs color translations during printing for RGB, CMYK, and Hexachrome colors.

Configuring Quark CMS

Here's how you configure Quark CMS:

1. **Choose QuarkXPress⇨Preferences on the Mac or Edit⇨Preferences in Windows, or press Option+Shift+⌘+Y or Ctrl+Alt+Shift+Y, and selecting Quark CMS from the list on the left.**

   The Quark CMS pane appears (as shown in Figure 9-9).

2. Click the Color Management Active check box in the upper-right corner to activate the window.

If you want to set program-wide color-management preferences, make sure that no layouts are open when you activate this box. At the top of the Color Management Preferences dialog box, three pop-up menus let you choose a default Monitor, Composite Printer, and Separation Printer.

3. Choose an output device from the Composite Printer and/or Separation Printer pop-up menus to correct the colors in your QuarkXPress layout.

The Composite Printer and Separation Printer pop-up menus let you correct the colors used in your printed output. A *composite printer* is often a proofing printer, such as a dye-sublimation printer, or *Matchprint* service, which simulates the colors of a printing press by using a series of laminated pages. A *separation printer* produces color by using multiple color printing plates. (Many composite printers do both.)

4. Choose a monitor in the Monitor pop-up menu.

The monitor you choose determines which color profile Quark CMS uses when displaying colors in QuarkXPress. It also lets you select which colors in the profile will show up on your screen. (For more details, see the sidebar "Your monitor's color profile.")

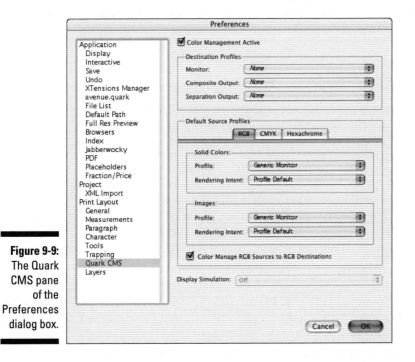

Figure 9-9: The Quark CMS pane of the Preferences dialog box.

5. **In the pop-up menu at the bottom of the Quark CMS pane, choose whether you want your monitor display to match your Monitor color space, your Composite Output color space, or your Separation Output color space.**

This Display Simulation option works only when you've chosen a color profile for your monitor display in your Monitor pop-up menu.

After you pick your Destination Profiles, you can use the three subpanes in the Default Source Profile section of the Quark CMS pane (RGB, CMYK, and Hexachrome) to choose an alternate color property for the times your output device can't print a particular color in your chosen color profile. In turn, two sections in the Default Source Profile section let you select color properties for two different variations of colors — Solid Colors and Images.

The Default Source Profile Section lets you choose options for modifying colors outside your selected color profile and preserve as many of the properties of the original color as possible.

For example, if you import EPS files into a layout that contains spot colors that aren't in your designated color profile and you set up the pop-up menus in the Solid Color menus to Adobe RGB 1998 and Saturation, QuarkXPress adjusts your color as closely to your original color as possible. Of course, getting the hang of these controls isn't easy. It takes practice, but if you study the QuarkXPress documentation, you'll find them to be extremely useful when you output your projects — the prepress crew will think you're a genius!

Changing a profile

When you import a picture into a QuarkXPress layout, Quark CMS uses the specified settings unless you choose to override those settings. After a picture is imported, you can display information about the picture and its color profile by displaying the Profile Information palette (shown in Figure 9-10). Choose Window⇨Show Profile Information to display this palette, which identifies the Picture Type, File Type, and Color Space of the picture in the active box. The Profile pop-up menu also displays the name of the currently selected color profile. You can change the selected profile by clicking the profile pop-up menu. You can also enable or disable Color Correction, in case you decide you don't want to color-correct the image.

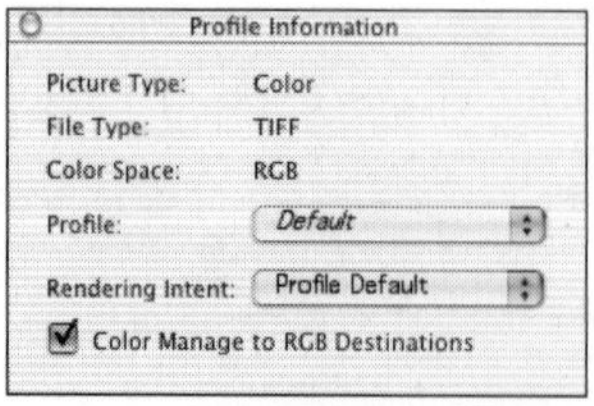

Figure 9-10:
The Profile Information palette.

Profile Information

Picture Type:	Color
File Type:	TIFF
Color Space:	RGB
Profile:	*Default*
Rendering Intent:	Profile Default

☑ Color Manage to RGB Destinations

Your monitor's color profile

If your monitor came with a color profile, use it. On the Mac, the Displays control panel (choose $\bullet$ ⇨System Preferences) has an option in the Color pane for setting color to a profile (stored in the Profiles folder in the ColorSync folder in the Library folder of the System folder), or you can use the ColorSync control panel to set profiles for several devices. In Windows, use the Display control panel (Start⇨Settings⇨Control Panel); the Settings pane has an option called Advanced that will open a dialog box that has a Color Management pane. The profiles are stored in the Color folder in the System folder in the Windows folder. Some monitors or video cards come with their own color-setup software.

Applying Color

After you create colors, you can get down to the fun of using them! You can apply colors to any of the following:

✔ A box's background or frame

✔ Text in a text box or on a path

✔ A grayscale TIFF image

✔ A black-and-white TIFF, PICT, BMP, or other bitmap image

✔ A line

The easiest way to apply colors is by using the Colors palette. Figure 9-11 shows the palette being used to apply color to a frame.

Figure 9-11:
You can change color for any element by using the Colors palette. The icons and lists give you access to all color controls.

In the Mac version of QuarkXPress 6, you can use such color-selection methods as swatches and crayons. The icons are displayed at the top of the Colors dialog box accessed from the Preferences dialog box's Display pane.

Three icons are at the top of the Colors palette in Figure 9-11. From left to right, these icons are Frame, Contents, and Background. Click the icon for what you want to color (the Content icon for text or grayscale and black-and-white images, for example) and then click the color that you want to apply. The palette changes when a line or a text path is selected, as in Figure 9-12.

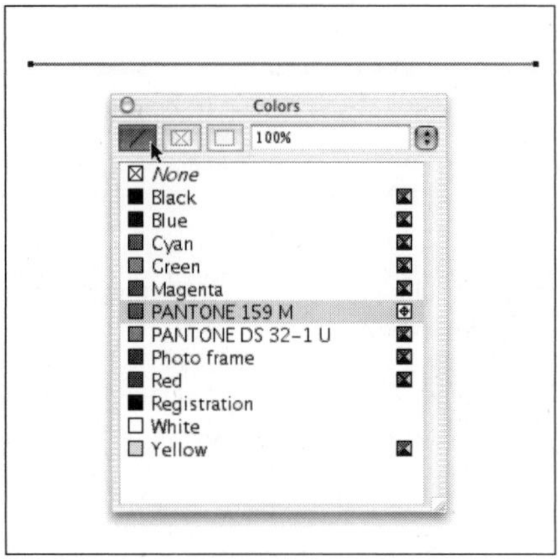

Figure 9-12:
The Colors palette lets you change the color of the selected items.

If you want to apply a shade (percentage) of a color, first apply the color and then enter a new shade value where you see the percentage in the top-right corner of the Colors palette. You can do either of the following:

✔ Click the triangle to the left of the current percentage (usually 100) to display a pop-up menu.

✔ Highlight the current percentage and type a new number.

If you click a color square in the Colors palette and hold down the mouse button, you apply the color to a box frame or background — but you cannot apply a color swatch to a picture image. To change the color applied to a picture, you must click the middle icon of the three located at the top of the Colors palette — and then click a color name.

Creating blends

One of the coolest effects you can achieve in the Colors palette is a *blend* — a gradual change of color from one end of a text or picture box to the other.

QuarkXPress lets you create several types of blends, as shown in Figure 9-13. Follow these steps to create a blend:

1. **Select a box and then click the background icon in the Colors palette.**

2. **Choose a blend type from the pop-up list that appears beneath the top-left icons.**

   Two radio buttons marked #1 and #2 appear, as well as a text box for entering the blend's angle in degrees.

3. **Click the #1 button and select a color.**

4. **Click the #2 button and select a different color.**

   QuarkXPress makes a blend from color #1 to color #2.

Change the angle (the default is 0 degrees) to change the blend direction.

For circular blends, changing the angle determines how quickly the color blends from the first to the second; a smaller number gives the blend a smaller core for the first color than a larger number.

In QuarkXPress 6, you can specify a background blend for an entire table by making None the table background color and placing the table over a box containing the blend.

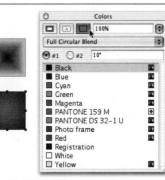

Figure 9-13:
Types of blends.

You can use white as the second color when you create a blend. The resulting fade-away effect is useful for one-color (black) publications.

About the only things you can't do are . . . well, actually, you can do everything you need to do. But the needed procedures aren't as straightforward as using the Colors palette. You can do one of three things:

  ✔ Choose Style⇨Color or Style⇨Shade options to change the color of a line or selected text (the Content tool must be selected to change the color of text).

✔ Use the Box pane of the Modify dialog box to change a box's background. (To display this dialog box, choose Item➪Modify, or press ⌘+M or Ctrl+M.)

✔ Use the Frame pane of the Modify dialog box to change a box's frame color. (To display this pane, choose Item➪Modify or Item➪Frame, or press ⌘+B or Ctrl+B.)

Editing colors

The Colors palette gives you access to the Colors dialog box. By holding down the ⌘ or Ctrl key when you click a color, you can jump directly to the Colors dialog box; the color that you clicked is highlighted. Then click Edit, Delete, Duplicate, and so on, for what you want to do with the selected color.

The contextual menu appears when you Control+click or right-click a color in the Colors palette. You can create, edit, or delete a color from that context menu, or convert a color from process to spot or vice versa.

A good effect is one that's used *sparingly*. Now that you're a color expert and you're ready to add color to your layout, make sure you don't overdo it and put color everywhere or use clashing colors.

Finding and replacing colors

When you edit a color, you can rename it. But if you want to replace all blues with reds, no specific find-and-replace function exists. But you have a makeshift way to find and replace colors:

1. **Choose Edit➪Colors.** You get a list of current colors in your QuarkXPress layout.

2. **Select the color you want to change.**

3. **Click the Delete button.**

   QuarkXPress asks what color you want to use to replace the deleted color in objects that use the deleted color.

4. **Select a replacement color from the Replace With pop-up menu.**

Of course, this makeshift procedure *deletes* the original color from the layout. To keep that color definition but still replace it in your layout with a different color, first use the Duplicate button to make a *copy* of the color that you want to change. Then delete the original color so that you can replace it with a different one. The duplicate color is kept with the other colors in your layout.

Chapter 10

Understanding XTensions

· ·

· ·

*I*magine that QuarkXPress, instead of being a layout program, is a prefabricated, one-room house. Your prefab copy of the house sits on a street with a dozen other houses just like it. Your next-door neighbor, a wild saxophone player who keeps you up at night with his playing, adds a music room onto his house. Your other next-door neighbor gives birth to triplets and builds a second story. You, on the other hand, add a greenhouse room so that you can keep your orchid collection healthy and growing in any season.

Like those neighbors, QuarkXPress users have different likes and needs. Just as the people in the imaginary neighborhood aren't satisfied with living in their identical prefab houses, publishers and designers also are not satisfied using only one flavor of QuarkXPress. For example, someone using the program to produce a two-color school newspaper has different needs than a designer who uses the program to create four-color process ads for magazines.

The creators of QuarkXPress wisely listened to their customers' needs and concerns and realized that every user is unique. The architecture of QuarkXPress meets these needs by allowing the development of *XTensions*. XTensions are add-on programs that target specific needs not addressed by QuarkXPress. Both Quark and third parties develop XTensions, which are available for the Macintosh and Windows versions.

To get an idea of why you need an XTension, suppose that you want to add some cool drop shadow effects to your boxes or a glow around some type. You could spend $900 on a sophisticated image-editing program and then import the images into QuarkXPress (without editable text). Or you can spend a few bucks on an XTension and get the same results — in QuarkXPress. Maybe you'd like a QuarkXPress feature that checks your layouts for trouble areas before you send it to the printer or prepress house. XTensions customize QuarkXPress for the kind of publishing that you do.

Getting Started with XTensions

You may not be aware of it, but you've been running — if not using — several XTensions every time that you've used QuarkXPress. If you personally installed your QuarkXPress 6 program and performed a Custom Install, you had the option to install or not install QuarkXPress XTensions. This setting simply determines which ones run by default — all the XTensions provided with QuarkXPress will be installed on your computer.

Installing XTensions with QuarkXPress

A Custom Install option in the installation dialog box lets you install the XTensions that ship with QuarkXPress. If you select this option and marked all the listed XTensions, over 25 XTension files are in the XTension folder inside your QuarkXPress program folder, as in Figure 10-1. These XTensions are features that you may never use (such as Jabberwocky for creating dummy text) and significant features (such as indexing and HTML export).

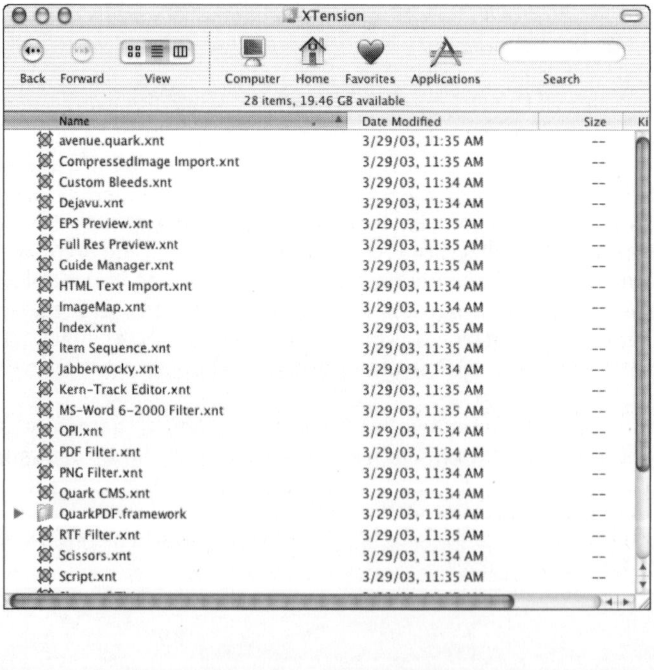

Figure 10-1: The XTension folder contains the XTensions you install.

Determining which XTensions are running

Displaying the QuarkXPress Environment dialog box (shown in Figure 10-2) shows you which XTensions are running. These are the XTensions that are currently operational and adding features to your copy of QuarkXPress. Here's how to open the Environment dialog box, depending on your platform:

- ✔ **Mac OS:** Hold down the Option key and choose QuarkXPress⇨About QuarkXPress.

- ✔ **Windows:** Hold down the Ctrl key and choose Help⇨About QuarkXPress.

QuarkXPress ™ Environment	
QuarkXPress Version:	6.0 Development 0
Patch Level:	0
Serial Number:	XY12345678901
Power Mac Native:	Yes
Machine Type:	Unknown
Floating Point Unit:	Yes
Main Monitor Depth:	24
Keyboard Type:	Apple USB Keyboard
Memory:	0/21003487
System Version:	10.2.4
Language:	U.S. English
Script Manager Version:	10.0.0
Printer Name:	DESKJET_940C
Max Files Open:	Indeterminate

XTensions Modules:

Cool Blends
GIF Filter
HTML Export
Hyperlinks
JPEG Filter
Layers
Placeholders
SpellChecker
Table
Web Tools
avenue.quark
LZW Import
Custom Bleeds
Dejavu
EPS Preview
Full Resolution Preview
Guide Manager
HTML Text Import
ImageMap
Index
Item Sequence
Jabber Wocky

Module Serial #:

User Reg. Info.   Create Reg. Disk   OK

Figure 10-2: The QuarkXPress Environment dialog box.

You can choose Utilities⇨XTensions Manager to see which XTensions are running. The XTensions with a check mark next to them in the Enable list are running. QuarkXPress 6 includes the following XTensions:

- ✔ **avenue.Quark:** A formerly separate product that lets Web-page creators extract QuarkXPress content files into Extended Markup Language (XML, a format often used for Web-content management systems).

- ✔ **Compressed Image Import:** This imports compressed TIFF files.

- ✔ **Custom Bleeds:** This creates what its name indicates, where the image on the page extends beyond the page boundary.

- ✔ **Dejavu:** This provides the ability to keep a list of previously opened QuarkXPress projects.

- ✔ **EPS Preview:** This creates the preview images for exported Encapsulated PostScript (EPS) files.

- ✔ **Full Res Preview:** This lets QuarkXPress 6 show the full resolution of imported bitmapped images. You must register QuarkXPress for this feature to be active.

- ✔ **Guide Manager:** This implements the guide-management functions.

- ✔ **HTML Text Import:** This imports HyperText Markup Language (HTML) files.

- ✔ **Hyph_CNS_1, Hyph_CNS_2,** and **Hyph_CNS_3:** These provide hyphenation rules.

- ✔ **ImageMap:** This lets you create image maps (graphical areas that include hyperlinks) in layouts for the Web. This function was brought over from the QuarkImmedia product to create dynamic Web pages.

- ✔ **Index:** This provides the indexing functions.

- ✔ **Item Sequence:** This lets you control the sequence of display for items on Web layouts. This function was brought over from the QuarkImmedia product to create dynamic Web pages.

- ✔ **Kern-Track Editor:** This manages font kerning pairs and tracking settings.

- ✔ **MS-Word 6-2000 Filter:** This imports and exports Microsoft Word files.

  The MS-Word 6-2000 Filter supports the current Windows XP and Mac OS X versions, despite the name.

- ✔ **OPI:** This lets Quark support the Open Prepress Interface.

  OPI stores high-resolution files on a separate server; and designers use a lower-resolution version in their QuarkXPress file. During printing, the OPI feature inserts the high-resolution images. This XTension adds an OPI pane or option to many dialog boxes involving images. QuarkXPress has supported OPI in previous versions, and this XTension includes those previous functions plus several enhancements.

- ✔ **PDF Filter:** This imports PDF files.

- ✔ **PNG Import:** This imports the Web-oriented PNG graphics format.

- ✔ **Quark CMS:** This provides the color management features.

- ✔ **RTF:** This lets QuarkXPress import the Rich Text Format.

  Microsoft developed RTF as a platform-neutral standard for text; it supports such formatting as boldface and font changes.

- ✔ **Scissors:** This displays a Tools palette item that can cut lines and boxes into segments.

- ✔ **Script:** This Mac-only Xtension better integrates AppleScripting into QuarkXPress.

- ✔ **WordPerfect Filter:** This imports and exports WordPerfect files.

- ✔ **XML Import:** This imports XML files.

- ✔ **XPress Tags Filter:** This imports and exports the XPress Tags format used to convert QuarkXPress formatting into codes.

Several included XTensions are free XTensions that Quark has long had on its Web site, including

- ✔ **Jabberwocky:** This puts random dummy text in a text box.

- ✔ **Shape of Things:** This provides the Starburst tool.

- ✔ **Super Step and Repeat:** This lets you tell QuarkXPress how many copies to make of an item and where to place the copies.

- ✔ **Type Tricks:** This adds fraction– and price-formatting functions.

Because Quark continues to modularize the application, QuarkXPress 6 has more XTensions than previous versions.

Installing additional XTensions

If you download or purchase a new XTension, all you usually need to do is drag the file into the XTension folder inside your QuarkXPress folder. Some commercial products include installer programs that place the XTension in the XTension folder automatically. (These programs often install other files in your Mac's System folder or the Windows System folder that the XTension needs to do its thing.) Either way, if QuarkXPress is running, you need to restart it to load the XTension and make its features available. You can disable an XTension by moving it to the XTension Disabled folder or choosing Utilities➪XTensions Manager.

XTensions developers often provide demo versions of their XTensions on CDs (handed out at trade shows or mailed to you) and on their Web sites. Sometimes these are full-featured versions of the XTension with a time limit. Other times, they shift QuarkXPress itself into demo mode, which doesn't allow you to save or print clean copies. After evaluating such XTensions, disable them to revert QuarkXPress to standard operating mode. You can also check our Web site, www.QXCentral.com, for information on XTensions.

QuarkXPress 6 cannot run XTensions written for previous QuarkXPress versions. The XTensions provided with QuarkXPress are already updated by Quark. For possible updates of third-party XTensions, contact the developer.

Handling XTension-loading errors

If any XTensions are unable to load at startup, an alert lists those XTensions. Click the name of the XTension to display a possible reason and then click About for additional information about the XTension (such as the version and developer). The XTension Loading Error alert displays the following buttons:

- ✔ **Ignore:** Click this if you want to launch QuarkXPress without launching the XTensions listed in the scroll list.
- ✔ **Manager:** Click this to display the XTension Manager dialog box, in which you can change the startup set of XTensions or create a new set.
- ✔ **Don't Show This Dialog Again:** Click this button if you don't want to be alerted when QuarkXPress is unable to load an XTension.

Managing XTensions

To help you control which XTensions are running — without forcing you to move files in and out of folders on your desktop — QuarkXPress provides an XTensions Manager. Preferences control how the XTensions Manager works, giving you options such as the ability to review the XTensions that load each time that you launch QuarkXPress.

Setting XTensions Manager preferences

The XTensions Manager preferences are application preferences, which means they are program-level defaults. If you make any changes to XTensions Manager preferences (whether a project is open or not), the changes are implemented the next time that you launch QuarkXPress.

To open XTensions Manager preferences, choose QuarkXPress⇨Preferences on the Mac or Edit⇨Preferences in Windows, or press Option+Shift+⌘+Y or Ctrl+Alt+Shift+Y. Then click the XTensions Manager option under the Application section, as shown in Figure 10-3.

Set the XTensions Manager preferences as follows:

- ✔ **Always:** Select the Always radio button if you want the XTensions Manager dialog box to open each time that you start QuarkXPress.

This setting is handy for service bureaus and other organizations that work with many client projects that have many different requirements. When the XTensions Manager opens, you can load a set of XTensions, create and modify XTension sets, and enable or disable individual XTensions for the current set.

✔ **When:** Select the When radio button if you only want the XTensions Manager dialog box to open under certain circumstances as dictated by the two accompanying check boxes.

- **"XTension" Folder Changes:** Check this check box to open the XTensions Manager dialog box when XTensions have been added to or removed from the XTension folder since the last time that you used QuarkXPress.

- **Error Loading XTensions Occurs:** Check this check box to open the XTensions Manager dialog box if QuarkXPress encounters a problem trying to load an XTension.

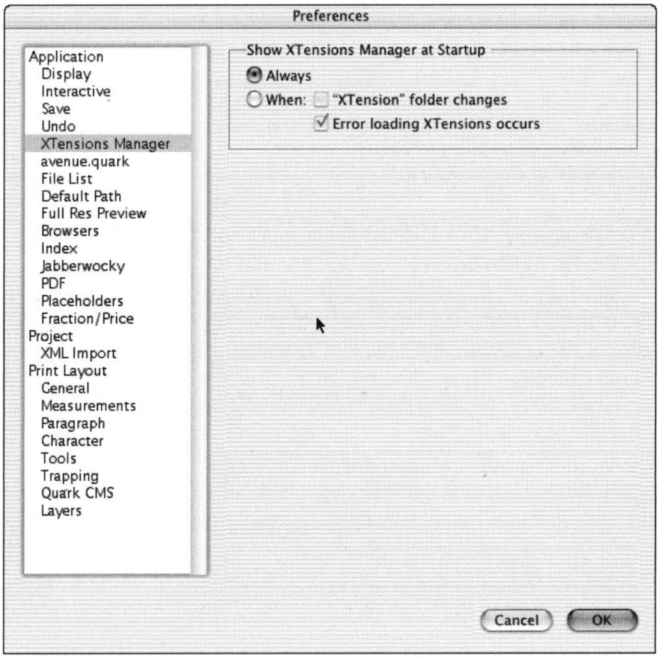

Figure 10-3:
The
XTensions
Manager
pane of the
Preferences
dialog box.

Using the XTensions Manager

Whether you run only a few XTensions with QuarkXPress or you run many, chances are you don't need all your XTensions every time that you use QuarkXPress. In workgroup environments, not every user requires the same kinds of XTensions. Instead of loading unnecessary XTensions, you can use the XTensions Manager feature to create startup sets of XTensions. An individual QuarkXPress user can use the XTensions Manager to create separate startup sets for page design, editorial, and output work. A workgroup site can create startup sets for each class of QuarkXPress user. For example, a page-layout artist may use a set of design and typographic XTensions, while an editor uses a different set of editorial-specific XTensions.

Changing XTensions

Anytime you want to change the XTensions that are running, choose Utilities⇨ XTensions Manager.

To run an XTension, click in the Enable column to place a check mark next to it, as shown in Figure 10-4.

To disable an XTension, click to remove its check mark.

Click OK to close the XTensions Manager dialog box and then restart QuarkXPress for the changes to take effect.

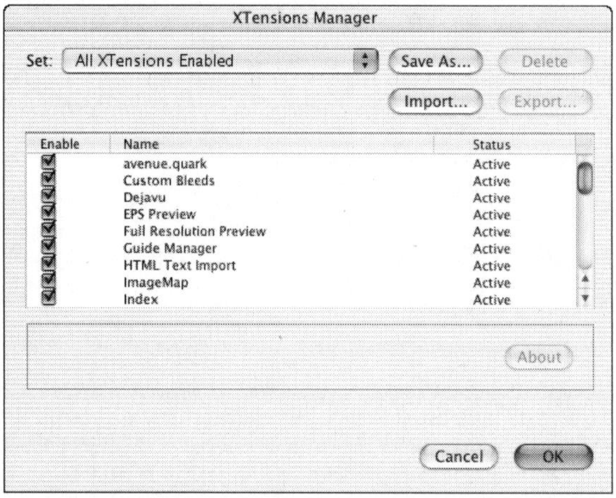

	XTensions Manager		
Set:	All XTensions Enabled	Save As...	Delete
		Import...	Export...

Enable	Name	Status
☑	avenue.quark	Active
☑	Custom Bleeds	Active
☑	Dejavu	Active
☑	EPS Preview	Active
☑	Full Resolution Preview	Active
☑	Guide Manager	Active
☑	HTML Text Import	Active
☑	ImageMap	Active
☑	Index	Active

About

Cancel   OK

Figure 10-4:
The
XTensions
Manager
dialog box.

Using XTensions sets

If projects or clients require specific XTensions, you can create sets of XTensions for them. You select the set that you want from the Set menu in the XTensions Manager dialog box. Click OK and then restart QuarkXPress to load only those XTensions. QuarkXPress provides these default sets:

✔ **No Set:** Okay, it's not really a *set;* it's an option in the Set menu. Choose this option to enable and disable XTensions on the fly, without using or changing sets. (This set appears only if you have added an XTension or disabled an XTension but didn't save the changes as a new set.)

✔ **All XTensions Enabled:** Choose this to move all XTensions in the XTension Disabled folder to the XTension folder; all XTensions in the scroll list are checked.

✔ **All XTensions Disabled:** Choose this for the opposite results. All XTensions in the XTension folder are moved to the XTension Disabled folder; all XTensions in the scroll list are unchecked.

To create an XTension set:

1. **Choose Utilities⇨XTensions Manager.**

2. **Enable the XTensions that you want in the set and disable all others.**

3. **Click Save As.**

4. **In the Save Set dialog box that appears, name the set according to its contents, the client, or the projects that it is intended for.**

5. **Click Save to create the set.**

   The set is automatically selected in the Set menu and will load when you restart QuarkXPress.

6. **Click OK to close the XTensions Manager dialog box and save the set in your XPress Preferences file.**

7. **Restart QuarkXPress to load the new set.**

The Import and Export buttons in the XTensions Manager dialog box let you share set definitions with other users who own the same XTensions. Exported sets have *information* about XTensions — not copies of XTensions.

XTension-related issues

The ability to set XTension-related preferences and to turn XTensions on and off via the XTensions Manager makes managing XTensions easy, but be aware of these XTension-related pitfalls:

✔ Some XTensions, often referred to as *required XTensions,* must be present whenever a QuarkXPress user opens a layout that was created when these XTensions were running.

✔ If you use a required XTension while creating a layout, you must include the XTension if you send the layout to a service provider for output.

✔ Some XTension developers offer freely distributable, viewer-only versions of their XTensions. A viewer-only XTension lets you open layouts created with the full working version of the XTension, but the functionality is disabled.

✔ You may encounter incompatibilities when running certain combinations of XTensions. If all XTensions were created correctly, any XTension would work flawlessly with any other XTension. But in the real world, problems can occur. If you experience odd or unpredictable results while working with QuarkXPress, look for XTension incompatibilities. Unfortunately, there are no tools that check for such problems. Your best bet is to disable suspect XTensions one by one until the problem goes away. It's also a good idea to keep your XTensions as up to date as possible. Many XTension developers offer free updates and fixes on their Web sites. Check these sites periodically for updated XTension versions.

Acquiring XTensions

The best way to obtain information about XTensions, upgrade XTensions that you own, and purchase new XTensions is on the Web. The Internet has plenty of information about desktop publishing, QuarkXPress, and XTensions.

If you're the adventurous type, perform a search for *QuarkXPress* or *XTensions* at your favorite search engine. Or start by heading to `www.QXCentral.com`, the companion site for this book, where we've included links to the major XTensions developers. In addition, Quark may post freebie and updated versions of its XTensions at `www.quark.com`.

Chapter 11

Outputting Projects

· ·

· ·

*A*fter your project is designed and laid out, you may actually want to see a printed copy or perhaps a PDF version of it on your computer screen. Go for it! This chapter covers outputting projects with QuarkXPress.

Setting Up a Printer

Suppose that you've developed a print project, and you'd like to see how it looks on paper. For this, you need a printer. Printers can have such a variety of features, and yours may require setup before you can use it.

Setting up Macintosh printers

Although you choose the printer type in the Setup pane of the QuarkXPress Print dialog box, you still need to set up the printer on your Mac before you can use it. To do that, use the Print Center program, which is well hidden. (Look in the Utilities folder in the Applications folder.) The Print Center lists any installed printers. Make sure that the printer you want to set up is connected to your Mac (directly or via the network) and turned on.

If you're using a network printer, make sure that the right network protocols, such as Internet Protocol (IP) and AppleTalk, are turned on via the Network control panel in the System Preferences dialog box, which you access by choosing⇨System Preferences.

To install a printer, you typically run a program that comes with the printer. Such programs often add the printer to the Print Center utility's Printer List. If not, click the Add button and locate the printer driver for your printer. (Again, you can usually find this on a CD that accompanies the printer.) If you can't find the CD, try going online to the manufacturer's site.

In Figure 11-1, you can see the Printer List dialog box that appears when you open the Print Center application.

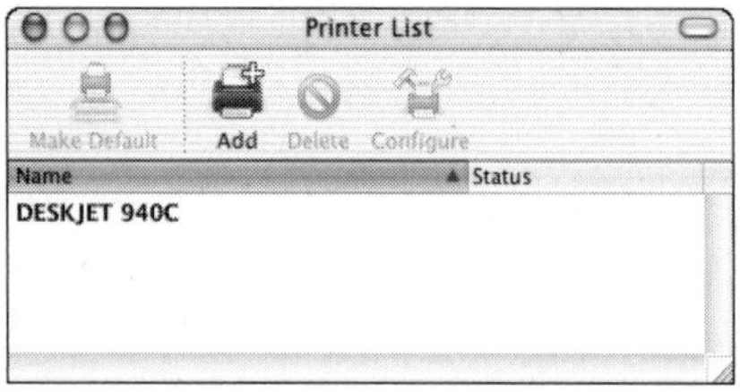

Figure 11-1:
The Mac's
Print Center
utility.

Printer List		
Make Default	Add	Delete	Configure
Name	▲ **Status**
DESKJET 940C	

Configuring an installed printer will vary based on the printer software that's provided with the printer. In some cases, a printer's configuration software is accessible via the Configure button in the Print Center utility. In other cases, you need to run a separate utility that came with the printer or use controls on the printer itself.

Setting up Windows printers

To set up a Windows XP printer, choose Start➪Control Panel➪Printers and Other Hardware. You then see a window (as shown in Figure 11-2) where you can double-click the Add a Printer icon.

For Windows 2000, choose Start➪Printer➪Add Printer. (Some installations of Windows XP Professional also let you use this method, as well as the option to choose Start➪Printers and Faxes and to then double-click the Add a Printer icon.) Either way, choosing Add a Printer opens a wizard that guides you through the setup process. You'll likely need a disk that came with the printer — or the Windows CD-ROM if you add a new printer — because Windows will need information specific to that printer. *Note:* Some printers have their own setup software that you should use instead of the Add Printer utility in Windows.

One pane matters greatly: The Device Settings pane lets you specify all the device settings, from paper trays to memory to how fonts are handled. For PostScript printers, this pane has several key options.

Figure 11-2:
The Printers
and Other
Hardware
window in
Windows
XP.

You may need to install a PostScript Printer Description (PPD) file that contains specific details on your printer. This file should come on a disk or CD with your printer and is often installed with the printer's setup program. Otherwise, download it from the printer maker's Web site. These files should reside in the `Preferences\PPDs` folder in the folder in which QuarkXPress is installed.

Printing Options in QuarkXPress

When you print in QuarkXPress, only the *current* layout prints, not *all* layouts in your project.

Before printing a layout, first make sure that the printer and project printing defaults are properly set up:

✔ To check while you're still creating your print layouts, choose File➪Page Setup.

✔ Otherwise, check when it's time to print via File➪Print.

They both provide the Print dialog box, as shown in Figure 11-3.

Purely PostScript no more

QuarkXPress has output options for non-PostScript printers because more non-PostScript printers (particularly inexpensive color inkjet printers) are being used by designers and publishers for proofing purposes.

With QuarkXPress, you can print pages as *thumbnails* (small images) to non-PostScript printers. Also, the Reduce or Enlarge field, the Page Positioning pop-up menu, and the Fit in Print Area check box features are now non-PostScript-friendly.

QuarkXPress also lets you print red/green/blue (RGB) composite picture files to non-PostScript printers, and you can print rotated TIFF pictures at full resolution to non-PostScript printers. Another cool non-PostScript enhancement is the addition of print styles for non-PostScript printers.

You can use the Frequency field in the Print dialog box Output pane to control the line frequency for imported pictures when printing to a non-PostScript printer. Before, these sorts of sophisticated, professional print features were thought worthy only of PostScript printers.

It's doubtful that PostScript output devices will be dethroned by non-PostScript devices anytime soon. And PostScript still remains the official language (printing language, that is) of the high-end publishing world. Still, it would seem that although PostScript is still far from being on its way out, some solid, less expensive alternatives are out there — making a home or small-business publishing system even more attainable than ever.

Blends (where one color switches to another) over a long area (say five inches or more) can end up looking banded (or striped) on PostScript Level 1 and Level 2 devices, but PostScript Level 3 has a function that prevents that banding. QuarkXPress 6 automatically enables that function, when printing to PostScript Level 3 printers or imagesetters, with its new *SmoothShading* capability.

QuarkXPress exports Web layouts to HyperText Markup Language (HTML) files for viewing in a Web browser when you choose File➪Export.

The Print dialog box has nine panes — Layout, Setup, Output, Options, Layers, Bleed, OPI, Preview, and Profiles — as well as a few options that are always available. Note that Profiles will not display if Quark CMS is not made active in the Preferences dialog box's Quark CMS pane, in the Print Layout section. (Choose QuarkXPress➪Preferences on the Mac or Edit➪Preferences in Windows, or press Option+Shift+⌘+Y or Ctrl+Alt+Shift+Y.)

In version 6, QuarkXPress adds one pane — Layers — to the Print dialog box to control output of specific layers in the project's print layouts. Also, the Layout pane is the new name for the former Document pane.

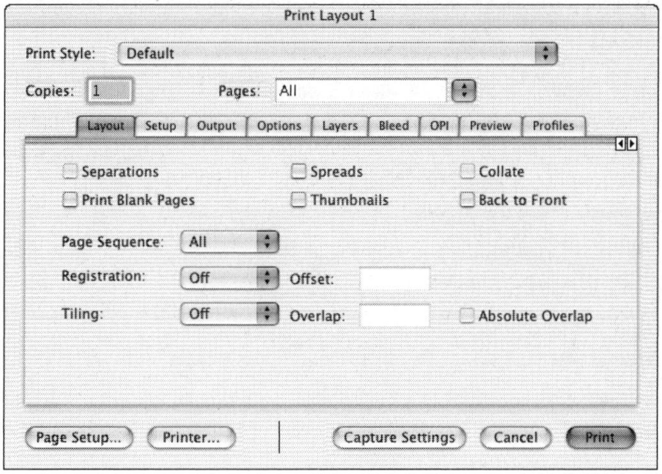

| Print Layout 1 |

Print Style: Default

Copies: 1   Pages: All

| Layout | Setup | Output | Options | Layers | Bleed | OPI | Preview | Profiles |

☐ Separations   ☐ Spreads   ☐ Collate

☐ Print Blank Pages   ☐ Thumbnails   ☐ Back to Front

Page Sequence: All

Registration: Off   Offset:

Tiling: Off   Overlap: ☐ Absolute Overlap

(Page Setup...) (Printer...) | (Capture Settings) (Cancel) (Print)

Figure 11-3:
The Print
dialog box.

Common options

No matter what pane is open, the following options are always available:

- ✔ **Print Style:** You choose the *print style* — a saved set of printer settings — from this list. We cover print styles in the section, "Using Print Styles."

- ✔ **Copies:** Enter here how many copies of the layout that you want printed.

- ✔ **Pages:** Choose here which pages to print. You can enter a range, such as 3–7; a single page, such as 4; a set of unrelated pages, such as 3, 7, 15, 28; or a combination, such as 3–7, 15, 28–64, 82–85. To print all pages, Select All from the pop-up menu or type **All**.

- ✔ **Capture Settings:** Clicking this button remembers the current Print dialog box settings and returns you to your layout. This way, you can make a change and return to the Print dialog box later without having to reestablish your settings.

- ✔ **Print:** Clicking this button prints the layout.

- ✔ **Cancel:** Clicking this button exits the Print dialog box without printing.

To change printers on the Mac, click the Printers button; in Windows, use the Printer pop-up menu. To change printer output settings such as paper size and collation, click the Page Setup button on the Mac and the Properties button in Windows.

The Layout pane

In this pane, shown in Figure 11-4, you set up the basic page printing attributes:

> **Print Layout 1**
>
> Print Style: Default
>
> Copies: 1   Pages: All
>
> | Layout | Setup | Output | Options | Layers | Bleed | OPI | Preview | Profiles |
>
> ☐ Separations   ☐ Spreads   ☐ Collate
> ☐ Print Blank Pages   ☐ Thumbnails   ☐ Back to Front
>
> Page Sequence: All
>
> Registration: Off   Offset:
>
> Tiling: Off   Overlap: ☐ Absolute Overlap
>
> (Page Setup...) (Printer...) | (Capture Settings) (Cancel) (**Print**)

✔ **Separations:** Selecting this check box prints color separations, putting each color on its own sheet (or negative) for use in producing color plates. Choose this if you're printing directly to an imagesetter and outputting separate plates or printing to file for such direct output.

✔ **Print Blank Pages:** Select this check box to output blank pages; clear it to print only pages with text or graphics on them.

✔ **Spreads:** If your printer can print facing pages on one sheet of paper (such as if you have an 11-by-17-inch printer and your pages are 8½ by 11 inches or smaller), and you want them printed that way, select this check box.

If you have *bleeds* (where ink will go all the way to the edge of the paper), you may not want to use the Spreads option when outputting to an imagesetter because there will be no extra space for the bleed between the spreads. If you use traditional *perfect-binding* (square spines) or *saddle-stitching* (stapled spines) printing methods, in which facing pages aren't printed contiguously, don't use this option. Check with your service bureau.

✔ **Thumbnails:** To get a miniature version of your layout printed several pages to a sheet, select this option.

✔ **Collate:** This option is available when you are printing more than one copy. If checked, it will print a full copy of the layout and then repeat for as many times as copies are specified. If unchecked, this option will print the number of copies of each page before going on to the next page (such as ten copies of page 1, followed by ten copies of page 2, and so on).

✔ **Back to Front:** If checked, this option reverses the printing order so that the last page comes first, followed by the next-to-last page, and so on.

✔ **Page Sequence:** You can select All, Odd, or Even, which will print the specified type of pages from whatever range that you select in the Pages box. Thus, if you select Odd and specify a page range of 2–6, pages 3 and 5 will print. This option is *grayed out* (unavailable) if you've checked the Spreads option.

✔ **Registration:** This option adds registration marks and crop marks, which you'll need if your project is being professionally printed. A printer uses registration marks to line up the page correctly on the printing press. Registration crop marks define the edge of the page (handy if you're printing to paper or negatives larger than your final page size). If you print color separations, enabling registration marks also prints the name of each color on its negative and includes a color bar in the output so that the printing press operator can check that the right colors are used with the right plates. You can choose to have registration centered, off-center, or turned off. Centered is the default.

With the new Offset field to the right of the Registration pop-up menu, QuarkXPress 6 lets you determine how far crop marks are offset from the page margins.

✔ **Tiling:** For layouts that are larger than the paper that you're printing them on, select Manual or Automatic to have QuarkXPress break your page into smaller chunks that fit on the page. QuarkXPress will print marks on your pages to help you line up the tiles. Here's how the options work:

- **Automatic:** If you choose Automatic, QuarkXPress determines where each tile breaks. You can select the amount of tile overlap by entering a value in the Overlap field: You can enter a value between 0 and 6 inches. If you enter a value in the Overlap field, QuarkXPress prints that overlapped area on both adjacent tiles, giving you duplicate material that you can overlap the tiles with to help with alignment.

- **Absolute Overlap:** If you check the Absolute Overlap check box, QuarkXPress makes sure that the overlap is always exactly the value specified in the Overlap field. If this option is unchecked, QuarkXPress centers the tiled image on the assembled pages, increasing the overlap if necessary.

- **Manual:** If you choose Manual, you decide where the tiles break by repositioning the ruler origin in your layout. For all pages selected, QuarkXPress prints the tiled area whose upper-left corner matches the ruler's origin. Repeat this step for each tiled area. Choose the Manual tile option if certain areas of your layout make more logical break points than others.

The Setup pane

The Setup pane is one that you'll rarely change after you set it up. Figure 11-5 shows the pane. It has the following options:

- **Printer Description:** This pop-up menu lists the printers for which a PostScript Printer Description file is available. These tell QuarkXPress how to format the output correctly.

- **Paper Size, Width, and Height:** In these three fields, you choose the size of the paper that will be used in the printer.

The size of the paper that you'll be using doesn't always correspond directly to the trim size of your final print layout.

- **Paper Offset and Page Gap:** The Paper Offset and Page Gap fields are controls used in imagesetters. Don't change them unless your service bureau directs you to.

Ask your the service bureau what they prefer.

- **Reduce or Enlarge:** You can scale a page before you print it by entering a value here between 25% and 400%. Printing at reduced scale is particularly useful if your layout's page size is large and if you can get by with a reduced version of the layout for proofing purposes.

- **Page Positioning:** This pop-up menu lets you align the page within the paper that it's being printed on. Your choices are Left Edge (the default), Center (centers both horizontally and vertically), Center Horizontal, and Center Vertical.

- **Fit in Print Area:** Almost every printer has a gap along at least one edge where the printer grasps the paper (usually with rollers) to move it through the printing assembly. The printer can't print in this gap, so a layout as large as the paper size usually has part of it cut off along one or more edges of the paper. Checking this check box ensures that nothing is cut off.

- **Orientation:** Click the icon that looks like a portrait to get a *vertical* orientation of the layout (taller than wide). Clicking the horizontal icon produces pages with a *landscape* orientation (wider than tall).

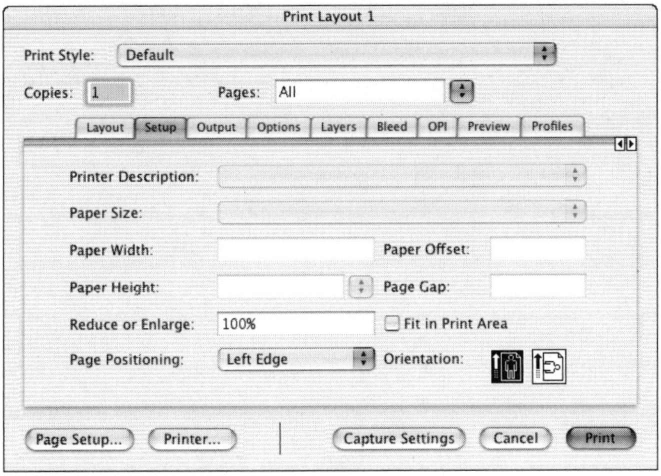

Figure 11-5:
The Setup
pane of the
Print dialog
box.

The Output pane

The Output pane, as shown in Figure 11-6, is where you set many attributes for printing to an imagesetter, whether you're producing black-and-white or color-separated print projects. You also use this pane for printing to a standard printer and to set resolution and color modes. The following two sections explain the options for both types of printers.

Using the section-numbering feature

If you use the QuarkXPress section-numbering feature to create multiple sections in your layout, you must enter the page numbers exactly as they're labeled in the layout. (The label for the current page appears in the lower-left corner of your layout screen.) Include any prefix used and enter the labels in the same format (letters, Roman numerals, or regular numerals) used in the section whose pages you want to print.

Alternatively, you can indicate the absolute page numbers by preceding the number with a plus sign (+). For example, suppose that you have an eight-page layout with two sections of four pages each. You label pages one through four as AN-1 through AN-4 and label pages five through eight as BN-1 through BN-4. If you enter BN-1 through BN-4 in the Pages field of the Print dialog box, QuarkXPress prints the first four pages in the section that uses the BN- prefix. If you enter +5 through +8, QuarkXPress prints layout pages five through eight — which again includes BN-1 through BN-4 in this example.

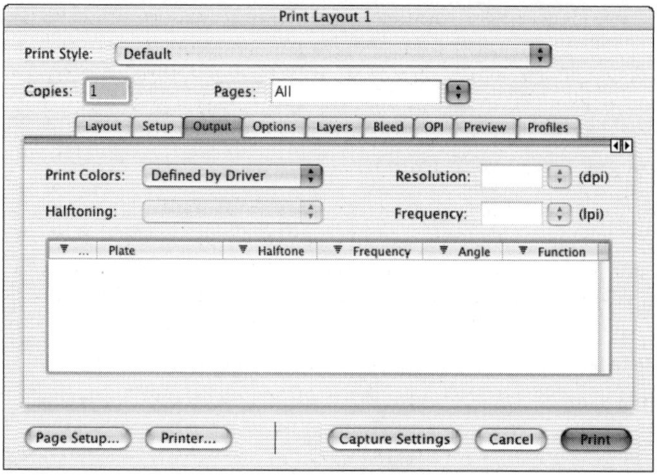

Print Layout 1

Print Style: Default

Copies: 1   Pages: All

Layout | Setup | Output | Options | Layers | Bleed | OPI | Preview | Profiles

Print Colors: Defined by Driver   Resolution: (dpi)

Halftoning: Frequency: (lpi)

▼ ...	Plate	▼ Halftone	▼ Frequency	▼ Angle	▼ Function

Page Setup...   Printer...   Capture Settings   Cancel   Print

Figure 11-6:
The Output
pane of the
Print dialog
box.

QuarkXPress offers several advanced printing options designed for professional publishing users. Options not available for non-PostScript printers (such as color options) are grayed out in the Print dialog box.

Here's how the settings work in the Output pane of the Print dialog box:

✔ **Print Colors:** This pop-up menu (available only if the Separations option is not checked in the Layout pane) lets you select Black & White; Grayscale; on a color printer, Composite RGB; and for some printers, Composite CMYK.

QuarkXPress 6 adds two options to the Print Colors pop-up menu:

- **As Is:** The new As Is option prints the colors in whatever color models they are defined in instead of converting them to RGB or cyan/magenta/yellow/black (CMYK). Use this when creating output that will be color-managed at the output device or by a service bureau using its own color management software.

- **DeviceN:** The DeviceN option is something that you don't need to worry about if you're just getting started with QuarkXPress. It formats color output in the PostScript Level 3 DeviceN format, which stores both the color names (spot colors) and their constituent CMYK values so that the output can be reproduced on both CMYK and spot-color-enabled printers. It's also handy when you create PDF files that you intend to print because it provides all the color information that any modern printer needs to make the best match. DeviceN is also available as an option when you save a page to EPS format via File➪Save Page as EPS.

✔ **Plates:** Use this list to determine whether all spot and process (CMYK) colors are output to their own individual plates (All Process & Spot) or whether all the spot colors (such as Pantone) are converted into the four process plates (Convert to Process). The answer depends on the capabilities of your printing press and the depth of your budget; typically, you'd choose Convert to Process.

✔ **Halftoning:** Use this pop-up menu to choose the halftone settings specified in QuarkXPress (the Conventional option) or to use the defaults in your printer. For black-and-white and composite-color printing, you'd typically choose Printer unless you used halftoning effects in the QuarkXPress Style menu. For color separations, only Conventional is available.

✔ **Resolution:** Select the dots per inch (dpi) at which the imagesetter will be printing. The minimum resolution for most imagesetters is 1,270 dpi. If you choose a lower setting in QuarkXPress than the printer is set for, all images will be halftoned at the lower resolution.

✔ **Frequency:** Specify the lines per inch (lpi) for your target printer. QuarkXPress will choose an initial setting based on the Resolution field's setting, but you can also select from the pop-up menu's other popular frequencies.

The Options pane

The Options pane is almost exclusively designed for people using an image-setter to create film negatives. Typically, your service bureau will adjust these settings or tell you how they want you to set them. Figure 11-7 shows the pane.

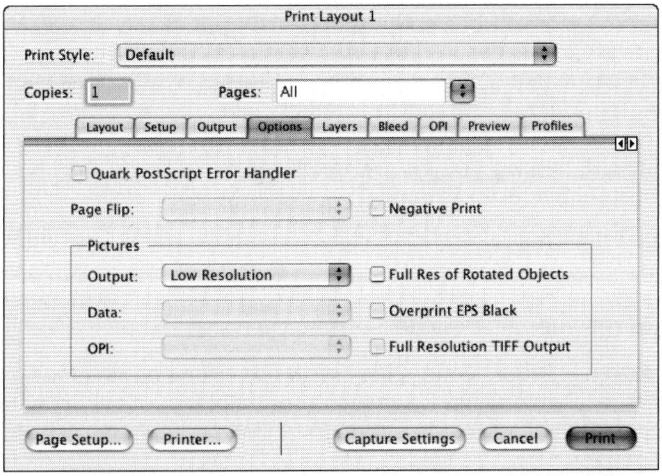

Figure 11-7:
The Options pane of the Print dialog box.

Screening angles explained

Screening angles determine how the dots comprising each of the four process colors — cyan, magenta, yellow, and black — or any spot colors are aligned so that they don't overprint (or print on top of) each other. The general guideline is that dark colors should be at least 30 degrees apart, and lighter colors (for example, yellow) should be at least 15 degrees apart from other colors. That rule translates into a 105° angle (also called −15°; it's the same angle) for cyan, 75° for magenta, 90° for yellow, and 45° for black.

But those defaults sometimes result in moiré patterns (swirling marks). With traditional color-separation technology, a service bureau would have to manually adjust the angles to avoid such moirés, which is an expensive and time-consuming process. With the advent of computer technology, modern output devices, such as imagesetters, can calculate angles based on the output's lpi settings to avoid most moiré patterns. (Each image's balance of colors can cause a different moiré, which is why there is no magic formula.) Every major imagesetter vendor uses its own proprietary algorithm to make these calculations.

PostScript Printer Description (PPD) files contain printer-specific, optimized settings, including screen output and resolution. (Many of these PPD files come bundled with various programs, including QuarkXPress, and are also often available from the manufacturer's Web as well as from the downloads sections of www.adobe.com.) QuarkXPress automatically uses the PPD values to calculate the recommended halftoning, lpi, and frequency settings shown in the Output pane of the Print dialog box.

The Page Flip and Negative Print options determine how the film negatives (or positives) are actually produced. The Output, Data, OPI, Full Res of Rotated Objects, Overprint EPS Black, and Full Resolution TIFF Output options determine how pictures are printed. The following list briefly describes how each option works:

- **Quark PostScript Error Handler:** PostScript is a language, and sometimes programs use it differently from what the printer expects, which leads to incorrect output or often no output at all. If this check box is selected, QuarkXPress prints a report when it encounters a PostScript error and will even print the problem page to the point where the error occurred, helping you narrow down the problem. (It may be in an imported image, for example.)

- **Page Flip:** This pop-up menu lets you mirror your page; your options are Horizontal, Vertical, and Horizontal & Vertical. You would use this feature if your service bureau requests that the page be flipped. Otherwise, leave this option at the default None setting.

- **Negative Print:** Selecting this check box prints an inverse image of your pages, exchanging black with white, and dark colors with light ones. Your service bureau uses this option if it has imagesetters that can print both positives and negatives (so that the service bureau can have the correct output based on what it's printing on). Your service bureau will tell you when to use this option.

✔ **Output:** The default is Normal, but you can also choose Low Resolution or Rough from this pop-up menu. Normal means that the pictures print normally; Low Resolution means that the pictures print at the screen resolution (usually 72 dpi); Rough means that the pictures don't print at all. You use the last two when you're focusing on the text and layout, not the images, because Low Resolution and Rough greatly accelerate printing time.

✔ **Data:** Typically your service bureau will tell you which of these three settings to use:

- Binary (smaller file sizes, faster printing, but not editable)

- ASCII (larger file sizes, slower printing, but editable)

- Clean 8-Bit (a hybrid of binary and ASCII, somewhere between the two in size, that can safely be sent to PC-based output devices).

✔ **OPI:** If you *don't* use an Open Prepress Interface (OPI) server, leave this option at the default setting of Include Images. If you use OPI, choose Omit TIFF if your OPI server has only high-resolution TIFF files (the most common type of OPI setup), and choose Omit TIFF & EPS if your OPI server contains both EPS and TIFF files.

✔ **Full Res of Rotated Objects:** This option ensures that rotated objects are printed at their full resolution on non-PostScript printers. This takes more imaging time and will slow down printer output, but it makes for the most accurate output of these images. (PostScript devices will output rotated images at their maximum resolution, so this option is grayed out when they're used.)

✔ **Overprint EPS Black:** Normally, QuarkXPress prints black by using the trapping settings set in the Trap Specifications dialog box (accessed via the Edit Trap button in the Colors dialog box, which you open by choosing Edit⇨Colors or pressing Shift+F12). But EPS files may have their own trapping settings for black defined in the program that created the EPS file. If you check the Overprint EPS Black check box, QuarkXPress forces all black elements in EPS files to overprint other colors. This doesn't affect how other black elements in QuarkXPress print.

✔ **Full Resolution TIFF Output:** If checked, this option sends TIFF images to the printer at the highest resolution possible based on the Resolution setting in the Output pane. You use this when you want your TIFF images (typically photos and scans) to be as sharp as possible.

The Layers pane

The new Layers pane, as shown in Figure 11-8, lets you control which layers are printed. Layers that are set to not output are in italics and are not checked in the Print column. You can force a layer to print (or not print) by using the Print pop-up menu, which is available when you select any layer in the pane.

The options are All, Yes, No, and None. Yes and No control the printing of the currently selected layer in the pane. All and None affect all layers. If you make an output-suppressed layer print *and* check the Apply to Layout check box, the layer's settings in the Layers palette will be changed. The same holds true if you uncheck Print for a layer — it then has Suppress Output checked in the Layers palette.

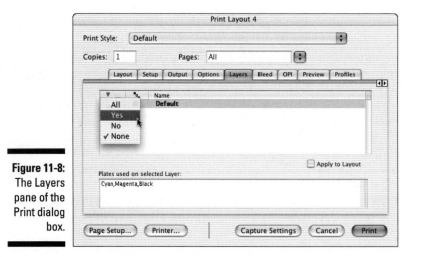

Figure 11-8:
The Layers pane of the Print dialog box.

The Bleed pane

This pane, as shown in Figure 11-9, is where you tell QuarkXPress how much room to leave around the layout edges for elements that bleed off the page. This is useful when printing to a file or to an imagesetter to ensure that the bleed is not inadvertently removed or shortened. A value of ⅛ inch (0.125 inch) suffices for most work.

If you select the Symmetric option in the Bleed Type pop-up menu, the bleed amount applies to all four sides. If you choose Asymmetric, you can set the bleed individually for each side. The Page Items option makes the page boundary the bleed boundary (no bleeds).

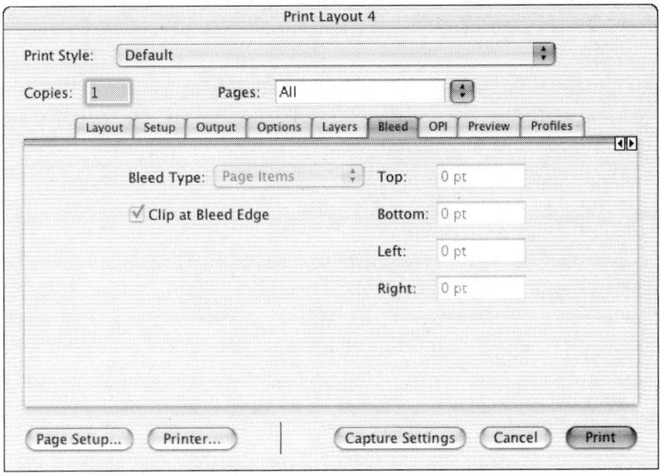

Figure 11-9:
The Bleed
pane of the
Print dialog
box.

If checked, the Clip at Bleed Edge check box prevents anything outside
the bleed rectangle from printing even if it's within the imageable area of the
output device. When Clip at Bleed Edge is unchecked, QuarkXPress prints all
objects that are at least partially within the bleed rectangle *if* they fit within
the imageable area.

The OPI pane

With this pane, you turn on the Open Prepress Interface feature, letting you
store high-resolution images on a remote server or at a service bureau while
you work on lower-resolution, more manageable-size versions. During printing, the high-resolution images are substituted from the OPI server, and your
QuarkXPress settings are applied to them. Figure 11-10 shows the pane.

In the pane, you also determine whether OPI is active for TIFF and EPS images
(by checking the Include Images check box) and whether to substitute a low-
resolution version of the TIFF file in local printing. By selecting Include Images,
you ensure that the PostScript output contains any special instructions in the
master OPI image. By checking the Low Resolution check box, you speed up
printing because QuarkXPress sends only a 36-dpi version of the TIFF file with
any functions applied in QuarkXPress instead of the full image.

The Preview pane

It's easy to set up your Print dialog box and print your job, only to find out
that something was off base after your pages printed. Use the Preview pane
to ensure that margins, crop marks, bleeds, and other element-fitting issues
actually work with your target paper size.

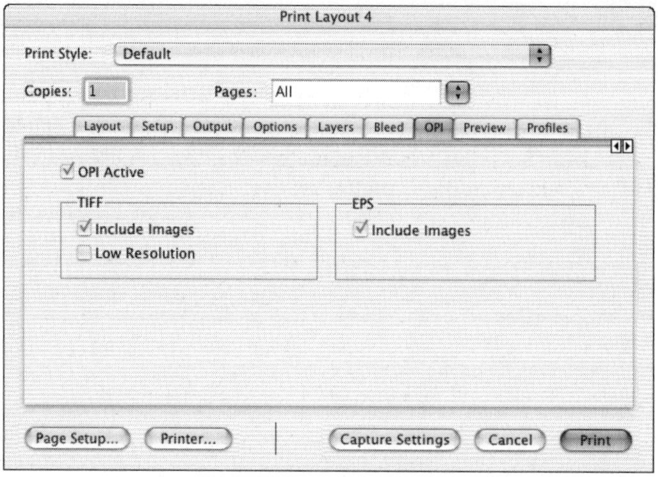

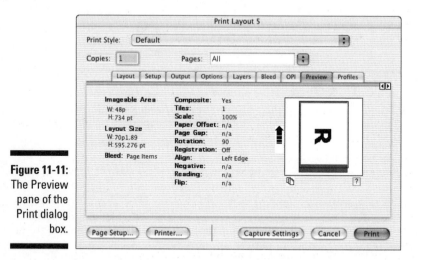

Figure 11-10:
The OPI
pane.

Figure 11-11 shows an example Preview pane in which the layout exceeds the right side of the page boundaries.

Figure 11-11:
The Preview
pane of the
Print dialog
box.

The Preview pane shows the layout area, bleed area, imageable area, and any clipped areas using specific colors. You can get a list of these colors by clicking the **?** icon below the preview, on the right side.

The big *R* indicates the reading order for the text, and the big arrow indicates the direction the paper feeds into the output device. The rest of the pane gives all the specific output settings.

The Profiles pane

If color management is active, you'll get a Profiles pane, as shown in Figure 11-12. The pane lets you select the color profile for RGB and CMYK output, as well as determine whether the composite output, such as to an inkjet printer for proofing, tries to simulate the CMYK output.

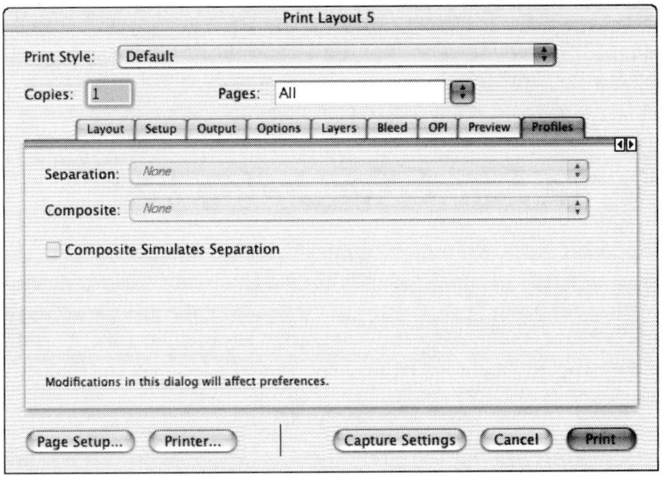

Figure 11-12:
The Profiles
pane in the
Print dialog
box.

Separation: None

Composite: None

☐ Composite Simulates Separation

Modifications in this dialog will affect preferences.

- ✔ **Separation profile:** Here you choose the output device (such as a printing press) that QuarkXPress should color-correct all images for when creating color separations. The default profile is whatever you specified in the Color Management dialog box.

- ✔ **Composite profile:** Here you choose the output device (typically an inkjet printer, thermal-wax printer, color laser printer, or dye-sublimation printer; sometimes a proofing system or a CMYK output device) that QuarkXPress should color-correct all images for when printing colors on a single page (rather than color-separating them). The default profile is whatever you specified in the Color Management dialog box.

- ✔ **Composite Simulates Separation:** If you check this check box, QuarkXPress alters the colors on your composite printer to make them match the separations printer as closely as possible. Use this when you're proofing color on a local composite printer before sending the final layout out for color separations.

Printing Color Separations

It's very easy to accidentally use spot colors such as red and Pantone 111 (say, for picture and text box frames) in a layout that contains four-color TIFF and EPS files. The result in this case is that QuarkXPress outputs as many as six plates: one each for the four process colors, plus one for red and one for Pantone 111. You might expect the red to be separated into 100 percent each of yellow and magenta (which is how red is printed in four-color work). And maybe you expect QuarkXPress to separate the Pantone 111 into its four-color equivalent (11.5 percent yellow and 27.5 percent black). So why doesn't QuarkXPress do this? Read on.

Using the Edit Color dialog box

By default, each color defined in QuarkXPress — including red, green, and blue, which are automatically available via the Edit⇨Colors menu — is set as a spot color. And each spot color gets its own plate unless you specifically tell QuarkXPress to translate the color into process colors. You do so when defining a new color by unchecking the Spot Color box in the Edit Color dialog box.

Regardless of whether a color is defined as a process or spot color, you can also choose the Convert to Process option in the Print dialog box's Output pane's Plates pop-up menu when printing to convert all spot colors to process colors. However, this technique is not good if you want to print a mixture of process colors and spot colors — for example, having red color-separated as 100 percent yellow and 100 percent magenta but Pantone 111 printed on its own plate as a spot color.

The Used Process & Spot option in the Plates pop-up menu in the Output pane comes in very handy to reduce this problem. It output plates just for the colors actually used.

The advantage to setting the colors to process — either in the Edit Color dialog box or via the context menu in the Colors palette — is that the colors are permanently made into process colors. The Convert to Process option must be used each time that you print, which you can automate via print styles, as we describe later in this chapter.

If your work is primarily four-color work, either remove the spot colors such as blue, red, and green from your Colors dialog box or edit them to make them process colors. If you make these changes with no layout open, they become the defaults for all new layouts.

Transferring duplicate color sets

If you do some spot-color work and some four-color work, duplicate the spot colors and translate the duplicates into process colors. Make sure that you use a clear color-naming convention. The same is true when you use Pantone colors (and Hexachrome, Trumatch, Focoltone, Toyo, DIC, and multi-ink colors). If you check the Spot Color check box in the Edit Color dialog box (choose Edit⇨Colors⇨New), these colors are output as spot colors. You can define a Pantone color twice, making one of the copies a process color and giving it a name to indicate what it is. Then all you have to do is make sure that you pick the right color for the kind of output that you want.

Mixing spot and process colors

You still can mix process and spot colors. For example, if you want a gold border on your pages, you have to use a Pantone ink because metallic colors cannot be produced via process colors. So use the appropriate Pantone color and don't uncheck the Spot Color check box when you define the color. When you make color separations, you get five negatives: one each for the four process colors and one for gold. That's fine because you specifically want the five negatives. (Just make sure that any other colors that you created from spot-color models were turned into process colors in the Edit Color dialog box; otherwise, each of these spot colors will print on its own negative, too.)

Setting imagesetter color separation options

If you're printing color separations to an imagesetter, you may want to adjust the output options at the bottom of the Output pane. You'll see a list of plates used in your layout. If you chose the Convert to Process option in the Plates pop-up menu, you'll see only the CMYK or Hexachrome plates. You can adjust the characteristics for each plate by selecting a plate and then using the pop-up menus (with the triangle after their names in the column header) to choose a new setting.

Printing to a File

Although you'll print mostly to a printer connected to your computer or to the network, sometimes you want to print to a file. Typically, this happens when you want to output a file exactly as you have created it for output on a service bureau's imagesetter. Another reason to print a file is as the first step of creating a PDF file via either the Adobe Acrobat Distiller program (which converts PostScript files to PDF) or the QuarkXPress PDF export option.

Printing to a file from a Mac

To print to a file from a Macintosh, click the Printer button in the Print dialog box, click the Output Options option in the pop-up menu, click Save As File, and then choose the output format (PDF or PostScript). You can also simply choose the Save As PDF button, which uses Mac OS X's built-in PDF-creation capabilities. But for PostScript printers, using the printer driver's PDF output usually results in high-quality output.

If you're using Acrobat Distiller to create PDF files (Distiller lets you set how fonts are embedded and specify the image resolution), output to PostScript format and then convert the PostScript file to PDF format via Distiller. Otherwise, use built-in PDF export in QuarkXPress (choose File⇨ Export⇨Layout as PDF), which is optimized for service bureau use.

Printing to a file from Windows

Some Windows programs have a Print to File option in their Print dialog boxes. But QuarkXPress does not, which forces you to create a separate virtual printer in Windows. To print to a file from a PC, use the following steps:

1. **Open the appropriate wizard to launch a printer.**

   • **In Windows XP:** Choose Start⇨Control Panel⇨Printers and Other Hardware to open the Printers and Other Hardware window. Then click the Add a Printer icon to launch its wizard.

   In some installations of Windows XP Professional, you can also choose Start⇨Printers and Faxes.

   • **In Windows 2000:** Choose Start⇨Printers. Double-click the Add Printer icon to launch the Add Printer Wizard.

2. **Use the dialog boxes to select the appropriate printer (the one that your print files will ultimately be output on).**

   You may need the Windows CD-ROM or a disk from the printer maker; if so, Windows will tell you. *Note:* When asked whether the printer is a local or network printer, choose local.

3. **When you get to the dialog box that lists available ports, be sure to choose FILE:, not a port such as LPT1: or COM1:.**

4. **Complete the installation (skip the printing of a test page).**

   Make sure that you name the virtual printer something like To File so that you'll know what it is later. From now on, select this printer in the QuarkXPress Print dialog box Printer pop-up list when you want to print to a file. (It will be available in all Windows programs' Printer pop-up lists.)

   You may need to create multiple virtual printers if you or your service bureau uses different output devices for which you want to generate print files.

Using Print Styles

The ability to create print styles is very handy. It lets you save settings for specific printers and/or specific types of print jobs. To create a print style, choose Edit⇨Print Styles to get the dialog box shown in Figure 11-13.

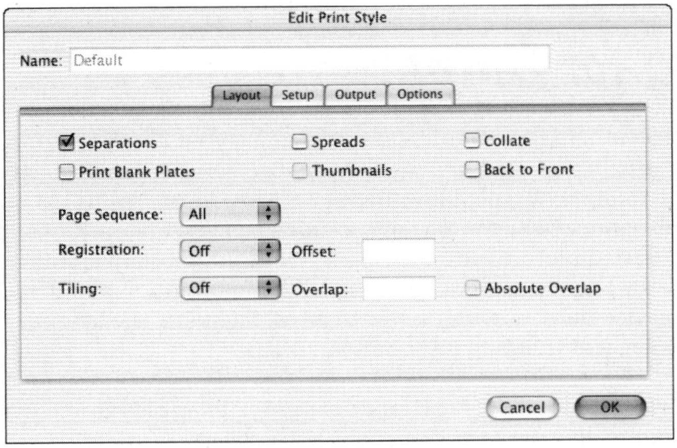

Figure 11-13: The Print Styles dialog box lets you save print settings.

When you choose to edit an existing style or create a new style, you get the Edit Print Style dialog box. It contains four of the Print dialog box's panes: Layout, Setup, Output, and Options. These panes are the same as in the Print dialog box, so set them here as you would there. When you've set the print style's options, click OK, and then click Save in the Print Styles dialog box. Keep in mind that QuarkXPress does not let you take Print dialog box settings and create a print style from them. You must re-create them in the Print Styles dialog box, so be sure to write them down.

Working with Service Bureaus

Service bureaus — companies that provide high-end output to prepare your files for professional printing — are great. They keep and maintain all the equipment, know the ins and outs of both your software and your printing press requirements, and turn around jobs quickly — at least most of the time. Working with a service bureau involves commitment and communication between both parties. They need your business; you need their expertise and equipment.

To ensure that you get what you want (fast, accurate service) and that the service bureau gets what it wants (no-hassle clients and printing jobs), make sure that you understand both your standards and needs. As a customer, keep in mind that the service bureau has many other customers, all of whom do things differently. Service bureaus likewise must not impose unreasonable requirements just for the sake of consistency because customers have good reasons for doing things differently.

Collecting for Output

If you've ever had the experience of giving a layout file to a service bureau, only to be called several hours later because some of the files necessary to output it are missing, you'll love the Collect for Output feature in QuarkXPress. This command, which you access by choosing File➪Collect for Output, copies all the text and picture files necessary to output your layout into a folder. It also generates a report that contains all the information about your layout that a service bureau is ever likely to need, including the layout's fonts, dimensions, and trapping information.

Like printing, the Collect for Output feature applies only to the current print layout, not to all print layouts in the open project.

How Collect for Output works

The Collect for Output feature generates very useful things to take to your service bureau:

  ✔ A folder that contains the layout and, depending on the options that you select, every file used by your layout (linked pictures, embedded pictures, color profiles, and fonts)
  ✔ A report listing all the specifications of the layout

To use Collect for Output, begin by saving the layout (choose File⇨Save, or press ⌘+S or Ctrl+S). Then choose File⇨Collect for Output (see Figure 11-14) and specify the location where you want to place the folder with the layout's collected files.

Before doing a full Collect for Output, it's a good idea to first generate a report about the layout so that you can review it for errors. To do this, select the Report Only check box in the Collect for Output dialog box. This generates a report about the layout without actually collecting the files.

Select the options that you want in the Collect for Output dialog box:

- ✔ **Report Only** is unchecked by default. A shortcut that automatically opens the Collect for Output dialog box with Report Only checked is to press Option or Alt while (at the same time) choosing File⇨Collect for Output.

- ✔ **Layout** copies the layout to a specified folder.

- ✔ **Linked Pictures** copies imported pictures into the Pictures folder inside the collection folder.

- ✔ **Embedded Pictures** copies pictures, such as PICT files on the Mac and BMP and WMF files on Windows, that are embedded in the layouts.

- ✔ **Color Profiles** (available only when the Quark CMS XTension is loaded and color management is turned on) copies color profiles associated with the layout itself, or with pictures imported into it, into the Color Profiles folder inside the collection folder.

The Collect for Output dialog box has different font options for Mac and Windows:

- **Screen Fonts** (Mac only) copies any screen fonts that are necessary for displaying the layout into the Fonts folder inside the collection folder. Check Screen Fonts if someone else will work on the QuarkXPress layout *before* outputting it.

- **Printer Fonts** (Mac only) copies printer fonts that are necessary for printing the layout into the Fonts folder inside the collection folder. Check Printer Fonts if someone else will *output* the layout. (This is usually why you use Collect for Output in the first place.)

- **Fonts** (Windows only) copies any fonts that are necessary for displaying and printing the layout into the Fonts folder inside the collection folder.

On the Mac, fonts are often composed of two files; in Windows, fonts usually are composed of one file.

After making selections in the Collect for Output dialog box, click Save.

Dealing with missing files

If a picture file is missing or has been modified, an alert is displayed. Click List Pictures (in the alert) to display the Missing/Modified Pictures dialog box. Note that if you click OK and then continue with Collect for Output without updating missing or modified pictures, Collect for Output can't collect all the necessary files to output your layout correctly. Select each modified picture and then click Update to automatically update the picture file. Select each missing picture and then click Update to display the Find dialog box. Locate the missing picture file, select it, and then click Open. Click OK in the Missing/Modified Pictures dialog box to continue with Collect for Output. Collect for Output creates a Report file and places it in the same folder as the copy of the layout and its associated font and picture files.

We strongly recommend using the Collect for Output feature. It ensures that your service bureau has all the necessary files and information to output your layout correctly.

Exporting Layouts as PDF Files

The *Portable Document Format* is a file format based on what Adobe calls its *Adobe imaging model*, which is the same device-independent representation used in the PostScript page-description language. The PDF file format is growing in popularity because it produces files that are independent of the program, operating system, and equipment used to create and display the files.

Going beyond Collect for Output

Although using Collect for Output is a big help, don't let it make you complacent. Relying only on this feature to make sure that you're giving the service bureau all the files that it needs can be risky. A file that looks good onscreen and is capable of being processed by Collect for Output is not necessarily one that will be processed smoothly at the service bureau. Two additional steps that you can take to avoid problems are to first review the layout's separations and then to use a separate preflight (or test before you output) software application.

Before collecting the files for output in QuarkXPress, take a close look at the color separations instead of the onscreen or printed composite. (*Hint:* Print separations to a local proofing printer to see what the final separations will look like on an imagesetter. Or use Adobe Acrobat 6 Professional's color-separation preview feature after making a PDF proofing copy of your layout in QuarkXPress.) Doing so could save you from sending off a file with an underlying error — one that you may otherwise find out about only after paying for film or (worse yet, if no one catches the error on the

film), not until after the job has been printed. Make sure that every element on each separation is supposed to be there. Also check that nothing is missing. Even the most experienced publishers find many errors by taking the time to do this type of review.

Another precaution to take before sending the file to your service bureau is to use an after-market software program such as Extensis Preflight Pro and PrintReady products or Markzware FlightCheck. (The companion Web site to this book, www.QXcentral.com, provides links to these products.) These programs check your layout against a predefined and customizable list of common errors and mistakes. Like the QuarkXPress Collect for Output feature, these programs gather all the files (graphics file, fonts, and so on) associated with the layout and place them into a folder for you to send to your service bureau. But the real value of preflight programs is that they automate the process, letting you preflight entire folders of files, including QuarkXPress, Adobe Illustrator, Photoshop, PageMaker, Macromedia FreeHand, and (in FlightCheck) Adobe InDesign files.

Version 6 of QuarkXPress adds technology for generating Adobe Portable Layout Format (PDF) files, which lets you create high-quality PDF files without needing to buy Acrobat software and its Acrobat Distiller PDF-creation component. However, many publishers will still want to use Adobe's PDF-creation tools. Benefits of using PDF are

- ✔ PDF files provide consistency because layouts appear — both online and on paper — as they were originally created.

- ✔ PDF provides security for transmitting digital files, resolves missing fonts, and prevents distorted graphics issues.

- ✔ For designers, using PDFs offers greater ease in collaboration, proofing, archiving, and digital use. You can use PDF files for high-resolution production requiring separations and composite color files.

Layouts intended for digital consumption can be fully indexed, searchable, and contain video, audio, and hyperlinks to other PDF layouts and Web sites. Interactive PDFs can incorporate forms, buttons, and links to other layouts.

Creating PDF Files Directly in QuarkXPress

To produce PDF files from QuarkXPress, you need nothing other than what comes with the program. (The PDF-creation components of QuarkXPress are stored in the Jaws directory in the folder containing QuarkXPress, so be sure not to delete or modify that new folder.)

Choose File⇨Export⇨Layout as PDF. In the resulting Export as PDF dialog box, choose the file name for the exported file and the folder in which you want to place it. You can also choose to generate the PDF files as *spreads* (where facing pages continue to display side by side) by selecting the Spreads check box.

Figure 11-15 shows the resulting PDF Export Options dialog box. After setting the options, you click OK to return to the Export as PDF dialog box, from which you click Save to create the PDF file.

Choosing File⇨Export Layout as PDF will not work if you're working on a Web layout. The only way to export Web layouts is by choosing File⇨Print, where QuarkXPress will always export Web layouts to HTML files for viewing in a Web browser. After making the HTML files, QuarkXPress displays the Print dialog box. On the Mac, that dialog box lets you create a PDF file via the Save as PDF button. In Windows, the Print dialog box doesn't have a Save to PDF option; you're expected to install either the Adobe PDFWriter driver or full Acrobat Acrobat Distiller program and make them available as printers in the dialog box. Note that your browser, not QuarkXPress, is actually printing the page.

Four panes help you control the PDF output, similar to the controls in Acrobat Distiller.

Document Info pane

This pane (see Figure 11-15) can be ignored in most cases. It has four text fields — Title, Subject, Author, and Keywords — that you can fill in. (The Title field is automatically filled in with the layout name.) This information will be included in the PDF file and is accessible via the Layout Properties dialog box in Acrobat when you open the PDF file. It has no effect on the output itself.

Hyperlinks pane

This pane, as shown in Figure 11-16, controls what happens to hyperlinks in your print layout. (You add hyperlinks to selected text and pictures by choosing Edit⇨Hyperlinks.)

The options are

- ✔ **Include Hyperlinks:** Checking this check box includes any hyperlinks set in the Hyperlinks palette and makes them active hyperlinks in the PDF file.

- ✔ **Export Lists as Hyperlinks:** Checking this check box creates hyperlinks from lists (such as tables of contents) created in the Lists palette to other pages in your QuarkXPress layout. This creates instant navigation from lists to the content that they refer to within the exported PDF file.

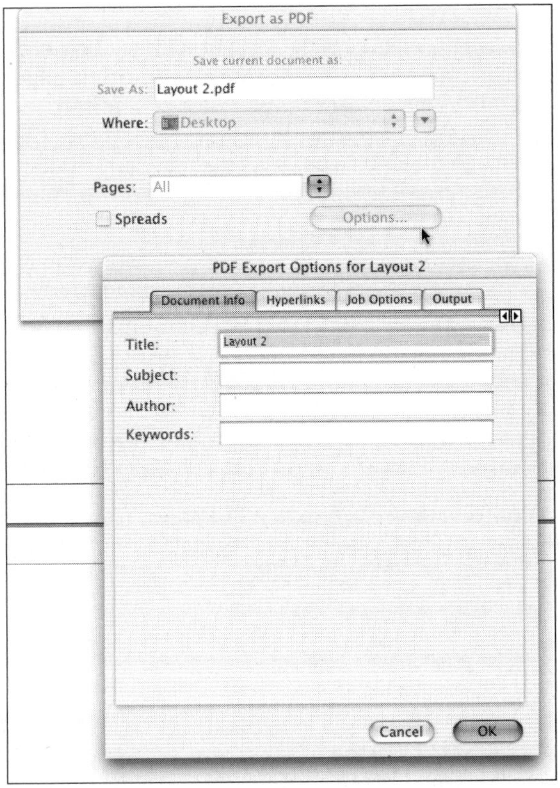

Figure 11-15: The PDF Export Options dialog box.

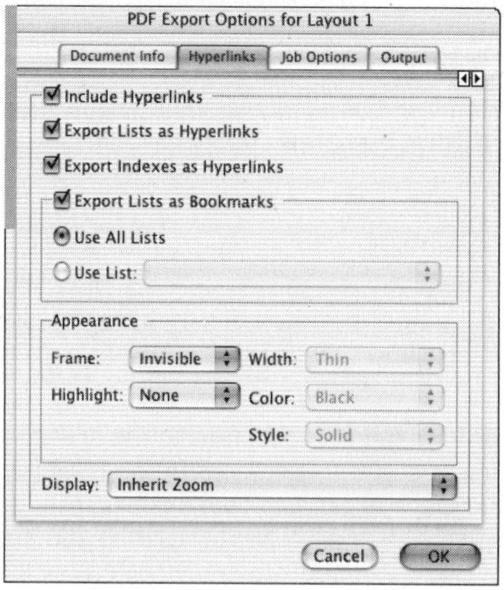

Figure 11-16:
The PDF
Export
Options
dialog box
and its
Hyperlinks
pane.

PDF Export Options for Layout 1

Document Info | Hyperlinks | Job Options | Output

☑ Include Hyperlinks
☑ Export Lists as Hyperlinks
☑ Export Indexes as Hyperlinks
☑ Export Lists as Bookmarks
◉ Use All Lists
◯ Use List:

Appearance

Frame: Invisible ⬍ Width: Thin ⬍
Highlight: None ⬍ Color: Black ⬍
Style: Solid ⬍

Display: Inherit Zoom ⬍

Cancel | OK

✔ **Export Indexes as Hyperlinks:** Checking this check box creates hyperlinks from indexes created in the Index palette to other pages in your QuarkXPress layout. This creates instant navigation from index entries to the content that they refer to within the exported PDF file. You can also choose between making hyperlinks from all lists via Use All Lists or select a single list to make hyperlinks via Use List. You cannot select more than one list — it's one or all.

✔ **Appearance:** This section sets how hyperlinks appear in the PDF file, setting a frame around the text and images that are hyperlinks via the Frame pop-up menu and its associated Width, Color, and Style pop-up menus. The Highlight pop-up menu lets you control how the links appear when a user clicks them. The options are Outline (place a box around the hyperlink), Invert (exchange black for white and white for black, as well as other color exchanges), and Inset (place the Frame color behind the text or picture).

✔ **Display:** This controls how the link to a PDF page appears in the browser or Acrobat Reader window. Choices are Inherit Zoom (which leaves the zoom level to be whatever the target file is set as), Fit Window, Fit Width, and Fit Length.

Job Options pane

This pane, as shown in Figure 11-17, controls the quality of the output. It's very similar to the Job Options controls in Acrobat Distiller.

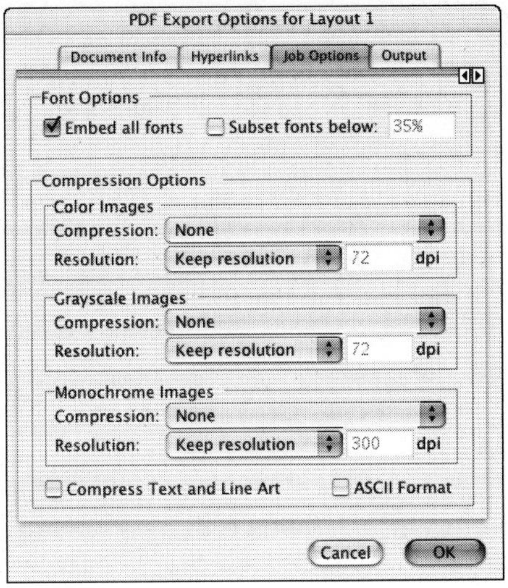

Figure 11-17:
The PDF
Export
Options
dialog box
and its Job
Options
pane.

PDF Export Options for Layout 1

| Document Info | Hyperlinks | **Job Options** | Output |

Font Options

☑ Embed all fonts ☐ Subset fonts below: 35%

Compression Options

Color Images

Compression: None

Resolution: Keep resolution 72 dpi

Grayscale Images

Compression: None

Resolution: Keep resolution 72 dpi

Monochrome Images

Compression: None

Resolution: Keep resolution 300 dpi

☐ Compress Text and Line Art   ☐ ASCII Format

Cancel   OK

For control over font embedding, first check Override Distiller's Font Option in the Job Options pane, which you get to by choosing File➪Export as PDF and then clicking the Options button). This enables the two options for embedding fonts:

✔ **If you want to distribute the PDF file without sending the font files as well, check the Embed All Fonts check box.**

Avoid using TrueType fonts in layouts targeted for PDF output. The fonts don't always embed properly.

✔ **To keep PDF file sizes smaller when you're embedding fonts, select the Subset Fonts Below check box.**

You can then specify a threshold of character usage below which a subset is created. For example, at the default setting of 35%, a subset is created if less than 35 percent of a font's characters are used in a layout.

You can override the way images in the PDF file are compressed by using the controls in the Compression Options section.

✔ The Compression menus in the Color Images and Grayscale Images areas let you specify how all color and all grayscale images are compressed in the PDF file. If you choose one of the Automatic options, QuarkXPress chooses the best option to achieve the indicated quality level. If you know exactly the appropriate compression technique and quality level, you can choose from the seven Manual options.

✔ The Resolution menus and fields in the Color Images and Grayscale Images areas let you resample images for the PDF. In each area, you can choose either Keep Resolution, Downsample To, or Subsample To and enter a resolution in the dpi field. (Keep Resolution doesn't change the images' native resolution, so you can't enter a dpi setting if it is chosen.)

✔ For Monochrome Images, you can specify the Compression and Resolution as well. The Compression menu lets you choose either CCITT Group 4, CCITT Group 3, or Zip compression for all monochrome images. The Resolution menu lets you resample the images with the same options as Color Images and Grayscale Images.

✔ Select the Compress Text and Line Art check box to use Zip compression for all text and line art (such as Bézier items) in the layout. This retains all the detail in the PDF file.

✔ To export the PDF file as ASCII instead of binary format, select the ASCII Format check box. The advantage to ASCII is that you can open and edit the PDF file in a text editor. However, ASCII files are larger, so only enable this if you — or your service bureau — really need to do this.

Output pane

This pane, as shown in Figure 11-18, controls how colors output, OPI images are managed, registration marks are handled, and bleeds are managed.

✔ **Printer Description:** This pop-up menu lets you choose what printer-specific settings the PDF file will incorporate. Use Generic PDF or, if you have Acrobat Distiller installed, Acrobat Distiller, to output PDF files that are the most flexible and universal for display and printing. Choose a specific printer description only if you're creating PDF files for use by a service bureau or commercial printer; be sure that you're using the correct PPD in such cases for the output device that will be used.

✔ **Color Output:** In this section, choose whether the files are color-separated or not via the Type pop-up menu. (Composite means that they are not color-separated.) In the Print Colors pop-up menu, you choose what inks are used to print the colors: Black & White, Grayscale, CMYK, RGB, As Is (which retains the process and spot color definitions in the source images), and DeviceN (which includes information for both process- and spot-color printing in the same PDF file, for use by PostScript Level 3 printers).

✔ **Produce Blank Pages:** This option is similar to the Print Blank Pages option in the Print dialog box's Layout pane.

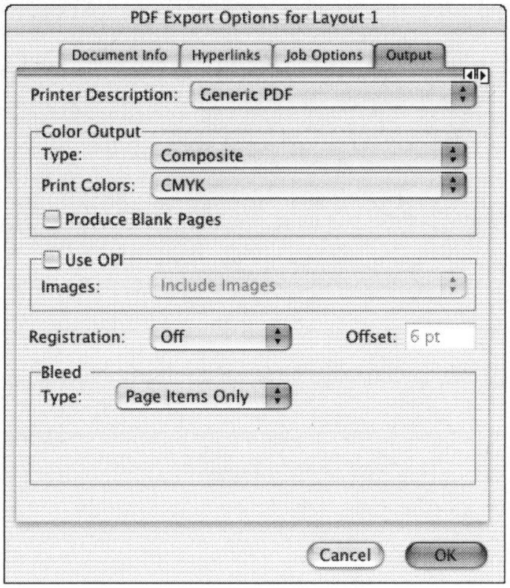

Figure 11-18:
The PDF
Export
Options
dialog box
and its
Output
pane.

✔ **Use OPI:** This option determines whether high-resolution images stored on an Open Prepress Interface server are substituted for the images used in the layout. You can choose to omit specific image types (TIFF and EPS) if you enable this check box.

✔ **Registration:** This pop-up menu indicates whether to print registration marks and, if so, how they are to be offset and located.

✔ **Bleed:** This pop-up menu controls how bleeds are output: cropped to the page boundaries (Page Items Only), the same bleed amount on all sides of the page (Symmetric), or user-specified bleed amounts for each side of the page (Asymmetric).

Part III
The Picasso Factor

The 5th Wave   By Rich Tennant

"You might want to adjust the value of your 'Nudge' function."

In this part . . .

We named this part of the book after the famous artist because it tells not only how to use QuarkXPress as an illustration tool, but also how to take normal-looking text and graphics and distort them. Why would you want to do this? Good question. The answer could be that, like Picasso, you want to present ideas in a visually interesting way. QuarkXPress lets you manipulate text and art in interesting ways, and we show you how. We also give you a brief primer on color. Put all these techniques together to create documents that dazzle.

Chapter 12

Using QuarkXPress as an Illustration Tool

*B*ack in the day, QuarkXPress was generally considered only a page layout program. Previous versions of QuarkXPress had limited drawing capabilities; if you needed to draw a curved line or curved shape, you needed a dedicated drawing program. Not anymore. Recent versions of QuarkXPress, including version 6, contain several nifty drawing-related features, such as the ability to draw Bézier (custom-shaped) lines and shapes, change text characters into picture boxes or text boxes, and flow text along a line or around the contour of a box. (We cover flowing text along a path in Chapter 15.)

Using Lines

In Figure 12-1, four tools are highlighted in the Tool palette. You use these tools to create straight and curved lines (as you may have already guessed).

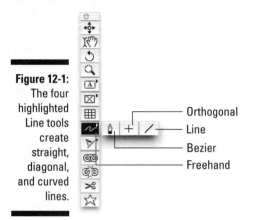

Figure 12-1:
The four
highlighted
Line tools
create
straight,
diagonal,
and curved
lines.

Orthogonal
Line
Bezier
Freehand

Each of the line-creation tools works a bit differently than the others. In addition to the basic Line tool, you have these four tools:

✔ **Diagonal Line tool:** Produces straight lines at any desired angle. If you hold down the Shift key while drawing a diagonal line, the line is constrained to be perfectly horizontal, perfectly vertical, or at a perfect 45-degree angle. (Note that the QuarkXPress user's manual simply calls this the *Line tool,* but we use the name *Diagonal Line tool* so that you don't mix it up with the other three Line tools.)

✔ **Freehand Line tool:** Lets you create Bézier lines by using the mouse as a freehand drawing tool. To create a freehand line, click and hold the mouse button while you drag the mouse in any direction. When you release the mouse button, QuarkXPress creates a line that follows the path of the mouse from where you first clicked to the point where you release the button.

✔ **Orthogonal Line tool:** Limits you to horizontal and vertical lines. Click and hold the mouse button, drag, and release the mouse to create a line with this tool.

✔ **Bézier Line tool:** Creates straight-edged zigzag lines, curvy lines, and lines that contain both straight and curved segments.

  • **To create a zigzag line:** Click and release the mouse button to establish the first endpoint. Continue clicking and releasing the mouse to add corner points with straight segments between points. Double-click to create the second endpoint or choose a different tool.

- **To create a curvy line:** Click the mouse button to establish the first point, drag the mouse a short distance in the direction of the next point, and then release the mouse button. While you drag, a line segment is drawn through the point where you first clicked. When you release the mouse button, the first endpoint (a symmetrical point) and two control handles are created. Create additional symmetrical points by clicking and dragging the mouse and then releasing.

  Don't worry too much about making the line perfect the first time. You can always go back and tweak if necessary.

- **To create a line with both straight and curvy segments:** Combine the two previous techniques.

If you use QuarkXPress for illustration tasks, you can use boxes as well as lines to create the pieces of your drawings.

Modifying lines

You can modify Bézier lines by clicking and dragging points, control handles, and segments. You can also choose from three types of points (corner, smooth, and symmetrical) and two types of segments (curved and straight):

✔ This is a corner point. Like with smooth and symmetrical points, a corner point can have control handles. But unlike the other kinds of points, when you move a handle attached to a corner point, the other handle doesn't move. You can delete a handle attached to a corner point by Option+clicking or Alt+clicking it. You can add handles to a corner point that doesn't have them by Control+clicking or by Ctrl+Shift+clicking.

✔ The point in the middle is a smooth point, indicated by a small square intersected by a short line with handles at both ends. The two segments that make up the line are unequal in length. You can control the length of the two segments independently by dragging either handle; however, the segments remain at opposite ends of a straight line (unlike corner point handles).

✔ This is a symmetrical point, which is like a smooth point. However, the line segment that passes through it is made up of two equal-length segments. If you change the length of a segment by dragging a handle, the other segment is also resized. A symmetrical point produces a slightly smoother curve than a smooth point.

The pointer displayed when you move the mouse over a Bézier line is different depending on whether the pointer is over a point (a small, black square appears), segment (a short, angled line appears), or handle (a small, open diamond appears). To move a point, segment, or control handle, click it and drag the mouse. Press Shift+click to select multiple points. You can use the Item tool or the Content tool to select and move points, handles, and segments. Press the ⌘ or Ctrl key while dragging to move the whole line.

Figure 12-2 shows a Bézier line with two points selected.

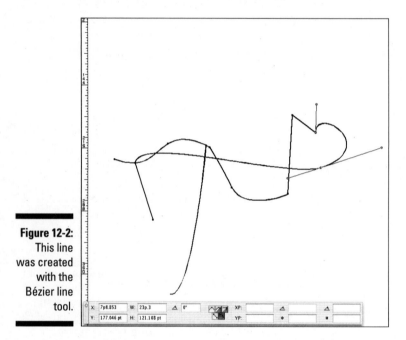

In Figure 12-2, you can see the five icons in the Measurements palette that let you change points and segments. The top three icons represent these three types of points:

- ✔ **The leftmost icon indicates a symmetrical point.** Click a nonsymmetrical point and then click this icon (or press Option+F3 or Ctrl+F3) to change it to a symmetrical point.

- ✔ **The center icon indicates a smooth point.** Click a point that's not a smooth point and then click this icon (or press Option+F2 or Ctrl+F2) to change it to a smooth point.

- ✔ **The rightmost icon indicates a corner point.** Click a point that's not a corner point and then click this icon (or press Option+F1 or Ctrl+F1) to change it to a corner point.

The bottom two icons relate to lines:

- **The left icon represents a straight segment.** Click it or press Option+Shift+F1 or Ctrl+Shift+F1 to change a curved segment into a straight segment. (A *straight segment* has corner points at each end.)

- **The right icon represents a curved segment.** Click it or press Option+Shift+F2 or Ctrl+Shift+F2 to change a straight segment. (A *curved segment* can end in smooth, symmetrical, or corner points. In all cases, control handles let you control the curve of the segment at both ends.)

In addition to the point/segment controls in the Measurements palette and their keyboard equivalents, you can also use the Point/Segment Type command in the Item menu to change the type of points and segments.

You can add a point to a Bézier line by Option+clicking or Alt+clicking the line. The kind of point that's added depends upon the type of segment that you click. Corner points are added to straight segments; smooth points are added to curved segments. To remove a point, Option+click or Alt+click it.

If you've never worked with Bézier lines before, don't worry. Getting the hang of dragging points, handles, and segments takes time, but like anything else, the more you practice, the better you get.

Changing the appearance of a line

When you create a line, the line is automatically given the default properties of the tool that you used to create it. Unless you change your tool defaults, the lines that you create will be black and 1-point in width. You can change the appearance of a line by using any of several methods.

Figure 12-3 shows the Line pane of the Modify dialog box. You can access the dialog box by choosing Item⇨Modify, or by pressing ⌘+M or Ctrl+M.

In the Line pane, you can

- **Choose a line style** — plain, dotted, dashed, or striped — from the Style pop-up menu.

- **Choose a width** from the Line Width pop-up menu or enter a width up to 864 points.

- **Move the active line** by entering new Origin Across or Origin Down values.

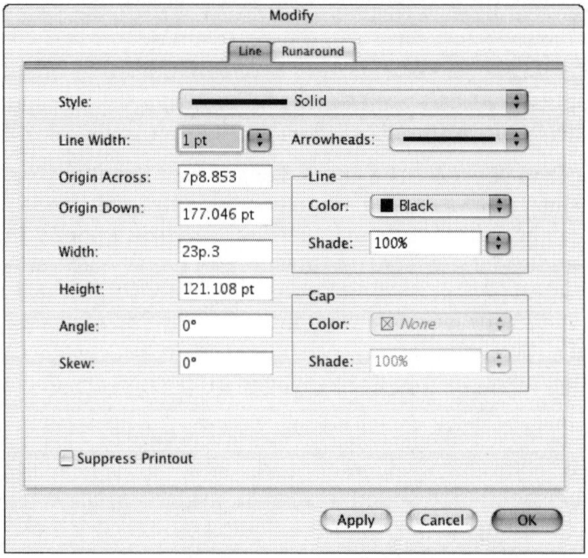

Figure 12-3:
The Line
pane of the
Modify
dialog box.

- ✔ **Change the length of the line** by entering a new value in the Width field. *Note:* If you change line length, all points are repositioned proportionally.

- ✔ **Change the overall *height* of the line** (the distance from the topmost point to the bottommost point) by entering a new value in the Height field. *Remember:* Again, all points are repositioned proportionally.

- ✔ **Rotate the line** by entering a value between 1 and 360 (degrees) in the Angle field.

- ✔ **Slant the line** by entering a Skew value (also in degrees; negative to slant to the left, and positive to slant to the right).

- ✔ **Add an arrowhead and tail feather** by choosing a style from the Arrowheads pop-up menu.

- ✔ **Change the color of the line** by choosing a new color from the Color pop-up menu. You can change the shade by choosing a 10% increment from the Shade pop-up menu or by entering a percentage value in the field.

- ✔ **Use the controls in the Gap area to apply a color and shade to the space between dots, dashes, and stripes** *if* you choose a dotted, dashed, or striped line in the Style menu. *Hint:* If you don't apply color and/or shade to the gaps, they remain white.

The Line pane isn't the only place where you can modify a line. Figure 12-4 shows some other things that you can do with a line:

✔ **Change line appearance:** The Style menu displays five commands for modifying the appearance of a line: Line Style, Arrowheads, Width, Color, and Shade.

✔ **Change line characteristics:** From left to right, the Measurements palette lets you change the location of a line (X and Y fields), the length and height of a line (W and H fields), the angle of a line (Angle field), and the thickness of the line (W field/pop-up). The two pop-up menus on the right side of the palette let you change a line's style and add arrowheads or tail feathers.

✔ **Change line color and shade:** The Colors palette lets you change the color and shade of a line.

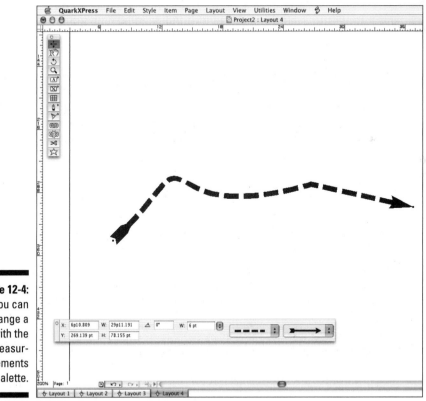

Figure 12-4:
You can change a line with the Measur- ements palette.

Converting Text into Boxes

Have you ever had the urge to import a picture into a box that's the shape of a text character? Not too long ago, you had to use a dedicated drawing program for such tricks. With QuarkXPress, you can convert highlighted text into picture boxes or text boxes. Not only is it easy, but the boxes that you produce by converting text into boxes behave as a single item. That means that you can run a background — a color, blend, or picture — across all the characters that you convert to text as though they were a single box. Features just don't get any cooler than this one.

Here's how you convert text into picture boxes:

1. **Highlight the text that you want to convert.**

   You can highlight an individual character or a range of text, but you cannot highlight more than one line of text. You can convert PostScript Type 1 fonts (in Windows, Adobe Type Manager must be installed before you can use such fonts) or TrueType fonts.

2. **Choose Style⇨Text to Box.**

   If you press the Option or Alt key when you choose Text to Box, QuarkXPress replaces the highlighted text with an individual Bézier picture box for each character and anchors the boxes within the text chain.

   If you don't press the Option or Alt key, QuarkXPress duplicates the highlighted text by using individual picture boxes for each letter. When you click any of the resulting boxes, all the boxes are selected, and they behave as a single box. You can put a frame around all the boxes in a single operation, import a picture that spans all boxes, apply a background color or a blend that spans the boxes, and so on.

At the top of Figure 12-5, you can see a text box with large text. The bottom of the figure shows the same text converted to picture boxes by using the Text to Box command; we then chose Edit⇨Get Picture (or you could press ⌘+E or Ctrl+E) to fill the picture boxes with the image.

You can split the merged boxes that are produced when you choose Text to Box by choosing the Split command from the Item menu. If you choose Outside Paths, all letters that have holes in them (such as O's, P's, and B's) remain intact. That is, if you click one of these letters, all component paths become active, or selected. If you choose All Paths, each path that makes up a letter becomes a separate shape that can be individually selected, moved, cut, and so on.

If you want to turn a Bézier picture box created with the Text to Box command into a text box, click it, then choose Item⇨Content⇨Text.

Figure 12-5:
Convert text
into picture
boxes by
using the
Text to Box
command.

Merging Boxes

The Bézier tools for text boxes, picture boxes, lines, and text paths let you create lines and closed shapes of all kinds. But what if you want to create something like a doughnut? (That is, you want a round box with a round hole in the middle.)

The Bézier drawing tools limit you to creating one path at a time; however, choosing Item⇨Merge lets you combine multiple items into complex Bézier shapes that contain multiple paths simultaneously, based on the submenu option that you select. For example, check out Figure 12-6; we used the Merge command with the empty picture boxes at the top of the page to produce the two variations. We created the Swiss-cheese look of the first variant by choosing Difference; the bottom one is similar but has circular pieces on each end, and we created it with Exclusive Or.

Understanding what each of the Merge options does to selected items takes some experimentation. The names of the options aren't exactly intuitive, some circumstances produce cryptic alerts, and some commands require that selected items overlap. Briefly, here's what each option does:

✔ **Intersection:** Calculates where each of the items (except the backmost item) overlaps the backmost item and retains only the overlap areas.

✔ **Union:** Combines all shapes into a single shape. The shapes don't have to overlap. If shapes overlap, the overlapped areas are retained along with the areas that don't overlap.

✔ **Difference:** Removes all shapes from the backmost shape. This option is useful for cutting pieces out of a shape. For example, you can use a circular shape to punch a round hole in a box.

✔ **Reverse Difference:** Retains what's left after the background shape and all shapes that intersect the background shape are removed.

✔ **Exclusive Or:** Cuts out all areas that overlap, retains areas that don't overlap, and creates new shapes for what remains.

✔ **Combine:** Similar to Exclusive Or except that the paths of the original items are retained.

✔ **Join Endpoints:** Available only when two lines or text paths are active, and endpoints from each line overlap each other or are within the snap-to distance, which is six pixels — unless you've changed the default Snap Distance. To change this setting, go to the General pane in the Preferences dialog box (choose QuarkXPress⇨Preferences on the Mac or Edit⇨Preferences in Windows, or press Option+Shift+⌘+Y or Ctrl+Alt+Shift+Y). Choosing Join Endpoints produces a single line or path, with a corner point where the endpoints previously overlapped.

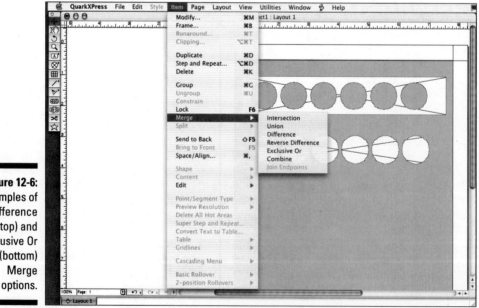

Figure 12-6:
Examples of
Difference
(top) and
Exclusive Or
(bottom)
Merge
options.

Figure 12-7 shows six pairs of examples of merged items. You can create the three on the left by choosing Item⇨Merge⇨Difference, and you can create the three on the right by choosing Item⇨Merge⇨Union. Each example shows the boxes before and after they are merged.

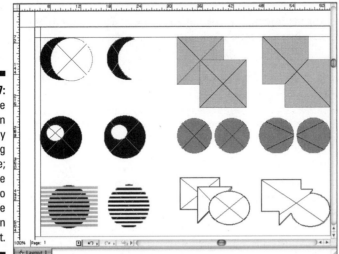

Figure 12-7: Create the boxes on the left by choosing Difference; choose Union to create the boxes on the right.

You can use the Split command in the Item menu to deconstruct any item that is a single box and contains more than one closed path — including complex Bézier shapes created with the Merge options — or a path that crosses itself. When you choose either of the Split options (All Paths or Outside Paths), multiple Bézier boxes are created. The contents and attributes of the original box are retained in each of the resulting boxes.

Grouping Items

If you group multiple items to create an illustration, the ability to select all the items simultaneously so that you can move, copy, or delete them in a single operation is helpful; otherwise, you have to take action on each separate part of the whole. Selecting individual items gets to be a drag. Instead, for such a project, you can create a group out of the items that make up the illustration. If you create a group, you can then use the Item tool to select all the items with a single click.

QuarkXPress provides several ways to select multiple items in preparation for creating a group. With either the Item or Content tool, you can hold down the Shift key while you click several items one by one. Each time that you Shift+click an item, you add that item to the collection of selected items.

You can also select several items by clicking and dragging a rectangle — by using either the Item or Content tool — that contains any part of the items that you want to select. If you want to select all the items on a page, choose Item⇨Select All, or press ⌘+A or Ctrl+A. (The Item tool must be selected.) To deselect an item that's among several selected items, Shift+click the item.

To create a group out of multiple-selected items, choose Item⇨Group, or press ⌘+G or Ctrl+G. At least two items must be selected for this command to be available. A group can contain as many items as you want, although the items must be on the same page or facing-page spread. A group can also contain other groups. Use the Ungroup command to break apart a group.

You can display all the grouped items together in a bounding box by clicking the Item tool and then clicking any item in the group. You can click and drag to move a group with the Item tool; however, you cannot move an individual item when the Item tool is selected.

You can select individual items within a group, move pictures within boxes, enter and edit text, and move lines by selecting the Content tool. If you want to move an item that's part of a group, select the Content tool, press the ⌘ or Ctrl key, and then click the item and drag it to a new location. When you press the ⌘ or Ctrl key, the Content tool — and all other tools — temporarily behave like the Item tool, meaning that they position the items while you move your mouse.

You can resize a group's items all at once. To do this, simply click any of the eight handles on a group's bounding box and drag. If you want to maintain the proportion of the items in the group but not the contents of boxes, press Option+Shift or Alt+Shift when you drag a handle. If you press Option+Shift+⌘ or Ctrl+Alt+Shift while you drag, both the items and the contents of boxes are resized proportionately.

In Figure 12-8, we combined three boxes — a picture box, text box, and a framed box without content — by choosing Item⇨Content⇨None.

The example in Figure 12-8 is a copy of the group that we scaled by clicking and dragging a handle while pressing Option+Shift+⌘ or Ctrl+Alt+Shift. The picture scale and the size of the text are reduced or enlarged along with the boxes that contain them.

Figure 12-8:
Items
created
by first
grouping
the items
and then
scaling the
group using
Option+
Shift+⌘ or
Ctrl+Alt+
Shift.

Setting the Thanksgiving Table

Changing the Shape of Items

QuarkXPress provides several different drawing tools for text boxes, picture boxes, lines, and text paths and lets you manually change the shape of an item by dragging handles — or, in the case of Bézier shapes, points or segments. You can also have QuarkXPress change the shape automatically. The Shape command in the Item menu, as shown in Figure 12-9, lets you perform a couple of nifty tricks. You can change the shape of an item and also change boxes into lines and lines into boxes.

When a single item is active, the nine options displayed in the Shape menu let you change the item into (from top to bottom):

✔ A rectangular box

✔ A rounded-corner box

✔ A beveled-corner box

✔ A concave-corner box

✔ An oval box

✔ An editable Bézier box (with no change in shape)

✔ A straight line (at any angle)

✔ A straight line that's either vertical or horizontal

✔ An editable Bézier line

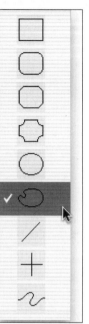

Figure 12-9:
The Shape submenu provides nine options for changing the shape of items and turning lines into boxes and boxes into lines.

As neat as the Shape options are, they can produce some unusual results, such as the following:

✔ If you convert a line into a Bézier box, the resulting box is as wide as the original line. If the original line was thin, opposite edges of the resulting box will be very close together — so much so that the shape may be difficult to edit.

✔ If you convert a dashed line, striped line, or a line with arrowheads into a Bézier box, each component is converted into a separate shape, as shown in Figure 12-10.

✔ If you convert a text box or picture box into a line, any box contents are deleted. (You are given a warning in this situation.)

If the active item is a Bézier line and the endpoints overlap or are close to each other, you can connect the endpoints to create a closed Bézier box by pressing the Option or Alt keys, choosing Item⇨Shape, and then clicking the Bézier box icon.

If you create a Bézier box by using the Shape submenu, you can change the shape of the box by clicking and dragging points and control handles, choosing Item⇨Edit, and then selecting the Shape option.

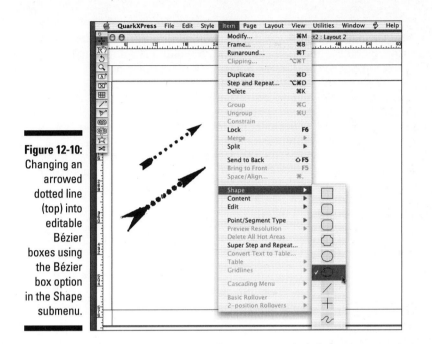

Figure 12-10:
Changing an
arrowed
dotted line
(top) into
editable
Bézier
boxes using
the Bézier
box option
in the Shape
submenu.

You can resize a Bézier box by clicking and dragging the handles of its bounding box, but you can't move points, handles, or segments. The Edit submenu also has a Runaround option that lets you modify runaround paths created with the Runaround pane of the Modify dialog box (choose Item⇨Modify, or press ⌘+M or Ctrl+M) and a Clipping Path option for modifying a clipping path specified in the Clipping pane of the Modify dialog box. (You can go directly to the Clipping pane by pressing Option+⌘+T or Ctrl+Alt+T.)

Creating Masks for Pictures by Using Clipping Paths

Rectangular picture boxes are like vanilla ice cream. Nice enough, but with so many other flavors available, why not try something different every once in a while?

In addition to letting you create Bézier picture boxes, which you can reshape in any way to crop the image within, QuarkXPress lets you crop an image within a box by using an embedded clipping path (created in an image-editing or illustration program) within QuarkXPress. A *clipping path* is a shape that isolates part of an image; everything outside the isolated area is transparent.

Figure 12-11 shows an image that's been imported into two picture boxes. In the top box, the entire picture is visible because no clipping path was used; in the bottom box, an embedded clipping path created in Adobe Photoshop was used to crop out the area in the upper portion of the image.

If you look at the Clipping pane of the Modify dialog box in Figure 12-11, you see that Embedded Path is selected in the Type pop-up menu. QuarkXPress lets you crop an image by using an embedded path or an embedded alpha channel. An *alpha channel* is an extra "plate" in an image that's often used as a mask to isolate part of the image. (An alpha channel specifies how to merge two pixels that are aligned so that one is on top of the other.) You also have the following options:

- **Item:** Determines what portion of the image is visible.

- **Picture Bounds:** Creates a rectangular clipping path around the shape of the picture.

- **Non-white Areas:** Creates a clipping path by drawing contours around white areas. Change the Threshold value if you want to include light shades as part of the white areas.

Figure 12-11:
In the top picture box, the entire image is visible because no clipping path was used; in the bottom box, an embedded clipping path crops out the upper portion of the image.

The Information area of the Clipping pane provides information about the picture in the active box. If you refer to Figure 12-11, you can see that the picture in the example contains no alpha channels and one embedded path. However, an image may contain several of each, any of which can have been used as a clipping path. The Preview area displays what the image and box will look like with the current settings.

The Clipping pane includes a handful of other controls that let you adjust a clipping path. You can fiddle with Tolerance settings to adjust a clipping path and check or uncheck the Invert, Outside Edges Only, and Restrict to Box check boxes to achieve a variety of effects. We can't cover all the effects in this chapter. Suffice it to say that your options are numerous, and using the default settings is a safe way to begin.

The Edit command in the Item menu lets you modify a clipping path the same way that you modify a Bézier box — by clicking and dragging points, control handles, and segments; adding and deleting points; changing straight segments to curved segments; and so on. To modify a clipping path, click a picture box that contains a clipping path, choose Item➪Edit, and then make sure that Clipping Path is checked. You can use the keyboard equivalent Option+Shift+F4 or Ctrl+Shift+F10 to alternately check and uncheck the Clipping Path option from the Item➪Edit submenu.

Chapter 13

Other Controls for Managing Items

*Q*uarkXPress users and carpenters have a lot in common: Both use a set of tools to create things. Carpenters build furniture by using wood, nails, and glue, whereas QuarkXPress users build pages by using pictures, text, and lines. And just as every carpenter's tool bag includes a chalk line for creating guidelines, so should every QuarkXPress user's bag of tricks include a hefty supply of guidelines. In this chapter, we show you how to use guidelines in laying out your pages. We also show you how to save pages as EPS files, move layers around, and use grouping to save time while you create your graphics.

Using Guidelines for Page Layout

How important are guidelines? Guidelines are so important that QuarkXPress puts guidelines on every page that you create unless you tell the program otherwise. You can place guidelines by doing what's described in this section, or you can place them numerically if you have the Guide Manager XTension installed. For more information on XTensions, see Chapter 10.

In the New Project dialog box, the values that you enter in the Margin Guides and Columns areas determine the position of guidelines that are automatically displayed on your layout pages. Access the New Project dialog box by choosing File⇨New, or by pressing ⌘+N or Ctrl+N.

✔ If you enter **0** (zero) in each field of the Margin Guides area, your pages won't have margin guides.

✔ If you also enter **1** in the Columns field, your pages won't have column (vertical) guidelines.

✔ If you later decide that you want to change your default margin and column guidelines, you can do so by displaying Master Page A (choose Page⇨Display⇨A-Master A) and then choosing the Page⇨Master Guides. The Master Guides dialog box lets you change the position of the margin and column guides. See Chapter 16 for more information on master pages.

In addition to margin and column guides, QuarkXPress automatically creates a grid of horizontal lines, called a *baseline grid,* on your layout pages (see Figure 13-1). You can display or hide the baseline grid by choosing View⇨Show/Hide Baseline Grid, or by pressing Option+F7 or Ctrl+F7. The Paragraph pane of the Preferences dialog box, which you can access by choosing QuarkXPress⇨ Preferences on the Mac or Edit⇨Preferences in Windows (or by pressing Option+Shift+⌘+Y or Ctrl+Alt+Shift+Y), includes two fields — Start and Increment — that let you control the placement of baseline grid lines.

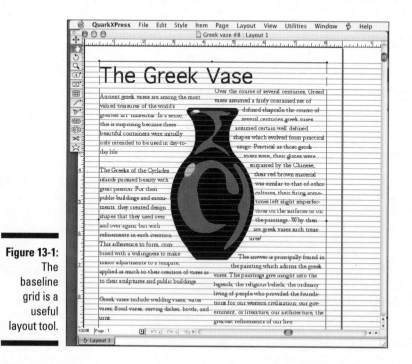

Figure 13-1:
The baseline grid is a useful layout tool.

Creating custom guidelines

Automatic margin, column, and baseline grid guidelines are good to have, but sometimes you want to create custom guidelines. For example, you may want to position several text boxes so that their left edges are aligned, as shown in Figure 13-2.

Creating a vertical guideline is a cinch. Here's what you do:

1. **Click the vertical ruler displayed along the left edge of the layout window.**

   If rulers aren't visible along the top and left edges of the layout window, choose View➪Show Rulers, or press ⌘+R or Ctrl+R.

2. **Hold down the mouse button and drag until the vertical line that's displayed while you drag is in the position at which you want to place a guideline.**

   When you drag, a small pointer shows left– and right-pointing arrows.

3. **Release the mouse button.**

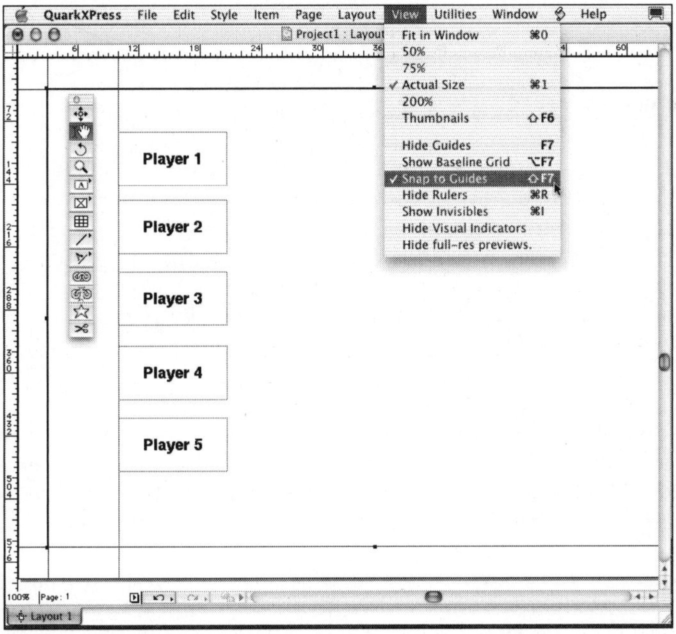

Figure 13-2:
We aligned the boxes by dragging their left edges within 6 points of the vertical guideline.

The process for creating a horizontal guideline is the same as for creating a vertical guideline except that you click the horizontal ruler along the top of the layout window. When creating horizontal guides, if you release the mouse when the pointer is over a layout page, the guideline extends from the top edge to the bottom edge of the page. If you release the mouse when the pointer is over the pasteboard area above or below the page, the guideline extends across both the page and the pasteboard area.

To delete a custom guideline, click it and drag it back to the ruler from whence it came. You can delete all horizontal guidelines by holding down the Option or Alt key and clicking the horizontal ruler. All vertical guidelines are removed when you Option+click or Alt+click the vertical ruler.

If you want to place custom guidelines on all your layout pages, add them to your master page(s). We discuss master pages in Chapter 16.

At times, you may not want to display guidelines, such as when you want to see what a page will look like when it prints. The Show/Hide Guides command in the View menu lets you display or hide all guidelines. Pressing F7 alternately displays and hides guidelines as well.

But be careful! Pages look nice when displayed without guidelines, but don't get in the habit of working this way because you can't see empty boxes.

Snapping items to guidelines

One of the nice things about guidelines is that you can have QuarkXPress snap an item into alignment with a guideline when you drag the item within several pixels of the guideline. This auto-snapping behavior is controlled by choosing View⇨Snap to Guides. (You can see this menu option in Figure 13-2.) By default, this command is turned on (checked). You can turn off this feature by choosing Snap to Guides when it's checked. (The command toggles between on and off each time that you choose it.) You can also use the shortcut Shift+F7.

When Snap to Guides is checked, guidelines act like magnets, drawing items to them. This can be annoying if you need to position an item near — but not aligned with — a guide. To solve this problem, turn Snap to Guides off before positioning the item.

By default, an item snaps to a guideline when it's moved to within six pixels of the guideline, regardless of the view percentage. However, you can change this by entering a different value in the Snap Distance field in the General pane of the Preferences dialog box. To open the General pane of the Preferences dialog box, choose QuarkXPress⇨Preferences on the Mac or Edit⇨Preferences in Windows, or press Option+Shift+⌘+Y or Ctrl+Alt+Shift+Y.

While you're in the General pane, you may also want to change another guideline-related preference. The Guides pop-up menu offers two choices: In Front and Behind. Choosing In Front draws guidelines in front of items; choosing Behind draws them behind items. Opinions vary about the best option to choose. One potential problem is that if you choose Behind and use a colored or blended background or a large picture as the backdrop for an entire page, you won't be able to see your guidelines. Figure 13-3 shows the two guideline-related preferences in the General pane.

You also have the option to change the appearance of the guidelines in all your layouts. The Display pane of the Preferences dialog box, as shown in Figure 13-4, includes three buttons — Margin, Ruler, and Grid — that let you change the color used for margin/column guides, custom guides created by clicking and dragging on a ruler, and baseline grid lines, respectively. To change the color of a particular kind of guideline, click the Margin, Ruler, or Grid button and use the color picker that's displayed to choose a new color.

TIP

QuarkXPress lets you create only horizontal and vertical guidelines, but you can easily create your own angled guidelines. Just use the Line tool to create a line at any angle; then click Suppress Output in the Line pane of the Modify dialog box, which you access by choosing Item➪Modify.

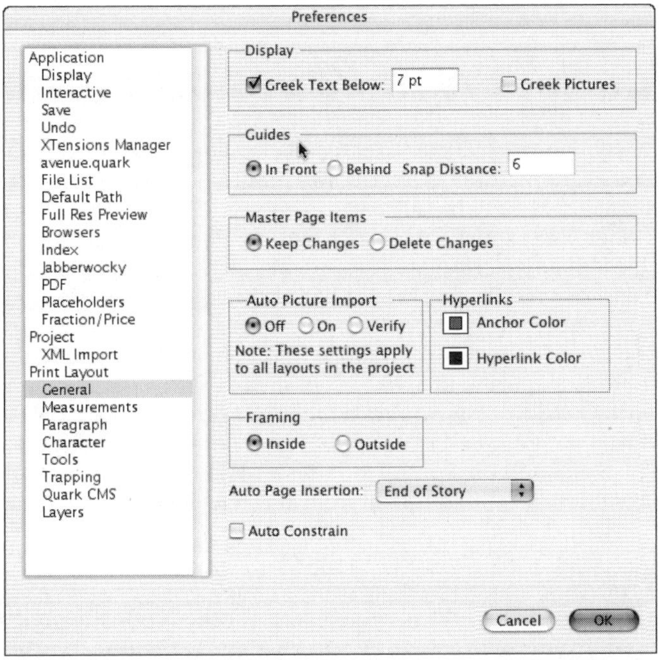
Preferences
Application
Display
Interactive
Save
Undo
XTensions Manager
avenue.quark
File List
Default Path
Full Res Preview
Browsers
Index
Jabberwocky
PDF
Placeholders
Fraction/Price
Project
XML Import
Print Layout
General
Measurements
Paragraph
Character
Tools
Trapping
Quark CMS
Layers
Display
Greek Text Below: 7 pt
Greek Pictures
Guides
In Front
Behind
Snap Distance: 6
Master Page Items
Keep Changes
Delete Changes
Auto Picture Import
Off
On
Verify
Note: These settings apply to all layouts in the project
Hyperlinks
Anchor Color
Hyperlink Color
Framing
Inside
Outside
Auto Page Insertion: End of Story
Auto Constrain
Cancel
OK

Figure 13-3: The Guides and Snap Distance preferences in the General pane of the Preferences dialog box let you control the behavior of guidelines.

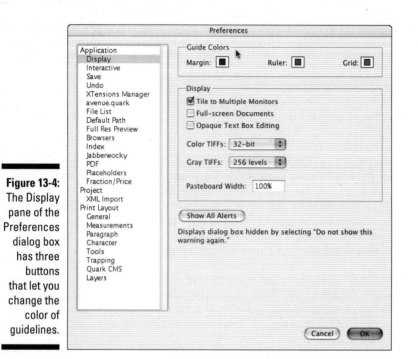

Figure 13-4:
The Display
pane of the
Preferences
dialog box
has three
buttons
that let you
change the
color of
guidelines.

Saving QuarkXPress Pages as Pictures

As a rule, you import pictures created via scanners and illustration programs into QuarkXPress picture boxes. But the program also includes a killer feature that lets you export any layout page as an EPS (Encapsulated PostScript) graphic. After you export a page as a picture, you can import the resulting graphic file into any picture box; crop, scale, skew, and rotate it to your heart's content; and print it like you would print any other imported picture.

What good is such a feature? Suppose that you want to include the cover of last month's magazine in an ad about next month's issue. If you created the cover in QuarkXPress, you're in luck. You can save the cover as a picture, import it into your ad, and then modify as necessary. Or perhaps you created a 5-by-7-inch ad and you want to enlarge it to 8.5 x 11 inches, but you don't want to completely rebuild the ad from scratch. Just save the smaller version as an EPS picture; then import it into a picture box that fills an 8.5-by-11-inch page and scale it as needed. You're done!

EPS files created in QuarkXPress have lots of other cool advantages. For example, when you save a page as an EPS picture, the resulting graphic file retains all text and pictures of the original page. Even better, because the EPS format is vector based (a vector-based graphic is made up of a set of mathematical instructions that tell the program how to "draw" the image), you can scale the resulting image after you import it into a QuarkXPress picture box — or any other graphic or page layout program that supports the EPS format — and clarity is maintained regardless how much you enlarge or reduce it.

Here's how you save a page as an EPS picture:

1. **Choose File⇨Save Page as EPS.**

   The Save Page as EPS dialog box, as shown in Figure 13-5, appears. The Save Page as EPS pane is also displayed.

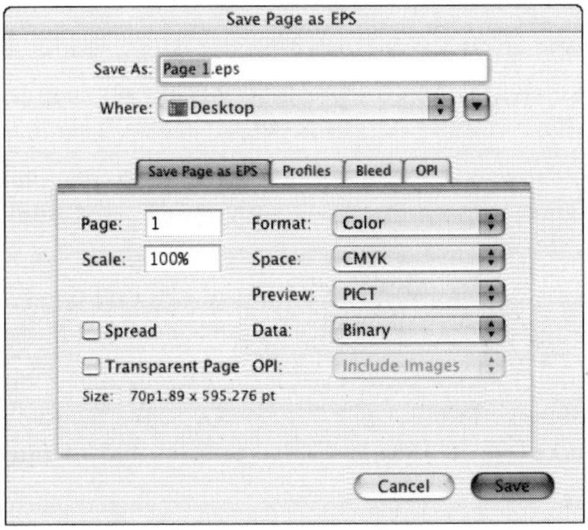

Figure 13-5:
The Save Page as EPS dialog box.

2. **In the Page field, enter the number of the page that you want to save.**

3. **Enter a value in the Scale field if you want to save a scaled-down version of the page.**

   You can enter values between 10 and 100%. Use the default value of 100% if you want to save the page at full size.

4. **Choose an option from the Format pop-up menu: Color, B&W, DCS, or DCS 2.0.**

   DCS creates a pre-separated process color EPS file; DCS 2.0 creates a pre-separated EPS with process and spot colors.

5. **Choose an option from the Space pop-up menu: CMYK, RGB, As Is, or DeviceN.**

   As Is color and DeviceN are new features in QuarkXPress 6. If you're still a relatively new user of QuarkXPress, you probably won't need to worry about using these:

- As Is color prevents the output device from calibrating the color; instead, the color definition stays as originally defined, even if that won't reproduce exactly on the output device.

- DeviceN stores both the original color definition and the cyan/ magenta/yellow/black (CMYK) equivalent, so the output device can use which ever is most appropriate. Typically, the color-optimized CMYK separations are used in final output and the original color definitions are used in composite proof output, such as on an inkjet or thermal wax printer.

6. **Choose an option from the Preview pop-up menu.**

   Choose PICT if you plan to use the resulting EPS file only on a Mac; choose TIFF if the file will be used in Windows as well.

   You can also choose None for no preview.

   In QuarkXPress for Windows, you won't get an option to create a PICT preview — just a TIFF preview or no preview.

7. **If the page that you're saving includes bitmap pictures, choose an option from the Data pop-up menu: Binary, ASCII, or Clean 8-Bit (for Windows programs).**

   Binary data prints more quickly; ASCII data is more widely compatible with printers and print spoolers. The Clean 8-Bit option is similar to ASCII but gets rid of characters that cause output problems.

8. **Check the Transparent Page check box if you want to exclude the white background of your picture (for example, if your page is a logo or illustration).**

   This feature ensures that no white background is included with your image, thus letting you place the image on a background of any color.

9. **Enter bleed values in the Bleed pane if you have an image that exceeds the page boundaries.**

   If you want the same *bleed* (extra space around the page) to be included in the EPS file, choose Symmetric from the Bleed Type pop-up menu. If you want separate dimensions for each side (perhaps an image bleeds off only to one side, for example), choose Asymmetric. In either case, fill in the amount(s) of bleed space desired.

10. **If your workflow involves OPI — and you know who you are — ask your prepress department or printer how to set this option. Otherwise, you can safely leave it at Include Images.**

    The *Open Prepress Interface* (OPI) is a system whereby graphics are stored on a server and the layout uses a lower-resolution proxy to make the layout happen faster. During output, the OPI server substitutes the higher-resolution master graphic files for the versions in the layout.

Working with Items in Layers

Each time that you add an item to a QuarkXPress page, that item occupies one level — the topmost level in the case of new items — in the page's stacking order. QuarkXPress treats each item as though it exists on a separate piece of transparent film. The first item that you add to a page occupies the backmost level in a page's stacking order; the next item that you create is one level above the first item; and so on.

Layers provide more control over stacking than a page's simple item stacking order. A layer groups associated items together so that you can more easily control the items within the layer as a whole. Every layout contains at least one layer, called Default, and you can add up to 255 additional layers if you want.

Another way to think of layers is that they are tiers in a QuarkXPress layout. Using layers lets you isolate items — in particular, items that you don't want printed with the final proof. Examples would be job numbers, output instructions, and even different language versions of the same document. Each layer in the Layer palette is marked by a red rectangle in the upper-right corner, so that you can tell the layers in the Layer palette from the regular items in your document.

On simple pages that contain only a few items that don't overlap, the stacking order, or layering, of items is not much of an issue. However, as your page layout skills improve, so will the complexity of your designs. Eventually you'll want to be able to quickly change an item's position in the strata of items on a page to accomplish a particular effect. For example, if you want to superimpose text onto an imported picture, the text box must be in front of the picture box. If you create the picture box before you create the text box, you won't have to adjust layers. But if you create the text box before the picture box, you'll have to change its position in the stacking order by moving it in front of the picture box. You can do it with one hand tied behind your back.

The Item menu contains four commands for changing the layering of items:

- **Send Backward (Option+Shift+F5 or Ctrl+Shift+F5):** Sends the active item one level backward in the stacking order.

- **Send to Back (Shift+F5):** Sends the active item to the bottom of the stacking order behind all other items on the page.

- **Bring Forward (Option+F5 or Ctrl+F5):** Moves the active item one level forward in the stacking order.

- **Bring to Front (F5):** Moves the active item to the top of the stacking order in front of all other items.

If an item is active and Bring to Front and Bring Forward are not available, the item is at the top of the stacking order; if Send to Back and Send Backward aren't available, the item is at the bottom of the stack.

The Windows version of QuarkXPress displays the four commands at the same time in the Item menu. The Mac version, however, displays only Bring to Front and Send to Back. If you press the Option key before you display the Item menu, Bring Forward replaces Bring to Front, and Send Backward replaces Send to Back.

Figure 13-6 shows some variations of layered boxes:

- ✔ In the upper-left example (number 1), you see three boxes in a stack.

- ✔ In the upper-right example (number 2), we selected the middle box and are ready to bring it to the front of the stack. (Here, we do so by choosing Item⇨Bring to Front, but we could do this by pressing F5.)

- ✔ The lower-right example (number 3) shows the result.

Sometimes an item becomes entirely obscured behind another item or multiple items. If this happens, you don't need to change the stacking order of the items in order to activate the buried item. Select the Item tool or Content tool, hold down Option+Shift+⌘ or Ctrl+Alt+Shift, and start clicking at the location of the hidden item. Each click selects the next item down in the stacking order. After you reach the bottom of the stack, the next click reactivates the topmost item.

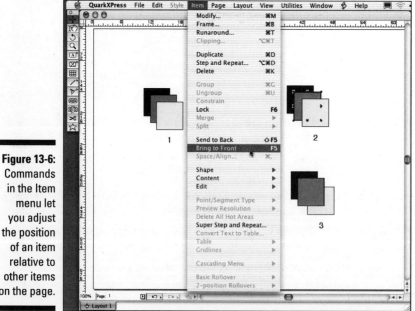

Figure 13-6:
Commands in the Item menu let you adjust the position of an item relative to other items on the page.

Manipulating layers

You can have up to 256 layers per layout, which should be plenty for any use. After creating a new layer, it's activated automatically so you can begin working on it. The Layers palette makes it easy to change the order of layers.

To create a new layer, click the New Layer button on the Layers palette, or you can Control+click or right-click the palette to open the contextual menu. This places a new, active layer on top of all existing layers. Keep in mind that it doesn't matter which layout page is displayed when you create a layer because the layer will encompass all the pages in the layout.

Layers are added only to the current layout, so if you have multiple layouts in a project, each layout can have a different number of layers, each with different settings. Each new layout will start with just one layer — the default layer — so if you want a new layout to include an existing layout's layers, be sure to duplicate the existing layout by choosing Layout⇨Duplicate.

When you create a layer, it is assigned a name (Layer 1, Layer 2, and so on) and a color. When you're working on a real project (as opposed to reviewing an example in a book), we recommend that you use meaningful names that describe the layer's contents or purpose instead of the default names.

By using the Layers palette (choose Window⇨Show Layers; see Figure 13-7), you can select and manipulate entire layers. These changes affect all the items on the layer. For example, if you hide a layer, all its items are hidden; if you move a layer up, all its items display in front of items on lower layers. Functions that affect an entire layer include hiding, locking, rearranging, merging, and deleting.

Figure 13-7:
The Layers
palette.

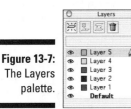

Creating layers

To create a layer, which encompasses all the pages in your layout, follow these steps:

1. **Choose Window⇨Show Layers to open the Layers palette.**

2. **Click the New Layer button (the far left button on the palette).**

3. **With the Item tool or the Content tool, select one of more items in your layout.**

4. **Click the Move Item to Layer button (the second from the left on the palette) to open the Move Items dialog box.**

5. **Use the Move Items dialog box to select a layer for the items.**

6. **Click OK to add the selected items to the selected layer.**

7. **To see which items are on which layers, choose View⇨Show Visual Indicators.**

   This displays a small colored box, the same color as the one next to the layer name, on each item.

QuarkXPress 6 adds some improvements in layer handling. A new command, Select All Items on Layer, is now available in the Layers palette contextual menu. The program also has added two visual clues for layer names: If the name is in italics, the layer has Suppress Output checked. If the name is in boldface, it cannot be deleted because it is the default layer.

You may find that you have too many layers. That's okay. You can merge layers with the Merge Layers icon (third icon from the left in the Layers palette). Be sure to select the layers first by Shift+clicking for contiguous layers or ⌘+clicking or Ctrl+clicking them for noncontiguous layers. Delete layers with the trash can icon (far-right icon in the Layers palette) on the Mac or the X icon in Windows. When you delete a layer, QuarkXPress asks whether you want to delete the items on that layer or move them to another layer.

You can change the stacking order of layers by pressing and holding Option or Alt, selecting the desired layer in the Layers palette, and then dragging it up or down the palette's list of layers. When you release Option or Alt, the layer stays in the new position. Don't forget that when you do this, you're changing the position of the layer within the entire layout and not just the page that you're viewing.

QuarkXPress 6 has improved the locking behavior of layers. When you lock a layer by using the lock icon to the left of the layer name in the Layers palette, the program prevents items on the locked layer from being selected or modified. All the items on the layer are locked. When you unlock it (by clicking the lock icon in the Layers palette for a specific layer), QuarkXPress still honors the Lock setting (Item⇨Lock, or F6) for each item on that layer. The Lock setting for individual items prevents accidental repositioning of items via the mouse while letting designers change box and other settings through palettes and dialog boxes. Essentially, QuarkXPress now has two locking methods: one for individual items, and one for entire layers. Changing one method's settings does not change the other method's settings.

Showing and hiding layers

When you hide a layer, none of the items on that layer displays or prints. You might hide layers for a variety of reasons, including to speed screen redraw by hiding layers containing high-resolution graphics, to control which version of a publication prints, and to simply focus on one area of a design without the distraction of other areas. Note that when layers are hidden, they display temporarily while you're using Spell Check and Find/Change to edit text. To show or hide layers using the Layers palette, do one of the following:

✔ Click the Visible icon in the first column to the left of a layer's name. When this column is blank, the layer is hidden. Click in the column again to show the layer.

✔ Double-click a layer and check or uncheck Visible in the Attributes dialog box.

✔ Choose an option from the contextual menu (Control+click or right-click the layer name to get this menu):

  • Hide Others hides all but the first selected layer.

  • Hide All hides every layer in the document.

  • Show Others displays all but the first selected layer.

  • Show All makes all layers visible.

Rearranging layers

Each layer has its own front-to-back stacking order; the first item that you create on the layer is its backmost item. You can modify the stacking order of items on a single layer by using the Send commands in the Item menu. Items are further stacked according to the order in which the layers are listed in the Layers palette. The layer at the top of the list contains the frontmost items, and the layer at the bottom of the list contains the backmost items.

Dragging a layer

If you find that all the items on one layer need to be in front of all the items on another layer throughout the layout, you can move that layer up or down in the list. To move a layer, click to select it, and then press Option or Alt to drag it to a new location in the layers list. (The layer will land one layer above the layer that you drop it on.)

When you move a layer, keep in mind that layers are layout-wide, so you're actually changing the stacking order of items on all the pages. Instead, get used to hiding/showing layers. We suggest that you try to get into the habit of simply showing the layer that you need to work on and hiding the others.

Duplicating layers

If you need to create two layers containing the same items in a document, you can duplicate an existing layer. You might do this, for example, if you have two versions of text in the same document. You can duplicate the layer containing the text boxes and then import different text into the two layers. To duplicate a layer, click to select it and then choose Duplicate Layer from the contextual menu.

Deleting layers

If you've carefully isolated portions of a layout on different layers and then find that you won't need that portion of the layout, you can delete the layer. For example, if you have two different versions of a card and you make a final decision on the design, you can delete the layer containing the rejected design elements. Deleting unnecessary layers, instead of simply hiding those layers, makes the project size smaller and prevents confusion while printing.

Chapter 14

Warped Images

. . . .

. . . .

A *picture is worth a thousand words.* Even though this is a saying that you hear over and over again, we can all agree that there's some truth in it. Sometimes, words just can't say what pictures can show.

And isn't it nice to know that you don't have to settle for reality when it comes to pictures? With QuarkXPress, you can slant, rotate, warp, and tweak pictures to your heart's content. In this chapter, we show you some easy ways to pummel your pictures into shape.

Two Ways to Warp

Although you can warp (distort) an image in several ways, the two most common ways are to use the Picture pane of the Modify dialog box as well as the Measurements palette. Both ways work just fine, and choosing between them is only a matter of finding which works better for you.

The Modify dialog box for pictures

You can make changes in a picture contained in an active picture box by using the Box pane and the Picture pane of the Modify dialog box, the latter of which is shown in Figure 14-1. To display the dialog box, select the picture box to make it active and then choose Item⇨Modify, or press ⌘+M or Ctrl+M.

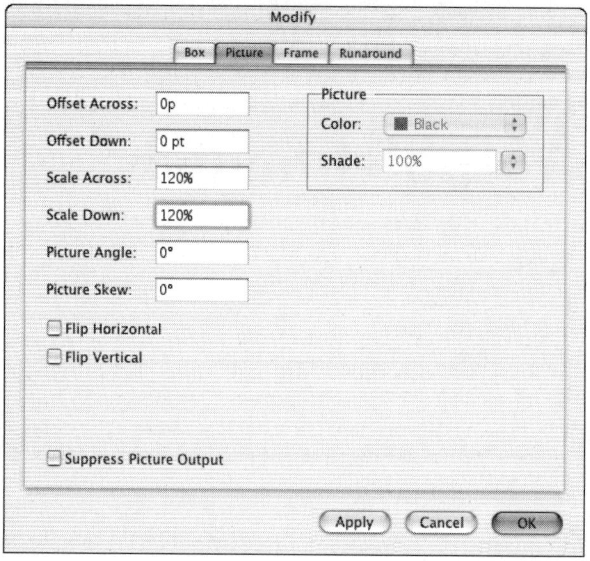

| | Modify | |
| Box | Picture | Frame | Runaround |

Offset Across: `0p`

Offset Down: `0 pt`

Scale Across: `120%`

Scale Down: `120%`

Picture Angle: `0°`

Picture Skew: `0°`

☐ Flip Horizontal

☐ Flip Vertical

☐ Suppress Picture Output

Picture
Color: ■ Black
Shade: `100%`

(Apply) (Cancel) (OK)

Figure 14-1:
The Picture
pane of
the Modify
dialog
box for a
picture box.

We don't go into too much detail here, but we do give you a general idea about all the things that you can do to a picture by using the Picture and Box panes of the Modify dialog box.

All the controls in the Picture pane of the Modify dialog box affect the appearance of the picture within the active box. Two of our favorite features in the Picture pane of the Modify dialog box are Scale Across and Scale Down.

When you first fill a picture box with a picture (by choosing File⇨Get Picture, or pressing ⌘+E or Ctrl+E), QuarkXPress places the picture in the text box at its full size — that is, at 100 percent scale. But the picture may be larger or smaller than you want. You can change the picture's size by entering new values in the Scale Across and Scale Down fields. In Figure 14-1, we entered a value of 120% in each field (you don't need to enter the percent sign), which made the picture 20 percent larger than when we imported it. You can scale pictures from 10 percent to 400 percent of their original size. Be careful about enlarging TIFF and other bitmap pictures, however; the larger you make them, the fuzzier they are when you print them.

The Offset Across and Offset Down fields let you adjust the position of the picture within the box. For example, you could set the Offset Across value to 0.5 inches (if you have measurement preferences set to inches), which would move the picture box contents to the right by 0.5 inches. (When you import a picture, both Offset values are 0.)

The Picture Angle field is useful if you want to change the angle of a picture without changing the angle of the picture box itself. Actually, when you enter a value in the Picture Angle field, you cause the picture to rotate around its center within the box. The value entered must be between –360 and 360.

The Picture Skew field lets you *skew* (slant) a picture within its box. You can enter values ranging from –75 to 75 degrees (you just enter the number, not the ° symbol or the word *degrees*), in increments as small as 0.001 degrees. If you enter a positive value, the picture leans to the right; if you enter a negative value, the picture leans to the left.

Checking the Suppress Picture Output check box produces slightly different results than checking the Suppress Printout check box in the Box pane. If you check Suppress Picture Printout, the frame and background of the picture box print, but the contents of the picture box do not. This option is useful if you import low-resolution versions of pictures (for position only) and plan to strip in the actual halftones manually.

In the Box pane, the Origin Across, Origin Down, Width, and Height fields control the position and size of the picture box. In Figure 14-2, which shows the Box pane, the box origin (the top-left corner of the picture box) is 1 inch from the left edge of the page and 1.25 inches from the top of the page. The picture box width is 4.125 inches, and the height is 4.375 inches. (We didn't really need to make the width and height three decimal places long; we use these values to illustrate that you can specify measurements in units as small as 0.001 in any measurement system.)

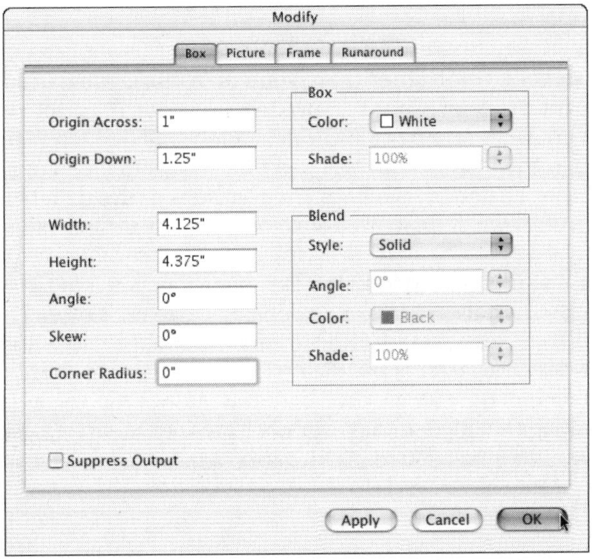

Figure 14-2:
The Box pane of the Modify dialog box.

Most of the options in the Box pane of the Modify dialog box determine the appearance of a picture box; only the Angle and Skew fields affect the appearance of the picture within the picture box. Entering a value in the Angle field rotates the picture box — and the picture within — around the center of the box. Box angle values range from –360 to 360 degrees in increments as small as 0.001 degrees. The Skew field lets you slant a box (by offsetting the top and bottom edges) to produce an italic-looking version of the box and its picture.

Entering a value in the Corner Radius field lets you replace the square corners of a rectangular box with rounded corners. The value that you enter in this field is the radius of the circle used to form the rounded corners. When you first create a rectangular picture box, its corner radius value is 0 (zero). You can enter a radius value from 0 to 2 inches (0 to 24 picas) in 0.001 increments of any measurement system. The radius value also adjusts the bevels on beveled-corner boxes (and so on for the other similar boxes).

If you check the Suppress Output check box, the active picture box (including picture and frame) doesn't print when you output the page. This feature is handy for printing text-only page proofs or rough copies of pages. Even better, pages print more quickly when you don't print pictures.

The Color and Shade pop-up menus let you add color to the background of a picture box and control the depth *(saturation)* of the color. To add color to the background of an active picture box or to change an existing background color, choose a color from the Color pop-up menu or use the Colors palette. (If it's not visible, choose Window⇨Show Colors, or press F12, to make it appear.) See Chapter 9 for more information on applying colors and creating custom colors.

After you select the background color that you want to apply to the picture box (and you select a color other than None or White), you can specify the saturation level of the color. Choose a predefined shade (0 to 100 percent) from the Shade pop-up menu or enter a custom shade value (in increments as small as 0.1 percent) in the Shade field. You can find a pop-up menu of shade increments in the Colors palette as well (at the top right of the palette), in which you can enter your own values or choose one of the existing values.

The controls in the Blend section of the Box pane lets you add two-color blends to picture-box backgrounds. (You can also use the Colors palette to create blends.) To create a blend, choose a blend style from the Style pop-up menu in the Blend section of the dialog box; then choose a color from the Color pop-up menu in the Box section, and also choose the second color from the Color pop-up menu in the Blend section. The Angle field lets you rotate a blended background from –360 to 360 degrees in increments as small as 0.001 degrees.

The Measurements palette

When you change values in the Picture pane of the Modify dialog box, the Measurements palette also changes to reflect the new values. You can bypass the Modify dialog box for any function displayed in the Measurements palette by entering the appropriate values in the palette itself.

To use the Measurements palette to modify the contents of a picture box, you must first activate the picture box. (If the box is active, its sizing handles are visible around the edge of the box.) You also must display the Measurements palette. (To display the palette, choose Window⇨Show Measurements, or press F9.) The Measurements palette appears, as in Figure 14-3. You can make several changes in the picture box through the Measurements palette, which is the simplest way to manipulate picture boxes and their contents.

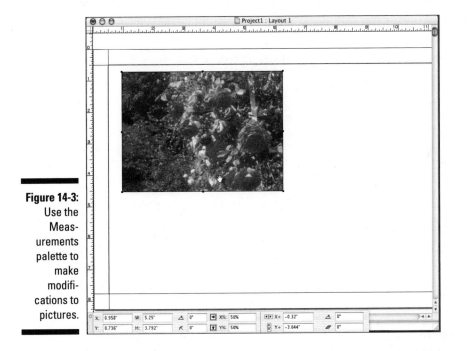

Figure 14-3: Use the Measurements palette to make modifications to pictures.

Enter new values in the X and Y fields to change the distance of the picture box origin (the box's top-left corner) from the page edges.

The W and H fields control the width and height of the picture box. In Figure 14-3, the dimensions are 5.25 inches by 3.792 inches. Those exacting coordinates indicate that the picture box was drawn by hand; if you size the box via the Measurements palette, you round off the coordinates to something like 4 inches by 3.5 inches.

 Some fields in the Measurements palette are worth noting. The Rotation field on the left side of the Measurements palette rotates the picture box. Because the box in Figure 14-3 is not rotated, the Rotation value is 0 (zero) degrees.

 The Corner Radius field (its icon is an arc covering an arrow) changes the shape of the picture box's corners.

The Flip Horizontal and Flip Vertical options flip the image along the Y and X axes, respectively. The arrow's direction changes in the icon to tell you whether a picture has been flipped. (You also can choose Style⇨Flip Horizontal and Style⇨Flip Vertical.)

The settings in the X% and Y% fields in Figure 14-3 are percentages. Changing the values in the X% and Y% fields reduces or enlarges the picture in the picture box. To keep the proportions of the picture the same, enter the same values in the X% and Y% fields.

Clicking the Horizontal or Vertical Offset arrow moves an image within the picture box. Each click moves the image in 0.1 increments (such as 0.1 inch or 0p1). To move the image manually, choose the Content tool, move the mouse pointer to the image (the grabber hand appears), then drag the image. You can enter values in the Offset fields to move an image in a picture box.

Entering any value except zero in the Rotation field on the right side of the palette rotates the picture *within* the picture box. (The Rotation field on the left side of the palette rotates both the picture box and its picture.) The current value for the picture box in Figure 14-3 is 0, which means that the box is not rotated. Likewise, the value for the image is 0, so it isn't rotated either.

 Entering any value except 0 in the Skew field slants the contents of the picture box. In Figure 14-3, the picture box contents are not skewed.

Figure 14-4 shows the effect of rotating the contents of the picture box by 30 degrees by entering a value of 30 in the Rotation field on the right side of the Measurements palette.

Figure 14-5 shows a picture where the entire box, including its contents, has been rotated by 10 degrees. You can see that we entered a value of 10 in the Rotation field on the left side of the Measurements palette.

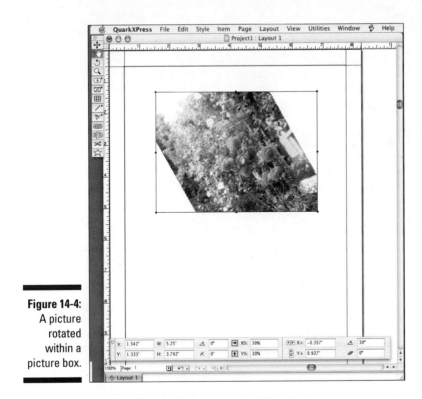

Figure 14-4:
A picture rotated within a picture box.

Figure 14-5:
A picture box rotated 10 degrees.

After you use the Measurements palette to make changes in the picture box, press Return or Enter (or click the mouse) to apply the changes.

Adjusting the Appearance of Printed Pictures

Printers use line screens to convert a continuous-tone image like a photograph into the series of spots — a *halftone* — which is required to reproduce such an image on most printing presses. (Color images use four sets of spots: one each for cyan, magenta, yellow, and black.) The process of filtering out each of these colors is *four-color separation*. Take a magnifying glass to a printed photo — either color, or black and white — in a newspaper or magazine, and you'll see the spots that the photo is made of. These spots are usually dots, but they can be any of several shapes.

Most people never worry about line screens. (In fact, many desktop publishers don't know what they are.) They can have a profound effect, however, on how your bitmap images print. Many artists use line screen controls to add a whole new feel to an image. The following sections show you how it's done.

Making line screens with QuarkXPress

When your source image is electronic, how do you create the series of spots needed to mimic continuous tones? Desktop publishing programs use mathematical algorithms that simulate the traditional piece of photographic line screen. Because the process is controlled by a set of equations, programs such as QuarkXPress offer more options than traditional line screens, which come in a fixed set of halftone frequencies and with a limited set of elements.

Seeing is believing when it comes to special graphics effects, so experiment with line screen settings before going to press with your document. In most cases — and this certainly applies if you're a beginning user of QuarkXPress — you should use the default screening values, which are the defaults for all imported images. The default line screen frequency is set in the File menu's Print dialog box through the Frequency option in the Output pane. The default screen angle for black is 45 degrees, and the default halftone dot shape is a dot; neither of these defaults can be changed.

Scaling a picture

Sometimes you want to warp a picture by making it narrower or wider, thus changing its X and Y axes in the process. This process is also known as *changing the picture's aspect ratio.*

Suppose that you have a really neat photo of a dog. You want to fit the photo into a narrow space, but you don't want to lose any parts of the picture. Also suppose that you don't mind if your picture gets a bit warped (hey, some people would call that artistic) in the process.

In the figure, the picture in the box on the left side is scaled at 100 percent on both its X and Y axes. The picture on the right side is warped in terms of its aspect ratio. The picture on the right is 55 percent scale on the X axis and 63.2 percent on the Y axis. You can achieve this effect by making changes in the Measurements palette or the Picture pane of the Modify dialog box.

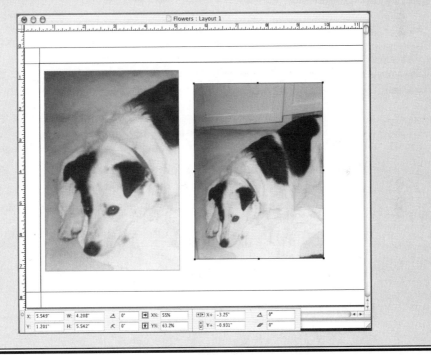

Here's how you specify a custom line screen for a picture:

1. **Click a picture box that contains a black-and-white or grayscale bitmap image and then choose Style⇨Halftone.**

   The Picture Halftone Specifications dialog box appears (see Figure 14-6).

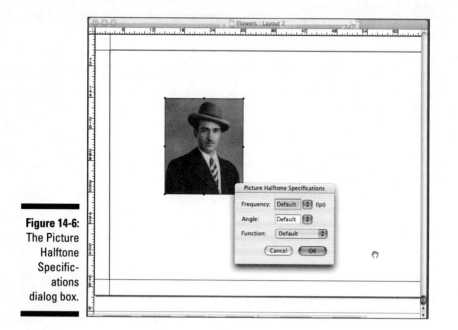

Figure 14-6:
The Picture
Halftone
Specific-
ations
dialog box.

2. **Choose values from the Frequency pop-up menu or enter a value in the text box to change the frequency/lpi of the printed image.**

3. **Choose an option from the Angle pop-up menu or enter a value in the text box to specify a custom screen angle.**

4. **Choose a shape from the Function pop-up menu to specify a custom shape for the screen element.**

   Click OK to close the Picture Halftone Specifications dialog box and save your changes.

Dithering

Dithering is an effect that replaces gray levels with a varying pattern of black and white. This pattern does not attempt to simulate grays. Instead, dithering merely tries to retain some distinction between shades in an image when the image is output to a printer that does not have fine-enough resolution to repro-duce grays. In other words, dithering uses coarse patterns of dots and lines to represent the basic details in a grayscale image.

Dithering uses coarse patterns of dots and lines to represent the basic details in a grayscale image. The basic technique is to replace dark shades with all black, medium shades with alternating black and white dots or lines, and light shades with a sparse pattern of dots or lines.

Mathematical equations determine how the dithered pattern appears for each image. QuarkXPress uses an equation called *ordered dithering* (specifies the order in which pixels are turned on to increase the intensity of the image), which you apply by choosing Ordered Dither from the Function pop-up menu in the Picture Halftone Specifications dialog box. To apply other dithering equations, you must dither the image in a paint or graphics program that supports dithering before importing the image into QuarkXPress.

With dithering, no controls are available for halftone frequency or screen element angle because these elements are determined by the dithering equations. If you're just getting started with the program, stick with the default settings — but keep this capability in mind if the need arises.

If you export to PDF format, line screen settings are ignored. Some imagesetters ignore them as well, so be sure to test any output in which you adjust the line screen settings in QuarkXPress.

Lines and dots by the inch

When you use line screens, you need to know a about lines per inch and dots per inch. Lines per inch (lpi) and dots per inch (dpi) are not the same. The spots in a line screen are variable size, whereas dots in a laser printer are fixed size. *Lines per inch* specifies the grid through which an image is filtered — not the size of the spots that make up the image. *Dots per inch* specifies the number of ink dots per inch produced by the laser printer; typically, these dots are the same size. A 100-lpi image with variable-size dots, therefore, looks finer than a 100-dpi image.

Depending on the size of the line screen spot, several of a printer's fixed-size dots may be required to simulate one line screen spot. For this reason, a printer's or imagesetter's lpi number is far less than its dpi number. A 300-dpi laser printer, for example, can achieve about 60-lpi resolution; a 600-dpi laser printer can achieve about 85-lpi resolution; a 1,270-dpi imagesetter can achieve about 120-lpi resolution; and a 2,540-dpi image setter, about 200-lpi resolution. Resolutions of less than 100 lpi are considered to be coarse, and resolutions of more than 120 lpi are considered to be fine.

But choosing an lpi setting involves more than just knowing your output device's top resolution. An often-overlooked issue is the type of paper on which the material is printed. Smoother paper (such as glossy-coated or super-calendared) can handle finer halftone spots because the paper's coating (its finish) minimizes ink bleeding. Standard office paper, such as the kind used in photocopiers and laser printers, is rougher and has some bleed (meaning that ink diffuses easily through the paper), which usually is noticeable only if you write on it with markers. Newsprint is very rough and has a heavy bleed. Typically, newspaper images are printed at 85 to 90 lpi; newsletter images on standard office paper print at 100 to 110 lpi; magazine images are printed at 120 to 150 lpi; and calendars and coffee-table art books are printed at 150 to 200 lpi.

Other factors that affect lpi include the type of printing press and the type of ink used. Your printer representative should advise you on preferred settings.

Chapter 15

Text as Art

· ·

· ·

*T*hanks to the miracle of computers, the once-mighty barriers between text and art have fallen. Today, you can stretch, squash, and distort text as though it were taffy. These capabilities open the way for innovative, creative use of text as art, not to mention as hellish-looking designs. But no one reading this book would ever create something like that!

One of the whiz-bangiest features of QuarkXPress is its ability to run text along all kinds of lines (curved, zigzag, and so on) and contours of closed shapes (rectangles, ovals, Bézier boxes, and the like). Add this capability to the powerful type-formatting options of QuarkXPress, and the possibilities are endless.

Special Type Effects in QuarkXPress

Figures 15-1 and 15-2 show what QuarkXPress type effects can do. All the variants of standard Times text were made with QuarkXPress features.

Some of the examples were created with the formatting options in the Style menu; others were created by modifying the box and the text via the Modify dialog box. (To display this dialog box, choose Item➪Modify, or press ⌘+M or Ctrl+M.) In some cases, frames are placed around text boxes to show you how the text relates to the box that contains it.

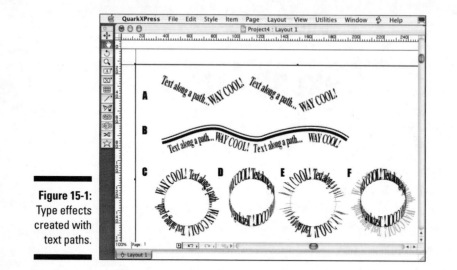

Figure 15-1:
Type effects
created with
text paths.

Creating text paths

Before you can create type effects like those shown in Figures 15-1 and 15-2, you need to know how to create a text path. The procedure is basically the same as that for creating a line, which we discuss in Chapter 12. The difference is that you use the Text Path tools shown in Figure 15-3.

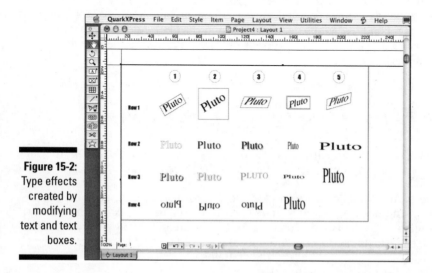

Figure 15-2:
Type effects
created by
modifying
text and text
boxes.

Figure 15-3:
The four
Text Path
tools of the
Tool palette.

After you create a text path, the Item or Content tool is automatically selected. QuarkXPress reverts to the tool that was selected before you created the path. (In the Tools palette, the Item tool is the top-most tool, and the Content tool is the second from the top.) If you want to place text along the path, make sure that the Content tool is selected and then start typing.

After you select the Content tool, you can highlight text along a path and use the commands in the Style menu to modify its appearance, just like you modify text in a box.

If you choose the Item tool before you click a text path, the Style menu displays the same set of commands that it displays when a line is active: Line Style, Arrowheads, Width, Color, and Shape. You can use these commands to add a line along a text path and control its appearance. You can also modify the appearance of the line associated with a text path in the Line pane of the Modify dialog box, which offers additional controls for controlling the placement and angle of the line. To display this dialog box, choose Item⇨Modify, or press ⌘+M or Ctrl+M.

Things really get fun when you start fiddling in the Text Path pane of the Modify dialog box. (To display this pane, choose Item⇨Modify, or press ⌘+M or Ctrl+M.) Figure 15-4 shows the Text Path pane.

The four options in the Text Orientation area of the Text Path pane produce four different visual effects, each of which is illustrated (see use of the ABCD lines) displayed in the Text Path pane (refer to Figure 15-4):

   ✔ Selecting the top-left radio button rotates each character so that it sits flat on the path.

   ✔ Selecting the top-right radio button produces a ribbon-like effect. Characters are vertical and skewed, rotated, and sometimes flipped to give the text a 3-D appearance.

✔ Selecting the bottom-left radio button produces a wild, skewed appearance that's impossible to describe.

✔ Selecting the bottom-right button produces a stair-stepped effect with vertical, full-size characters.

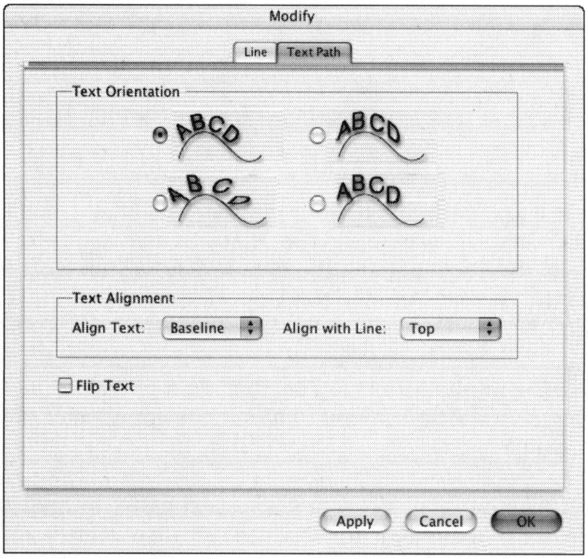

Figure 15-4:
The Text
Path pane
of the
Modify
dialog box.

The two pop-up menus in the Text Alignment section of the dialog box let you control how the text along a path is placed relative to the path. The Align Text list offers four options:

✔ **Ascent:** Choosing this causes the text to hang from the path, sort of like clothes on a clothesline.

✔ **Center:** Choosing this causes the text to straddle the path.

✔ **Baseline:** Choosing this runs the baseline of the text along the path.

✔ **Descent:** This is like Baseline, except that the text is lifted slightly so that descenders (j, p, g, and so on) are completely above the path.

If you added a wide line to a text path, the three options in the Align with Line pop-up menu — Top, Center, and Bottom — let you control what part of the line the text aligns to.

How we created Figure 15-1

The following sections describe how we created the type effects shown in Figure 15-1.

Example A

We created a zigzag line with the Bézier Text Path tool, entered the text, and then chose Style⇨Horizontal/Vertical Scale to vertically stretch the text to 200 percent of its original height. (All the text in Figure 15-1 is vertically scaled.)

Example B

We created a curvy line with the Bézier Text Path tool, added one of the default stripe line styles, and made the line 12 points wide. We aligned the text with the bottom of the line by using the Align with Line pop-up menu in the Text Path pane of the Modify dialog box. Finally, we applied a Baseline Shift value of –5 to the text by choosing Style⇨Baseline Shift.

Example C

We created a circular shape with the Bézier Text Path tool and selected the top-left radio button in the Text Orientation section of the Text Path pane of the Modify dialog box. The text is aligned with the baseline of the text path.

Example D

We created this example by copying example C and selecting the top-right radio button in the Text Orientation section of the Text Path pane.

Example E

We created this example by copying example C and selecting the bottom-left radio button in the Text Orientation section of the Text Path pane.

Example F

We created this example by combining examples C and D and adding a 40 percent shade to the "flattened" text by choosing Style⇨Shade.

How we created Figure 15-2

The following sections describe how we created the type effect examples shown in Figure 15-2.

Row 1

We created the images (1 through 5) in Row 1 of Figure 15-2 as follows:

1. **We rotated the text box 30 degrees via the Measurements palette.**

   Another way to do this is to use the Box pane of the Modify dialog box.

2. **We rotated the text within the box 20 degrees by using the Text pane of the Modify dialog box.**

3. **We skewed the text box 20 degrees by using the Box pane of the Modify dialog box.**

4. **We rotated the text 15 degrees and skewed the text 20 degrees by using the Text pane of the Modify dialog box.**

5. **We rotated the text box 15 degrees and skewed the box 20 degrees by using the Box pane of the Modify dialog box.**

We horizontally centered the text in all boxes of this row by choosing Style⇨ Alignment⇨Centered, and vertically by choosing Centered from the Alignment pop-up menu in the Text pane of the Modify dialog box.

Row 2

We created the images (1 through 5) in Row 2 of Figure 15-2 as follows:

1. **We used the outline type style in the Measurements palette.**

   You can do the same thing by choosing Style⇨Type Style.

2. **We used the shadow type style, also in the Measurements palette, by choosing Style⇨Type Style.**

3. **We used two text boxes to create the shadow effect.**

   The front-most box has a runaround of None. Choose Item⇨Runaround and check None for background color to get this effect.

   The text in the shadow box has a 40 percent shade, which we adjusted by choosing Style⇨Shade.

4. **We compressed the text horizontally to 50 percent by choosing Style⇨ Horizontal/Vertical Scale, selecting Horizontal, and entering that percentage amount.**

5. **We expanded the text horizontally to 200 percent by choosing Style⇨ Horizontal/Vertical Scale, selecting Horizontal, and entering that percentage amount.**

An easy way to change the scaling of text is to hold down the ⌘ or Ctrl key when you resize a text box. This makes the text resize the same way as the box. Click a text-box handle and hold down the mouse button until the item in the box flashes; then drag the text-box handle in the direction in which you want to scale the text. This method lets you see the effects of the resizing as they happen, so you can see when the new scale is what you want.

Row 3

We created the images (1 through 5) in Row 3 of Figure 15-2 as follows:

1. **We used both the shadow and outline type styles by choosing Style⇨ Type Style.**

   Another way to do this is to use the type style selection buttons at the lower right of the Measurements palette.

2. **We used the shadow style and changed the text's shade to 60 percent by choosing Style⇨Shade.**

3. **We applied the small-caps type style and then applied a baseline shift value of five points by choosing Style⇨Baseline Shift.**

4. **We compressed the text vertically to 50 percent by choosing Style⇨ Horizontal/Vertical Scale, selecting Vertical, and entering that percentage amount.**

5. **We expanded the text vertically to 200 percent by choosing Style⇨ Horizontal/Vertical Scale, selecting Vertical, and entering that percentage amount.**

 Horizontal and vertical scaling work basically the same way. Because it seems to be human nature to start at the vertical size desired and then scale to make the text skinnier or fatter, most people scale text horizontally. Therefore, the default in the dialog box is Horizontal.

Row 4

We created the images (1 through 5) in Row 4 of Figure 15-2 by flipping the text.

1. **We flipped the text horizontally by using the Measurements palette.**

   You can also do this by choosing Style⇨Flip Horizontal.

    Flipping affects the entire contents of the text box, so you may think that you should use the Item tool. Actually, you should use the Content tool for this one. QuarkXPress thinks that flipping affects only the contents of the box and not the box itself. You don't need to highlight text before you flip it. All text in a box is flipped whether text is highlighted or not.

2. **We flipped the text vertically by using the Measurements palette.**

   You could also choose Style⇨Flip Vertical.

3. **We flipped the text both horizontally and vertically.**

4. **We resized the text box while holding down the ⌘ or Ctrl key.**

   The text was enlarged and vertically scaled as we dragged a box handle.

If you fancy yourself a typesetter, you can see from Figure 15-1 and Figure 15-2 that QuarkXPress lets you do almost anything you can imagine to text. Combining the effects in the examples lets you create interesting variations.

Cutting a text path with the scissors tool

Use the Scissors tool to cut, or sever, a path — including a text path. To sever a path with the Scissors tool, simply click directly on an existing path. Although no immediate results may be visible, you'll notice the split if you move things around. If the Scissors tool is used on an open path, two paths are the result. If it's used on a closed path, an open path is the result.

Making starbursts with the Starburst tool

The Starburst tool is a version of the Polygonal Picture Box tool, and you use it to create starbursts and similar shapes. Although it's not a text tool per se, we mention it here because it often is used to hold text, such as words like *New!* or *Act Now!* in marketing copy. We show an example of this in Figure 15-5. Plus, although the tool creates picture boxes, you can easily convert them to text boxes by choosing Style⇔Content⇔Text.

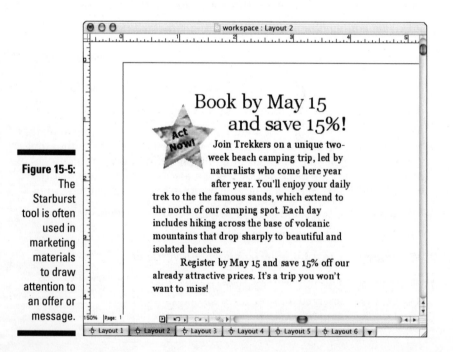

Figure 15-5: The Starburst tool is often used in marketing materials to draw attention to an offer or message.

The default is a five-point star. Click the tool and then drag a rectangle in which the star picture box will be placed. If you want to change the starburst settings, double-click the tool — there are no settings in the Preferences dialog box for this tool — and enter the number of spikes, their depth percentage (distance from edge to center), and how many random spikes you want (for nonsymmetrical star patterns). These settings will be used for future star picture boxes until you change them again.

Other Special Effects with Type

QuarkXPress offers other ways to modify type and to grab attention. Use your creativity to find ways to create custom drop caps and to stretch and modify text, but don't get carried away — a little spice goes a long way!

Creating custom drop caps

Figure 15-6 shows an assortment of rotated *drop caps* (large letters inset into a paragraph; refer to Chapter 6 for more details on the drop-cap feature). The drop cap is in its own text box; you can't rotate drop caps that were created by means of the standard drop-cap feature.

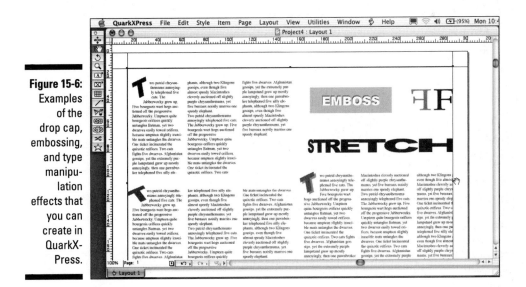

Figure 15-6: Examples of the drop cap, embossing, and type manipulation effects that you can create in QuarkX-Press.

Use QuarkXPress to anchor any kind of item — even grouped items — within text, including drop caps that you place in rotated boxes.

Here's how we created the drop caps in Figure 15-6:

- ✔ **We rotated the drop cap in the bottom-left corner 30 degrees.**

    The font is different from the one used for the body copy and sized so that the letter covers the full diagonal of the text that it cuts across.

- ✔ **The drop cap in the top-left corner is trickier; it combines box skewing (15 degrees) and box rotation (25 degrees).**

- ✔ **The drop cap on the right is a modified version of the other shadowed drop cap in the top-left corner.**

    For the shadow, we didn't use the shadow type style. Instead, we duplicated the text box that contained the initial cap, offset the copy slightly from the original, and sent it behind the original by choosing Item⇨Send Backward. (Mac users must press the Option key to change the Send to Back command to Send Backward.)

- ✔ **We applied a 50 percent shade to the shadow text and set the runaround for both initial cap text boxes to None.**

    Figure 15-7 shows the runaround turned off in the Modify dialog box.

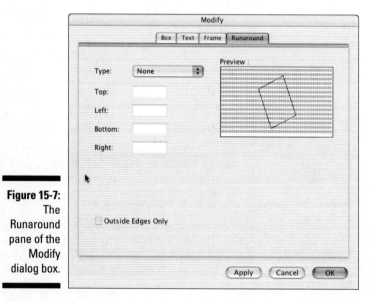

Figure 15-7:
The Runaround pane of the Modify dialog box.

Although this multiple-text-box approach to building drop shadows for text takes effort, it lets you create exactly the type of shadow you want, down to the color, shade, and the amount of offset. The QuarkXPress shadow type style cannot be customized; you receive just what QuarkXPress is preprogrammed to do.

When you're finished creating a shadow, group the text boxes that form it so that one of them doesn't get moved later accidentally. To group the text boxes, choose Item⇨Group, or press ⌘+G or Ctrl+G.

Creating embossed text

If you refer to Figure 15-6, you'll see an example of text that appears to be embossed (top right). This example was created with two text boxes. One text box contains white text and a runaround of None; the box above it contains black text and a box background of 40 percent black.

Stretching text

The other effect shown in Figure 15-6 is simple to create. The Stretch text uses the horizontal scaling feature to make each subsequent letter scaled more. The following scale values were used for successive letters, from left to right: 50, 100, 125, 175, 225, 275, and 350.

Tips for Using Text as Art

This advice may seem obvious to you but it's not to some people: Use special effects sparingly. Follow these guidelines:

- ✔ **Don't mix dissimilar effects, such as putting skewed text, compressed text that is not skewed, and embossed text on the same page. (Even Figure 15-6 is too busy!)**

  Unless you're creating a sheet of examples, all you'll do is make the reader notice the dissimilarities and wonder just what you were thinking.

- ✔ **For the best appearance, design special text effects to work with other graphical elements.**

  If several items are slanted, for example, have them slant the same amount whether they're text or lines.

✔ **Pay attention to spacing. If text looks like a graphic, give it more space than you would if it looked like just a weird part of the text.**

A good rule to follow is to put minimal space around warped text if that text is meant to be read with other text. Drop caps, for example, should not be so far away from the rest of the paragraph that the reader doesn't realize that they are drop caps.

✔ **Conversely, don't position a graphic that's made of a symbol (such as a logo) so close to text that people try to read it as part of the text.**

The more different the warped text looks from the regular text, the easier it will be for the reader to know that the text is different, and you won't have to worry so much about spacing.

That's it! Congratulations! Manipulating text as art is the most difficult stuff because it requires an active imagination, an understanding of the tools in QuarkXPress (so that you can turn that imagination into reality), and patience in learning how to effectively apply these tools. Have fun!

Part IV
Going Long and Linking

The 5th Wave   By Rich Tennant

FLY-BY STATUS BAR HAT BANDS

In this part . . .

Did you know that you can create books using QuarkXPress? It's true. If your project has more than a dozen or so pages, there's no need to feel antsy about keeping track of figure numbers, table numbers, index entries — well, you get the idea. QuarkXPress handles all this drudge work for you. In fact, crafting long published works is a piece of cake. In this part, we not only show you how to put books together, we also tell you how to make lists, tables of contents, and indexes.

Chapter 16

Building Books and Standardized Layouts

In This Chapter

▶ Creating books

▶ Using master pages

▶ Using the book palette

▶ Numbering sections and chapters

*I*t's been said that each person has a book in them, waiting to be written. You may have several books — stories that are sometimes funny, sometimes serious — needing to be told. Or you may have a job that requires you to create highly structured, technical, or nonfiction books for a living.

Whatever the book you have inside you, QuarkXPress is a good tool to use when you're ready to bring your book from inside to out. This chapter describes features in QuarkXPress that are designed to help ease the process of getting books and other long print projects to look their best.

Planning Your Book

Whatever your dreams of writing the Great American Novel, a book is basically a collection of chapters. Each chapter is a separate layout, and you knit the chapters together into a whole book — mentally and physically.

In QuarkXPress, a book is also something more: It's a palette. To be precise, it's a book palette. Like other palettes in QuarkXPress, a *book palette* is a list of information displaying the chapters that make up the book.

Building a book isn't difficult, especially if you take it one step at a time. The following sections show you how to do it. But before exploring book palettes and how to use them, you need to do some planning. Here are some pointers to consider before you begin building a book in QuarkXPress:

✔ **Organize your chapters beforehand.** Start by outlining the book, either the old-fashioned way (with pencil and paper) or the modern way (on your computer).

✔ **Use style sheets to format the chapters uniformly as you write the book.** See Chapter 6 for more about style sheets.

✔ **Decide on the number, names, and order of the chapters.** You can make changes to a chapter's number, name, and order at any time, but figuring out these basics in advance can save you time in the long run.

✔ **Make decisions about the format of the book (style sheets, typeface, pagination style, and so on) at the chapter level, beginning with the first chapter.** Choosing the format is important because the work is smoother without style sheet conflicts and other inconsistencies.

After you write the chapters and are ready to assemble them, create a book palette (that we describe in the following sections) to combine the chapters into a book. After assembling the chapters, you can update the page numbers, create a table of contents, and create an index for the book (see Chapter 17).

Creating and Opening Books

To open a book palette and create a new book, choose File➪New➪Book (as shown in Figure 16-1). Like libraries, you can have multiple book palettes, and each has a name you provide.

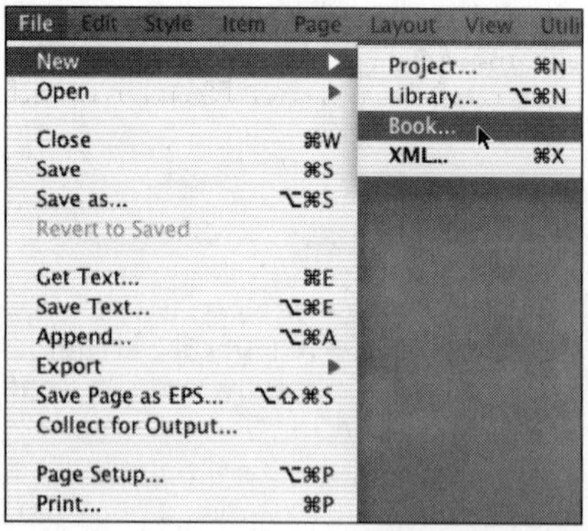

Figure 16-1: Creating a new book.

In Figure 16-2, you see a new, open book palette for a book we named *The Rattlesnake Book.* The upper part of Figure 16-2 also shows the controls that you use in the Add New Chapter dialog box to locate the chapters that you want to place in the book. To open an existing book palette, choose File⇨Open, the same as you would to open a layout or a library. To display the Add New Chapter dialog box, click the Book icon at the upper-left of the book palette.

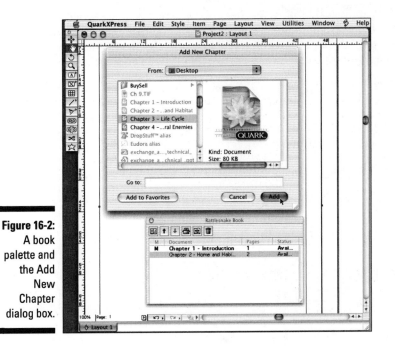

Figure 16-2:
A book palette and the Add New Chapter dialog box.

Working with master pages

When you're building a book, you're likely to want some elements repeated on multiple pages. For example, you may want a running head at the top, outer edge of every page to identify the book. Or you may want a page number to appear at the bottom of every page. Whenever you have elements that repeat on more than one page, you want to use master pages. A *master page* is a nonprinting page that automatically formats pages in a layout. A master page may contain such items as page numbers, headers, footers, and other elements that repeat on multiple pages throughout a layout.

Master pages aren't just for books — they're very handy for any type of document that has a standard layout, from textbooks to magazine articles, from manuals to newsletters. But they're *really* handy for books, since they let you ensure that text formatting is consistent across all chapters.

Open a master page by choosing Page⇨Display⇨A-Master A (as shown in Figure 16-3). To return to the layout page, choose Page⇨Display⇨Layout. You can tell that the master page is displayed if you see the icon for a chain link in the upper-left corner of the page.

On the master page in Figure 16-3, we created a text box and typed the running head *The Rattlesnake Book*. Now, whenever we use a new layout page that's based on the A-Master page, the running head appears. Of course, you can always decide to delete any master page item while you have the layout open.

In QuarkXPress 6, you work on one layout at a time — as if each layout is a separate document — and you can convert a layout to another form (different size, single-sided into two-sided or vice versa, Web to print, and print to Web) at almost any time (see Chapter 1). The exception? You can't change a layout from print to Web while that layout is included in a book. Note that although QuarkXPress 6 permits multiple layouts in a project file, project files that are brought into book palettes may contain only one print layout and no Web layouts.

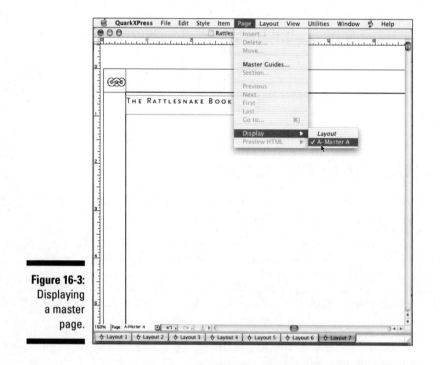

Figure 16-3:
Displaying a master page.

Working with master chapters

After you open a new book palette and list the book's first chapter, QuarkXPress treats that chapter as the master chapter. The *master chapter* contains attributes that all chapters of the book use. For example, let's say we decided to establish a spot color for *The Rattlesnake Book* running head in our book. If this spot color is in the master chapter, it will appear in all subsequent chapters of the book after you click the Synchronize button on the book palette. If you add the spot color to a chapter other than the master chapter, the color will appear only in that chapter, not throughout the book.

You can tell which chapter is the master chapter by looking for an *M* next to the chapter name in the book palette. In Figure 16-4, you can see an *M* next to Chapter 1, indicating that Chapter 1 is the first chapter we added and is, therefore, the master chapter. Note that QuarkXPress creates a master chapter even if you choose not to use master pages.

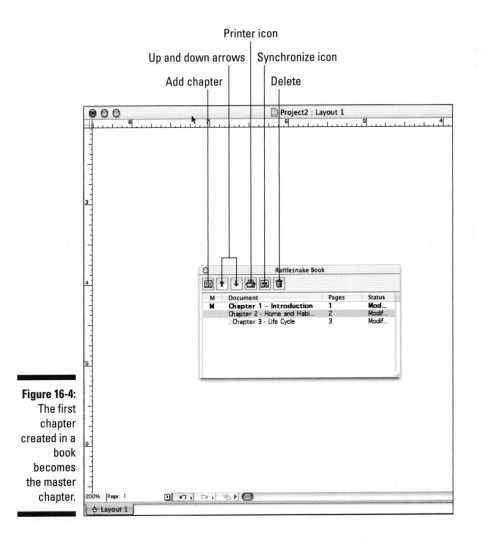

Figure 16-4:
The first chapter created in a book becomes the master chapter.

Making any chapter the master chapter is easy, so you're not stuck with the first chapter added to the book. To change the master chapter, just click to the left of the chapter name under the M column in the book palette. The *M* will move next to that newly chosen master chapter.

Adding, deleting, and moving layout pages

While building the chapters in a book, you may need to insert, delete, or move pages. To do any of these operations, you use the Page menu:

- ✔ To insert pages, choose Page➪Insert to display the Insert Pages dialog box.

- ✔ Deleting pages is a similar function. Choose Page➪Delete; a dialog box appears in which you're able to choose pages to delete.

- ✔ To move pages, choose Page➪Move to access a dialog box where you can specify which pages to move and the locations to move them to.

These page techniques work in any QuarkXPress project.

Navigating through a layout

As long layouts get longer, QuarkXPress offers a couple of quick and easy ways to navigate through their pages:

- ✔ One way is to enter the number of the page to which you want to go in the Page Number field on the left side of the bar below the layout page. QuarkXPress takes you directly to that page.

- ✔ Another option is to choose Page➪Go to or press ⌘+J or Ctrl+J, which displays the Go to Page dialog box.

If you simply want to get from the top to the bottom of a page, use the scroll bar at the right side of the layout window.

Using the Book Palette

In QuarkXPress, books are files that help you keep chapters organized. A book palette indicates the number of pages in each chapter and tells you the status of the chapters that you've added (as shown in Figure 16-5).

Figure 16-5:
A book
palette,
showing the
status of
individual
chapters.

Figure 16-5:
A book palette, showing the status of individual chapters.

A book palette indicates the status for each chapter:

- ✔ **Available:** You can open, edit, or print this chapter.

- ✔ **Open:** This chapter is currently open, and you can edit or print it. In Figure 16-5, Chapters 3 and 5 are open.

- ✔ **Modified:** This chapter has been changed since the last time the book palette was open on this computer. In Figure 16-5, Chapters 2 and 4 have this status.

- ✔ **Missing:** This chapter is unavailable to the book palette or cannot be located at this time.

Multiple users can open copies of the same book if the book is stored in a shared location on a server. Then book users can either *check out* chapters of the book (to edit the chapters over the network) or drag a copy of the chapter to their hard drives to edit it. In this case, if you're in a workgroup and want to prevent other people in your group from editing an original chapter while you're editing a copy of it, move the original chapter to a separate folder. If someone tries to edit the chapter, QuarkXPress lists it as Missing.

QuarkXPress offers another way to control access to your chapters, one that lets you make a chapter *read-only* (Mac) or *locked* (Windows). When a chapter in a book is in read-only or locked mode, edits can be made only from the computer where it was locked or changed to read-only mode. All the other computers on the network can display the chapter on-screen for reading purposes, but they can't make changes to the chapter.

Book palette control icons

The icons across the top of the book palette control the chapters in the book. In order from left to right, here's how the icons work:

- ✔ **To add chapters:** The first icon is the Add Chapter icon. After you click this icon, an Add New Chapter dialog box appears (refer to the upper dialog box in Figure 16-2) and lets you locate a chapter that you want to add to the book palette.

✔ **To rearrange chapters:** Use the icons with up arrows and down arrows to rearrange chapters within the book palette. (For example, to move Chapter 4 so that it follows Chapter 3, click Chapter 4 to select it and then click the down arrow to move it down a chapter.)

To speed things up, you can also move a chapter in the list by pressing the Option or Alt key and clicking and dragging the chapter up or down.

✔ **To delete chapters:** The icon of a small trash can (in Windows, the icon is a big *X*) is the Delete button. By highlighting one or more chapters and then by clicking this icon, the chapters are deleted from the book.

The file itself is not deleted; just the link that lists the file as a chapter in the book palette is deleted.

✔ **To print a chapter:** The icon that looks like a printer is the Print button.

✔ **To synchronize chapter formatting:** The icon with a left- and a right-pointing arrow is the Synchronize button. It lets you format the other chapters in the book so that they're consistent with the master chapter. (See the following section, "Synchronizing chapter formatting," for more information.)

Synchronizing chapter formatting

QuarkXPress lets you make *local changes* (changes that affect only the chapter you're working on) to chapters at any time, and then add, or *synchronize,* some or all the chapters in a book consistently. Synchronize chapters by using the Synchronize button on the book palette (the button with a left– and a right-pointing arrow; refer to Figure 16-5). When you synchronize chapters, QuarkXPress compares each chapter with the master chapter and then modifies the chapters as necessary so that they conform to the master chapter's colors, style sheets, hyphenation and justification (H&J) sets, lists, and so on.

The Append dialog box, which you open by choosing File⇨Append, lets you synchronize chapters (as shown in Figure 16-6) — and lets you pick and choose which elements you'd like to synchronize throughout your chapters. To select and synchronize an element, you simply highlight one or more of the items in the list on the left side of the Append dialog box and click the right-pointing arrow to move them to the list on the right side of the dialog box. When an item is in the right dialog box, it will be synched when you close the menu. If you want to synchronize all the modified items, just click the Synch All button at the bottom of the dialog box.

Don't worry about losing chapter-specific styles, colors, H&J sets, or other things when you synchronize chapters. Synchronizing only adds new styles or modifies existing styles. In other words, let's say Chapter 1 (the master chapter) has a style named Body and a style named Side Note, and Chapter 3 has a style named Body and a style named Caption. When you synchronize, Chapter 3's Body style is modified to match Chapter 1's version, Chapter 3 gains the Side Note Style used in Chapter 1, and the unique Caption style in Chapter 3 is unaffected.

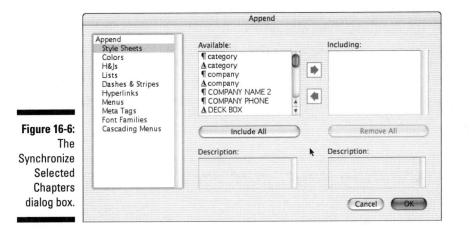

Figure 16-6:
The
Synchronize
Selected
Chapters
dialog box.

Printing chapters and books

In a book palette, the icon of a printer is the Print button. You click this icon to print either the entire book or selected chapters listed in a book palette. Chapters with a status of Missing or Modified won't print, and an error message notifies you of this situation. Following is a list of printing options:

- ✔ To print selected chapters, highlight the chapters that you want to print and click the Print icon. (Shift+click to select a range of chapters and ⌘+click or Ctrl+click to select noncontiguous chapters.) The Print dialog box appears, as shown in Figure 16-7. (To print the entire book, make sure that no individual chapter is highlighted when you click the Print icon.)

- ✔ To print all the pages in the selected chapters (or to print the entire book if no chapters are selected), choose All from the Pages pop-up menu at the top of the Print dialog box.

- ✔ To print a range of pages from selected chapters, choose Selected from the Pages pop-up menu and enter the page numbers.

- ✔ After entering your printing selections in the Print dialog box, click the Print button at the lower right (or press Return or Enter) to print the book or the selected chapters.

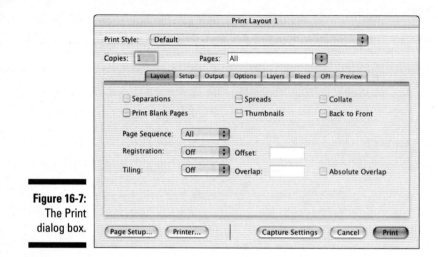

Figure 16-7:
The Print
dialog box.

Numbering pages and sections

In long layouts, dividing chapters into *sections* is not uncommon. For example, you may have a Chapter 2 with Sections 1, 2, and 3. QuarkXPress can help you paginate chapters that have sections. For example, you may want the pages in Section 2 of Chapter 2 to be numbered 2-2.1, 2-2.2, and so on. The following sections show you how this is done.

Creating a section

To create a section in a chapter, open the chapter and then choose Page⇨ Section to access the Section dialog box (as shown in Figure 16-8).

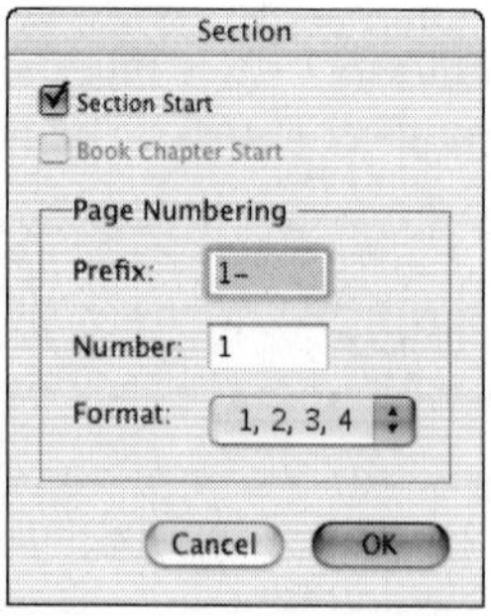

Figure 16-8:
The Section
dialog box.

TIP

Synchronizing chapters

Synchronizing chapters is a great idea if you have a long, involved book that you've worked on over several months (in which case you can easily make a paragraph style change in one chapter and forget to make the change in all other chapters).

Synchronizing is also a good idea if the project has several authors, any of whom may have made local changes without informing the entire group.

Suppose that you already specified Chapter 1 as the master chapter, but you really want to make the whole book look like Chapter 3. The book palette should first show an *M* to the left of the name of Chapter 1. Click to highlight Chapter 3 and then click the blank area to the left of the chapter name. Chapter 3 then becomes the new master chapter, and the *M* is now to the left of Chapter 3's name.

To paginate the pages in a section, do the following:

1. **In the Section dialog box, check Section Start to disable (uncheck) the Book Chapter Start option (which we describe in "Using the Book Chapter Start feature," later in this chapter.**

   After you add, delete, or rearrange pages or chapters, QuarkXPress paginates subsequent chapters with the settings in the Section dialog box.

2. **If you want, in the Page Numbering area of the Section dialog box, you can enter a page prefix up to four characters in length in the Prefix box.**

   For example, you may want to number the pages in an attachment as *Att-1, Att-2;* in this case, *Att* would be the prefix.

3. **In the Number box, type the page number that you want to assign to the first page of a new section.**

   The Number field requires Arabic numbers, regardless of the format of the section numbers; for example, if you're using lowercase Roman numerals for the front matter of a book and want the first page of the section to be page iii, type **3** in the Number field.

4. **Use the Format pop-up menu to select a style for page numbers in a section, and click OK once you've made your selections.**

   Choices include numeric (1, 2, 3, 4), uppercase Roman (I, II, III, IV), lowercase Roman (i, ii, iii, iv), uppercase alphabetic (A, B, C, D), and lowercase alphabetic (a, b, c, d).

In the book palette, an asterisk next to the numbers in the Pages field indicates chapters that contain section starts (beginnings of sections in a multi-section file).

Using the Book Chapter Start feature

If a chapter doesn't have sections, QuarkXPress considers it as having a *Book Chapter Start,* which is the default setting. After you check the Book Chapter Start box in the Section dialog box, QuarkXPress starts numbering the pages of a chapter after the last page of the preceding chapter. If the last page in a book's first chapter is page 15, for example, the first page in the second chapter is page 16. Here's the lowdown on the Book Chapter Start feature:

✔ Whenever you add a chapter without any sections to a book, QuarkXPress numbers pages sequentially throughout the book.

✔ As you add and delete pages from chapters, QuarkXPress also updates the page numbers.

Chapter 17

Making Lists and Indexes

Chances are, you know someone who is a *listmaker* (you know, the person who writes a list of everything to do today, tomorrow, and next week). Listmakers know that lists can help them keep information organized.

Lists, such as a table of contents, work well in publishing, too. In QuarkXPress, a list is actually nothing more than a compilation of paragraphs or text selections that are formatted with the same style sheet (paragraph or character style sheets). As you can imagine, lists are very handy for long documents.

After you create a book (or even a single layout), QuarkXPress can build a list by scanning the chapters for the style sheets that you specify. For example, if you create a book and have a style sheet that you apply to the figures in the layout, you can generate a list of those figures by asking QuarkXPress to list all the paragraphs that use the style sheet named *Figure.* The process that we describe in this chapter works for any kind of list you want to build in QuarkXPress, including tables of contents.

Planning a List

Before you start whipping up a list in QuarkXPress, you have some decisions to make. What will be the content of your list? Will your list include all the Heads and Subheads (indicated by their respective style sheets) in your layout? Or will the list include all the text in your Figure Title style sheet?

You need to be sure that style sheets are applied consistently to generate a list. If you're not sure, check the layouts. Chapter 6 explains how to create and apply style sheets.

Lists are linear, listing from top to bottom the text in the order it appears in a layout (or in alphabetical order). If your final list is not meant to be linear, the Lists feature may not be for you.

After you decide what you want in your list, use a little bit of dummy (or *placeholder*) text to format a sample list. Your formatting should include any indents for different levels in your list, and it should also include tabs and fill characters as necessary. When you're satisfied with the formatting of your sample list, create style sheets from it. Be sure to use clear names, such as TOC-Level 1.

Creating a list

In QuarkXPress, a list defines the text you want in a table of contents (or other list), what order it appears in, how page numbers are added, and how the list is formatted. Because you specify the list's final formatting through paragraph style sheets, it's best to create those style sheets before you define the list (as discussed in the preceding section). Here's how you create a list:

1. **To create a new list, choose Edit⇨Lists.**

   If you're working in a book, make sure you do this in the master chapter.

2. **Click New and enter an obvious name, such as** Table of Contents, **in the Name field.**

   The Edit List dialog box appears (as shown in Figure 17-1).

3. **To specify what text belongs in your list, click the first style sheet in the Available Styles list; then click the right arrow to transfer the style to the Styles in List area.**

   Although the Styles in List do not need to be in the same order as they will appear in your final list, it will be easier for you to decipher what's going on in the Edit List dialog box if you define them in that order. You can include up to 32 style sheets in a list, which should be plenty.

4. **For each style sheet you add to the list, choose an option from the Level menu to indicate its position in the list hierarchy.**

   For example, if you're including chapter heads, they might be level 1, and section heads might be level 2. QuarkXPress provides levels 1 (highest) to 8 (lowest).

5. **Use the Numbering menu to specify whether and how page numbers are listed for each item in the list.**

A traditional table of contents might use the Text...Page # option, but you may use Text Only for chapter names, so page numbers would not be listed for chapter introduction pages. You can also place page numbers prior to text in your list by choosing Page #...Text.

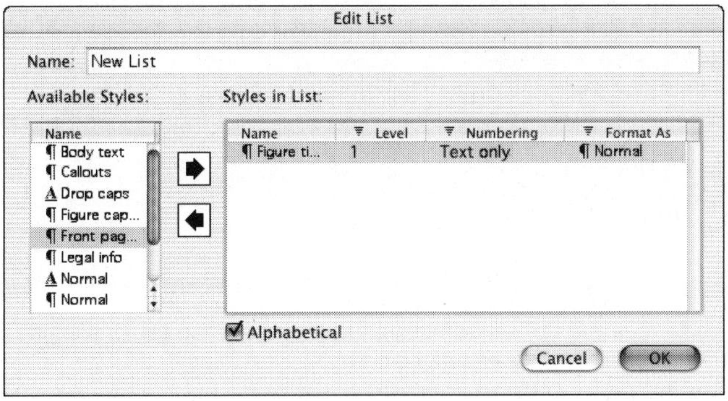

Figure 17-1:
The Edit List
dialog box.

6. **Use the Format As menu to select the paragraph style sheets to be applied to your formatted list.**

   For example, text in your Chapter Heads style sheet may be formatted with TOC-Level 1. It's through these paragraph style sheets that text in your list is formatted — if you don't select well-created paragraph style sheets, your list could end up making no sense.

7. **If you want the text in your list to be alphabetical (rather than sequential through the layout or book), check Alphabetical in the Edit List dialog box.**

   This step overrides any levels you've specified — you will not get alphabetical lists within each level.

8. **If you change your mind about including any styles in your list, select the style sheet and click the left-facing arrow to send that style back to the Available Styles area.**

9. **When you're satisfied with your list definition, click OK, then click Save.**

After you define a list, you can go to the Lists palette and display it. If you're working on a book and the list is not included in all the book's chapters, be sure to synchronize the chapters, as covered in the preceding chapter. This synchronization adds the lists from the master chapter to all other chapters.

Don't be surprised if you need to come back and edit your list — you may have included too much information to start with, resulting in a list that's too long, or you may not like the page numbering that you've selected. Using the Lists dialog box (Edit⇨Lists), you can always edit an existing list. (Again, if you're working in a book, synchronize to update the list throughout the chapters.)

Compiling a list

To view a list, you use the Lists palette (Window⇨Show Lists, or Option+F11 or Ctrl+F11), as shown in Figure 17-2. The Lists palette works as follows:

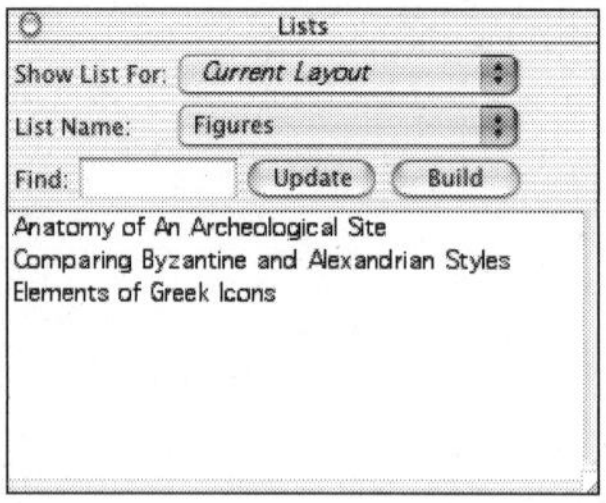

Figure 17-2:
The List
palette.

The Show List For menu lets you display a list for the current layout or for an entire book. (To create an accurate list for all the chapters in a book, all the chapters need to be available.)

The List Name menu shows all the lists you've created for the current layout. Pick one to display it. In the palette, QuarkXPress indents each level of your lists. Note that the list will only include the first 256 characters of a paragraph.

In a longer list, use the Find field to locate specific text within the list. All you have to do is type in the field to jump to the first instance of that text in the list.

Click the Update button any time you modify text in the layout, add new chapters to a book, modify your list definition, or make any other change that affects the content of your list. Lists don't update dynamically as you work.

Double-click any item in the list to jump to that location in the layout. If the location is in another chapter in a book, the chapter will be opened to that location (provided that the chapter is still available).

Flowing a formatted list

When the Lists palette is open, you can flow (or place) a formatted list, with up-to-date page numbers, into any selected text box. Before you do this:

Make sure that you've saved space in the layout for the list. This space should be a single text box or a series of linked text boxes. You can also use the automatic text box if you set Auto Page Insertion to End of Story in the General pane of the Preferences dialog box (choose QuarkXPress⇨ Preferences on the Mac or Edit⇨Preferences in Windows, or press

Option+Shift+⌘+Y or Ctrl+Alt+Shift+Y). When you're creating a table of contents for a book, it may be useful to flow the table of contents into its own chapter.

✓ **Click Update and then take a look at the Lists palette to make sure the list content looks right.** (If not, use the Edit➪Lists command to modify the list and fix any problems with style sheets incorrectly applied to text.) If you're working in a book, be sure all the chapters are available while updating and building your list. If you change the list definition at all, be sure to do so in the master chapter and to synchronize the book.

After you're satisfied with the contents of your list, select the Content tool and click in the text box where you want to place the list. On the Lists palette, click Build. If you want to apply any local formatting to the list, such as colors or typeface changes, be sure that you're working with the final version of the list or be prepared to apply that formatting again.

Make sure that you don't change page numbering when you flow your list. For example, if you add five pages to the beginning of a layout to hold a table of contents, the page numbers listed may be five pages off (if your pages are numbered sequentially). If you need to update page numbering after flowing a list, simply rebuild the list.

Updating and rebuilding a list

If you edit a layout after you build a list, be sure to update the list by clicking the Update button in the Lists palette. If you previously used the Build button, you need to use it again to replace the old list with the new, updated list.

Creating an Index

If you've ever had trouble finding information in a book, you can appreciate how important a good index can be. Indexing used to be a laborious process, involving lots of index cards. QuarkXPress makes indexing much easier, while still relying on you to make key decisions about formatting. The following sections show you how to do your part in creating an index.

Choosing an indexing style

Before you develop an index, you need to decide on the indexing style that you want to use. Large publishers usually have their own house style guides for indexes. One option is to use an index you like as a model and then take the steps necessary in QuarkXPress to achieve that index style. Before you begin indexing, ask yourself the following questions:

✔ Do you want to capitalize all levels of all entries, or do you just want to use initial caps?

✔ Should headings appear in boldface?

✔ Do you want to capitalize secondary entries in the index?

✔ Should the index be nested or run-in style? For examples of these indexes, check out the "Nested or run-in index?" sidebar, elsewhere in this chapter.

Setting index preferences

To index words in QuarkXPress, you *mark* the words that you want to use as index entries in the chapters of your book. These markers appear as colored brackets around the entry. The Index pane of the Preferences dialog box lets you choose the color of *index markings* (the markers that indicate text is part of the index) and the punctuation (called *separation characters*) used in your final, built index. Choose QuarkXPress⇨Preferences on the Mac or Edit⇨ Preferences in Windows, or press Option+Shift+⌘+Y or Ctrl+Alt+Shift+Y, to access the Index pane shown in Figure 17-3. The following sections explain the dialog box options.

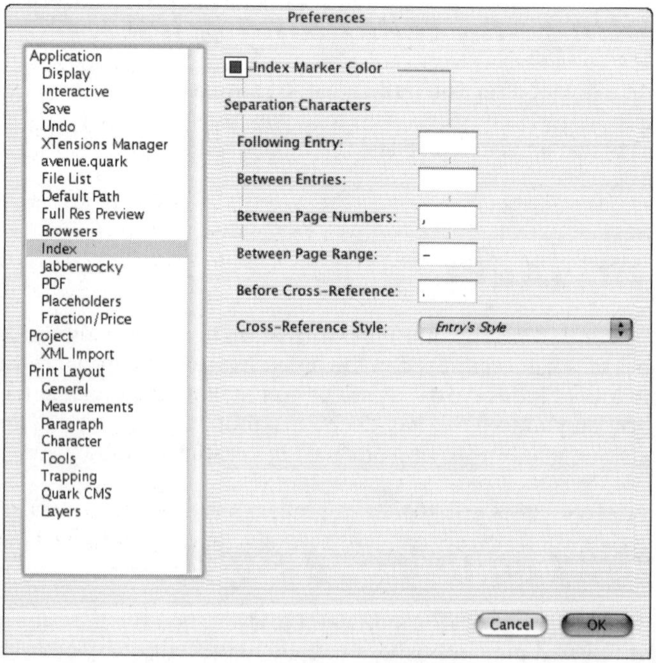

Figure 17-3:
The Index Preferences dialog box.

Changing the index marker color

To change the color of the index markers, click the Index Marker Color button in the Index pane; this action displays a color picker. Use the controls in the color picker to define the new color for index markers. Click OK to close the color picker and then click OK in the Index pane to complete the process.

Choosing separation characters

In the Index pane, you can also choose the characters and spaces that separate entries in the index. The options in the Separation Characters section of the pane work as follows:

- ✔ **Following Entry:** Defines the punctuation that immediately follows each index entry. This punctuation is usually a colon (:). For example, the index item *Santorini: vi, 14, 22–24* uses a colon and space following the index entry *Santorini*.

- ✔ **Between Page #s:** Defines the characters or punctuation that separates a list of page numbers. This punctuation is usually a comma (,) or semicolon (;). For example, the index item *Santorini: vi, 14, 22–24* uses a comma and a space between its page numbers.

- ✔ **Between Page Range:** Defines the characters or punctuation that indicates a range of pages. This option is usually the word *to* or a dash. For example, the index item *Santorini: vi, 14, 22 to 24* uses the word *to* between the numbers, indicating a range of pages.

- ✔ **Before Cross-Reference:** Defines the characters or punctuation that appears before a cross-reference. This option is usually a period and space, or a semicolon. For example, the index item *Santorini: vi, 14, 22–24. See also Ancient Thira* uses a period and space before the cross-reference.

- ✔ **Cross-Ref Style:** Specifies a default style sheet for cross-references in your index. For example, if you'd like to use the same style sheet for your cross-references that you used for your body copy, you can choose the style sheet for your body copy in the pop-up menu provided.

- ✔ **Between Entries:** Defines the characters or punctuation between entry levels in a run-in index. This option is usually a period or a semicolon. For example, the index item *Santorini: vi, 14, 22–24; Thira: 19* uses a semicolon between entry levels.

If you are new to indexing, you may want to create a few lines of a sample index to determine your index preferences. As with lists, if the first index you generate doesn't work for you, you can easily change settings and try again.

Nested or run-in index?

Index style is a matter of personal taste, but common sense should be a guide. Determine which index format you use by the number of levels in the index's hierarchy. If the index has only two levels, a run-in format works well, but an index with three or more levels requires a nested format for the sake of clarity.

Nested indexes look like this:

Crete

    beaches, 191

    climate, 242–248

    Cretan caves 92–94, 96, 99–101

    festivals, 275–284

    hotels, 180–195

    map, 91

    restaurants, 196–199

    vernacular architecture 282–283

Run-in indexes look like this:

Crete: Beaches, 191; Climate, 242–248; Cretan caves 92–94, 96, 99–101; Festivals, 275–284; Hotels, 180–195; Map, 91; Restaurants, 196-199; Vernacular architecture 282–283

Although QuarkXPress doesn't force you to make this decision until you actually build the index, you really need to make it before you get started. If you tag words for a four-level index but then build a run-in index, your index will have some logic problems.

Using the Index palette

When your layout is ready to index, open the Index palette by choosing Window⇨Show Index, or by pressing Option+⌘+I or Ctrl+Alt+I. Use this palette to add words to the index in as many as four indent levels, to edit or delete index entries, or to create cross-references. The Index palette appears in Figure 17-4.

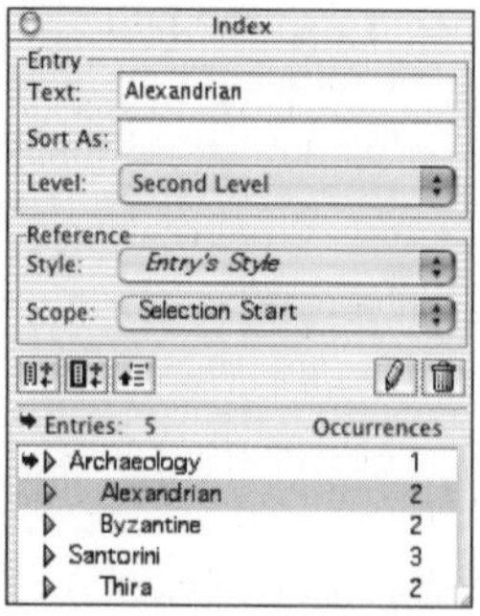

Figure 17-4: The Index palette.

The controls in the Index palette include the following:

✓ **Text:** The Text field in the Entry section of the Index palette is where you type in an index entry or where the text appears that you tagged with index markers. If you highlight text in an open layout when the Index palette is open, the first 255 characters of the highlighted text appear automatically in the Text field (saving you the effort of typing) and are ready to be captured as an index entry.

You can automatically reverse the order of text in the Text field as you add it to the index. For example, you can change *Byzantine Icons* to *Icons, Byzantine*. All you need to do is press the Option or Alt key while you click the Add button or the Add All button.

✓ **Sort As:** Entries in the Sort As field override the default, alphabetical sorting of the index entry. For example, you may want *16-day tour* to be indexed as if the entry appeared as *Sixteen-day tour;* you can accomplish this task by entering the spelling **Sixteen-day tour** into the Sort As field.

✓ **Level:** This pop-up menu lets you control the order and structure of index entries.

✓ **Style:** The Style pop-up menu (within the Reference section of the palette) lets you apply a character style to the page numbers for the current index entry or cross-reference. One example of how you may want to use this option is with a cross-reference like "See also *Cycladic art*" where you want to use an italicized character type for the words *Cycladic art.*

✓ **Scope:** This pop-up menu in the Reference section lets you control the scope, or range, of the index. For example, you can use it to:

• Make an entry a cross-reference

• List an entry as covering a specific number of paragraphs

• Suppress the printing of the entry's page number (for example, if the entry is a cross-reference to another entry).

✓ **Add button:** This button lets you add an entry to the index.

✓ **Add All button:** If you have more than one occurrence of an index entry, this button lets you add all occurrences of that entry to the index simultaneously.

✓ **Find Next Entry button:** This button finds the next occurrence of an index entry in the active layout.

✓ **Edit button:** You can edit an active index entry by clicking the Edit button (pencil icon) or by double-clicking the entry name.

✓ **Delete button:** You can delete a selected entry by clicking the Delete button (trash can icon on the Mac or the big *X* icon in Windows). If you delete an entry, its subentries are deleted as well.

Creating an index entry

To create an index entry, highlight the text that you want to use for the index entry. (Don't highlight the whole area that you want the index entry to reference; just highlight the word that you want to appear in the index.) Then click the Add button in the Index palette to add the index entry to the list by using the currently selected values in the Entry and Reference areas. When you add index entries, make sure that the capitalization of the words in the Text field matches the style of your index. QuarkXPress does not automatically capitalize (or lowercase) words in your index.

Editing an index entry

To edit an index entry, you must first select it in the Index palette and then go into editing mode; you can either double-click the index entry, or you can click the index entry and then click the Edit button. You can select an entry and make changes to the Entry and Reference areas, but unless you go into editing mode first, you're only changing the settings that will be used when you create the *next* index entry.

Creating page-number references

Each index entry includes a reference. A reference usually consists of the page number(s) to which the entry refers, but it may also be a cross-reference. To see the page number reference (or cross-reference) for an index entry, click the icon to the left of the entry in the lower section of the Index palette.

Creating cross-references

Cross-references enhance an index because they give the reader another way to find pertinent information. The following steps show you how to add a cross-reference to an indexed entry:

1. **If you're creating a new index entry, highlight the text and make sure that the Text, Sort As, and Level field settings are set as you would like them to be.**

   If you're adding a cross-reference to an existing entry, click on that entry in the index to place its information in the Text field.

2. **Choose Scope⇨Cross-Reference. Then choose an option from the pop-up menu: See, See Also, or See Herein (as shown in Figure 17-5).**

   Use See to point readers to the appropriate index entry; use See Also to point the readers to additional useful information elsewhere in the index; use See Herein to point readers to a subentry for this index entry.

3. **To point readers to another index entry, you have two choices: You can type an index entry's text in the field, or you can click on an existing entry in the Index palette.**

If the entry you're referencing is in another chapter, you have no choice but to enter its text in the field. You may want to refer to the other chapter to make sure that you get the wording exactly right.

4. **Within your cross-reference, you can change the formatting of the text for the referenced index entry.** For example, if your cross-reference is *See also Greek icons,* you can change the formatting of *Greek icons* to italics. A setting in the Index preferences pane controls the default character style sheet applied to cross-reference text, but you can change it by selecting an option from the Style menu.

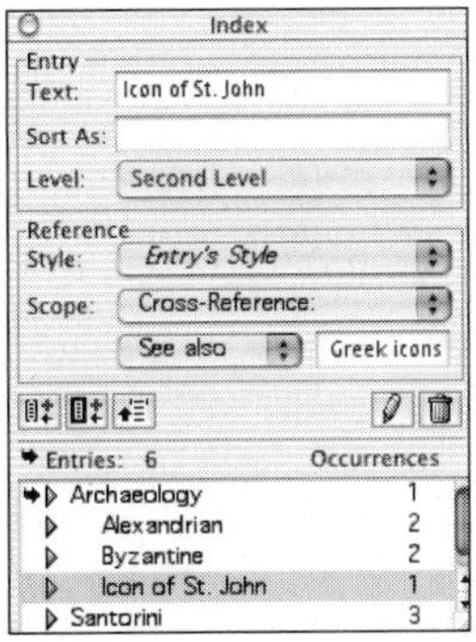

Figure 17-5:
In this example, we cross-reference the index entry *Icon of St. John* to *Greek icons.*

5. **From the See pop-up menu, choose an option (See, See Also, or See Herein) to govern how the cross-reference appears under the index entry.**

In Figure 17-5, for the index entry *Icon of St. John,* we have a cross-reference to *Greek icons.*

Using index levels

QuarkXPress supports four levels of indexing. The most important thing to remember about creating a level-two, level-three, or level-four index entry is that you must tell QuarkXPress where to put it — that is, you must indicate a higher-level index entry for the subentry to fall under. You provide a higher-level index entry by using the arrow column at the left edge of the index entry list at the bottom of the Index palette. Follow these steps to create a level-two entry to an existing level-one entry:

1. **Select the text that you want to add.**

2. **In the arrow column, click next to the level-one entry under which you want the new entry listed.**

3. **Choose Second Level from the Level pop-up menu in the Entry area.**

4. **Click the Add button to add the new entry.**

Building an index

To build an index from a list that you generate in the Index palette, choose Utilities⇨Build Index to open the Build Index dialog box, as shown in Figure 17-6. This command is available only when the Index palette is open.

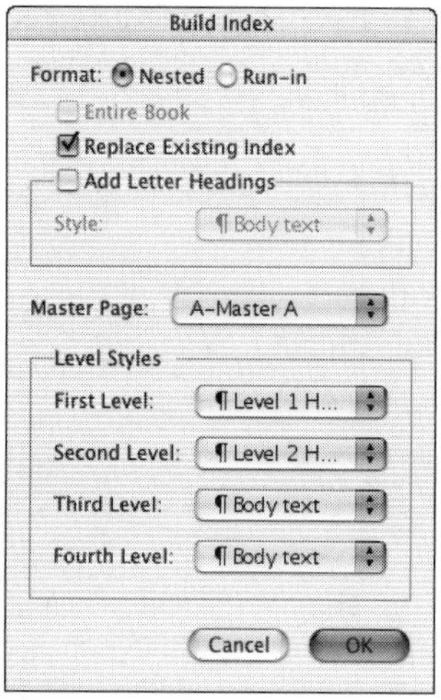

Figure 17-6:
The Build
Index
dialog box.

The options in the Build Index dialog box work as follows:

- ✔ **Choosing a nested or run-in index:** Your first decision is whether the index is nested or run-in. (See the "Nested or run-in index?" sidebar, elsewhere in this chapter, to help you make a decision.)

- ✔ **Building an index for an entire book:** The Build Index dialog box lets you build an index for the entire book rather than for just the open chapter. You select this option by clicking the Entire Book box.

- ✔ **Replacing an existing index:** Indexing is an iterative process, and you'll probably want to build an index a few times through the course of a book project. When you click Replace Existing Index in the Build Index dialog box, QuarkXPress overwrites the existing index with the most current version.

- ✔ **Adding letter headings:** In long indexes, you may want to divide the index alphabetically so all the index entries that begin with *A* are in a category with the heading *A,* for example. Check Add Letter Headings to use this feature. You can select a paragraph style sheet for the letter headings from the Style pop-up menu.

✓ **Basing an index on a master page:** The Master Page pop-up menu lets you select a master page on which to base the index page. For long indexes, you should consider developing a master page just for that purpose. See Chapter 16 for more about master pages.

✓ **Choosing level styles:** The Level Styles pop-up menus let you choose the paragraph style sheet(s) you want to apply to the various index levels. If you select the run-in format, all the index levels flow into one paragraph so that only the First Level pop-up menu is available. If you select the nested format, make sure that you specify indentation values for the index level styles that you choose.

After you make your choices in the Build Index dialog box, create the index by clicking OK or pressing Return or Enter.

Part V
Taking QuarkXPress to the Web

The 5th Wave   By Rich Tennant

Okay, enlarge the chicken bone by 900 percent and attach it to an e-mail to the museum saying, "Getting close...send more money."

In this part . . .

Publishing pages on the Web is a relatively new frontier for publishers, but the challenges of creating material that is useful, legible, and interesting is the same online as it is in print. QuarkXPress is up for the challenge. In this part, we explain some of the basics you need to know to publish in this medium. We also show you some new QuarkXPress Web features and give you tips on how and when to use them. Then we give you pointers on how to get those nicely designed pages up on the Web.

Chapter 18

Web Projects: An Overview

In This Chapter

▶ HTML basics

▶ Differences between print and Web layouts

▶ Connecting ideas together with hyperlinks

▶ HTML terms that you need to know

▶ Creating a Web page

▶ Choosing a layout for your Web page

▶ Using Web tools and features in QuarkXPress

QuarkXPress is known for its precision and flexibility. And it should be. After all, it can adjust the leading in a paragraph to within $\frac{1}{1000}$ of a point — and it can do so by using inches, picas, ciceros, centimeters, or agates as a measuring system.

For now, forget about all that stuff because now we're going to show you how to use QuarkXPress 6 to build Web pages, and a lot of the regular QuarkXPress rules don't apply. Many of the features that work with print layouts don't work quite the same as they do with Web layouts, or they don't work at all. This is especially important if you already have some experience in print design because in the world of Web design, you will not have the same extraordinary degree of control over your design.

Web Layouts and Projects

QuarkXPress 6 integrates print and Web layouts into a single file called a *project*. Web and print layouts within the same project can share text. With the new Synchronize Text feature, the program can automatically synchronize edits between print and Web layouts, updating the written content of your project while you work.

The differences between QuarkXPress Web and print layouts stem from the internal construction of the layouts themselves:

🖊 Print layouts are built with sophisticated programming languages, including PostScript, that precisely output print layouts to your screen and to your printer.

🖊 Web layouts are built with a language called *Hypertext Markup Language (HTML),* which can be interpreted and displayed differently by the computer of every person who visits your Web page. Simply, HTML lacks the exacting precision of PostScript. But do not fear, because QuarkXPress 6 uses several methods to keep text and pictures lined up on your Web page. The one exception to this: Text wraps are almost impossible to control in HTML.

HTML: The lingua franca of the Web

HTML is the native tongue of the Web. All Web pages are founded in HTML, and they are completely free of computer platform restraints. Despite what you may think, HTML is a pretty simple computer language to master, and no special applications or tools are needed to write the HTML code for Web pages. If you had a mind to, you could buy a beginner's guide to HTML and start composing your first Web page in any text editor or word processing program, such as Mac OS X's TextEdit, Windows' WordPad, or Microsoft Word. Figure 18-1 shows a page being produced in TextEdit.

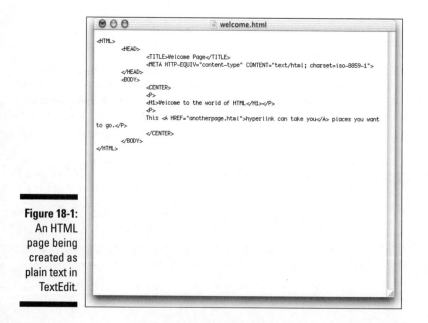

Figure 18-1:
An HTML page being created as plain text in TextEdit.

Browsing through the browsers

After you create your HTML page, you can view it on virtually every computer platform as long as you have a monitor and browser (as shown in Figure 18-2). No doubt you've got the monitor part down, but even creating a simple page can be exciting when you craft it from raw code.

Figure 18-2:
Figure 18-1 when viewed in a Web browser with a hyperlink in the second line.

HTML and QuarkXPress

Right about now, you're probably thinking, "This is all fine and good, but I think this HTML programming stuff looks complicated. And what the #$% does QuarkXPress have to do with all this?" Good question. You don't need to know squat about HTML or programming to create a basic Web page in QuarkXPress (although it doesn't hurt).

Don't plan on using QuarkXPress all by itself to produce highly sophisticated Web sites. QuarkXPress lets you create Web pages in a WYSIWYG (What You See Is What You Get) environment, so you'll never really see those little brackets and codes shown in Figure 18-1. This is great if you have simple Web publishing needs or are nervous about HTML, but the tools here are not robust enough to handle full-blown Web production, where getting your fingers into the underlying code is essential. Other products, such as Adobe GoLive or Macromedia Dreamweaver, are much more appropriate for serious Web development.

If you're interested in Web production and willing to give it a try, QuarkXPress offers a quick and easy way to build Web pages that you can publish on the Internet.

Just remember that a QuarkXPress Web layout is simply a WYSIWYG view of pages and pages of HTML code, and it's the HTML code that the Web browser uses to display a Web page. The basic process for creating Web pages to be seen by anyone on the Internet requires three steps in QuarkXPress:

1. **Design your page in a Web layout in QuarkXPress.**

   This chapter shows you how to design Web pages in QuarkXPress.

2. **Output, or *export*, the Web layout to HTML files.**

   With Chapter 19, you're a QuarkXPress export maven.

3. **Copy, or *upload*, the exported HTML files to a Web server.**

   Again, Chapter 19 is your one-stop resource.

When you complete all three steps, everyone can see your Web page with a Web browser.

With the exception of some Web-specific tools and a slightly modified layout display, creating Web layouts in QuarkXPress is nearly identical to creating print layouts. In fact, the only reason why we bring up these HTML basics at all is because they help you understand some of the obvious differences that you'll encounter when creating a Web layout, as opposed to a print layout, in QuarkXPress.

These are the most glaring differences and limitations that you'll run across:

- ✔ **Measurements:** Obviously, print and Web layouts serve two entirely different purposes. As a result, the two use different types of measurements. When you build a Web layout, you use pixels instead of inches or centimeters.

  - A width of 600 to 800 pixels is a good size for a Web layout; this width can be accommodated on a majority of computer screens.

  - The *length, or height,* of a Web page isn't really a factor. Because most browsers have scroll bars on their windows, the length of a Web page could conceivably run on for hundreds of feet.

  QuarkXPress limits the vertical length (height) of your Web layout workspace to 3,450 pixels (or 48 inches), like how it limits print layouts.

- ✔ **Fonts:** When you view a Web layout on your computer's browser, 99 out of a 100 times it looks fine because you are building it on *your* computer with *your* fonts. When someone in Saltlick, USA, opens it on another computer, the fonts used with your Web page may be totally replaced with an entirely different set of fonts at different sizes.

Build your Web layouts with a small palette of fonts (Arial, Verdana, Times New Roman, and Georgia are Web favorites). This increases the chances that other systems will have the same fonts as yours.

✔ **Graphics:** 72 dpi (dots per inch; the universal screen resolution) JPEG and GIF files are the standard graphics for Web pages instead of EPS and TIFF files. JPEG and GIF are recognized by browsers because of their inherently small file size, which saves a lot of download time.

Don't panic if you're copying high resolution EPS or TIFF images from a print layout to a Web layout; QuarkXPress will convert them to JPEG or GIF for you automatically.

✔ **Layout:** In Web layouts, tables are used differently than in print layouts. Most often, tables are used in Web layouts as a layout tool for pictures and text — much like how text and picture boxes are used on the print side. In fact, after you build your Web layout in QuarkXPress and you prepare to upload it to the Web (a topic that we cover in Chapter 19), QuarkXPress converts your text and picture boxes to HTML tables — most of which look more like asymmetric rat nests than traditional charts.

✔ **Page numbering:** Traditional page numbering is not used in Web layouts. Although you can insert any number of pages in a QuarkXPress Web layout, there's no implied connection or sequence to those pages. After all the pages in your Web layout are completed, rounded up, and stored in a folder together, they are connected to each other with hyperlinks in whatever order you've chosen with the Hyperlinks palette.

Getting around with hyperlinks

A *link* (short for hyperlink) is an item embedded in an HTML page that you can click to perform a specific action, such as going to another HTML page, either within your Web site or on a different Web site. Hyperlinks can be used to perform all sorts of functions, including accessing an e-mail address or downloading a music or picture file. These clickable items can be a word or phrase, a picture (normally referred to as a *hot spot*), or even an isolated area in a page or picture. You create hyperlinks by choosing Style➪Hyperlinks➪New.

Unlike the other Web layout tools in QuarkXPress, the Hyperlinks palette is available when a print layout is open, too, because hyperlinks also work with Portable Document Format (PDF) files. At least they do when the page is being displayed onscreen. So you may want to apply hyperlinks to a print layout if you plan on also saving it as a PDF file to be opened in Adobe Acrobat.

If you refer to Figure 18-2, you see we already created our first hyperlink: namely, the phrase <u>hyperlink can take you</u>. You know it's a hyperlink because it's underlined and a different color than the rest of the text. To give you an idea of how hyperlinks work, we've created a second page entitled Just Another Web Page (see Figure 18-3) that is linked to that hyperlink on the Welcome to the World of HTML page. If you look closely at the HTML code back in Figure 18-1, you'll see that the hyperlink in that code links to `anotherpage.html`. The browser interprets the HTML code to display the hyperlink in blue and underlined. When you click the Back button of the browser toolbar shown in Figure 18-3, you return immediately to the original page.

Figure 18-3:
When you click the link, the linked page takes its place.

Other Web-related definitions

After you've mastered hyperlinks, you can get pretty far in the Web world. You should also be familiar with several phrases and acronyms if you want to get serious about creating professional Web pages. Several are listed below:

✔ **URL (Uniform Resource Locator):** Most people refer to this as a *page's address*. The URL of a page appears in a field at the top of the window of most browsers (as shown in Figure 18-4). In Internet Explorer, this field is the Address field. In Netscape Communicator, it is the Web Site field. URLs usually begin with `http://` and end with an extension like `.com`, `.net`, `.org`, or something similar. If the address is for a specific page instead of a site, it will end in `.html` or `.htm`. You may also encounter sites that start with `https://`. The *s* stands for secure, meaning that hackers cannot easily penetrate it.

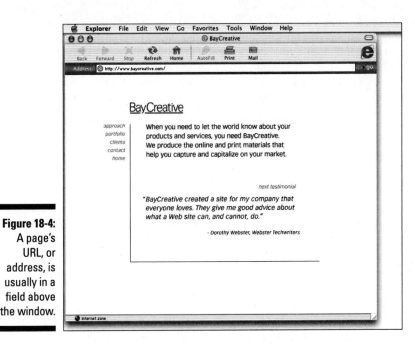

✔ **Meta tags:** *Meta tags* are nothing more than a fancy way of saying "notes from the author to other Web masters and search engines." Meta tags let the designer of the page provide information about the page so that search engines can index it and browsers can display it correctly. Meta tags usually include such specifications as the name of the author, the subject of the page, and the language that the page should be displayed in (such as English, Russian, or Japanese). ***Remember:*** It is the *World Wide* Web.

The most important use of meta tags is identifying words that describe the content of the page, thus making it easier for others to find the page via a search engine. In QuarkXPress, meta tags are entered in the Meta Tags dialog box found in the Edit menu.

People viewing the Web site in their browsers cannot see meta tags unless they view the Web page's *source code,* which is a standard menu option in most Web browsers. Viewing the source code is a bit like peeking behind the curtain, and it can be very helpful if you want to know more about a Web page than what is displayed in your browser window. Although beginners may not care about the complex-looking HTML code, viewing the source can be one of the fastest ways to learn more about meta tags and to see how HTML works.

✔ **Site navigation:** Just like it is helpful to have a means of getting your bearings in a fluid environment — like using a compass while sailing a ship — a dependable means of navigation is exceedingly helpful in the fluid realm of the Web. Unlike the numbered, bound pages of a book, the pages of a Web site can be linked together in any manner that you choose. Because of this, visitors to your Web site will thank you if you provide them with a consistent way of getting around. Although it may sound simple, nothing more than including a hyperlink that appears on every page that links back to your home page can have a very comforting effect on visitors to your site. The best way to understand how to create good site navigation is to go visit lots of other Web sites and see how their creators do it. There are no specific rules for building a Web site's navigation except that consistency is generally rewarded with happy, returning visitors.

✔ **Rollover:** One of the coolest things about Web pages is that they can be designed to be interactive, and one of the most common of these interactive features is the rollover. In HTML, a *rollover* is a picture (usually text saved as a JPEG or GIF) that changes color or appearance when you move the mouse pointer over it. Rollovers are easy to create in QuarkXPress. We show how to make rollovers later in this chapter.

✔ **Two-position rollover:** A neat bit of HTML magic, the *two-position rollover* lets you affect a graphic on one part of the page when you move your mouse over another part. It's kind of like a remote-control rollover.

✔ **Image map:** As we mention in the earlier "Getting around with hyperlinks" section, different areas of a picture on a Web page can be given different hyperlinks. The sum of these hyperlinks on a single image is an *image map*.

✔ **Forms:** *Forms* are those parts of Web pages, frequently found on e-commerce sites, that have information fields where site visitors can enter personal information, such as a credit card number, an e-mail address, and a shipping address.

✔ **Cascading menus:** You can create menus similar to the drop-down menus used in most operating systems and applications. The menus can even contain submenus. The advantage of cascading menus is that they take up very little space on the Web page, yet they can give the visitor to your Web site a very comprehensive way of getting to the information that they want with just a click or two.

✔ **CSSs (cascading style sheets):** This refers to the way that fonts on your Web pages can be specified so that they most closely approximate your original design. The *cascading* part refers to the way that CSSs begin with the desired font and then fall back on second and third font choices if the desired font can't be found on the computer that is displaying your Web page.

✔ **Live text:** As we show later in this chapter, QuarkXPress can transform your carefully created print designs into Web pages. To do this, the program can either create live text that flows as a Web page is resized, or it can create a static graphic image of the text that looks almost exactly like the original but does not flow. A great deal of the Web's value lies in its ability to move information around into different formats. When you're converting print layouts into Web pages, you want to decide which is more important: to create live text that can flow but which lacks the finer points of typographic control; or to create graphical representations of text that are less flexible but more true to your design.

Creating a Web page

Aside from a small list of differences, building a Web page is very much like building a QuarkXPress print layout. You create the layout (using such elements as text boxes, picture boxes, and lines) and then you export it. Exporting a Web page to HTML is just like outputting a print page to a printer, but as you can imagine, outputting a Web document differs quite a bit from outputting a print document. With a few exceptions, you even use the same tools to create a QuarkXPress Web page. As for HTML code (refer to Figure 18-1), you cannot see or edit it in QuarkXPress, but you can open, view, and edit it with just about any text editor after exporting the page.

If you want to connect a series of Web pages together as a site, one approach is to first design the text and images and then add the site navigation and hyperlinks. This way, you can break the tasks into two areas: designing the pages and creating interactivity for the Web. This approach is easy to follow in QuarkXPress because hyperlinks can be added to images and text at any time.

When you create a Web layout in QuarkXPress, you find tools, palettes, and dialog boxes for creating Web-specific features such as forms, pop-up menus, rollovers, and scrollable lists. Here's a complete rundown.

QuarkXPress 6 creates files called *projects* that can contain both print and Web layouts. You create a QuarkXPress Web page layout in the same way that you create a QuarkXPress print layout:

1. **Choose File➪New➪Project.**
2. **Choose Web from the Layout Type pop-up menu to make a new Web layout.**

The New Project dialog box is shown in Figure 18-5. This dialog box doesn't share any of the print layout options except page width; don't worry; it's actually easy to configure.

```
                        New Project

Layout Name:  [ Layout 1                    ]
Layout Type:  [ Web                       ◆]

  ┌ Colors ──────────────────┐  ┌ Layout ──────────────┐
  │                          │  │                       │
  │ Background: [☐ White   ◆]│  │ Page Width: [ 600 px ◆]│
  │                          │  │                       │
  │ Link:       [■ Blue    ◆]│  │ ☑ Variable Width Page │
  │                          │  │                       │
  │ Visited Link:[■ Web Purple ◆]│ Width:   [ 100%      ]│
  │                          │  │                       │
  │ Active Link:[■ Red     ◆]│  │ Minimum: [ 300 px    ]│
  └──────────────────────────┘  └───────────────────────┘

  ☐ Background Image: [                    ]   ( Select... )

  Repeat:          [ None          ◆]

                                      ( Cancel )  ( OK )
```

Figure 18-5:
The New Project dialog box for a Web layout.

Colors

The first area in the New Project dialog box is the Colors section. This is where you choose the default colors for several of the items in your Web page. They are as follows:

✔ **Background:** Use this pop-up menu to pick the background of your Web layout. You may want to choose a background color before you choose a text color because the color of your text will depend largely on the color of the background.

✔ **Link:** Use this pop-up menu to decide the color of your hyperlinks.

This color applies to text hyperlinks only. Image maps remain invisible.

✔ **Visited Link:** It's a good idea to choose a different color for hyperlinks that have already been clicked, or *visited*. That way, visitors know that they've already been there. You can choose any color from this pop-up menu, although we recommend that you use a lighter shade of the color that you choose from the Link pop-up menu. This lighter shade gives the visited link a *grayed-out* appearance, thus making it easier for visitors to make the association between the visited links and the unvisited ones.

✔ **Active Link:** Use this pop-up menu to choose a color for the link that you're currently visiting. This may sound a bit ridiculous at first. After all, you just clicked the link that got you where you are now. You should have no trouble remembering which one it is, right? The active link color is visible during the moment that people click their mouse buttons, which provides a nice bit of feedback that their clicks have selected the link.

About colors on the Web

When you open the pop-up menus in the New Project dialog box, QuarkXPress offers a nice palette of colors for you to work with, just in case you aren't ready to make your own color choices yet. But if you want to dive right in and pick your own colors, choose Other from any of the pop-up menus in the Color area; this opens the Edit Color dialog box where you'll find all your favorite color-matching systems in the Model pop-up menu. Ignore these systems; they won't do you any good on a Web page because they're for print layouts. Monitors don't bother matching colors like printers do; they just display whatever equivalent is at hand — and in many instances, that color won't be the same as the color that you picked.

Instead, choose the Web-safe color palette at the bottom of the Model list. These colors have been created specifically for Web pages. The naming is a little weird; blues, for example, have bland tags like #000066 and #0033CC. Unfortunately, this is how HTML codes refer to colors. If the numbers really freak you out, try the Web Named Colors palette. This palette isn't nearly as extensive as the Web-safe palette, but the names are much more user-friendly. Some are even kind of cute. How do PeachPuff and PapayaWhip grab you?

Layout

The Layout section of the New Project dialog box lets you decide the width of your Web page. There is no default measurement for height because there is no need for one. Theoretically, a Web page can be any vertical height; however, QuarkXPress limits the height of Web layouts to 3,450 pixels (or 48 inches), just like it does for print layouts. QuarkXPress automatically increases the height of the white "live" area to accommodate your design while you build down the page. Here is a rundown of the choices in the Layout section:

✔ **Page Width:** The width choices in this section are very limited, for good reason. Even though Web browsers have both horizontal and vertical scroll bars, most people find it annoying to scroll from left to right while reading a Web page, particularly if they're already scrolling from top to bottom. So QuarkXPress limits your width options to four choices to fit your Web page inside the standard widths of most monitor screens on the market:

- 600 pixels (px)
- 800 px
- 1,024 px
- 1,268 px

We recommend that you use either 600 px or 800 px to ensure that people with smaller (less that 17-inch) monitors can read the full width of your page. The larger settings are for wide-screen monitors.

✔ **Variable Width Page:** To make the page a *variable* width page — that is, one that expands or contracts to fit the width of the reader's Web browser — check the Variable Width Page check box and then enter values in the following fields:

✔ **Width:** Specify here the percentage of the viewable browser area that the page will occupy.

✔ **Minimum:** Specify here a minimum page width. If the reader's browser window is smaller than this width, items will stop being resized.

The minimum setting is a great fix for readers with many varying monitor widths, with a couple of exceptions:

- This feature is not compatible with all Web browsers, particularly older versions.

- If the reader's monitor is much larger than your specified page width, the page will stretch to fit the larger monitor. In the process, it may take on a lopsided look.

Test your Web page designs on many different browsers to get an idea of how it will look after it is released "into the wild."

Background

The last choices in the New Project dialog box configure the background of your Web page. One of the neat (or sometimes, not-so-neat) features of HTML is its ability to change a graphic into a wallpaper-like background for your Web page. If used wisely, this wallpaper effect can add depth and dimension to a Web page; more often, these backgrounds are annoying and interfere with the rest of your layout.

This isn't the same as the Background pop-up menu in the Colors section.

Figure 18-6 shows two examples of this background effect: a high and a low contrast background. Note how a low contrast background makes reading text much easier.

Fortunately, the tiled background (left side of Figure 18-6, where the image is repeated in the background) isn't the only option offered. From the Repeat pop-up menu, you can choose to repeat the image either vertically or horizontally.

To use a background image, we recommend the following steps. This process creates a background image that bleeds on all four sides of the Web browser.

1. **Create a very large, very light image.**

2. **In the New Project dialog box, check the Background Image check box and then click the Select button.**

3. **Locate and select the background image that you created.**

4. **Select None from the Repeat pop-up menu.**

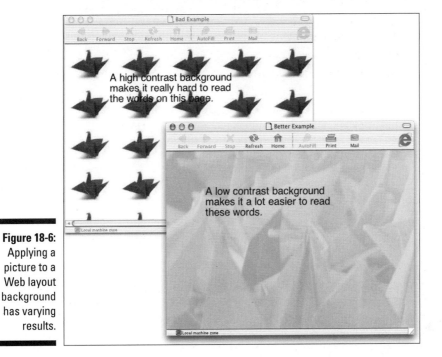

Figure 18-6:
Applying a
picture to a
Web layout
background
has varying
results.

This effect has its pitfalls, however. A large picture like the one described can take a long time to download, especially for those using 56 Kbps dial-up modems. Still, with some experimentation, you may be able to come up with some striking effects by using the background features in the New Project dialog box. (If you've already created a Web layout and you want to add a background image, choose Layout➪Layout Properties to access these same controls.)

After you make your choices in the New Project dialog box, click OK. You now have a brand new canvas on which to build your first QuarkXPress Web page.

If you aren't happy with your choices after you see them onscreen, you can change them. Simply choose Layout➪Layout Properties and make the changes there.

Using the Web Tools palette

When you open or switch to a Web layout of a QuarkXPress project, choosing Window⇨Show Tools displays a submenu, namely the Tools submenu. There, you find two choices:

✔ **Show/Hide Tools**

✔ **Show/Hide Web Tools**

The Web Tools palette is an extension of sorts of the regular Tools palette (which we cover in Chapter 1). In fact, it looks very similar to the Tools palette, with the obvious exception that the tools in the Web Tools palette are completely different than those in the regular Tools palette. The Web Tools palette is shown in Figure 18-7.

Figure 18-7:
The Web
Tools
palette.

Both the Tools palette and the Web Tools palette can be open at the same time within a Web layout. We recommend that you have both open at the same time because you'll be using tools from both palettes constantly while you're working on a Web layout.

Image Map tools

Image maps are those *hot spots* placed on images. You can click hot spots to get to another page, send an e-mail, submit information, and so on. An image map is, in effect, a hyperlink assigned to an entire area. Figure 18-8 shows an image map drawn over one large main image.

You create an image map very much like you'd create a text or picture box. Just follow these steps:

 1. **Select the Image Map tool that you want to use from the Image Map pop-up menu in the Web Tools palette. Here are your choices:**

- **Rectangle Image Map tool:** This produces a standard rectangular box much like what you'd create with the Text Box tool and the Picture Box tool. The big difference, of course, is that the boxes that you're creating now are used as hyperlinks. To create a square, hold down the Shift key while drawing the box.

- **Oval Image Map tool:** This tool produces an ellipse shape. Hold down the Shift key while drawing to create a circle.

- **Bézier Image Map tool:** This tool produces *polygons* (shapes composed of a series of flat sides) and *polycurves* (shapes composed of a series of curves) as well as shapes that combine both sides and curves. To create a Bézier shape, you click and release at each corner (technically known as a *node*). When you want to complete the box, click back on the origin point. (Notice how the pointer changes to a circle from the normal cross.) If you click and drag for a little bit at each desired node, you see the Bézier control handles that let you create a curve. You can have both straight and curved sides based on how you use the mouse at each node — experiment to get the hang of it.

2. **Place the cursor over the imported picture where you want the image map to appear.**

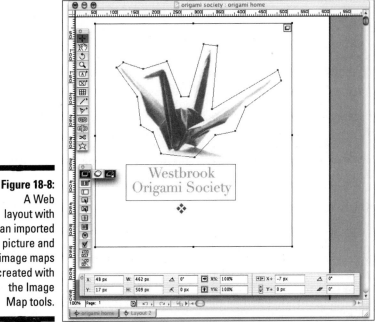

Figure 18-8:
A Web layout with an imported picture and image maps created with the Image Map tools.

3. Click and drag the mouse until you cover the portion of the image that will be the hot spot.

A white tinted area appears, indicating where the image map is so that you can assign a hyperlink to it. This light color can be difficult to see on a light-colored image, but the map boundaries will turn back into a red outline when you click the image again with the Move tool. (We show you how to assign a hyperlink to the individual map areas later in the chapter in the "Applying Links with the Hyperlinks Palette" section.) A red outlined box is a visual indicator in the upper-right corner of the picture box. This is just a simple reminder that the picture box contains image maps in addition to the picture.

Creating forms

Forms let people interact with your Web page. People can enter information in fields, choose items from lists, and — in more complicated instances — buy merchandise online.

The Form Box tools

Building forms in QuarkXPress is actually simple. However, getting those forms to work with your Web server can be more complicated because of the need for relatively complex programming scripts to make everything work.

Although the meat of most forms comprises a combination of buttons, fields, and other doodads, the form itself is contained in a rectangular box (a *form box*) that you create by using the Form Box tools, which are located directly below the Image Map tools in the Web Tools palette. The first of these two tools is the Form Box tool. The other tool in the Form Box pop-up menu is the File Selection tool.

With QuarkXPress 6, you can change the content of an existing box by changing its content to Form. This makes it easier to quickly create form boxes.

Form Box tool

Creating a form box is pretty much like creating any other kind of box in QuarkXPress. Just follow these steps:

1. Select the Form Box tool from the Web Tools palette.

2. Move your pointer to the area where you'd like to place the form.

3. Click and drag the mouse pointer until you cover the area where you'd like your form to be.

A form box looks exactly like a text box when it is first created with the exception of the visual indicator in the upper-right corner that looks like the form icon (as shown in Figure 18-9).

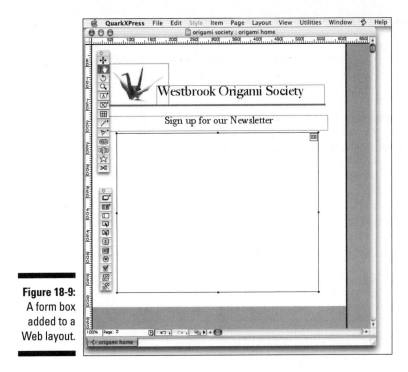

Figure 18-9:
A form box added to a Web layout.

4. **Choose Item⇨Modify, or press ⌘+M or Ctrl+M.**

   The Modify dialog box appears.

5. **Go to the Form pane and enter the name of the form box in the Name field.**

6. **From the Method pop-up menu, choose a method for submitting your form's information. You have two choices:**

   • **Get:** This tells the Web browser to append the data from your reader's form to the end of the URL of the target script or application.

   • **Post:** This tells the Web browser to send the data from your reader's form to the target script (or application) as a separate Hypertext Transfer Protocol (HTTP) transaction (HTTP is the underlying messaging protocol used by the Web).

   If you select Post from the Method pop-up menu, you must specify a Multipurpose Internet Mail Extension (MIME) type for the form's data in the Encoding pop-up menu.

Additional Form Box options

You must also make some other choices in the Modify dialog box, including how your page should reply when it receives the reader's submitted information (the *action*) and which script you'd like to use to process the submitted information.

With the exception of perhaps the first couple of fields, the rest of the choices in this dialog box are no doubt utterly confusing, but don't worry. Remember when we said that it was fairly easy to build an HTML form but more difficult to make it work? This is what we were talking about. QuarkXPress can build all the pieces of your form for you. It can even provide you with a map of what you need to get it working. The one thing that it can't do is to tell you what to put in those fields. To make a form that lets you and your reader interact, you must send commands to the server where your Web page will eventually be stored. The server processes the information from your form by using a script, which is usually written in one of the various programming languages, such as Perl, C, or Microsoft Active Server Pages (ASP).

Does this mean you'll have to take a class in Java or CGI scripting just so that you can make your simple little form work? Not at all. If you want to try tackling the backend processing yourself, poking around on the Web may turn up some good primers about CGI scripting, and these primers usually have some prewritten scripts that you can copy and paste or download to your machine for use in QuarkXPress. (A good place to start is at this book's companion Web site, www.QXCentral.com.) Additionally, many Web hosting companies also provide you with ready-made CGI scripts for creating forms. Unless your form is very basic, you may ultimately need to enlist the services of a Web programmer to get everything up and running. Getting complex HTML forms to work properly can be a challenge for even the most seasoned HTML coders.

You can also create a form box automatically by drawing a *form control* (such as a button or menu) in a blank section of a Web layout. QuarkXPress automatically renders a form box around your chosen form control according to the specification for the Form Box tool in the Tools pane of the Preferences dialog box (choose QuarkXPress⇨Preferences on the Mac or Edit⇨Preferences in Windows, or press Option+Shift+⌘+Y or Ctrl+Alt+Shift+Y). Unfortunately, much of the information here is putting the proverbial horse in front of the proverbial cart.

The File Selection tool

This tool creates a form field that lets visitors upload files from their local computers to your remote server. When readers click the Browse button, for example, the Open File dialog box appears in their Web browsers, where they can select the file that they want to upload. After they've located the file, they click the Submit button, and the file is sent to your remote server. (Chances are that you won't use this feature much.)

To create a file submission control, follow these steps:

1. **Choose the File Selection tool from the Web Tools palette.**

2. **Move the pointer to someplace within your form box; then click and draw your submission control like you would an ordinary text box.**

3. **Choose Item⇨Modify, or press ⌘+M or Ctrl+M.**

   The Modify dialog box appears.

4. **On the Form pane, enter the name of the control submission in the Name field.**

5. **In the Accept field, enter a list of acceptable MIME types, which must be separated by commas.**

   If you're not sure what to enter, check with your company's Web master or the administrators of your Web server.

6. **Click Required.**

   This ensures that the attached file will upload with the form data.

7. **Click OK.**

Text Field tool

The Text Field tool lets you create fields in which readers can enter text. On the Web, you often see these text fields in the form of name, address, city, and so on. For passwords, QuarkXPress lets users enter text that appears only as a series of asterisks. A hidden field control then translates the text but does not display that value to the user — only to you.

To add a text field to your form, follow these steps:

1. **Select the Text Field tool from the Web Tools palette.**

2. **Move the pointer to a spot within your form box, and then click and drag until the text field is close to the length that you desire.**

   The entire text field must remain in the form box.

3. **Choose Item⇨Modify, or press ⌘+M or Ctrl+M.**

   The Modify dialog box appears.

4. **Go to the Form pane.**

5. **In the Name field, enter an appropriate name for the field.**

   For example, if it is a field for an address, use the name *Address*.

6. **From the Type pop-menu, choose one of the following four options:**

   • **Text – Single Line:** This lets the reader enter only one line of text: for example, a name or an address.

   • **Text – Multi Line:** This lets the reader enter multiple lines of text. These types of fields are generally reserved for additional comments or messages in custom greeting cards.

   • **Password:** This displays text in asterisks or bullets.

   • **Hidden Field:** This is submitted with a form but doesn't display in the reader's Web browser. These fields can be used to calculate information about the visitors submitting the form, such as what type of browsers they're using, without displaying that information on their screens.

7. **Complete the other options in the pane as appropriate for the text field that you're creating:**

   • **Max Chars:** Enter the maximum number of characters that the control will accept.

   The number that you choose doesn't necessarily have anything to do with the length of your field. For example, you can fit 40 characters in a field that's 25 characters in length. However, readers might be more inclined to make a mistake if their typing begins to scroll outside the range of the visible character field.

   • **Wrap Text:** Check this check box if you want the text entered into a multiple-line text box to break to the next line in a multiple-line text field. We recommend that you always keep this checked. Otherwise, visitors' typed text begins to scroll outside the range of the field; before long, they won't be able to see what they're typing.

   • **Read Only:** Check this check box to indicate that the readers should not be able to edit the contents of a field.

   • **Required:** Check this check box to indicate that a response is required in the field.

8. **Click OK.**

When you create fields, keep in mind that they should never overlap. Only hidden fields can overlap other fields, and in all honesty, you will probably never use a hidden field for anything.

Button tool

The Button tool is used to — get this! — *create buttons*. You can create two kinds of buttons:

✔ **Submit:** The Submit button is used to submit the information that the visitor has entered in your Web page to your remote Web server, which is in turn rerouted to your personal computer.

✔ **Reset:** The Reset button is simply a "start over" button that wipes a form clean.

Chances are that after you know how to create a proper form, you'll be using these two buttons more than any others. Usually you see these buttons side by side in a form.

To create a Submit or Reset button:

1. **Select the Button tool from the Web Tools palette.**

2. **Move the cursor within your form box and then click and drag to draw the button.**

3. **Choose Item⇨Modify, or press ⌘+M or Ctrl+M; then go to the Form pane.**

4. **In the Form pane, enter the name of the button in the Name field.**

   If you want text in the button, such as *Submit,* choose the Content tool in the Tools palette and then enter the text that you want displayed in the button.

5. **From the Type pop-menu, choose either Submit or Reset.**

6. **Click OK.**

For these buttons to actually do anything, you must attach them to a CGI script of some sort. Figure 18-10 shows an example of a Submit button coupled with a text field.

Image Button tool

In QuarkXPress 6, you needn't limit your buttons to text. You can also turn pictures into buttons. Not to be confused with image maps, *image buttons* are used to submit forms. They, like the regular text buttons, require some scripting before they are any use on a Web page.

To create an image button:

1. **Choose the Image Button tool from the Web Tools palette.**

2. **Move the cursor to the place in the form box where you'd like to place the image button, and then click and drag the cursor until the image is the size that you desire.**

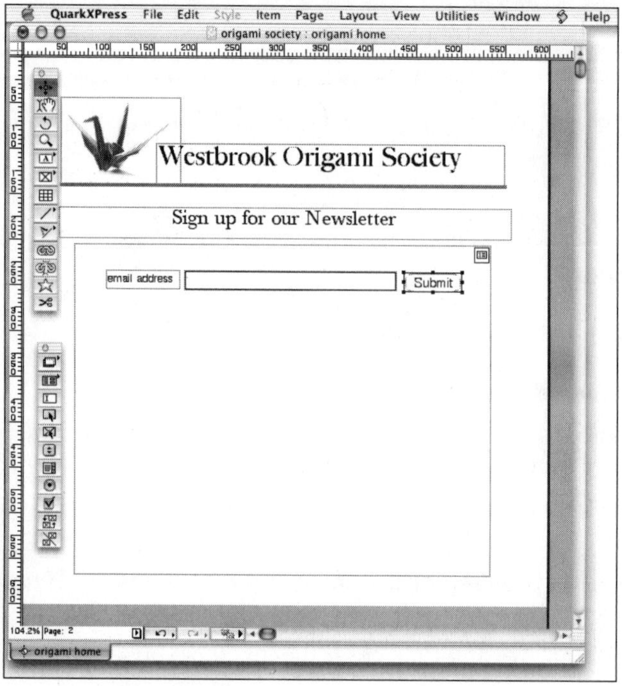

Figure 18-10:
We've
added a text
field and
a Submit
button at the
bottom of
our Web
layout.

3. **Choose File⇨Get Picture, or press ⌘+E or Ctrl+E.**

   The Get Picture dialog box appears.

4. **Select the picture file that you'd like to make into a button and then click Open.**

5. **Choose Item⇨Modify, or press ⌘+M or Ctrl+M.**

   The Modify dialog box appears.

6. **Enter the name of the button in the Name field.**

7. **Go to the Export pane in the Modify dialog box.**

8. **In the Export pane, choose a graphic format from the Export As pop-up menu.**

   The Export pane displays different options, depending on the graphic format that you choose. You can choose from three graphic formats:

   • **JPEG:** Use this format when the graphic is a photograph.

     When you choose this format, you are asked to enter a description of the picture in the Alternate Text field. If the picture doesn't show up in someone's browser (usually because of lack of memory), the text that you enter in this field shows up in its place. When you select this option, a new pop-up menu appears in the Export pane: namely, Image Quality, with options ranging from Lowest (pure resolution, but quicker download time) to Highest (crispest resolution, but slower download time). Choose the option that you think will be best for the majority of Web site visitors, based on image size and the typical method that users will have to access your pages. (Lower-quality images would not cause large page-loading delays for users with slow dial-up connection, for example.) Last, check the Progressive check box so that the image displays as a progressive JPEG. (When you download a Web page with a *progressive* JPEG image, the whole image appears and is blurry, and then gets clearer.)

- **GIF:** This format is the best solution for illustrative art or animated images.

  When you choose the GIF format, you are asked to enter a description of the image in the Alternate Text field. Check the Use Dithering check box if you want the picture displayed with dithered colors. Likewise, check the Use Interlacing check box to display the images as interlaced GIF images; like the progressive JPEG option, this option helps the user realize during slow connections that an image is appearing. Also choose a color palette from the Color Palette pop-up menu. Your best choice is probably Web-Safe, which ensures that the picture's color will remain consistent on different platforms. However, you can also choose Windows, Adaptive (the picture is displayed according to what colors are available on a given monitor), and Mac OS.

- **PNG:** This format is the Portable Network Graphics format that works on both the Web and for single-image files.

  Although the PNG format loads quickly on Web pages, it is not widely supported by browsers. The choices that go along with a PNG are essentially the same as those that go with a GIF, with one added choice. In the Export pane, you can tell the Web browser to display a PNG picture as either *True Color* or *Indexed Color*. True Color displays the maximum number of colors that it can muster from a given computer monitor. Indexed Color lets you apply dithering and/or interlacing to the picture via the Use Interlacing and Use Dithering check boxes.

  More browsers support the PNG format now than a few years ago, so this image format will become more popular.

  9. Click OK.

With the proper CGI scripts, your picture can be used as a button to submit information just like any other button.

Pop-Up Menu and List Box tools

In QuarkXPress 6, you can create two kinds of selection lists:

- ✔ **Pop-up menus**

  A *pop-up menu* lets you choose *only one* item from its menu.

- ✔ **List boxes**

  A *list box* (which looks something like a multi-line text field) lets you choose *one or more* items from its menu.

To add a pop-up menu or list control to a form, follow these steps:

1. **Choose the Pop-Up Menu tool or List Box tool from the Web Tools palette.**

2. **Move the cursor to the place (within the form box) where you'd like to place the pop-up menu or list box, then click and drag the cursor to draw the pop-up menu or list box.**

   Make sure that the perimeter stays within the form box.

3. **Choose Item⇨Modify, or press ⌘+M or Ctrl+M, and then go to the Form pane.**

   The Form pane of the Modify dialog box appears.

4. **Enter a name for the pop-up menu in the Name field.**

   If you'd like to convert your pop-up menu to a list box, you can do so in the Type pop-up menu.

5. **Pick the menu list that appears in the pop-up menu, or click New to create a new pop-up menu.**

   We show you how to create these menus in the Edit Menu dialog box later in the chapter.

6. **Select the appropriate options for your menu or list box:**

   - **Allow Multiple Selections:** If you want users to have the option of selecting more than one item in the list, check the Allow Multiple Selections check box.

     Only list boxes allow multiple selections.

   - **Required:** If you want to make sure the reader has to click at least one item in the list, check the Required check box.

7. **Click OK.**

You can change the menu items after you make either a pop-up menu or list box. Choose Edit⇨Menus to edit the items. Figure 18-11 shows both a pop-up menu and a list box.

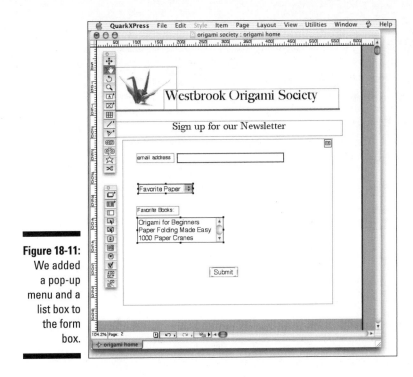

Figure 18-11:
We added a pop-up menu and a list box to the form box.

Radio Button tool

A group of radio buttons, which lets a visitor choose only one value from an entire list of values, are great for gathering demographic information about visitors. For example, you can use a radio button to allow users to sign up to receive e-mail, as shown in Figure 18-12.

To add a group of radio buttons to a form:

1. **Select the Radio Button tool from the Web Tools palette.**

2. **Move the cursor to the place in the form where you'd like to position the radio button, and then click and draw a selection control for each button that you want.**

3. **Select one of the radio buttons.**

4. **Choose Modify⇨Item, or press ⌘+M or Ctrl+M, and then go to the Form pane.**

   The Form pane of the Modify dialog box appears.

5. **Choose Radio Button from the Type pop-up menu (if it isn't already selected).**

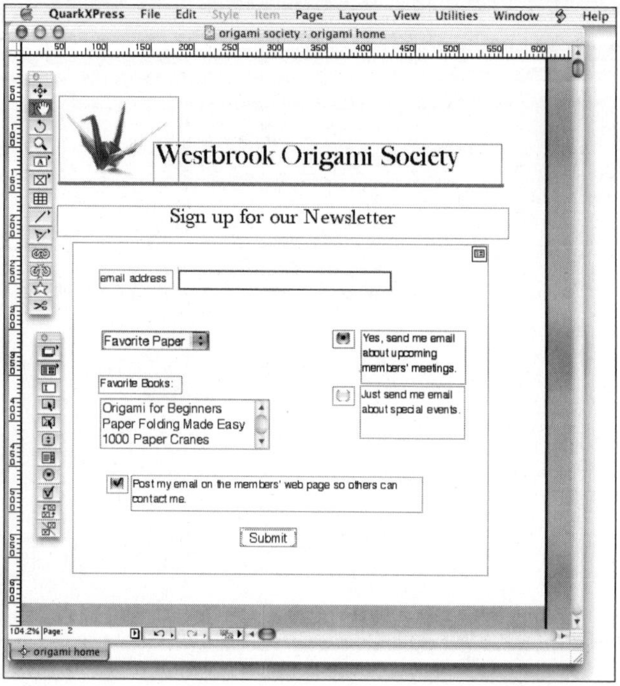

Figure 18-12:
Two radio
buttons
collect
information
from
visitors.

6. **Decide on a name for the radio button group and enter that name in the Group field.**

   Radio button controls with the same name are considered to be part of the same group.

7. **Enter a value for the selected radio button in the Value field.**

8. **Repeat Steps 1 through 7 until you have created all the radio button controls in the group.**

9. **To select a default radio button, select the radio button, choose Item⇨ Modify, go to the Form pane, and check the Use as Default check box.**

10. **To indicate that a button must be selected before the form can be entered, check the Required check box in the Modify dialog box.**

    It isn't necessary to check Required if you checked Use as Default. The Default button will always be selected if one of the other buttons isn't.

11. **Click OK.**

Check Box tool

A check box button can be used for all sorts of things. It can be used to answer yes/no questions, to create a list, or even to activate a function in a form.

You create check box buttons the same way that you create radio buttons, with a few slight differences. Follow these steps to create a check box button:

1. **Select the Check Box tool from the Web Tools palette.**

2. **Move the cursor to the place in the form where you want to position the check box, and then click and draw a selection control for each check box that you want.**

3. **Select one of the check boxes.**

4. **Choose Modify⇨Item, or press ⌘+M or Ctrl+M, and then go to the Form pane.**

   The Form pane of the Modify dialog box appears.

5. **Choose Checkbox from the Type pop-up menu (if it isn't already selected).**

6. **Enter a name for the check box in the Name field.**

7. **Enter a value for the check box in the Value field.**

8. **Select the appropriate options:**

   - **Initially Checked:** To indicate that the check box control should be enabled when the Web page first displays, check Initially Checked.

   - **Required:** To indicate that one of the check boxes must be selected before the form can be entered, check Required (in the Modify dialog box).

9. **Click OK.**

Making a menu

Simply put, a *menu* is a list of items. In the Web world, these items are generally displayed in a list control or a pop-up menu control. You create menus from the Menus dialog box, which you open by choosing Edit⇨Menus.

The menus that you create in the Menus dialog box can do different sorts of things. For instance, you can use menus to let users choose from a list of options, or you can create navigation menus where each item has a corresponding URL. To create a menu, follow these steps:

1. **Choose Edit⇨Menus.**

   The Menus dialog box appears, as shown in Figure 18-13.

2. **Click the New button.**

   The Edit Menu dialog box appears, as shown in Figure 18-14.

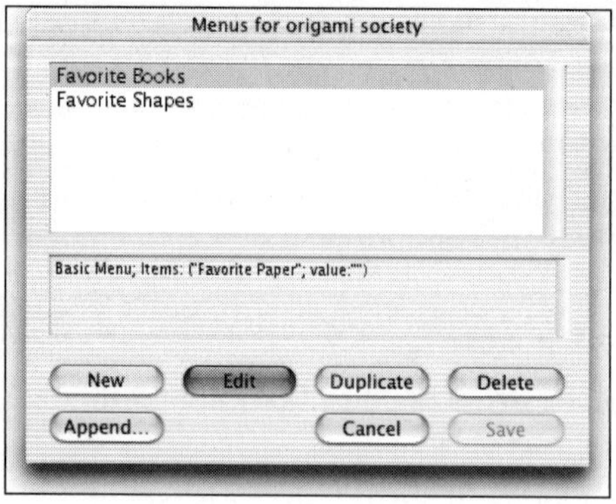

Figure 18-13:
The Menus
dialog box.

3. **To specify a menu as a navigation menu, check the Navigation Menu check box.**

   A *navigation menu* lets you link a menu item to a specific URL. When the visitor chooses a particular item in the navigation menu, the browser opens the URL for that item.

4. **Click the Add button to add an item to a new or selected menu.**

   The Menu Item dialog box appears.

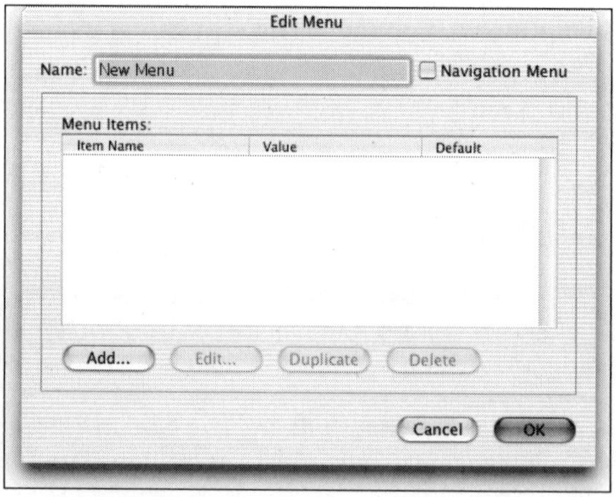

Figure 18-14:
The Edit
Menu
dialog box.

5. **Enter the name of your new menu item and (if you need it) the value of the menu item.**

   • If the menu is a navigation menu, you enter a URL in the Value field.

   • If the menu isn't a navigation menu, choosing the item simply means that the value in the Value field is sent to the Web server with the rest of the form data when the form is submitted.

6. **To specify that the menu item should be selected by default, check the Use as Default check box.**

7. **Click OK to close the Menu Item dialog box.**

8. **Click OK to close the Edit Menu dialog box.**

9. **Click Save to close the Menus dialog box.**

   Menus are saved in the project file so that the next time you create a pop-up menu or list box, your new menu is listed both as a choice in the Menu pop-up menu in the Forms pane of the Modify dialog box and in the Menus dialog box.

Applying links with the Hyperlinks palette

Hyperlinks can be used to stitch the pages of a Web site together, and they can be used to access everything from music files to e-mail addresses. In this section, we show you exactly how to accomplish these feats and the tool to accomplish them: the Hyperlinks palette (as shown in Figure 18-15).

If you prefer, you can also build a hyperlink by selecting an image or text and then choosing Style⇨Hyperlink. The commands in this submenu take you through the same steps as the Hyperlinks palette.

Figure 18-15:
The
Hyperlinks
palette.

To open the Hyperlinks palette, choose Window⇨Show Hyperlinks. After the palette is open, you can begin applying links immediately. It's a simple process, too. You begin by highlighting text or selecting an image map that you'd like to link to another page or another site. In this case, we will link the image map surrounding the large paper crane on the first page of Web site — the Westbrook Origami Society home page — to the second page of our Web site — the Sign Up for Our Newsletter page. To do this:

1. **Select an image map area and click the New Hyperlink icon in the top-left corner of the Hyperlinks palette.**

   The New Hyperlink dialog box appears.

2. **In the New Hyperlink dialog box, enter the URL for the page that you're linking to and then choose a Target for the page.**

   There are two Target options:

   - **Self:** The target is the same browser window.
   - **Blank:** This opens up a new browser window while leaving the original window available.

   This is a great option when you link to other sites.

3. **After you've established the URL, click OK.**

   In our example, the image map surrounding the paper crane is now linked to the Sign Up for Our Newsletter page as shown in Figure 18-16. When you click the paper crane in the Web browser, it displays the sign up page in its place. The link appears in the Hyperlinks palette after you've entered it.

Adding an Anchor

Anchors are little embedded targets within a Web layout that let you jump to a particular word or section of a page. A hyperlink can be directed to the anchor — not just the page on which it resides. You can also jump to specific text on the current page this way. You can create an anchor by choosing Style⇨Anchor, then selecting from its submenu. The commands in this submenu take you through the same steps as the Hyperlinks palette.

To create an anchor, follow these steps:

1. **Choose the spot that you want to pinpoint in the page.**
2. **Click the Anchor button atop the Hyperlinks palette.**
3. **In the Anchor dialog box that appears, enter a name for the anchor and then click OK.**

When you create a hyperlink, you can direct it directly to the anchor, thus making it easier for the visitor to navigate to specific parts of a page.

Creating rollovers

Almost every Web site has a menu bar, composed of hot spots that lead visitors to other pages, such as contact information and biographies. When you move your cursor over some of these hot spots, they do all sorts of cool things. They light up, turn different colors, and even transform into entirely different images. These tricky little hot spots are *rollovers,* and they are surprisingly easy to create.

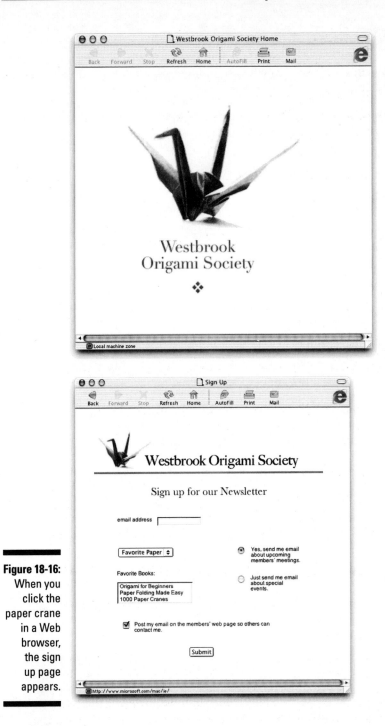

Figure 18-16:
When you click the paper crane in a Web browser, the sign up page appears.

Preparing a rollover

Rollovers are easy to make, but they do require some prep work. A rollover is an optical illusion created by two superimposed graphics, not unlike a cartoon. So to create this little two-picture cartoon, you need two pictures of the same size. You create these pictures in an image-editing program like Macromedia Fireworks or Adobe Photoshop. In this case, we've created our pictures in Photoshop. Both pictures are displayed in Figure 18-17.

Figure 18-17:
Two pictures that will be merged to make a rollover.

Making a basic rollover

After you create your two pictures, you can go back to QuarkXPress and make that rollover happen. Here's how:

1. **Import your default picture — that is, the picture that will usually appear onscreen — somewhere in your Web layout.**

2. **Choose Item⇨Basic Rollover⇨Create Rollover.**

   The Rollover dialog box appears. (The path to your default picture has already been placed in the Default Picture field in the Rollover dialog box. That means QuarkXPress has already done half the work for you.)

3. **Click Browse next to the Rollover Image field and locate your other picture — that is, the rollover picture; then select the picture and click OK.**

4. **In the Hyperlinks field, select the URL to which you'd like to link the rollover.**

   A rollover is really just a fancy *hyperlink*. When you click it, it should take you somewhere. In our example, we've linked our rollover image to take us back to the home page of our Westbrook Origami Society site.

5. **Click OK.**

That's it. Now you can open your page in a Web browser and watch it do its stuff. Many Web sites have an entire menu bar dedicated to these sorts of links. You can get a glimpse of ours in Figure 18-18.

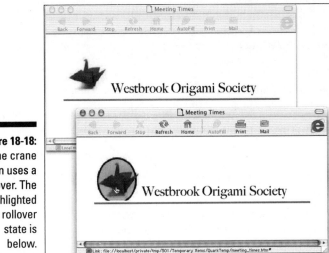

Figure 18-18:
The crane
icon uses a
rollover. The
highlighted
rollover
state is
below.

Creating a two-position rollover

Two-position rollovers are new to QuarkXPress 6.

A *two-position rollover* is like a basic rollover with a remote control. Unlike a basic rollover image, which changes the image directly *under* your cursor, a two-position rollover changes a second image *away* from your cursor. The Rollover Link tool at the bottom of the Web Tools palette creates this Web magic.

1. **Create two picture boxes with the Picture Box tool.**

   • The first picture box is the *target,* which is a picture box that will change its image.

   • The second picture box is the *trigger* that makes the target change.

   The Rollover Link tool will link the two picture boxes together.

2. **Select the Item tool.**

3. **Click the picture box that will be the target.**

4. **Choose File⇨Get Picture, or press ⌘+E or Ctrl+E.**

5. **Select the image that you want to be the default image for the target.**

   The default image is the one that first appears on the page until the target is triggered.

6. **Click OK.**

7. **Choose Item⇨2-Position Rollovers⇨Create a 2-Position Target.**

8. **Select the Content tool from the Tools palette.**

   This step begins importing the second image that the target picture box will change over to when it is triggered.

9. **Click the target picture box.**

10. **Choose File⇨Get Picture, or press ⌘+E or Ctrl+E.**

11. **Select the image that you want to be the rollover image for the target.**

12. **Click OK.**

13. **Select the Rollover Link tool from the Web Tools palette.**

   This step begins creating the interactive relationship between the target and trigger picture boxes.

14. **Click the second picture box (the trigger) once and then click the first picture box (the target created in Step 7) once.**

   An icon of a pointing hand should appear on the trigger picture box. Add the image for the trigger picture box.

15. **Select the Content tool from the Tools palette.**

16. **Click the trigger picture box (the one with the pointing finger).**

17. **Choose File⇨Get Picture, or press ⌘+E or Ctrl+E.**

18. **Select an image that you want to be the trigger.**

That's it! Choose Page⇨Preview HTML⇨[your browser] to test the two-position rollover in the browser (as shown in Figure 18-19).

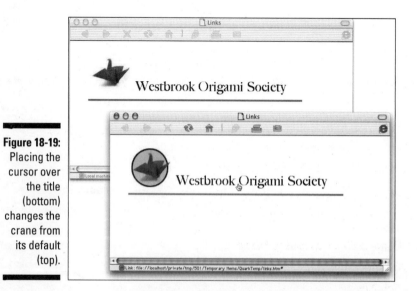

Figure 18-19:
Placing the cursor over the title (bottom) changes the crane from its default (top).

Cascading menus

Cascading menus are like very fancy rollovers that can simulate the way that drop-down menus work in most operating systems and applications.

Building a cascading menu

To build a cascading menu, there are three steps:

1. **Choose Edit⇨Cascading Menu, and then define the menu and sub-menu items for your cascading menu in the Edit Cascading Menu dialog box (as shown in Figure 18-20).**

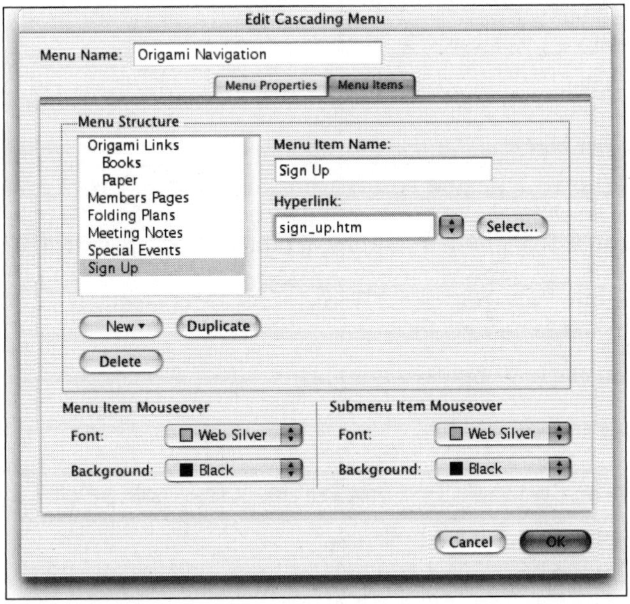

Figure 18-20:
The Menu Items pane of the Cascading Menu dialog box.

2. **Add a graphic to your page; the graphic can serve as the starting point for the menus.**

3. **Connect the menus to the graphic.**

Create the menu items in the Cascading Menu dialog box

Follow these steps to create the menu items:

1. **Choose Edit⇨Cascading Menu.**

   The Cascading Menu dialog box appears.

2. **Click New.**

   The Edit Cascading Menu dialog box appears.

3. **Type a name in the Menu Name field.**

   There are many choices to make in the Menu Properties pane that affect the cascading menu's visual appearance that you can try out. We recommend that you experiment to find the right visual appearance for your cascading menu.

4. **Go to the Menu Items pane by clicking the Menu Items tab.**

5. **For each menu item, follow these steps:**

   a. Click the New button in the Menu Structure section.

   b. Type a name in the Menu Item Name field.

   c. Type a URL in the Hyperlink field.

6. **Select the font and background colors for the menus and submenus.**

7. **Click OK.**

8. **Click Save.**

Make a text box that contains graphic text

You need to create a picture box as a starting point for the cascading menus to appear. The simplest way of creating a picture box for this purpose is to make a text box that contains graphical representations of text.

✔ You can turn any text into a Web graphic by checking the Convert to Graphic on Export check box.

✔ You can use any imported graphic.

Follow these steps:

1. **Select the Rectangle Text Box tool from the Tools palette.**

2. **Drag out a text box on your page.**

3. **Select the Content tool.**

4. **Click the text box and enter some text into it.**

   We've used the text *Origami Navigation* to help people find the menu on the page (refer to Figure 18-20).

5. **Choose Item⇨Modify, or press ⌘+M or Ctrl+M.**

6. **Go to the Export pane.**

7. **Check the Convert to Graphic on Export check box at the bottom of the pane.**

8. **Click OK.**

Now you have a text box that can be the starting point for your cascading menu.

Add a cascading menu to the Web page

The following steps connect the text box with the graphical text up to the cascading menu:

1. **Connect the box with either of these steps:**

   • Select the text box with either the Content tool or the Item tool.

   • Select any picture box with an imported image.

2. **Choose Item⇨Cascading Menu and select the cascading menu name from the submenu.**

Figure 18-21 shows the fruits of our efforts in the browser.

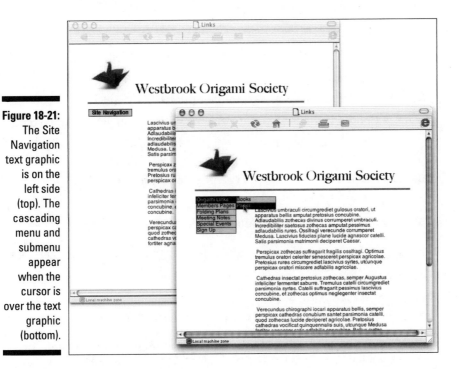

Figure 18-21: The Site Navigation text graphic is on the left side (top). The cascading menu and submenu appear when the cursor is over the text graphic (bottom).

Moving between print and Web

QuarkXPress 6 lets you convert print layouts into Web layouts and vice versa. You can convert a print layout's text boxes, pictures, lines, and boxes into a close approximation with the design of the print layout. This process is not perfect but will help to move your print pieces onto the Web.

QuarkXPress 6 offers a *synchronized text* feature to automatically synchronize text among text boxes within the same QuarkXPress project. This very useful feature makes it much easier to have standardized text across print and Web layouts that have different physical arrangements (where the Web page is simply not a replica of the print layout).

Converting a print layout to Web

QuarkXPress will automatically transfer the size, scaling, and placement of your images over to the Web version while making them suitably small files for the Web. Text is slightly more complex, so we get to that in a moment.

Convert a *copy* of a print layout and not your original. Converting your design and information between print and Web is not perfectly reversible.

Convert the layout

This conversion process is very simple:

1. **Open a print layout.**

2. **Select one of these copy or original options:**

   - Choose Layout⇨Duplicate to work on a *copy* of your print layout.

   - Choose Layout⇨Layout Properties to change your *original* print layout.

3. **Select Web from the Layout Type pop-up menu.**

4. **Click OK.**

5. **Click Yes in the warning dialog box.**

Congratulations! You've just made a Web layout. There's a lot more than that to it, but you're most of the way there.

Preserve the live text

When you publish or export your Web layout, QuarkXPress tries to preserve the original look of the design as accurately as possible. To do this, it converts the text in text boxes to images. Although this helps keep the look of your design, it can make your Web page less "Web-like" and cause it to take longer to download. QuarkXPress shows you which text boxes that it will convert into an image by placing a small icon of a camera in the top-left corner of the text boxes on Web layouts.

Now you need to decide which text boxes of your print layout that you want keep as live text and which ones you'd prefer to have QuarkXPress convert into images.

How do you choose which text boxes to keep live? We recommend these guidelines:

✔ Let QuarkXPress convert the larger type, like headlines and titles, into images.

✔ Keep the text boxes with stories and articles as live text.

To preserve text elements that you want as live text, follow these steps:

1. **Click a text box containing the words that you want to keep live.**

2. **Select Item⇨Modify, or press ⌘+M or Ctrl+M.**

3. **Go to the Export pane and uncheck the Convert to Graphic on Export check box.**

4. **Click OK.**

Making synchronized text boxes

Synchronized text lets you keep content in text boxes up to date when you make changes to the text in any of the text boxes that are synchronized. This can be used to match up the text in a print layout and a Web layout, even while one or the other is edited.

Suppose that you have a layout of a printed brochure and a Web page based on it. If you use synchronized text boxes for important information such as phone numbers, you can change a phone number on the print layout and rest assured that the Web page will continue to match your brochure. This saves you from having to double-check the phone number when you export and publish the Web page. Chapter 3 covers the process in detail.

Cascading style sheets

One of the ways that you can maintain the look of your text on the Web is to use cascading style sheets (CSSs). *Cascading style sheets* tell a reader's browser to substitute other specific fonts if your first choice of font is not available.

For example, you may want to use Adobe Caslon as the font for the text of your Web page. Most people don't have Adobe Caslon on their systems. So you decide that if Caslon can't be used by the browser that will display your page, it would be okay for the page to be displayed with Baskerville instead. Cascading style sheets lets you define the order of your font choices. In the preceding example, you can specify fonts in this order:

✔ Adobe Caslon, your preferred font

✔ Baskerville

✔ Georgia (which comes with Microsoft Office)

> ✔ The PostScript font Times (which is common on Macs)
>
> ✔ The TrueType font Times New Roman (which is almost universal)

You specify the exact order of the font choices in the Font Families dialog box by choosing Edit⇨CSS Font Families (as shown in Figure 18-22).

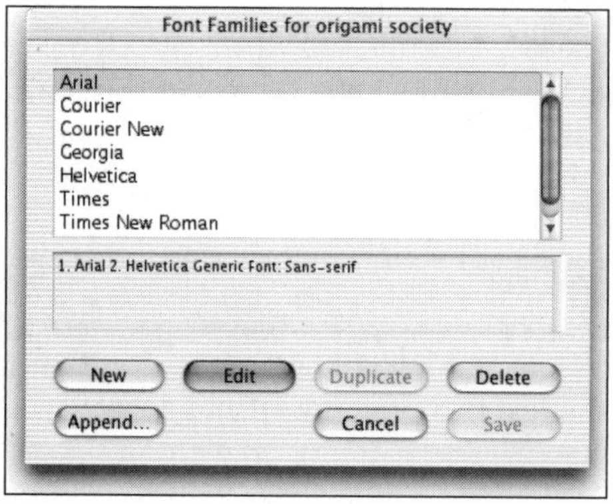

Figure 18-22.
The Font
Families
dialog box.

You can add a new font family by clicking New, which opens the Edit Font Family dialog box (as shown in Figure 18-23).

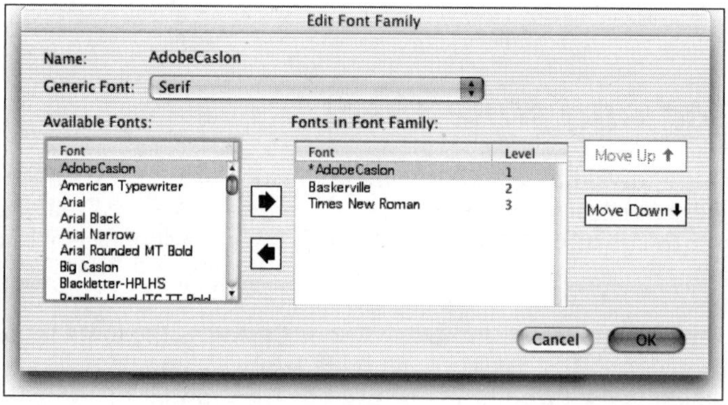

Figure 18-23.
The Edit
Font Family
dialog box.

To create a new CSS font family:

1. **Choose Edit⇨CSS Font Families.**

2. **In the Edit Font Family dialog box, select the name of the font that you want to use as your first choice from the Available Fonts list.**

3. **Click the top, black right-arrow to add it to the Fonts in Font Family list. Keep adding second and third (and fourth) choices the same way.**

   You can change the order of the fonts in the Fonts in Font Family list with the Move Up and Move Down buttons. The font name at the top of the Fonts in Font Family list as Level 1 is the primary font and is used for the font family's name.

4. **Select a generic font from the Generic Font pop-up menu.**

   Generic fonts are unnamed and only determine the general kind font family to be used as a last resort if your choices in the Fonts in Font Family list can't be located.

5. **Click OK.**

Now you when you use the first font in the font family on your Web page, the reader's browser will look for each font in the order that you specified.

Chapter 19

Getting Your Site Up and Running

In This Chapter

▶ Preparing your layout for the Web

▶ Exporting your layout to the Web

▶ Taking a brief look at XML

*W*e all know the ultimate destination of printed layouts — the printer, right? But how do you get your Web site up and running? That's what we discuss in this chapter. But first, we want to show you how to preview your pages in a Web browser so that you know what to expect when they're posted on the Web. You can skip this step in the process, but you shouldn't. The layouts that you create in QuarkXPress may look very different in your Web browser. QuarkXPress Web layouts aren't actual Web files — yet. As we explain at the beginning of Chapter 18, a Web layout is just a WYSIWYG (What You See Is What You Get) view of what amounts to pages and pages of HyperText Markup Language (HTML) code, and it's the HTML code that the Web browser is interested in.

A browser takes the HTML code from your QuarkXPress Web layouts and displays its own WYSIWYG version of what you've created. Often the two don't match up. Lines may get bumped up or down, pictures may shift, and text may reflow. Chances are that you'll have to make some adjustments to your pages before you're happy with them.

Prepping Layouts for the Web

No matter what type of layouts you're preparing for the Web, the tasks of getting them ready are important ones. This section explains the processes involved in getting pages ready to go online:

1. Output or *export* the Web layout to HTML files.

2. Copy or *upload* the exported HTML files to a Web server.

Chapter 18 covers page design for a Web layout in QuarkXPress.

Naming your Web pages before exporting

You probably thought that you already named your Web pages, didn't you? Actually, several types of names are used in Web projects. These two name types make the export work:

- **Page Title:** This is the name that you want people to see in the title bar of their browser when they load your Web page.

- **Export File Name:** This is the name that the HTML files will get when you export your Web layout.

First, there are the names that you assigned to your QuarkXPress Web layouts and projects: that is, those that show up in the title bar in QuarkXPress. The export process ignores these project and layout names.

To begin, open your QuarkXPress Web layout and then choose Page➪Page Properties. In the Page Properties dialog box that appears (as shown in Figure 19-1), enter the name of the page in the Page Title field. Below the Page Title field is the Export File Name field, where you enter the HTML name for your page. You'll need to do this for each page in your Web layout because each Web page is exported to its own HTML file.

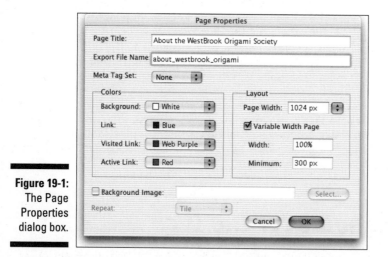

Figure 19-1:
The Page
Properties
dialog box.

When you enter a name in the Export File Name field, remember three rules:

- **Never** leave *spaces* in the name.

- **Always** keep letters in the name all *lowercase*.

  Uppercase letters in the name may confuse on some types of Web servers and make it harder to build working hyperlinks in your projects.

> ✔ **Never** use strange or punctuation *characters,* other than perhaps a hyphen or an underscore (for example, `about_westbrook_origami`).

If you stray from these three rules, browsers may not recognize your pages. Another problem is that, when it comes time to export your pages, browsers will use these names and not the names from the Save Project dialog box.

QuarkXPress adds the necessary `.htm` filename extension to the end of the name when you export it to HTML, so you don't need to add that extension to the export file names of your pages.

To assign export file names to many Web pages, follow these steps with the Page Layout palette, as shown in Figure 19-2:

1. **Choose Window⇨Show Page Layout if it is not showing.**

2. **Click the page name once under a page icon in the palette to select it.**

3. **Give the page a name that is used during file export.**

    Remember the three preceding rules of Web page file naming.

Figure 19-2: The Page Layout palette.

Adding meta tags

Meta tags are, in essence, just author notes about such informative points as who wrote the Web page and why certain scripts were used. However, meta tags can also serve a different and very useful purpose. Meta tags let you add lists of words describing your page to your HTML file. After your page has been uploaded to the Web, online search engines search for as many matches to a query as possible, including the words found in meta tags.

With a meta tag list, your chances of being found by a search engine increase immensely because you can enter descriptions of your page that wouldn't otherwise be in your HTML file. For the Westbrook Origami Society site, for example, we could include words and phrases such as *paper folding, hobbies, Japanese culture,* and so on, in the meta tags file.

Follow these steps to create a meta tag:

1. **Choose Edit⇨Meta Tags.**

   The Meta Tags dialog box appears (as shown in Figure 19-3).

2. **Click the New button.**

   The Edit Meta Tag Set dialog box appears (as shown in Figure 19-4).

3. **Give the new meta tag set a name (for example *Search Words*) in the Name field and then click the Add button.**

4. **Add words and phrases to your meta tag list.**

   For each word or phrase, repeat this process:

   a. Enter the *name* in the Meta Tag field.

   b. Enter the *description* in the Name field

   c. Enter your *word* or *phrase* in the Content field.

   d. When you're finished with the entry, click OK.

5. **When you're finished with adding words or phrases, click Save.**

6. **Choose Page⇨Page Properties.**

   The Page Properties dialog box appears.

7. **From the Meta Tag Set pop-up menu, select your meta tags list and then click OK.**

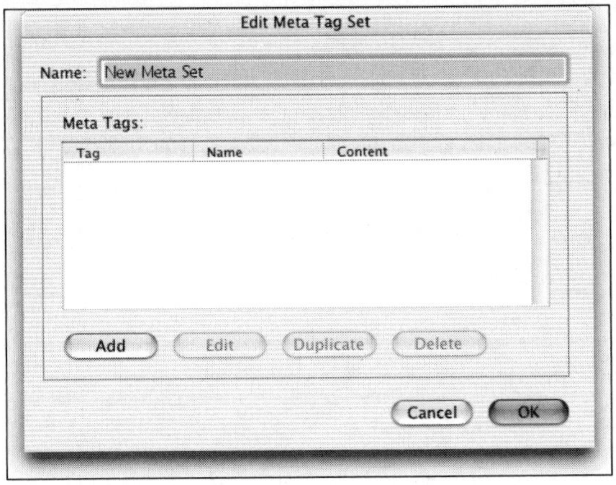

Figure 19-4:
The
Edit Meta
Tag Set
dialog box.

Your description list is included with your HTML page when it is exported.

You can include several types of meta tags in your HTML file. If you are interested in learning more about the types of meta tags, we recommend *HTML 4 For Dummies,* 4th Edition, by Ed Tittel and Natanya Pitts (Wiley Publishing, Inc.) for the straight skinny.

Choosing a browser

After you prepare your pages, you choose a browser (or several browsers) in which to preview the pages. You do this in the Browsers pane in the Preferences dialog box (as shown in Figure 19-5). To open this pane, choose QuarkXPress⇨Preferences on the Mac or Edit⇨Preferences in Windows, or press Option+Shift+⌘+Y or Ctrl+Alt+Shift+Y, and then click Browsers in the list on the left.

If you're serious about your Web site, we recommend that you have the latest and next-to-latest versions of the Microsoft Internet Explorer, Netscape Navigator/Communicator, and Opera browsers installed. Install them on at least one Mac testing system and one Windows testing system. This lets you see what your Web pages will look like in the real world because different browsers don't always show the same thing. All three browsers are free downloads from their respective corporate sites:

```
www.microsoft.com
www.netscape.com
www.opera.com
```

If you're using a Mac, try testing your pages on Apple's Safari browser, available at www.apple.com/safari.

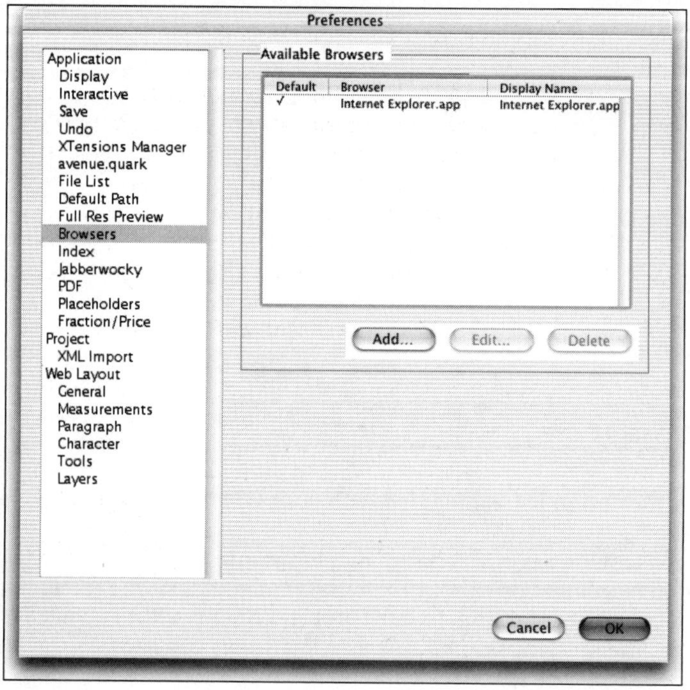

Figure 19-5:
The
Browsers
pane in the
Preferences
dialog box.

To add a browser, follow these steps in the Browsers pane of the Preferences dialog box:

1. **Click the Add button.**

   A dialog box appears that is similar to the standard Windows or Mac Open dialog boxes.

2. **Navigate your way to the Web browser that you'd like to add to the list and then click Open.**

   QuarkXPress adds it to the list of browsers in the Browsers pane.

3. **Repeat Steps 1 and 2 to add additional browsers (optional).**

4. **If you want one of the browsers in the list to be your default browser, click to the left of the browser's name.**

   A check mark appears next to the browser's name, indicating that this is now your default browser.

5. **If you want to delete a browser from the list, just highlight the name of the browser in the list and then click the Delete button.**

6. **After you finish making your changes, click OK.**

   You're ready to preview your pages.

Previewing your Web pages

To preview QuarkXPress Web pages in a browser, open the layout in QuarkXPress, find the small icon at the bottom of the QuarkXPress layout window that has a globe (to the left of the scroll bar and arrow), and then click and hold. Surprise! That globe icon is actually a pop-up menu for all the Web browsers that you entered in the Browsers Preferences dialog box (as shown in Figure 19-6). Just choose a browser from the menu, and QuarkXPress automatically opens the page.

There is your Web page is in all its colorful and, er, flawed splendor.

Pages in QuarkXPress may differ a bit when opened in a Web browser:

✔ Text or images may not be exactly where you planned.

✔ Some items may overlap.

All sorts of weird things may be going on, but nothing you can't fix! Study the page, make notes, and then return to your original QuarkXPress page and make the necessary adjustments. It may take you a few times to get everything just right, but what a great learning exercise!

Figure 19-6:
The Browsers pop-up menu (bottom of screen).

Exporting Your Web Pages

When your Web page is finished, the next step is to export it as HTML. Follow these steps to organize your files before you begin to export:

1. **Create a directory to round up all the pieces (such as pages and pictures) and name it.**

    This folder acts as your Site Root Directory.

2. **Copy all the pieces to the Site Root Directory.**

    Make sure that none of the pieces are in subfolders.

3. **Open the Preferences dialog box (either choose QuarkXPress⇨ Preferences on the Mac or Edit⇨Preferences in Windows, or press Option+Shift+⌘+Y or Ctrl+Alt+Shift+Y) and then select the General pane.**

    Two fields appear: Image Export Directory and Site Root Directory.

4. **In the Image Directory, enter a name such as *images* or *image_folder* to specify where QuarkXPress will store all your pictures when it exports your pages.**

5. **For the Site Root Directory, click the Select button to the right of the field and navigate to your directory folder. Highlight that folder in the window and then click the Select button at the bottom of the dialog box.**

With the directories prepared and the pieces in place, you're ready to export. To do so, follow these steps:

1. **Choose File⇨Export⇨HTML.**

    The Export HTML dialog box appears (as shown in Figure 19-7).

2. **Either keep the Pages field set to All or enter a range of pages just as you would in the Print dialog box.**

3. **Check the External CSS File check box if you want QuarkXPress to place the style information in the exported Web layout as a CSS (cascading style sheet) file in the export folder.**

    Cascading style sheets (CSSs), like the style sheets that you use in word processors or in QuarkXPress layouts, are a simple mechanism for ensuring consistent use of style (such as colors and fonts) in Web pages.

4. **Check the Launch Browser check box to display the first exported page in your default browser.**

5. **Click the Export button.**

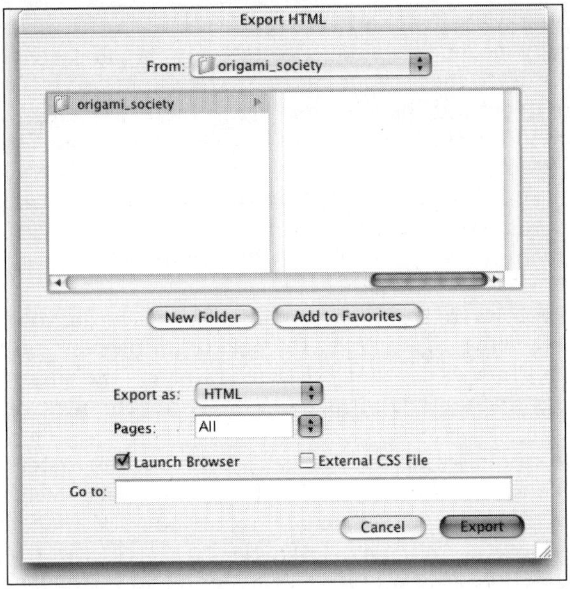

Figure 19-7:
The Export
HTML
dialog box.

You can upload files to the Web in a number of ways, but however you choose to do this, you need to perform the following:

✔ **Subscribe to a Web hosting service or an Internet service provider (ISP) that offers Web hosting.** If you have a Web address, you may already be working with a hosting provider. You may even be entitled to some free storage space along with your e-mail service. You might also ask some of your Web-savvy friends what host provider they recommend. Ask lots of questions because host providers offer all sorts of perks with their services, including technical support, monthly stats, and ready-made CGI scripts designed specifically for their servers. These scripts are free and can be incorporated with the forms in your QuarkXPress Web layouts easily.

✔ **Register a domain name.** Some people might tell you to do this first, in case some hotshot out there is ready to pounce on the name before you do. But we recommend that you wait until you decide on your host provider. A good host provider can have your domain name up and running in an hour. It makes sense to let the folks at the host provider do the work because they have the experience.

 • Your host provider representative can help you register your domain name on the spot.

 • The host provider can screen the Web to make sure that the name you want isn't already taken.

✔ **Find a reliable FTP client software application.** *File Transfer Protocol* (FTP) basically means the path for getting your HTML pages from here (your computer) to there (your ISP). *FTP client software* is the software that you use to get your pages from here to there. FTP client software packages are inexpensive, and some — such as Transmit, Fetch, WS_FTP Pro, CuteFTP, and AbsoluteFTP — are well worth the money. It is also worth noting that Fetch offers a Macintosh version of its product, whereas many FTP clients are for Windows only. If you are using Mac OS X, Panic Software's Transmit is a very full-featured and reliable FTP client.

If you're using a Web server to which you have direct access, you can simply copy the files there with a disk or over the network. However you get your files onto the Web, chances are that you'll need to copy the various files in specific directories that match the page hierarchy of your site.

Often, images are stored within an Images folder inside the folder that contains their Web pages, but they can also all be stored in one master folder. Work with your Web master to determine how the pages are saved on the server. In many cases, the Web page designer won't have to worry about this, but in smaller operations, the Web page designer could be the Web master.

To XML or Not to XML

eXtensible Markup Language (XML), is a system of tags for labeling information and controlling its structure.

You can use XML in QuarkXPress 6, thanks to Avenue.Quark. Avenue.Quark lets you extract and store QuarkXPress layout content in XML format. After content is in XML, it can be reused almost anywhere — in print, on CD-ROM, and on the Web. Chapter 10 explains how to install and use XTensions.

QuarkXPress integrates the Avenue.Quark tool to create and manipulate XML documents.

XML lets you create the tags, or labels, for various kinds of content (called *data type descriptions,* or DTDs) based on what makes sense for your content. Then you specify what happens to each of the types of labeled content; how it is presented, and so forth. Compare that with the more rigid HTML and PDF formats where there are only certain tags available (that furthermore cannot be changed) and where the presentation is fixed based on the label chosen.

XML code is similar to HTML in the sense that tags are surrounded by angle brackets (< and >) and commands and labels are turned on and off (such as `<standardHeader>` at the beginning of a header item and `</standardHeader>` at the end of it). Comments begin with `<!--` and end with >, whereas custom commands and declarations begin with `<?` and end with `?>`.

The Value of XML

Why do you need XML? Well, once upon a time writers and editors used to write books, newspapers, and magazines, and then publishers printed them on paper. Then along came the Web, and before long, those publications had to be converted to HTML after they were published in print format. A few years later came personal digital assistants (PDAs), Web-enabled cell phones, and WebTV-style boxes, so writers and editors were stuck with yet another task: writing and editing their words once for print, and again, and again, for many different Web devices. Writers and editors were not happy. Neither were the publishers who paid them.

Some programming genius took pity on these writers and their plight, and invented XML. With XML, writers and editors (or whoever) only have to write a document or book one time. From there, they can use XML tags to extract information or rearrange its structure according to the device that interprets it. Cool, eh?

XML is probably not something that you'll need to worry about if you're new to QuarkXPress. If you need to understand XML in the QuarkXPress context, refer to the documentation on XML that comes with the software and is also available from the Quark Web site, www.quark.com.

The Avenue.Quark XTension can relate styles and structures in QuarkXPress projects with elements in XML. After it's tagged in XML, the content can be stored separately from your QuarkXPress projects. When the time comes, you can translate XML content into HTML and serve it on the Web as HTML. Simple! And if you later want to create a more truncated version of the same project for a handheld device, such as a PDA or Web-enabled cell phone, you can translate the project for that platform as well.

You get to Avenue.Quark preferences by choosing QuarkXPress⇨Preferences on the Mac or Edit⇨Preferences in Windows, or pressing Option+Shift+⌘+Y or Ctrl+Alt+Shift+Y and then selecting Avenue.Quark from the list on the left of the Preference pane. See Figure 19-8.

The right side of the pane has three options that control how tags are applied:

✔ **Always Insert Repeating Elements at the End of the Current Branch.** If you enable this check box, any DTD elements marked as repeating are added to the end of the active branch. (This is how the preference should usually be set.) If you leave the box cleared, you're asked to manually determine the position of a new repeating element when you move text with a repeating element (such as a new instance of text set as `<Text>`) into the XML Workspace palette.

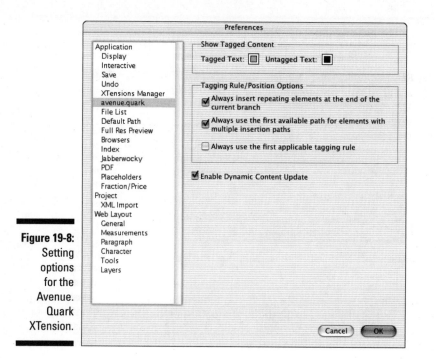

✔ **Always Use the First Available Path for Elements with Multiple Insertion Paths.** If you select this check box, QuarkXPress uses the first of multiple rules in the DTD for an element that has multiple rules. For example, if the DTD defines `<Paragraph>` element to be created at both the end of a current branch and after a new `<Sidebar>` element, QuarkXPress uses whichever rule is first. Otherwise, you're prompted when adding the element to the XML Workspace palette.

✔ **Always Use the First Applicable Tagging Rule.** If you select this check box, QuarkXPress uses the first tagging rule if there is a conflict between tagging rules. Otherwise, you're prompted when adding the element to the XML Workspace palette.

Of course, this begs the question, "If I can just translate a QuarkXPress print layouts to HTML, and upload it to the Web, why fiddle with XML in the first place?" Conceivably, you could do that. In fact, many corporations are converting their QuarkXPress layouts to XML. However, most of the world hasn't caught up with XML. Most Web browsers, particularly the older ones, still support only HTML. And most people still haven't gotten the hang of HTML. However, it is expected that XML soon will replace HTML as the language of choice for the Web and other platforms.

Part VI
Guru in Training

The 5th Wave   By Rich Tennant

GRICHTENNANT

It's another cow box mutilation, Sheriff. Look how cleanly the case has been severed. And if my hunch is right, you won't find the motherboard within a thousand miles of here.

In this part . . .

After you master the basics, why not pick up some of the tricks the pros use? In this part, we show you how to customize QuarkXPress so that it works the way you want it to. We also explain how QuarkXPress works on Windows PCs and on Macs.

Chapter 20

Customizing QuarkXPress

· ·

In This Chapter

▶ Setting application preferences

▶ Setting print and Web defaults

▶ Customizing tools

· ·

*P*eople who publish come in all shapes and sizes, and they approach their work from different directions. Fortunately, QuarkXPress offers many controls that let you customize the program to the way that *you* work. Use the Preferences dialog to control how your copy of QuarkXPress works with all print and Web projects.

In this chapter, we cover how to set application, print layout, and Web layout defaults in these dialog boxes.

Understanding Global and Local Controls

Global settings affect everything that you do — every project and layout and item that you create. They govern how QuarkXPress behaves when you perform certain actions. *Local* changes, on the other hand, affect only selected objects, such as an active page or item. Most preference settings are found in the Preferences dialog box (choose QuarkXPress⇨Preferences on the Mac and Edit⇨Preferences in Windows, or press Option+Shift+⌘+Y or Ctrl+Alt+Shift+Y). In QuarkXPress, global and local changes work as follows:

 ✔ **Application preferences are global.** They define how various features in your copy of QuarkXPress work with any type of file open.

 ✔ **Project preferences can be global or local.** If you change these preferences *with no projects open,* they change how QuarkXPress features behave for all future projects. If you change preferences *with a project open,* they affect only the active project.

✔ **Default settings are changes you make to the list of available colors, H&J sets, style sheets, print styles, and so forth.** Some of these lists, such as print styles, are always global. Other lists, such as style sheets, become program defaults when no projects are open but apply only to the active project when projects are open.

The Quark CMS, Index, and Fraction/Price options are now in the main Preferences dialog box (in version 5, they had been in separate dialog boxes), as are new panes for Undo, Full Res Preview, Placeholders, and XML Import. The Project label is also new. Gone is the StreetPost pane, which controlled how Extensible Markup Language (XML) projects connected to the Web. QuarkXPress 6 uses a different XML engine, and this pane is no longer relevant.

Setting Application Preferences

Application preferences control how QuarkXPress works with all projects. Any changes that you make in application preferences apply to all files that you create or edit with your copy of QuarkXPress. Note that preferences are saved in the XPress Preferences.prf file and not with each project.

To change application preferences, you first click the corresponding pane under the Application heading in the Preferences dialog box.

Display pane

Options in the Display pane, shown in Figure 20-1, control how QuarkXPress displays guides, projects, picture previews, and more. The way that you set these preferences will vary depending on your own taste and on your system.

Guide Colors area

You can change the color of Margin, Ruler, and Grid guides used for positioning items and text. The Margin color displays on the item; the Ruler color displays on the clipping path; and the Grid color displays on the text runaround path.

Display options

Three options in the Display pane control how QuarkXPress projects relate to the monitor's screen area. The *default view,* which appears each time that you start up the application or open a new project, is Actual Size (100%). The following list describes each option.

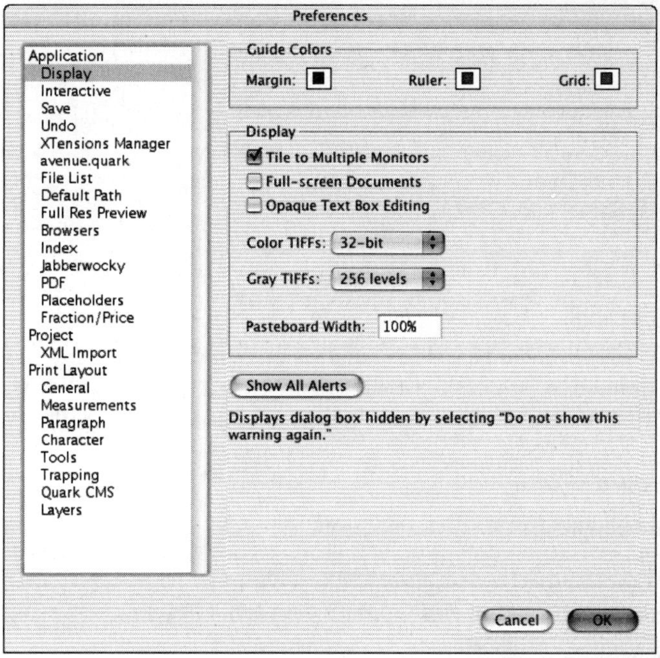

Figure 20-1:
The Display
pane of the
Preferences
dialog box.

Macintosh users have two options that aren't available for Windows:

- ✔ **Tile to Multiple Monitors:** If you have multiple monitors attached to your Mac, selecting this check box tells QuarkXPress to automatically put some project windows on your secondary monitor(s) when you choose Tile Projects.

  Use the Displays control panel in the Mac OS X System Preferences dialog box to set up your system for multiple monitors.

- ✔ **Full-Screen Documents:** If you select this Mac check box, the project window will appear at the screen's far left, under the default position for the Tool palette. If you use it, make sure that you move your Tool palette so that you can click the close box.

Opaque Text Box Editing

If you mark this check box, text boxes temporarily turn opaque while you are editing them. When the background of a text box is opaque, it's easier to see the text so that you can edit it. When the box is not opaque, you can see any background illustrations or graphics and edit text in relation to them.

Image display options

The Color TIFFs and Gray TIFFs settings control the accuracy of the colors and shades in the onscreen previews generated for imported TIFF images. Lower bit depths can result in considerably smaller project files because of the low bit depth of the resulting TIFF image previews. If you're trying to match colors onscreen and you have a higher-end system, you can set the bit depths higher.

The Color TIFFs and Gray TIFFs settings apply only to screen previews and do not affect the resolution of the printed picture.

QuarkXPress for Windows has a unique option called Display DPI Value. This should remain at 96 dots per inch (dpi); using a larger number permanently zooms the monitor view, and a smaller number zooms out the view.

Pasteboard Width

This option sets the width of the *pasteboard,* which is the area outside the edges of the layout where you can store layout elements until you are ready to position them. The default is 100%, which means the pasteboard is as wide as the page, thus giving you the equivalent of a half-page working area on either side of your layout.

Show All Alerts button

This feature is a reset button for the alerts in QuarkXPress that gives you the option to turn them off. You can turn off most alerts by enabling a Do Not Show This Warning Again check box. Sometimes, you regret turning off alerts, so to turn on the alerts again, just click Show All Alerts.

Interactive pane

The Interactive pane, as shown in Figure 20-2, controls scrolling, smart quotes, and the display of dragged items.

Scrolling

Use the Scrolling slider to control how fast the page scrolls when you click the arrows in the scroll bars. Most people prefer a Scrolling setting somewhere in the middle range. If you set the slider closer to Slow, QuarkXPress moves more slowly across your project window, which is helpful if you want to pay close attention to your project while scrolling. If you set the slider closer to Fast, QuarkXPress zips across the window, which may cause you to move past a desired element.

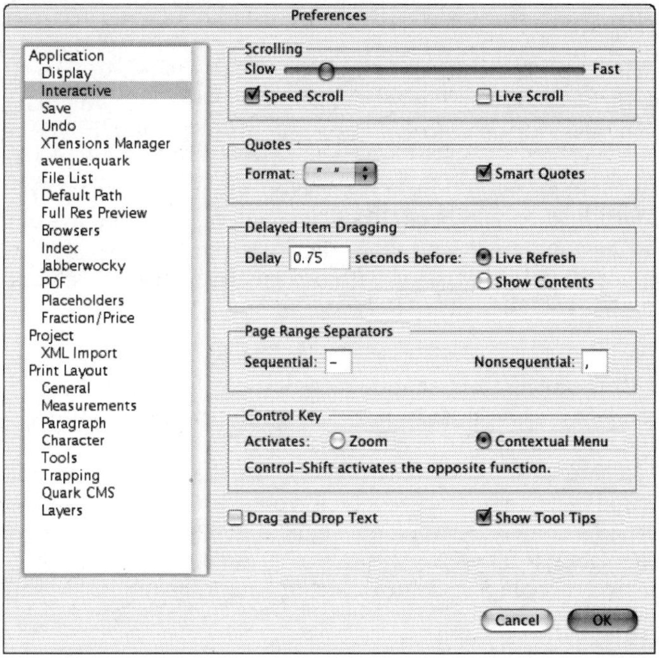

Figure 20-2:
The
Interactive
pane of the
Preferences
dialog box.

Two other options in the scrolling section of the dialog box are:

- ✔ **Speed Scroll:** This option speeds up scrolling by masking out the graphics and blends when you scroll. After you stop scrolling, the graphics and blends are redrawn. Generally, you should check this check box.

- ✔ **Live Scroll:** If you check this check box, QuarkXPress redraws pages while you are dragging the box in the scroll bar. Check this option unless you're working on a slow computer.

Quotes

The style of quotes that you select from the pop-up list is used when you check Convert Quotes in the Get Text dialog box (File⇨Get Text, or ⌘+E or Ctrl+E). The Smart Quotes check box controls whether straight quotes are converted to typographers' (curly) quotation marks while you type.

Delayed Item Dragging

The options in the Delayed Item Dragging area control how items display when you drag them with the Item tool. If you simply select an item and drag it immediately, these controls are ignored. (All you see is the outline of the item until you finish moving it; then the text reflows as necessary, and the item displays again.) However, if you click and hold and then drag the item, you have the option to either see the text wrap change or simply the contents of the item. The value that you enter in the Delay Seconds field controls the time (in seconds ranging between 0.1 and 5.0) that you must press and hold the mouse button before Show Contents or Live Refresh is activated.

If the Live Refresh radio button is selected when you press and hold the mouse button when you begin dragging an item, the contents of the item are visible while you drag it, and the screen also refreshes to show item layers and text flow. If you're working with designs with lots of text wraps, we recommend that you check Live Refresh.

Page Range Separators

The Page Range Separators option defines the characters used to define a range of pages that you're printing. It's only necessary if you're using the Section feature — and then only if you're using a hyphen or a comma within your section page numbers. By default, you use a hyphen in a sequential range of pages and a comma between nonsequential pages, but with the Section feature, you might use a hyphen within a page number (page A-1, A-2, and so on). If you do end up using separators within your page numbers, you can change the defaults here.

Control Key

This Mac-only feature lets you decide whether pressing the Control key lets you zoom in or access one of the contextual menus. (Pressing Control+Option will still let you zoom out.) If the Zoom radio button is selected, the Control key acts as a short cut for the Zoom tool. If the Contextual Menus radio button is selected, the Control Key displays the contextual menu of an item when you click and hold on it. Windows users always access contextual menus by right-clicking.

Drag-and-drop editing

When the Drag and Drop Text check box is checked, you can highlight a piece of text and then drag it to a new location (as you can in most word processors) instead of cutting it from the old location and pasting it in the new one. If you hold down the Shift key, a copy of the highlighted text is moved to the new location while the original text stays put.

Show Tool Tips

Checking the Show Tool Tips check box displays the official names of the palette or tool icons when the mouse pointer is positioned on them. This is checked by default, and because it does no harm, you might as well leave it that way.

Save pane

The Save pane lets you control how QuarkXPress saves projects and libraries as well as how it makes backup copies of your projects. The Save pane is shown in Figure 20-3.

Here are the options that you can select:

- ✔ **Auto Save:** When this check box is checked, QuarkXPress saves opened projects at regular intervals. You determine that interval through the value that you enter in the Every Minutes text box. If your computer crashes, an auto save occurs. QuarkXPress does not actually save your project to its regular project file; instead, it creates an auto-saved project (with a filename that ends in .AutoSave on the Mac and .asv in Windows). If your computer crashes, you can revert your file to its last auto-saved condition by opening the auto-saved project.

- ✔ **Auto Backup:** When this option is selected, QuarkXPress creates a backup copy of your project every time that you manually save it. You determine how many (up to 100) previous versions are retained by making an entry in the Keep Revisions text box.

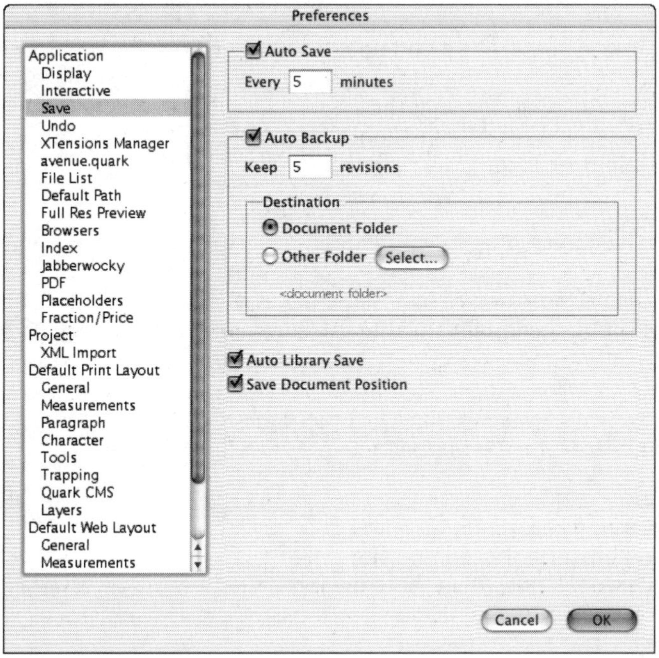

Figure 20-3:
The Save pane of the Preferences dialog box.

✔ **Destination:** You determine where backups are stored by choosing one of the two Destination radio buttons. The default location is in the same folder as the current project, but we highly recommend that you change it because it's otherwise very easy to open the wrong version of a file. Select the Other Folder radio button and then click the Select button to select or create a backup folder.

✔ **Auto Library Save:** When the Auto Library Save check box is checked, as it is by default, any changes that you make to libraries are instantly saved. Otherwise, QuarkXPress saves changes to libraries when you close them or quit QuarkXPress. We recommend that you keep Auto Library Save checked. As our dear grandmothers always used to say, "Better safe than sorry."

✔ **Save Document Position:** Unless you're sharing projects among users with monitors of varying sizes, keep this check box selected, too. Why? When checked, Save Document Position automatically remembers the size, position, and proportions of your project window, thus saving you the time of finding your place the next time that you open the project.

Undo pane

QuarkXPress now includes multiple undos and redos, and the Undo pane (see Figure 20-4) lets you control how undos and redos work.

In this pane, you set the Redo hot key — your choices are the default Shift+⌘+Z or Ctrl+Shift+Z, ⌘+Y or Ctrl+Y, or ⌘+Z or Ctrl+Z — and the maximum number undoable steps (in the Maximum History Actions field, with a maximum of 30).

You get the choice of redo commands because different programs use different shortcuts, and QuarkXPress lets you pick the one you prefer or that your other applications tend to use. Selecting ⌘+Z or Ctrl+Z sets Redo to be the same as Undo, essentially making the command toggle back and forth.

XTensions Manager pane

The XTensions Manager pane, as shown in Figure 20-5, controls if and when the XTensions Manager dialog box displays when you launch QuarkXPress. In a service bureau, for example, you might want to see the XTensions Manager at every launch. (See Chapter 10 for more information on XTensions.)

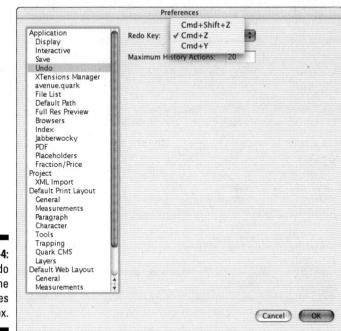

Figure 20-4:
The Undo
pane of the
Preferences
dialog box.

Figure 20-5:
The
XTensions
Manager
pane of the
Preferences
dialog box.

The options that you can choose include

- ✔ **Always:** Selecting this radio button makes the XTensions Manager display each time that you launch QuarkXPress.

- ✔ **When "XTensions" Folder Changes:** Selecting this radio button/check box combination causes the XTensions Manager dialog box to appear when you launch QuarkXPress, but only if you have previously added or removed XTensions from the XTensions folder.

- ✔ **When Error Loading XTensions Occurs:** Selecting this radio button/check box combination causes the XTensions Manager dialog box to appear when you launch QuarkXPress, but only if you had a problem loading an XTension.

Avenue.Quark pane

The Avenue.Quark pane of the Preferences dialog box lets you establish some tagging standards for XML files (see Chapter 19 for pointers on using XML).

File List pane

The File List pane, as shown in Figure 20-6, adds a list of recently opened files to the File menu or to the File⇨Open submenu, as you prefer. This makes it easier to access files — instead of hunting for a file, you simply let QuarkXPress find and open it for you.

The options in this pane include

- ✔ **Number of Files:** Enter a number here for the number of files that you want QuarkXPress to keep track of in the file list. The default number of files is 3, but you can enter up to 9 if you want to keep track of lots of files (as many of us do).

- ✔ **File List Location:** The two options here let you determine where to put the names of the files. The first is Append Files to File Menu. When you select this radio button, your file names are listed toward the bottom of the File menu. The other option is the Append Files to Open Menu Item. Selecting this radio button adds a submenu to File⇨Open that contains those recent filenames in the Open submenu so that you will only see them when you try to open a project.

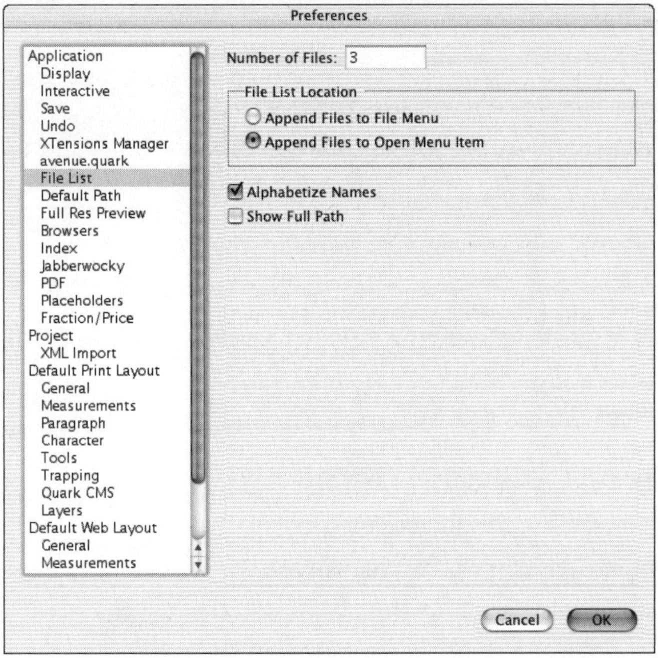

Figure 20-6:
The File List
pane of the
Preferences
dialog box.

✔ **Alphabetize Names:** Checking this check box alphabetizes the names in your list; otherwise the file names appear in the order in which they were opened.

✔ **Show Full Path:** Checking this check box shows you the path to your file as well as the name of the file. The full paths can be useful if you need to find a file to send it elsewhere or if you have multiple versions of a file in different locations.

Default Path pane

Use the preferences in the Default Path pane, as shown in Figure 20-7, to establish a consistent path to specified folders on your hard drive, thus making it easier for you to locate items in your project if they are properly organized. QuarkXPress lets you set separate default locations for the Open, Save/Save As, and Get Text/Get Picture dialog boxes.

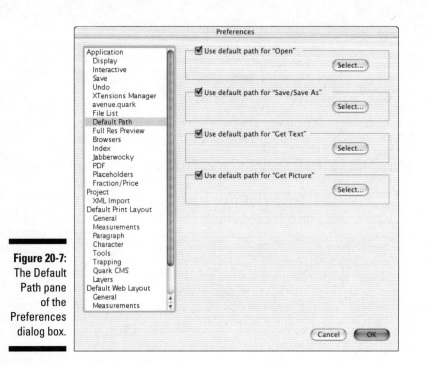

Figure 20-7:
The Default
Path pane
of the
Preferences
dialog box.

Full Res Preview pane

A new feature in QuarkXPress, the Full Res Preview pane (see Figure 20-8), displays images at their full resolution instead of at screen resolution. Full-resolution preview produces higher fidelity for clipping paths when you zoom in, but using it takes more computer horsepower and can slow down display. *Note:* This new feature only works in registered copies of QuarkXPress.

The options in this pane include

✔ **Preview Cache Location:** To display images at full resolution, QuarkXPress creates *cache files* — electronic scratchpads — that it uses when you zoom and scroll, so it loads only the necessary data for the current operation or view. This minimizes display slowdown. The Preview Cache Location options determine where these cache files are stored. The default is the QuarkXPress Folder radio button, but we recommend that you enable the Other Folder radio button and then click the Browse button to pick a folder dedicated to these cache files. That way, your QuarkXPress folder does not get filled up with temporary files. You might want to create a Cache folder within your QuarkXPress folder so that these files are kept in one location but stay with other QuarkXPress files.

You also set the maximum cache folder size in this pane. The default is 100MB, which is fine for most users. If you use full-resolution preview in image-heavy projects, you should increase this folder size to something like 250MB or greater.

✔ **Display Full Resolution Preview For:** Because Full Res Preview can slow performance, QuarkXPress lets you have only selected pictures displayed this way. You select them by choosing Item⇨Preview Resolution. In the Full Res Preview pane, you can override that setting so that all cached pictures are displayed in full resolution as well as any new images that you select via the Item menu. Or you can prevent display of the high-resolution previews from previously selected images so that only currently selected images have full-resolution previews. Use the radio buttons in the Display Full Resolution Preview For section of this pane.

You can disable full-resolution previews entirely by checking the Disable Full-Resolution Previews on Open check box. Although a designer might want full-resolution previews displayed, a copy editor may not. The copy editor could have QuarkXPress automatically turn off full-resolution previews in her copy of the program by using this option instead of requiring the designer to remove full-resolution preview from each image.

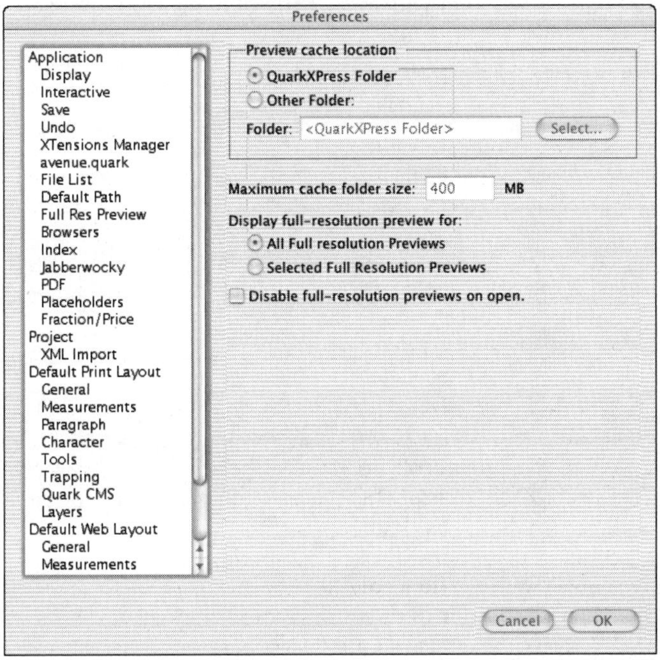

Figure 20-8:
The Full Res Preview pane of the Preferences dialog box.

Browsers pane

The Browsers pane, as shown in Figure 20-9, lets you specify the Web browsers that you want to use for previewing Web layouts. Most Web designers preview layouts in at least the latest versions of Internet Explorer and Netscape Navigator. Chapter 19 has more information about the Browsers pane.

Index pane

Index preferences relate mostly to punctuation within an index, so if you create standard indexes for all publications, you want to set program defaults. These preferences are saved with the active project. Figure 20-10 shows the Index pane.

Jabberwocky pane

Jabberwocky lets you generate customized dummy text that you can use in preliminary designs while you wait for final copy. The Jabberwocky pane, as shown in Figure 20-11, lets you specify the default word set used for dummy text and its format.

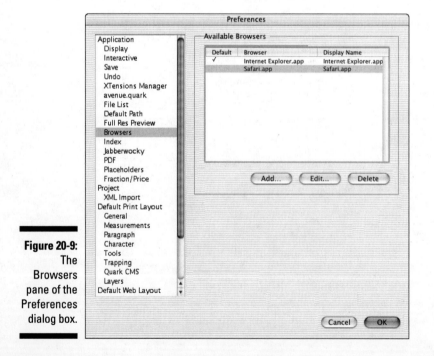

Figure 20-9:
The
Browsers
pane of the
Preferences
dialog box.

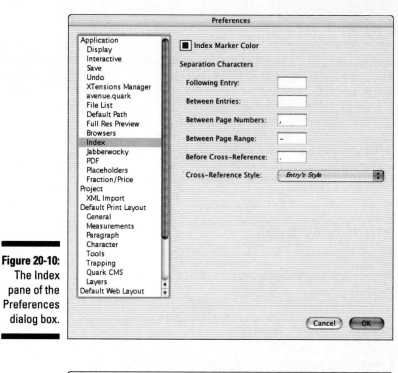

Figure 20-11:
The Jabber-
wocky pane
of the
Preferences
dialog box.

PDF pane

The new PDF pane (see Figure 20-12) lets you specify whether the PDF files are created via the QuarkXPress new, direct PDF-creation capability or via Adobe's Acrobat Distiller software. You also have the options to set a Watched folder for Acrobat Distiller — this is a folder that Acrobat Distiller checks periodically for files to convert.

In the Default Settings section, click the Options button to specify how hyperlinks are translated and change output settings. Chapter 11 has more information about creating PDF files with QuarkXPress.

Placeholders pane

The new Placeholders pane lets you set the colors for text and graphics placeholders used in XML projects.

Fraction/Price pane

The Fraction/Price pane sets defaults for fractions and prices, including character size and position as well as the fraction separator character and the price symbol. (*Note:* If the Type Tricks XTension isn't running, this pane won't be available.)

These settings are saved only in the XPress Preferences file as application preferences instead of as project-level preferences, as shown in Figure 20-13. This is unfortunate because the settings may vary according to the actual type sizes and fonts in use. If you change these settings for specific designs, make a note of them.

XML Import pane

With the XML Import pane, shown in Figure 20-14, you control whether a project's associated XML file is imported when you open it.

This pane works in similar fashion to the Auto Picture Import option in the Print Layout pane, letting you choose whether to use the project's existing XML information or to update it with the external source file. We recommend that you enable the Verify radio button, which prompts you whether to update the XML data when and XML file is opened. Chapter 19 has more information on XML.

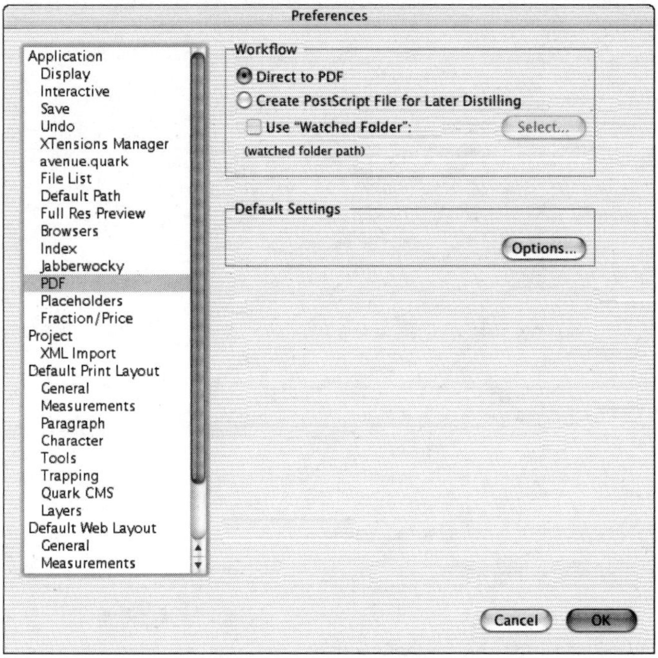

Preferences

Workflow
- ● Direct to PDF
- ○ Create PostScript File for Later Distilling
- ☐ Use "Watched Folder": [Select...]
- (watched folder path)

Default Settings

[Options...]

Application
  Display
  Interactive
  Save
  Undo
  XTensions Manager
  avenue.quark
  File List
  Default Path
  Full Res Preview
  Browsers
  Index
  Jabberwocky
  PDF
  Placeholders
  Fraction/Price
Project
  XML Import
Default Print Layout
  General
  Measurements
  Paragraph
  Character
  Tools
  Trapping
  Quark CMS
  Layers
Default Web Layout
  General
  Measurements

[Cancel] [OK]

Figure 20-12:
The PDF pane of the Preferences dialog box.

Preferences

Numerator
- Offset: 35%
- VScale: 50%
- HScale: 50%
- Kern: -15

Slash
- Offset: 0%
- VScale: 100%
- HScale: 100%
- ☑ Virgule

Denominator
- Offset: 0%
- VScale: 50%
- HScale: 50%
- Kern: -15

Price
- ☑ Underline Cents
- ☑ Delete Radix

Application
  Display
  Interactive
  Save
  Undo
  XTensions Manager
  avenue.quark
  File List
  Default Path
  Full Res Preview
  Browsers
  Index
  Jabberwocky
  PDF
  Placeholders
  Fraction/Price
Project
  XML Import
Default Print Layout
  General
  Measurements
  Paragraph
  Character
  Tools
  Trapping
  Quark CMS
  Layers
Default Web Layout
  General
  Measurements

[Cancel] [OK]

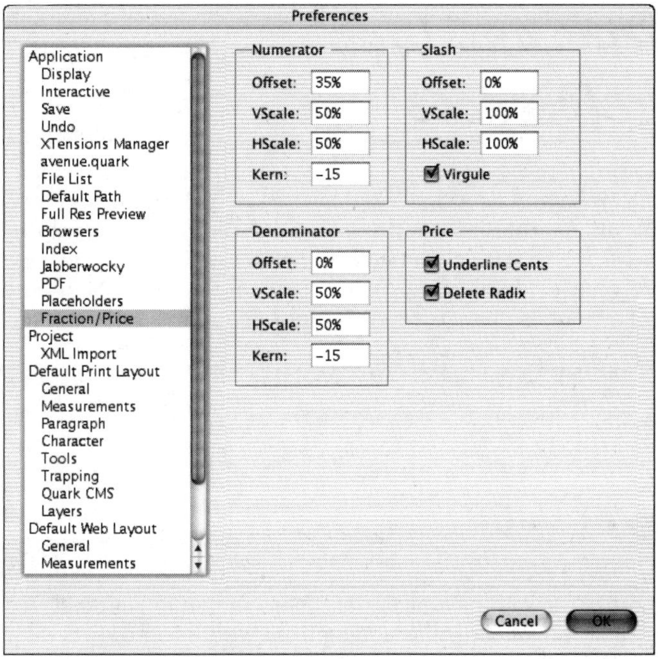

Figure 20-13:
The Fraction/ Price pane of the Preferences dialog box.

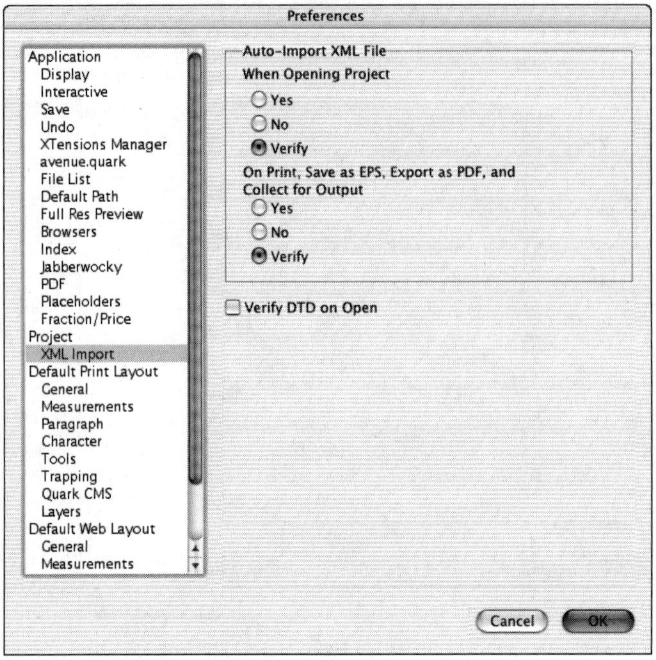

Preferences

Application
Display
Interactive
Save
Undo
XTensions Manager
avenue.quark
File List
Default Path
Full Res Preview
Browsers
Index
Jabberwocky
PDF
Placeholders
Fraction/Price
Project
  XML Import
Default Print Layout
  General
  Measurements
  Paragraph
  Character
  Tools
  Trapping
  Quark CMS
  Layers
Default Web Layout
  General
  Measurements

┌─ Auto-Import XML File ──────────────────┐
  When Opening Project
    ○ Yes
    ○ No
    ◉ Verify

  On Print, Save as EPS, Export as PDF, and
  Collect for Output
    ○ Yes
    ○ No
    ◉ Verify
└──────────────────────────────────────┘

  ☐ Verify DTD on Open

    [Cancel] [OK]

Figure 20-14:
The XML
Import pane
of the
Preferences
dialog box.

Setting Print and Web Layout Preferences

When no projects are open, any changes that you make to panes in the Default Print Layout section — and in the Default Web Layout section, which offers essentially the same options — are saved in the XPress Preferences file. This means that these defaults will affect all future projects. However, if you have a project open, changes to these preferences affect only that active project. The names change, too, to Print Layout and Web Layout.

The Default Web Layout panes are available only if a Web layout is open or if no project is open.

General pane

There are two versions of the General pane: one for Print Layout preferences and the other for Web Layout preferences. Shown in Figure 20-15, both contain a cornucopia of controls ranging from whether graphics display to how boxes are framed. The following sections describe in detail how you can use the options in the two versions of the General pane.

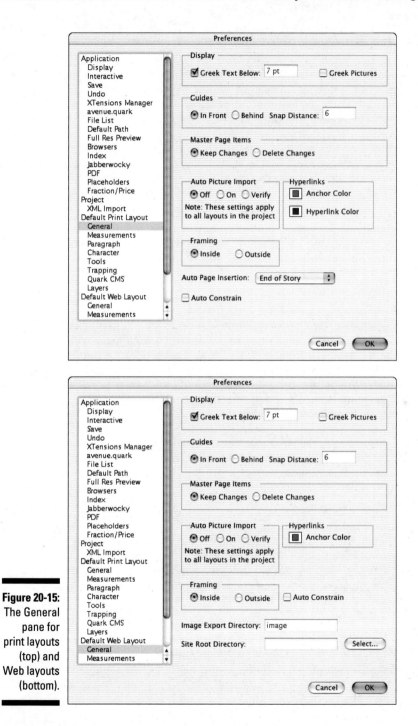

Figure 20-15:
The General
pane for
print layouts
(top) and
Web layouts
(bottom).

Greek Text Below and Greek Pictures

When you use *greeking*, QuarkXPress displays a gray area to represent text or pictures on the page; this makes the page display more quickly on your monitor. Turning on greeking speeds the display of your QuarkXPress layout. When you print, images and text are unaffected by greeking; in other words, they print. The greeking options include

- ✔ **Greek Text Below:** Checking this check box tells QuarkXPress to greek the text display when text is below a certain point size. The default value is 7 points (pt), but you can enter a value ranging from 2 to 720 pt. To disable greeking, clear the Greek Text Below check box.

- ✔ **Greek Pictures:** Checking this check box tells QuarkXPress to display all unselected graphics as gray shapes, which speeds up display. This feature is useful after you position and size your images and no longer need to see them in your layout. You can still look at a greeked picture by clicking it.

Guides

The Guides menu specifies whether *guides* (lines that help you see where margins are and help you position items on the page) appear in front of boxes (the default setting) or behind them. These guides do not print or appear in finalized Web pages but simply help you with arranging items in a layout. When guides are behind boxes, you can more easily see what's in the boxes, but you may find it harder to tell whether elements within the boxes line up with margins, gutters, or baselines.

You can also specify the *snap distance* here. This simply means you can specify how far away you want an item to be from a guide before it "snaps to," or aligns with, a nearby guide.

Master Page Items

The Master Page Items options control what happens to text and picture boxes that are defined on a master page when you apply a different master page to your layout pages. Your options are Keep Changes (the default) and Delete Changes. We recommend that you leave this setting on Keep Changes. Then, after applying a new master page, you can manually remove any unwanted elements that are left behind.

Auto Picture Import

Use Auto Picture Import options to update links to your source images automatically. This preference is handy if your picture may change frequently and you don't want to forget to update your layout to accommodate the changes. The options are

✔ **Off:** QuarkXPress does not check whether the source graphic files have been modified.

✔ **On:** This setting tells QuarkXPress to automatically import the latest version of changed graphics files.

✔ **Verify:** QuarkXPress checks the date and time stamp of the graphics files to see whether they have been modified. The program then displays a list of all the modified graphics files in your project so that you can decide whether to update the layout with the newest versions.

Use Verify or On even if you don't expect graphics files to change much; that way, if the graphics files do change, your project will contain the most recent versions of the files.

This option works only with graphics that you imported by choosing File⇨Get Picture, or pressing ⌘+E or Ctrl+E. Graphics that you paste into QuarkXPress via the Clipboard are not affected because the pasted file is copied into your layout, not linked to an outside file.

Framing

The Framing options tell QuarkXPress how to draw the *ruling lines* (frames) around text and picture boxes. You can access this option by choosing Item⇨ Frame, or pressing ⌘+B or Ctrl+B). You can place these frames Inside or Outside the box edge.

Hyperlinks

This section of the General pane lets you choose default colors for hyperlinks and anchors in a Web page (see Chapter 18 for information on how to use hyperlinks and anchors).

Auto Page Insertion

Auto Page Insertion (a print layout preference) tells QuarkXPress where to add new pages when all your text does not fit into an automatic text box. You must define the text box containing the overflow text as an automatic text box in the layout's master page. Your options are:

✔ **End of Section:** Places new pages at the end of the current section. (You define sections by choosing Page⇨Section.) If no sections are defined, End of Section works the same as the End of Document option.

✔ **End of Story:** Places new pages immediately following the last page of the text chain.

- **End of Document:** Places new pages at the end of the layout.
- **Off:** Adds no new pages, leaving you to add pages and text boxes for overflow text wherever you want. The existence of overflow text is indicated by a red box at the end of the text in the text box.

Auto Constrain

The Auto Constrain option (a print layout preference) controls the behavior of boxes that are created within other boxes. If you check the Auto Constrain check box, a box is created within another box — a picture box drawn inside a text box, for example — and may not exceed the boundaries of the parent box (in this case, the text box). Neither can you move the box outside the parent box's boundaries. Unless you have a good reason to do otherwise, leave this default option unchecked.

Measurements pane

In the Measurements pane, as shown in Figure 20-16, you can set the default measurement system displayed in most fields, although some options (such as type size) are always expressed in points. Although you set up Web projects in pixels (equal to points onscreen), the measurement systems work the same for both print and Web layouts.

Paragraph pane

The Paragraph pane, as shown in Figure 20-17, offers options for horizontal and vertical spacing: leading, baseline grid, and hyphenation. The hyphenation setting is only there to keep QuarkXPress compatible with previous versions, but the leading and baseline grid options have a significant impact on spacing in projects.

The Paragraph pane has its own keyboard shortcut: Option+⌘+Y or Ctrl+Alt+Y.

Character pane

You can customize character attributes such as type styles in the Character pane, as shown in Figure 20-18. For the most part, you'll make these decisions only once because they are likely to be the same for most projects. Some, however, are related to your designs and workflow. For example, if you work in a cross-platform environment, you may wish to turn off Ligatures because they're not supported on Windows. Or, if a particular design uses Small Caps frequently, you might tweak its settings in one project.

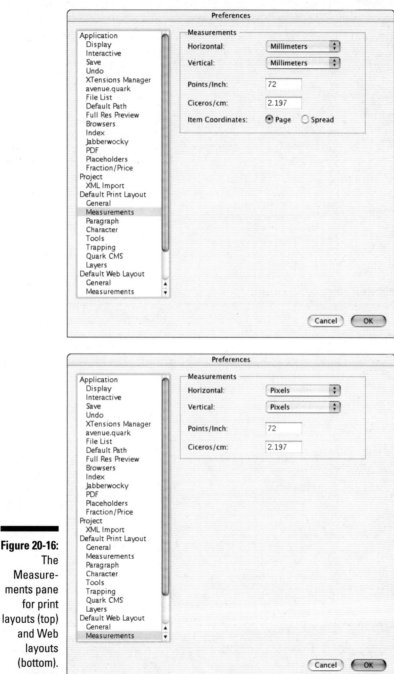

Figure 20-16:
The Measure-ments pane for print layouts (top) and Web layouts (bottom).

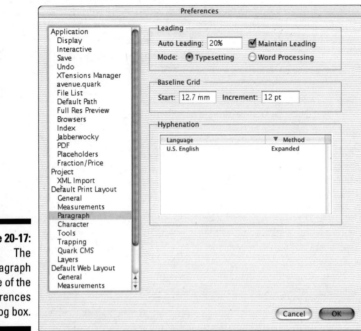

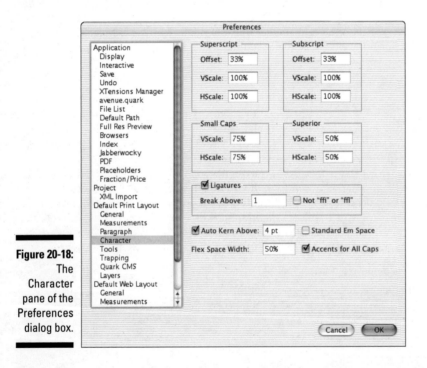

Several options in the Character pane affect character styles. These options include the four areas labeled Superscript, Subscript, Small Caps, and Superior. *Superiors* are special superscript characters that always align along the *cap line,* which is the height of a capital letter in the current typeface. Superiors typically are used in footnotes.

Superscript and Subscript

The Superscript and Subscript sections share the following options:

- ✔ **Offset:** Dictates how far below or above the baseline QuarkXPress shifts a subscripted or superscripted character. The default settings are 33% for both Subscript and Superscript. We prefer 35% for superscript and 30% for subscript.

- ✔ **VScale** and **HScale:** Determine scaling for the subscript or superscript. Although the default is 100%, typeset projects typically use a smaller size for subscripts and superscripts — usually between 60 and 80 percent of the text size. The two values should be the same.

Small Caps and Superior

The options in the Small Caps and Superior sections are identical even though these attributes are very different. VScale and HScale determine the scaling for the small cap or superior, or both should be set to the same value.

Usually, a small cap's scale should be between 65 percent and 80 percent of the normal text, and a superior's scale should be between 50 percent and 65 percent.

Ligatures

A *ligature* is a set of joined characters. The characters are joined because the shapes almost blend together by default, so typographers of yore decided to make them blend together naturally. When you select the Ligatures check box, QuarkXPress automatically replaces occurrences of *fi, ffi, fl,* and *ffl* with their respective ligatured equivalents (*fi, ffi, fl,* and *ffl*), both when you enter text and when you import it. If you uncheck the Ligatures check box, all ligatures in your project are translated to standard character combinations. (Not all fonts support ligatures, and many sans serif typefaces look like their nonligature equivalents.) This feature is nice because it means that you don't have to worry about adding ligatures manually; it's also nice because it doesn't affect spell checking.

- ✔ **Not "ffi" or "ffl":** Some people don't like using ligatures for *ffi* and *ffl.* Check the Not "ffi" or "ffl" check box to prevent these ligatures from being used automatically.

✔ **Break Above:** The Break Above option for ligatures lets you set how a ligature is handled in a loosely tracked line. You can enter a value ranging from 0 to 100. That value is the number of units of tracking (each unit is ¹⁄₂₀₀ of an em space) at which QuarkXPress breaks apart a ligature to prevent awkward spacing.

QuarkXPress for Windows does not support ligatures. As a result, Mac files with Ligatures option selected — when moved to QuarkXPress for Windows — are converted so they use the standard characters. But when they are moved back to the Mac, the ligatures are re-enabled automatically.

Auto Kern Above

Use Auto Kern Above to define the point size at which QuarkXPress automatically kerns letter pairs. *Kerning* is the process of adjusting the space between two letters so that the letters have a better appearance.

Standard Em Space

This option determines how QuarkXPress calculates the width of an *em space,* which is a standard measurement in typography upon which many other spacing measurements are based. If you check this check box, QuarkXPress uses the typographic measurement (the width of the letter *M,* which is usually equal to the current point size). Unchecked, QuarkXPress uses the width of two zeroes.

Flex Space Width

This option lets you define the value for a *flex space,* which is a user-defined space. The default is 50%, which is about the width of the letter *t,* called a thin space. A better setting — because you're more likely to use an em space than a thin space — is 200%, which is equal to an em space.

Accents for All Caps

In many publications, the style is to drop accents from capitalized letters. If checked, this option lets accented characters retain their accents if you apply the All Caps attribute to them.

Tools pane

QuarkXPress lets you customize how its basic tools — in particular the item creation tools and the Zoom tool — work by changing settings in the Tools pane (see Figure 20-19). The ability to customize certain settings comes in handy. You can, for example, give oval picture boxes an offset of 1 pica or set text boxes to have a 3-point frame and a transparent background. To open the Tools pane, you can double-click any tool that can be modified. You can modify tools for both print and Web layouts.

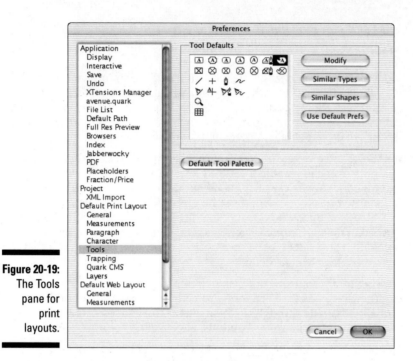

Figure 20-19:
The Tools
pane for
print
layouts.

Selecting tools to customize

After the Tools pane is open, you select the tools that you want to modify:

- ✔ **To select one tool,** simply click on it.

- ✔ **To select noncontiguous tools,** ⌘+click or Ctrl+click them.

- ✔ **To select a range of continuous tools,** Shift+click them.

- ✔ **To select all the item creation tools of one type** (text box, picture box, line, or text path), select one and then click Similar Types.

- ✔ **To select all the tools that create items of the same shape** (for example, all oval boxes), select one and then click Similar Shapes.

After the tools are selected, you can click Modify to access the customizable options that the tools have in common. If you select all the text-box creation tools, for example, you'll be able to specify a default number of columns for all text boxes. Commands that do not make sense as defaults — such as size and placement — are not included.

Tools that you can customize

The tools that you can customize fall into the following groups:

- ✔ **Zoom tool:** You can change the minimum and maximum zoom views to any value between 10 and 800 percent. You also can specify how much QuarkXPress zooms into your project each time that you click the project with the Zoom tool active. To do this, enter any value from 10 to 800 percent, in increments of 1 percent, into the Increment field.

- ✔ **Box tools:** You can set the item settings for all the Text Box and Picture Box tools. You can establish settings for options normally available for the individual boxes via the Item menu's Modify, Frame, and Runaround options. If you select one of these box tools from the Tools pane and click Modify, a dialog box containing three panes — corresponding to those Item menu options — appears, and you can set these options just as you do if you select a box on a project page. The difference is that you are setting them as defaults.

- ✔ **Drawing tools:** You can establish defaults for new lines that you draw with the Line and Text Path tools. You can set most line options that are normally available through the Item menu. You can also set other line-specification and runaround options, such as line color and weight.

- ✔ **Tables tool:** You can modify some default characteristics of tables, such as the number of rows and columns in a table and the table's borders.

- ✔ **Image Map tools:** You can control the shape's complexity by limiting the number of points that defines the clickable area as well as control the granularity — that is, how closely the clickable area follows the image contours. This is available only in the Web Layouts section's Tools pane.

- ✔ **Form tool:** You can determine the default width and height for new form boxes. This is available only in the Web Layouts section's Tools pane.

Reverting to default tools

If you find that modifications made to tools are not appropriate to one or all of your projects, you can revert the changes made in the Tools pane. Simply select the tools whose settings you want to revert and then click Use Default Prefs.

One tool that you won't see in the Tools pane is the Starburst tool. To change its settings, double-click the Starburst icon on the Tools palette.

Trapping pane

The Preferences dialog box contains another pane, Trapping, that lets you specify defaults for how QuarkXPress traps colors and objects when you separate a project into its color plates. This feature is very advanced, and we recommend that beginners do not change the defaults.

Quark CMS pane

With the Quark Color Management System (CMS) XTension, QuarkXPress can help you ensure accurate printing of your colors, both those in imported images and those defined in QuarkXPress. What Quark CMS does is track the colors in the source image, the colors displayable by your monitor, and the colors printable by your printer. If the monitor or printer doesn't support a color in your project, Quark CMS alters the color to its closest possible equivalent.

To activate the Quark CMS, make sure the Quark CMS XTension is active (choose Utilities⇨XTensions Manager) and that Color Management is on. Turn on color management by checking the Color Management Active check box in the Quark CMS pane, as shown in Figure 20-20.

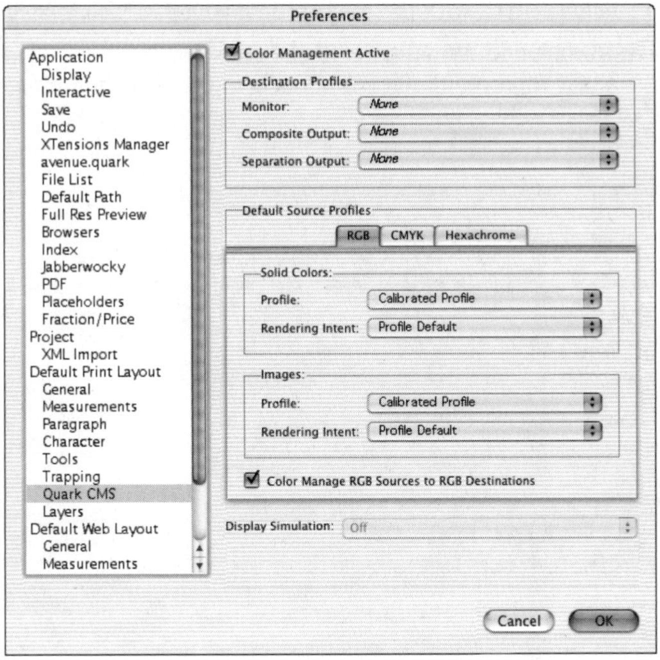

Figure 20-20:
The Quark
CMS pane
of the
Preferences
dialog box.

Layers pane

Layers are slices of a project that are stacked on top of each other. Layers, which are project-wide rather than page-specific, help you organize content and store multiple versions of the same publication in a single project file. The Layers pane, as shown in Figure 20-21, lets you specify defaults for layers:

- ✔ **Visible:** When this check box is checked, all new layers added to a layout are visible, and the eye icon appears next to each layer in the Layer palette. When the Visible box is unchecked, new layers are invisible until you click where the eye icon normally appears in the Layers palette.

- ✔ **Locked:** When the Locked check box is selected, all items on a layer are unmovable unless they are first "unlocked" in the Layers palette.

- ✔ **Suppress Output:** This box works hand in hand with the Visible check box. If Visible is not checked, Suppress Output is automatically grayed out. If Visible is checked, however, the Suppress Output button is reactivated. When Suppress Output is checked, layers are automatically kept from being output with the rest of the layout.

- ✔ **Keep Runaround:** When this check box is checked, items on a layer can have a text runaround. If it isn't checked, the text runaround option defaults to None.

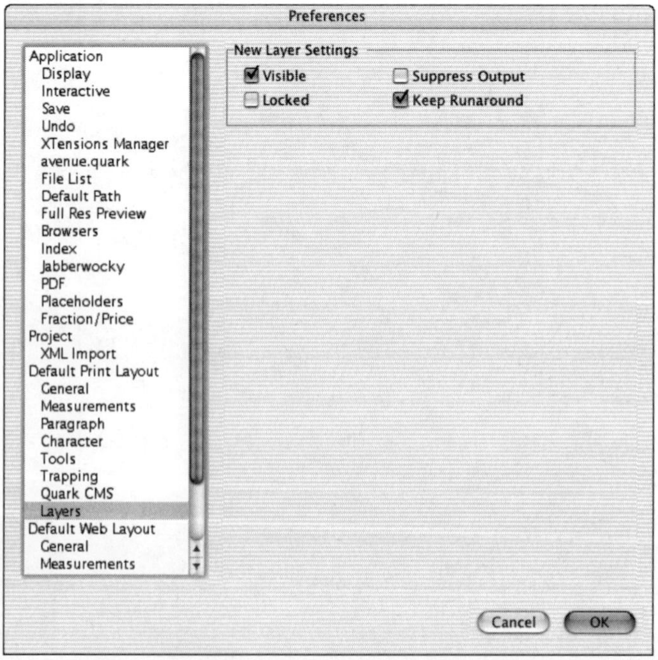

Figure 20-21:
The Layers
pane of the
Preferences
dialog box.

Changing Default Settings

Default settings, such as the list of colors available, are settings that you can make with no projects open. The settings then become part of all new projects that you create. Some of the default settings that you change globally can be modified for individual projects. Other settings remain defaults that apply throughout your QuarkXPress projects. The default settings that you can change are in the Edit menu and the Utilities menu.

Edit menu defaults

The Edit menu has two types of defaults: some that you can change globally and edit locally; and others that you can only change globally. The ones that you can edit both globally and locally are located after Find/Change. The ones that cannot be saved with individual projects are grayed out when the menu is pulled down and no project is open. Figure 20-22 shows the menu.

You can change these settings for all new projects but then change them for an individual project that is active:

✔ **Style Sheets:** You can modify the Normal style sheets (changing the default font, for example) and add your own style sheets.

✔ **Colors:** You can delete colors you never use — such as the default Red, Green, and Blue — and then add commonly used colors, such as the Pantone color in your company logo.

Figure 20-22:
When no projects are open, commands for default settings remain active in the Edit menu.

Edit	Style	Item	Page
Can't Undo			⌥⌘Z
Can't Redo			⌥⇧⌘Z
Cut			⌘X
Copy			⌘C
Paste			⌘V
Paste In place			⌥⇧⌘V
Clear			
Select All			⌘A
Show Clipboard			
Find/Change			⌘F
Style Sheets...			⇧F11
Colors...			⇧F12
H&Js...			⌥⌘J
Lists...			
Dashes & Stripes...			
Print Styles...			
Tagging Rules...			
Hyperlinks...			
Jabberwocky Sets...			
Underline Styles...			
Menus...			
Meta Tags...			
CSS Font Families...			
Cascading Menus...			

- ✔ **H&Js:** You can modify the Standard hyphenation and justification set to suit your editorial style and then add other H&J sets that you use often (although H&J sets often need to be modified within projects depending on fonts, column width, and so on).

- ✔ **Lists:** If you're generating automatic tables of contents (from paragraph style sheets), you can create default lists to be included in all new projects.

- ✔ **Dashes & Stripes:** You can customize the dash and stripe patterns for lines and frames and include your patterns with all new projects.

- ✔ **Print Styles:** You can import and export these print settings to share them with other users, because they're not saved with projects.

- ✔ **Hyperlinks:** These are sets of URLs, mailtos, and other hyperlinks for Web and PDF documents.

- ✔ **Jabberwocky Sets:** These are sets of words that make up "dummy" text for use in preliminary designs; like with print styles, you can import and export Jabberwocky text.

- ✔ **CSS Font Families:** These are sets of fonts used in Web pages' cascading style sheets.

- ✔ **Meta Tags:** These are sets of behind-the-scenes information stored in Web pages that, for example, help search engines properly categorize Web pages as well as indicate the site's owner.

- ✔ **Cascading Menus** and **Menus:** These, which are created for interactive projects, are also saved with QuarkXPress.

The Hyperlinks, CSS Font Families, and Cascading Menus options are new to QuarkXPress 6.

Utilities menu defaults

When no projects are open, changes that you make to any active options in the Utilities menu affect all new projects. These include Auxiliary Dictionaries and Hyphenation Exceptions (which manage hyphenation settings) and Tracking Edit and Kerning Table Edit (which manage intercharacter spacing). You can also make changes in the XTensions Manager, which controls which XTensions load with QuarkXPress but has no effect on individual projects. The PPD Manager works similarly, letting you load printer description files for global use in QuarkXPress instead of for specific project use.

When a project is open, any changes to the Auxiliary Dictionaries and Hyphenation Exceptions menu options affect only the current layout in that project.

Part VII
The Part of Tens

The 5th Wave   By Rich Tennant

"Look into my Web site, Ms. Carruthers. Look deep into its rotating, nicely animated spiral, spinning, spinning, pulling you in, deeper... deeper..."

In this part . . .

This part of the book gives a quick rundown of tools and techniques that help you get the most out of QuarkXPress with the least amount of muss and fuss: shortcut keys, some great terms to know, and common mistakes to avoid. This part is so packed with useful information that you might even be tempted to start reading here and then go back to Chapter 1, but don't. The concepts in this part will make more sense to you if you read the other sections of the book first.

Chapter 21

The Ten Most Common Mistakes

. . . .

In This Chapter

▶ Using too many fonts

▶ Putting too much on a page

▶ Overdoing the design

▶ More bits of QuarkXPress-related advice that may someday save your life (or at least your job)

. . . .

*L*earning how to use QuarkXPress takes time. Learning how to use it right takes even longer! Knowing that, we thought we'd try to save you some time (and maybe even a few tears) by pointing out some of the most common mistakes that people make when they start dabbling in desktop publishing. Take a few minutes to read this chapter. Why? Because we *like* you.

Using Too Many Fonts

Avant Garde. Bellevue. Centaur Gothic. Desdemona. Fonts have cool names, and looking at a font list and seeing all the possibilities is fascinating.

Yes, we know that trying out a great many fonts is tempting. This urge overcomes nearly everybody who's new to publishing. (The few who don't begin their QuarkXPress careers by liberally sprinkling fonts throughout a page are often those who are traditional designers or who have typesetting backgrounds. In other words, they already know better.) Try keeping the number of fonts that you use on a page to two. When you have three, four, or five fonts, the layout takes on an amateurish appearance, quite frankly. Experts in page design never use several fonts together.

These rules apply doubly to new Web designers who not only have font issues to contend with (including fonts that may or may not be on other people's computers, as we describe in Chapter 18), but the color issue as well. How many times have you visited a Web site and shuddered at the grape background splattered with 28-point neon green headlines and 16-point pink body copy — bleeding on all four sides of the Web browser as if it were a margin-free zone? Artists aren't generally a conservative lot, but they are conservative with their work. You should be, too.

Not Trying Out the New Features

Each generation of QuarkXPress — including this one, version 6 — is an evolution from an earlier rendition. The people who work for Quark listen to a lot of users and take great care to keep adding features with each version that make the program better than ever. Not trying out the new features is akin to buying a new digital camera with all the bells and whistles and then leaving it in the box.

Go ahead, be brave, and try some of the latest and greatest tricks. For QuarkXPress 6, you won't want to miss nifty new features, such as synchronized text, multiple undos, enhanced tables, and the ability to create and apply cascading style sheets on Web pages, among other things. Go ahead, buckle up, and take the new features of QuarkXPress out for a test drive!

Putting Too Much on a Page

You've probably seen them before: pages that are overflowing with *stuff* — words, pictures, lines, colors — you name it.

One of the best things that you'll ever learn about page design is the value of *white space* — the places on the layout that have no text, no pictures, no lines — just the plain paper (or a nice uncluttered area of screen, in the case of a Web page) showing through. Pages that are crammed full of text and pictures are pages that readers avoid. Keep some space between text columns and headlines as well as between items on the page and the edges of the page.

Finding white space on a layout is like going to a crowded beach and finding a perfectly smooth, empty spot in the middle of the crowd that offers you a gorgeous view from your beach blanket. The white space "feels" great to your viewers' eyes and makes them more likely to get the message that's being conveyed by the words and pictures on the page. Of course, this is easier said than done. Professional designers have spent years perfecting this Zen-like approach to design.

Again, this applies to Web designers as well. Funny little cartoon GIFs or clever Flash sequences can be cute to a point. However, more than one in a design can destroy an otherwise competent Web site.

Overdoing the Design

This entry is kind of an extension for the previous one; avoiding over-designing a page can't be stressed enough. QuarkXPress is a powerful application that lets you do all kinds of nifty things. But just because you *can* do all of those things doesn't mean that you *should*.

Nothing looks worse than a complex design created by a publishing novice. Professionals know that less is more. Yes, it's possible to rotate text, skew text and graphics, make cool blends, set type on a curvy line, add multiple colors, stretch and condense type, and bleed artwork off the page. But using all these effects at the same time can overwhelm your audience and make them miss the whole point of the message you're trying to convey.

Here's a good rule to remember: Limit special effects to a maximum of three on a two-page spread. Here's an even better rule: If you're ever in doubt about whether to add an effect to a page, *don't.*

Not Consulting a Designer

We know that it's not rocket science, but designing a layout still can get fairly complicated. Knowing when to consult a professional graphic designer is a good idea.

You can best make the decision by taking into consideration how you'll use the project that you're creating. Are you developing a one– or two-color newspaper for a small club or organization, or a simple Web site? Then it's probably perfectly fine for a new QuarkXPress user to tackle the job. But if the project is a full-color display ad that will run in a national magazine or a company's Web site, leave it to the pros.

When you have to design a high-end print or Web project, professional graphic designers are worth their weight in gold. Sure, you may have to spend a few bucks to hire a talented designer, but you may save that much and more by having that person craft your project for you. Designers are trained to know what works visually (and, even more important, what doesn't), how to select the right paper, how many colors are appropriate, and how to have the project displayed on the Web or output to paper. In short, a good graphic designer can make your pages sing, and you end up smelling like a rose.

Not Using Master Pages

Before you start working on a layout, you need to have an idea about what it will look like. Will the text be in two columns? Will the top half of every page have a graphic? Where will the page numbers appear?

After you figure out these things, set up master pages for all the elements that will repeat in the same spot, page after page (such as page numbers). Master pages make things much easier, and they are easy to create. People who don't use master pages are people who like to do things the hard way. And we know you'd rather use the easy way so that you can save time for the really hard stuff.

To create a master page, open a layout and choose Page⇨Display⇨A-Master A. Anything that you create on that page becomes part of the master page and appears on every page in the layout that is based on that particular master page. See Chapter 16 for help in mastering master pages.

Not Using Smart Quotes and Dashes

Nothing, and we mean nothing, bothers a professional designer or publisher more than seeing inch marks where typesetter's quote marks should appear or skinny little hyphens — or worse yet, *two* skinny little hyphens — in place of em dashes. (An *em dash* is a dash that is the same width as the current font's capital *M*. You can create an em dash by using the key command Option+Shift+– (hyphen) or Ctrl+Shift+=.)

Using the correct quotes and dashes is easy in QuarkXPress. You can choose among a variety of quote formats, including some that work with foreign languages. You want to use typographically correct quotes and dashes because they make your layout look much more professional.

To use typographically correct quotes, choose QuarkXPress⇨Preferences on the Mac or Edit⇨Preferences in Windows, or press Option+Shift+⌘+Y or Ctrl+Alt+Shift+Y, and then check the Smart Quotes check box in the Interactive pane.

To get the right kinds of quotes and dashes when you import text from a word processing application, make sure that the Convert Quotes box is checked in the Get Text dialog box.

Be aware, however, that if you're dealing with measurements in your text — in particular inches and feet — the inch and foot marks will appear curly, too (and bother those professionals even more). You can get around this problem by using the shortcut key combination of Control+Shift+" for inch marks and Control+' for foot marks on the Mac, or Ctrl+" for inch marks and Ctrl+Alt+' for foot marks in Windows.

Forgetting to Check Spelling

Typos are like ants at a summer picnic — they show up all the time, no matter how careful you are. You can avoid some typos if you always remember that the last thing to do before outputting your print project or posting your Web layout is to check spelling. Checking spelling won't catch every possible error (you still need to proofread thoroughly to catch all errors), but using the built-in spell checker in QuarkXPress is easy to do, and it can prevent embarrassing typos and misspellings.

Not Talking with Your Commercial Printer

If you're creating a print project that will be commercially printed, be sure to talk with your printer early in the game. These folks know their business. Your printer can help you plan your project, pick the right number of colors to use in it, and produce it cost-effectively. He or she will appreciate your concern, too, and will likely invest extra effort in doing a great job for you if you show that you care enough to consult the pros early on.

Not Giving the Service Bureau Every File

If you've never worked with a *service bureau* — the place where you take or send your QuarkXPress print projects to be output to an image-setting device — you may think that the people who work there are downright snoopy. They poke and prod, ask millions of questions, and want to know every little thing about your project. They give you the third degree, asking about every file for every graphic on every single page.

These people are not out to pick on you; they truly do need to know about all the fonts and files necessary to output your project.

Why? Because they just do, that's why. Seriously, the equipment that a service bureau uses needs to have everything that you used to create your print project. If you have layouts that include an EPS file that contains text, for example, the service bureau needs to have the font that is used in the text. If that font is not available, the EPS file prints incorrectly, and the job has to be output again.

The Collect for Output feature in QuarkXPress can help. This feature copies all the text, fonts, color profiles, and picture files that are necessary to output your print project. It also generates a report with useful information, including fonts, dimensions, and trapping information used in the project. To use this feature, choose File➪Collect for Output (see Figure 21-1).

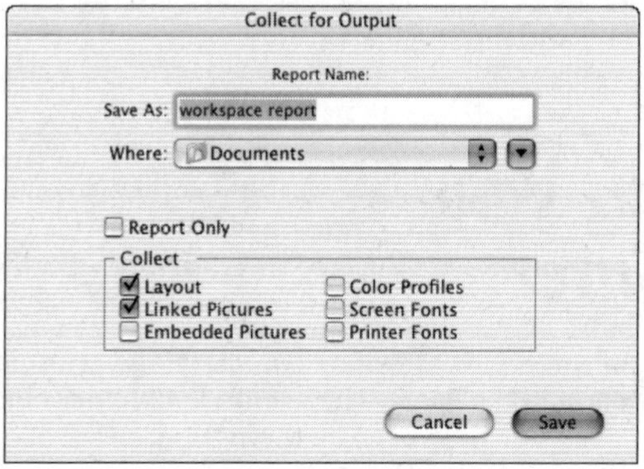

Figure 21-1: The Collect for Output dialog box.

The Collect for Output feature can't replace your *brain*. You still need to think about your project. You are the person who is responsible for making sure that your service bureau has everything that it needs to output your project the right way, the first time. Make sure that all the pieces are there before you waste hundreds of dollars outputting a series of incorrect layouts.

Chapter 22

More Than Ten Terms to Know

In This Chapter

▶ Definitions of terms used in Web and print publishing

▶ QuarkXPress-specific terms

*L*ike many specialized functions, print and Web publishing have their own unique terms. You're likely to encounter some of these words during the course of developing layouts in QuarkXPress. You eventually become so wise about all this layout and production business that you'll notice when novices use terms incorrectly. But it is a good idea to learn the lingo, because doing so makes communicating with others easy. Here are definitions (grouped by topic area) that you need to know about.

Typography Terms

Ascender: The part of the letter that extends above the *x* height (as in the letter *b*).

Baseline: An imaginary line that letters appear to sit on. While some letters like j, p and q extend below the baseline, other letters like h, n and m just touch it.

Cap height: The size of the average uppercase letter (based on the letter *C*).

Descender: The part of the letter that goes below the baseline, such as the "tail" in the letter *q*.

Drop cap: A drop cap is a large capital letter that extends down several lines into the surrounding text. (The rest of the text wraps around it.) Drop caps are used at the beginning of a section or story or chapter.

Fill character: When you set tabs, you can also specify a *fill character,* which is the character used to fill the empty space that usually precedes a tab stop. Often, this is something like the dots used to separate a table of contents entry from its page number.

Font: A font is a set of characters at a certain size, weight, and style (for example, 10-point Palatino Bold). Often used as a synonym for *typeface,* which is a set of characters of a certain style in *all* sizes, weights, and styles (for example, Palatino).

Font family: A group of related typefaces (for example, the Franklin family includes Franklin Gothic, Franklin Heavy, and Franklin Compressed).

Italic type: Type that is both slanted and curved (to appear more like calligraphy than roman type).

Oblique type: Roman type that has been mathematically slanted to give the appearance of italic type.

OpenType: This new version of PostScript, co-developed by Adobe and Microsoft, combines some TrueType technology and is meant to eventually replace both Type 1 and TrueType. Its biggest attribute is that it supports a wide range of international characters, symbols, and character variations within the same font, such as true small caps and ligatures — called *glyphs* as a group. Mac OS X, Windows 2000, and Windows XP support OpenType natively, but you need to make sure that your imagesetter or other prepress device can handle OpenType — many cannot.

PostScript Type 1: This is the publishing industry's standard for fonts. Anyone outputting to an imagesetter or other prepress device must use these fonts. PostScript Type 1 font support is native to Mac OS X. Windows does not support PostScript natively and so requires a font-management utility (such as Adobe Type Manager, DiamondSoft Font Reserve, or Extensis Suitcase) to work with PostScript fonts.

Raised cap: This is the same as a *drop cap* except that it does not extend down into the text. Instead, this large capital letter rests on the baseline of the first line and extends several lines above the baseline.

Roman type: Upright type.

Serif: A horizontal stroke used to give letters visual character.

TrueType: Co-developed by Microsoft and Apple Computer, this is Windows' standard font format, and it also is supported natively on the Mac OS. However, TrueType fonts are not supported by most imagesetters and prepress devices, and their use in your layouts can cause output problems. Do not use them in any professionally published document.

Weight: Typeface thickness. Typical weights, from thinnest to thickest, are *ultralight, light, book, medium, demibold, heavy, ultrabold,* and *ultraheavy.*

X height: The height of the average lowercase letter (based on the letter *x*).

Layout Terms

Active layer: In QuarkXPress, this is the layer that you are creating items on — whether you're using tools, dragging items in from a library or another project, or pasting items from other layers or layouts.

Contents: Text and pictures that go into text boxes and picture boxes, respectively. (QuarkXPress calls any imported graphic a picture, whether it's a logotype, a chart, a line drawing, or a photograph.) Contents are always placed within an item — so you can have items without contents, but you cannot have contents without items.

Frame: Most publishing and graphics arts programs use the term *stroke* to mean adding a border to an item, whether it's a box or line. QuarkXPress never uses that term, preferring *frame* for strokes on boxes and simply *width* for strokes on lines and text paths. To make matters more confusing, other programs use the term *frame* for what QuarkXPress calls a *box*. When it comes to QuarkXPress, remember that a shape is a box, and the border around it is a frame.

H&Js: Hyphenation and justification settings that determine how QuarkXPress hyphenates and aligns text.

Items: Things you draw on a page — such as squares, circles, lines, and wavy shapes — and then fill with color, rotate, and the like. You can also import text and graphics — *contents* — into items. The primary items in QuarkXPress are picture boxes and text boxes, but there are also lines, text paths, and tables.

Layout: In QuarkXPress, a *layout* or *layout space* is the design space where you create the content for a specific print or Web job. In earlier versions of the program, the term *document* was used in place of *layout*.

Library: A floating palette designed to hold formatted items — such as blocks of text and graphics — until you need them.

Lines: See *Rules*.

Project: The QuarkXPress file that serves as a folder for one or more layouts and the attributes and specifications (style sheets, colors, H&Js, and the like) that define them. Every project contains at least one layout but may contain as many as 25 layouts.

Rules: QuarkXPress uses this term (interchangeable with *lines*) to indicate a paragraph attribute that automatically places lines above and below paragraphs.

Runaround: An area in a page's layout where you don't want text to flow. *Text runaround* lets you place copy around an active element (such as a text box, picture box, or line), fitting the text as close to the contours of the element as you want.

Template: The shell of a document — the basic structure — that is used as a starting place for new documents.

Graphics Terms

Alpha channel: An invisible outline picture used to crop or isolate a portion of the image to which it is attached.

Bézier: An industry-standard way of defining curved paths, named after its creator, Pierre Bézier. Bézier technology relies on *curve handles* (Quark's term for what the industry calls *control points*) to manipulate the curvature of each segment in a path.

Clipping path: A shape, created in an image-editing program, which isolates a portion of a picture.

EPS: The Encapsulated PostScript vector format favored by professional publishers — also Adobe Illustrator's native format. (QuarkXPress also supports the DCS color-separated variant of EPS, whose full name is Document Color Separation.)

GIF: The Graphics Interchange Format common in Web projects. A very simple bitmap graphic format with a limited color palette and resolution, designed to take little file space. It's very popular on the Web because of its small file size.

JPEG: The Joint Photographers Expert Group compressed bitmap format, often used on the Web. A compressed color-image format used for very large images and the individual images comprising an animation or movie. Images compressed in this format may lose detail, which is why print publishers prefer TIFF. But JPEG is fine for the relatively coarse resolution of a monitor, and its file sizes are much smaller than TIFF files, so it's very popular in Web projects.

PDF: Portable Document Format, also known as Acrobat format, a variant of EPS that is commonly used for distributing formatted documents.

PICT: The Mac's former native graphics format (it can be bitmap or vector); little used in professional documents but common for inexpensive clip art. Also supports bitmaps and is the standard format for Macintosh screen-capture utilities. QuarkXPress imports PICT files with no difficulty. Colors cannot be color-separated unless the Quark CMS XTension is installed and active.

Point: A kind of magic dot that is plotted wherever a Bézier path is supposed to change direction significantly. (It is also called a *vertex.*) For the simplest example, think of a triangle shape. A triangle consists of three points. In Bézier terminology, we would call these *corner points* because the transitions are sharp. Now think of an S-curve. The simplest S-curve has no sharp transitions, but its curvature does change direction significantly midstroke, so you still need at least one point (in this case, a smooth point) between the two endpoints.

Posterization: The removal of gray levels in an image.

TIFF: Tagged Image File Format, the bitmap standard for professional image editors and publishers. The most popular bitmap format for publishers. Supports color up to 24 bits (16.7 million colors) in both RGB and CMYK models. Every major photo-editing program supports TIFF on both the Macintosh and in Windows. TIFF also supports grayscale and black-and-white files. The biggest advantage to using TIFF files rather than other formats that also support color, such as PICT, is that QuarkXPress is designed to take advantage of TIFF. QuarkXPress can work with the contrast settings in grayscale TIFF images to make an image clearer or to apply special effects — something the program can't do with any other bitmap format.

WMF: The Windows Metafile Format, native to Windows but little used in professional documents.

Color Terms

Build: An attempt to simulate a color-model color by overprinting the appropriate percentages of the four process colors.

CIE LAB: This standard specifies colors by one lightness coordinate and two color coordinates — green-red and blue-yellow.

CMS: Color Management System. With the bundled Quark CMS XTension installed, QuarkXPress color-separates non-CMYK files. It also calibrates the output colors (whether printed to a color printer or color-separated for traditional printing) based on the source device and the target output device.

CMYK: This standard specifies colors as combinations of cyan, magenta, yellow, and black. These four colors are known as *process colors.*

Color gamut: This is the range of colors that a device, such as a monitor or a color printer, can produce.

Color model: An industry standard for specifying a color, such as CMYK and Pantone.

Color separation: A set of four photographic negatives — one filtered for each process color — shot from a color photograph or image. When over-printed, the four negatives reproduce that original image.

Color space: A method of representing color in terms of measurable values, such as the amount of red, yellow, and blue in a color image. The color space RGB represents the red, green, and blue colors on video screens.

Four-color printing: The use of the four process colors in combination to produce most other colors.

Hexachrome: Pantone's six-color alternative to CMYK. It adds green and orange inks for more accurate color reproduction in those hues, as well as enhanced versions of black, magenta, cyan, and yellow inks.

Pantone: Pantone is an international reference system for specifying and matching ink colors. Pantone, Inc. is a company responsible for this color-matching system.

Process color: Refers to any of the four primary colors in publishing: cyan, magenta, yellow, and black (known as a group as CMYK) that are mixed to reproduce most color tones visible to the human eye. In printing, a separate negative is produced for each of the four process colors. This method, often called four-color printing, is used for most color publishing.

RGB: The color standard used by monitors, and the abbreviation from the three colors in it: red, green, and blue. One of the biggest hurdles to producing color documents that look as you'd expect is that computers use RGB while printers use CMYK, and the two don't always produce colors at the same hue.

Spot color: A single color applied at one or more places on a page. Spot colors can also be process colors. Spot color refers to any color — whether one of the process colors or some other hue — used for specific elements in a document. For example, if you print a document in black ink but print the company logo in red, the red is a spot color. A spot color is often called a *second color* even though you can use several spot colors in a document. Each spot color is output to its own negative (and not color-separated into CMYK).

Swatchbook: A set of color samples. If you send a QuarkXPress project to a commercial printer, the printer uses a premixed ink based on the color model identifier you specify; you look up the numbers for various colors in a table of colors in a series of color samples known as a swatchbook).

Production Terms

Crop marks: Indicators on a layout that tell a printer where to cut the negatives; anything outside the crop marks is not printed. Crop marks are used both to define page size and to indicate which part of an image is to be used.

Registration marks: Indicators on a layout that tell a printer where to position each negative relative to other negatives; the registration marks must line up when the negatives are superimposed.

Screen: An area printed or displayed at a particular percentage of color. For example, a border on a page might have a 20 percent black screen.

Trapping: A method of adjusting the boundaries of colored objects to prevent gaps between abutting colors on the final printed page.

Web Publishing Terms

Browsers: HTML browsers are separate programs, such as Netscape's Communicator, Opera Software's Opera, Apple's Safari, and Microsoft's Internet Explorer, that interpret HTML codes so formatted pages display properly on-screen. Browsers and HTML are designed to give users some power over how pages display.

Cascading style sheets: These are style sheets that define the formatting of text on a Web page; they are similar to QuarkXPress style sheets for print. Abbreviated as CSS, cascading style sheets specify the color, font, and styling information of text that is displayed in a Web browser.

Home page: An HTML page (a Web page) that usually summarizes what a Web site, or entire group of Web pages, offers.

HTML: Hypertext Markup Language; a page-description language that's interpreted (turned into page images) by HTML browsers.

Image map: A graphic on a Web page that, when clicked, brings the user to a different Web page.

Link and jump: Also known as *hyperlink*. An area in a Web page that, when users click on it, takes users to a different location on a Web page or to an altogether different Web page. A link often consists of an icon, button, or underlined word that users click to activate.

Rollover: A picture (usually text saved as a JPEG or GIF file) that changes when you move the mouse pointer over it in a Web browser.

Two-position rollover: A rollover where one part of the Web page changes when you move your mouse over a different part of the same page.

Other QuarkXPress Terms

Global settings: Settings that affect everything you do — every project you create, every item you make, and the like. They govern how the software behaves when you perform certain actions.

Jabberwocky: A popular XTension from Quark that lets you generate customized greeking text ("fake" copy) for preliminary designs.

Local changes: Unlike global settings, local changes affect only selected objects, such as highlighted text or an active page or item.

Required Components: Small software modules that add features to QuarkXPress. These features include such things as tables, HTML export, and GIF import. Unlike XTensions (optional add-ons for QuarkXPress), Required Components must be present for QuarkXPress to run. Many of Quark's old XTensions, such as Cool Blends, now exist as Required Components. The idea is that Quark can update and distribute these small modules without updating the entire program. Required Components are stored in a folder called Required Components inside your QuarkXPress folder, which is where you should leave them.

XPress Tags: ASCII (text-only) text that contains embedded codes telling QuarkXPress which formatting to apply.

XTensions: Plug-in software programs that add features to QuarkXPress. For a list of XTensions, go to www.QXCentral.com.

Index

• *M* •

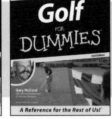

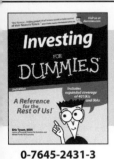

FOR DUMMIES®

A world of resources to help you grow

TRAVEL

Italy FOR DUMMIES
0-7645-5453-0

Hawaii FOR DUMMIES
0-7645-5438-7

Walt Disney World & Orlando FOR DUMMIES
0-7645-5444-1

Also available:

America's National Parks For Dummies
(0-7645-6204-5)

Caribbean For Dummies
(0-7645-5445-X)

Cruise Vacations For Dummies 2003
(0-7645-5459-X)

Europe For Dummies
(0-7645-5456-5)

Ireland For Dummies
(0-7645-6199-5)

France For Dummies
(0-7645-6292-4)

Las Vegas For Dummies
(0-7645-5448-4)

London For Dummies
(0-7645-5416-6)

Mexico's Beach Resorts For Dummies
(0-7645-6262-2)

Paris For Dummies
(0-7645-5494-8)

RV Vacations For Dummies
(0-7645-5443-3)

EDUCATION & TEST PREPARATION

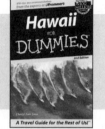

Spanish FOR DUMMIES
0-7645-5194-9

Algebra FOR DUMMIES
0-7645-5325-9

U.S. History FOR DUMMIES
0-7645-5249-X

Also available:

The ACT For Dummies
(0-7645-5210-4)

Chemistry For Dummies
(0-7645-5430-1)

English Grammar For Dummies
(0-7645-5322-4)

French For Dummies
(0-7645-5193-0)

GMAT For Dummies
(0-7645-5251-1)

Inglés Para Dummies
(0-7645-5427-1)

Italian For Dummies
(0-7645-5196-5)

Research Papers For Dummies
(0-7645-5426-3)

SAT I For Dummies
(0-7645-5472-7)

U.S. History For Dummies
(0-7645-5249-X)

World History For Dummies
(0-7645-5242-2)

HEALTH, SELF-HELP & SPIRITUALITY

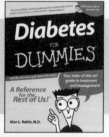  

Diabetes FOR DUMMIES
0-7645-5154-X

Sex FOR DUMMIES
0-7645-5302-X

Parenting FOR DUMMIES
0-7645-5418-2

Also available:

The Bible For Dummies
(0-7645-5296-1)

Controlling Cholesterol For Dummies
(0-7645-5440-9)

Dating For Dummies
(0-7645-5072-1)

Dieting For Dummies
(0-7645-5126-4)

High Blood Pressure For Dummies
(0-7645-5424-7)

Judaism For Dummies
(0-7645-5299-6)

Menopause For Dummies
(0-7645-5458-1)

Nutrition For Dummies
(0-7645-5180-9)

Potty Training For Dummies
(0-7645-5417-4)

Pregnancy For Dummies
(0-7645-5074-8)

Rekindling Romance For Dummies
(0-7645-5303-8)

Religion For Dummies
(0-7645-5264-3)

FOR DUMMIES®

Plain-English solutions for everyday challenges

HOME & BUSINESS COMPUTER BASICS

0-7645-0838-5   0-7645-1663-9   0-7645-1548-9

Also available:

Excel 2002 All-in-One Desk
Reference For Dummies
(0-7645-1794-5)

Office XP 9-in-1 Desk
Reference For Dummies
(0-7645-0819-9)

PCs All-in-One Desk
Reference For Dummies
(0-7645-0791-5)

Troubleshooting Your PC
For Dummies
(0-7645-1669-8)

Upgrading & Fixing PCs For
Dummies
(0-7645-1665-5)

Windows XP For Dummies
(0-7645-0893-8)

Windows XP For Dummies
Quick Reference
(0-7645-0897-0)

Word 2002 For Dummies
(0-7645-0839-3)

INTERNET & DIGITAL MEDIA

0-7645-0894-6   0-7645-1642-6   0-7645-1664-7

Also available:

CD and DVD Recording
For Dummies
(0-7645-1627-2)

Digital Photography
All-in-One Desk Reference
For Dummies
(0-7645-1800-3)

eBay For Dummies
(0-7645-1642-6)

Genealogy Online For
Dummies
(0-7645-0807-5)

Internet All-in-One Desk
Reference For Dummies
(0-7645-1659-0)

Internet For Dummies
Quick Reference
(0-7645-1645-0)

Internet Privacy For Dummies
(0-7645-0846-6)

Paint Shop Pro For Dummies
(0-7645-2440-2)

Photo Retouching &
Restoration For Dummies
(0-7645-1662-0)

Photoshop Elements For
Dummies
(0-7645-1675-2)

Scanners For Dummies
(0-7645-0783-4)

Get smart! Visit www.dummies.com

- **Find listings of even more Dummies titles**

- **Browse online articles, excerpts, and how-to's**

- **Sign up for daily or weekly e-mail tips**

- **Check out Dummies fitness videos and other products**

- **Order from our online bookstore**

Available wherever books are sold. Go to www.dummies.com or call 1-877-762-2974 to order direct

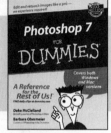